Skip·Beat!

Shojo Beat

Skip·Beat!

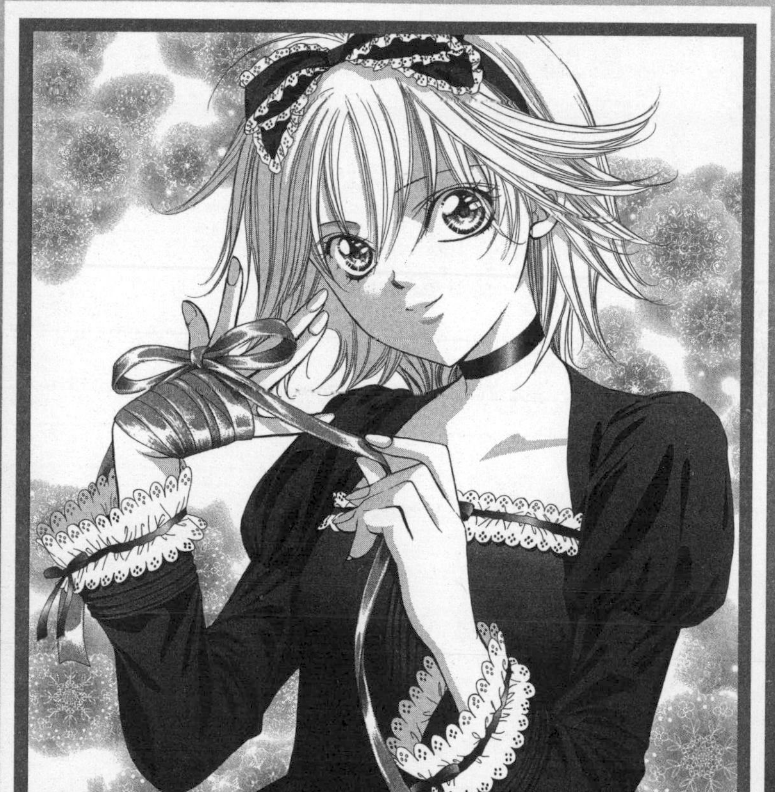

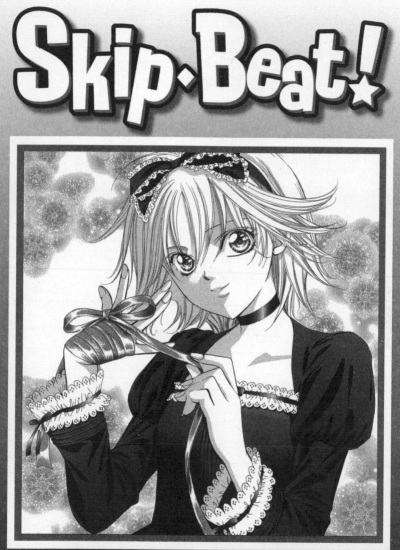

36

Story & Art by Yoshiki Nakamura

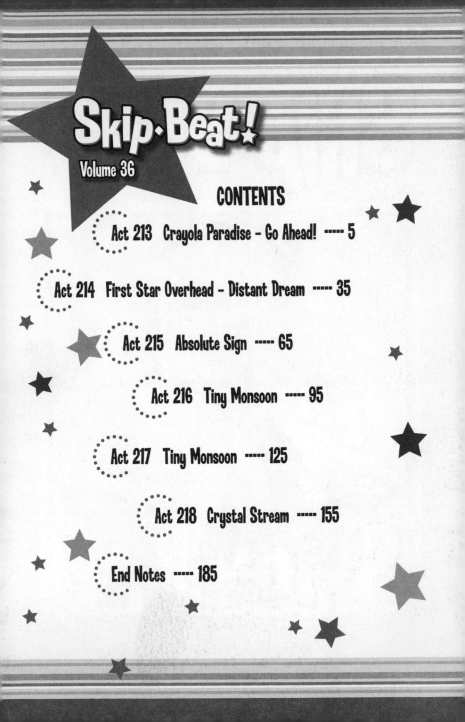

Skip·Beat!

Volume 36

CONTENTS

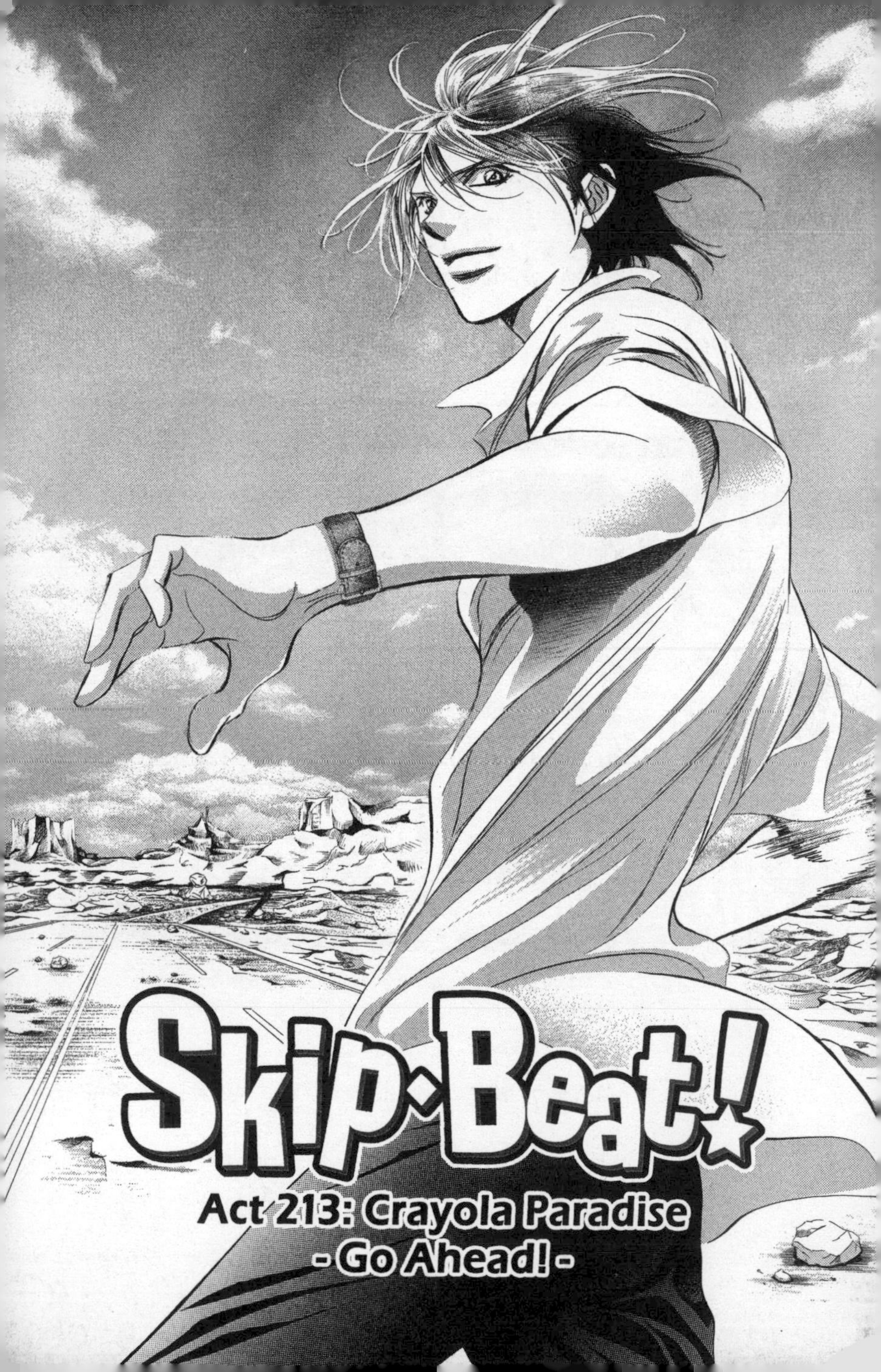
Skip·Beat!
Act 213: Crayola Paradise
- Go Ahead! -

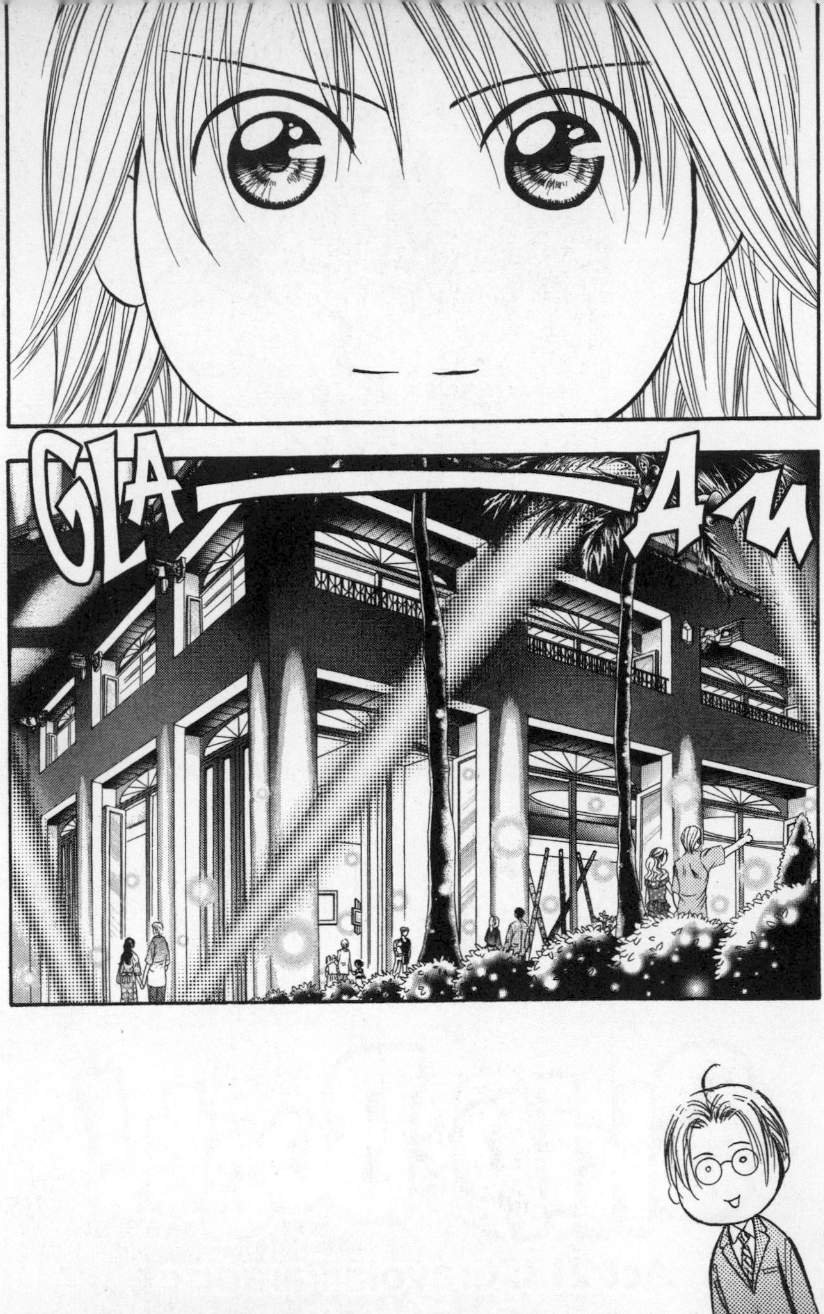
GLA——AM

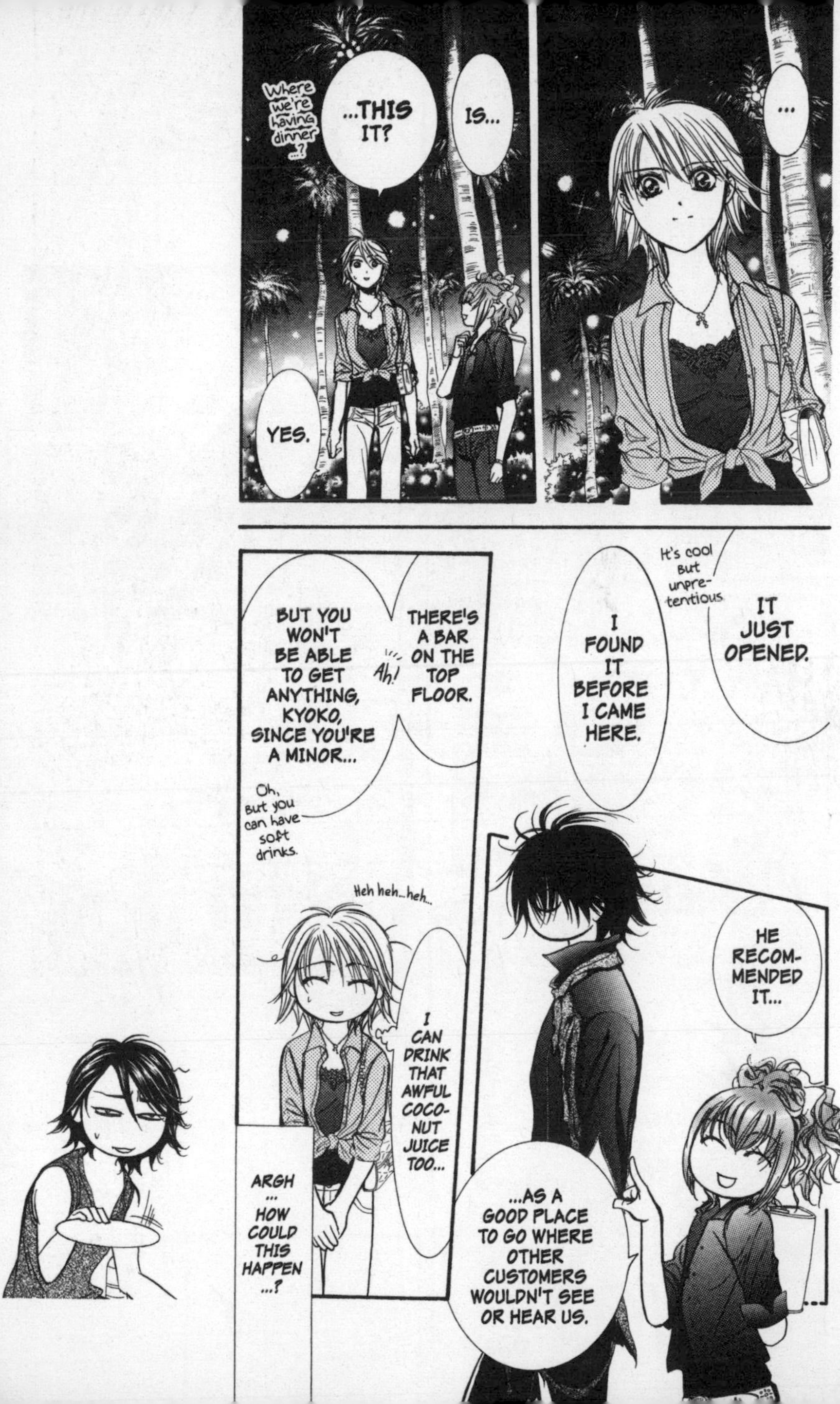
...
IS...
...THIS IT?
Where we're having dinner ...?
YES.
IT JUST OPENED.
It's cool but unpre-tentious
I FOUND IT BEFORE I CAME HERE.
HE RECOMMENDED IT...
...AS A GOOD PLACE TO GO WHERE OTHER CUSTOMERS WOULDN'T SEE OR HEAR US.
THERE'S A BAR ON THE TOP FLOOR.
Ah!
BUT YOU WON'T BE ABLE TO GET ANYTHING, KYOKO, SINCE YOU'RE A MINOR...
Oh, but you can have soft drinks.
Heh heh...heh...
I CAN DRINK THAT AWFUL COCO-NUT JUICE TOO...
ARGH ... HOW COULD THIS HAPPEN ...?

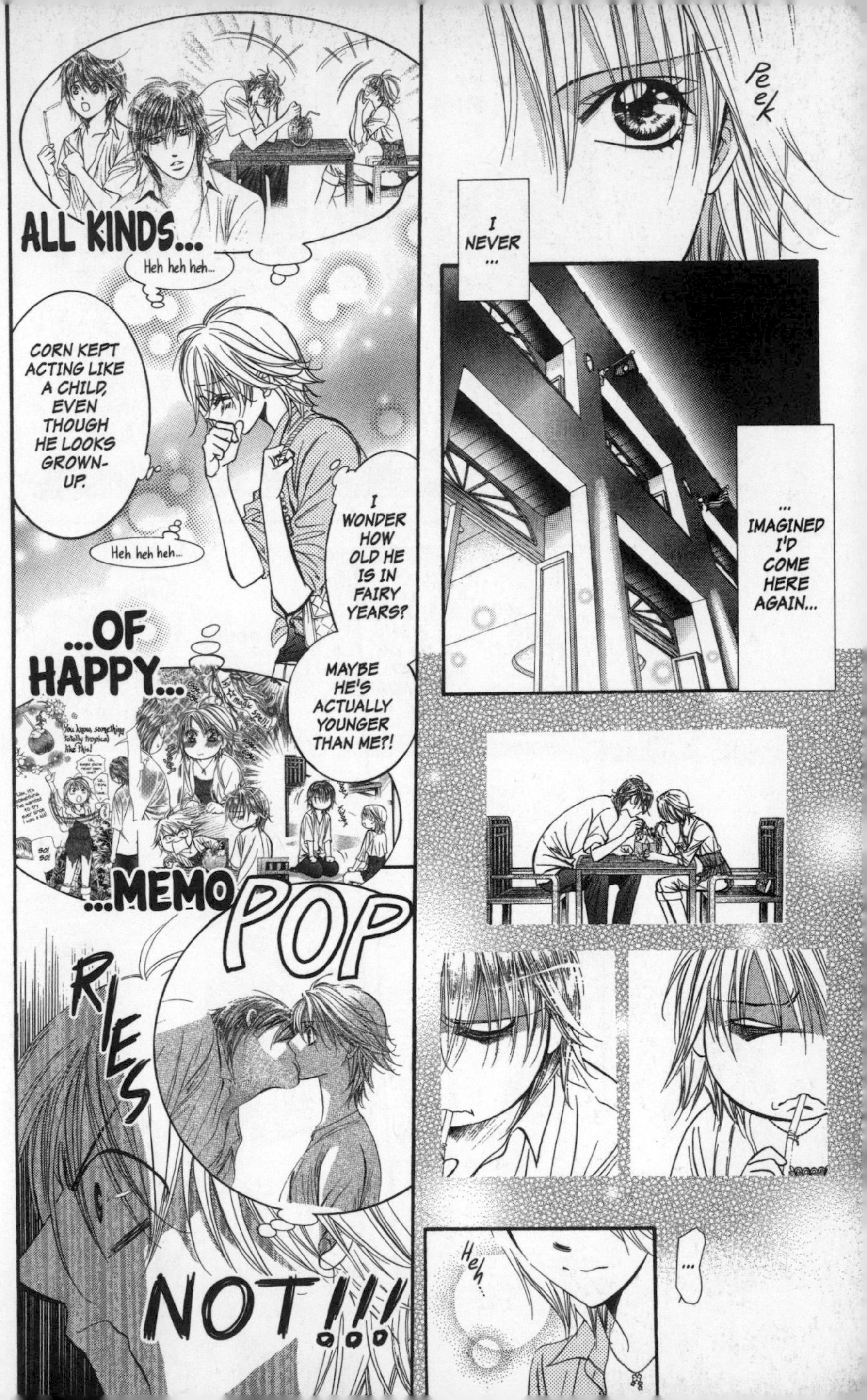

Peek
I NEVER ...
... IMAGINED I'D COME HERE AGAIN...
Heh...
...
ALL KINDS...
Heh heh heh...
CORN KEPT ACTING LIKE A CHILD, EVEN THOUGH HE LOOKS GROWN-UP.
Heh heh heh...
I WONDER HOW OLD HE IS IN FAIRY YEARS?
MAYBE HE'S ACTUALLY YOUNGER THAN ME?!
...OF HAPPY...
You know, something totally tropical like this!
...MEMO
POP
RIES
NOT!!!

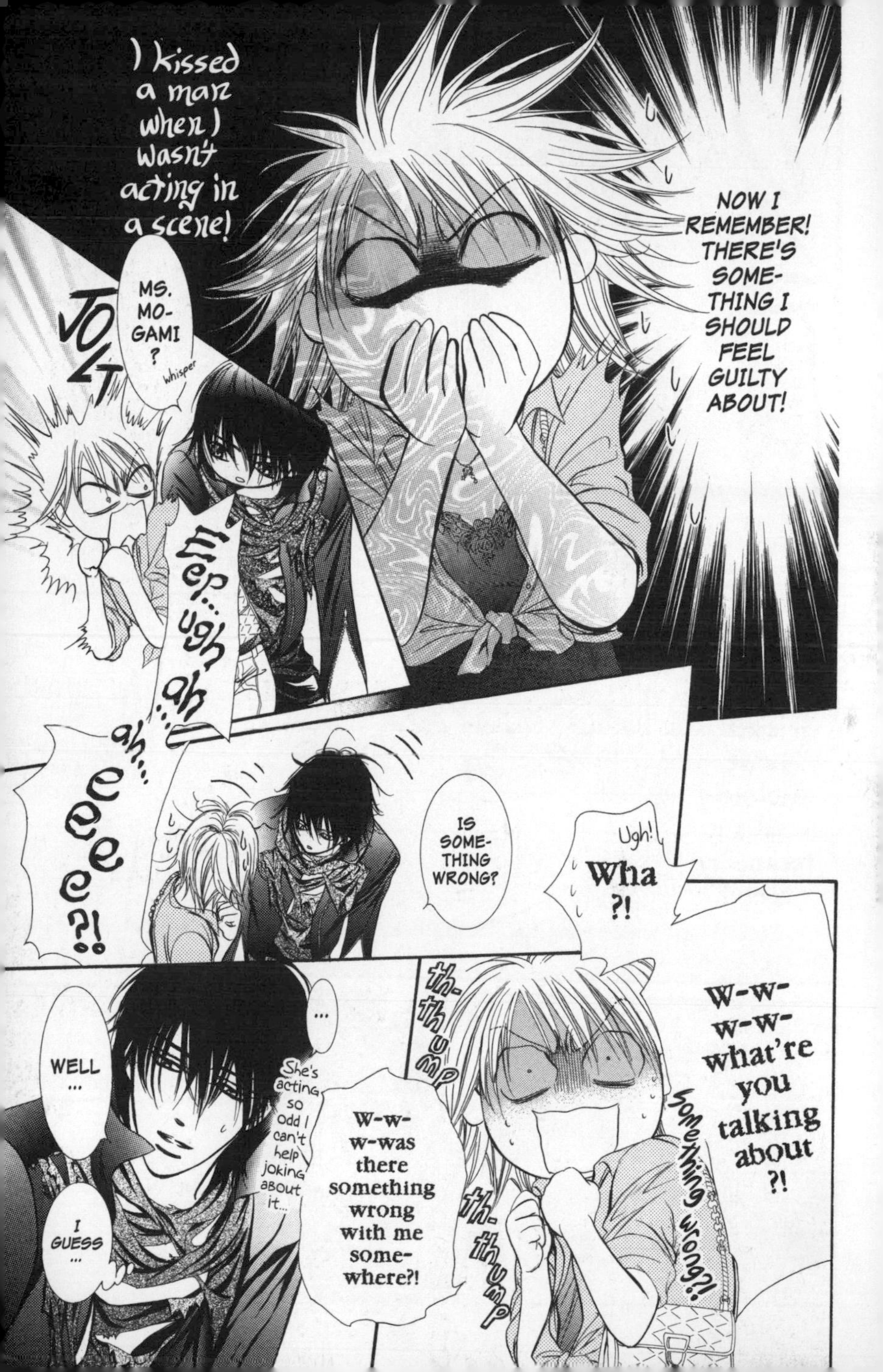
NOW I REMEMBER! THERE'S SOME-THING I SHOULD FEEL GUILTY ABOUT!
I kissed a man when I wasn't acting in a scene!
MS. MO-GAMI?
whisper
JOLT
Eep... ugh ah...
Ugh!
Wha?!
IS SOME-THING WRONG?
ah... eeee?!
W-w-w-w-what're you talking about?!
something wrong?!
th-thump
th-thump
W-w-w-was there something wrong with me some-where?!
...
WELL...
She's acting so odd I can't help joking about it...
I GUESS...

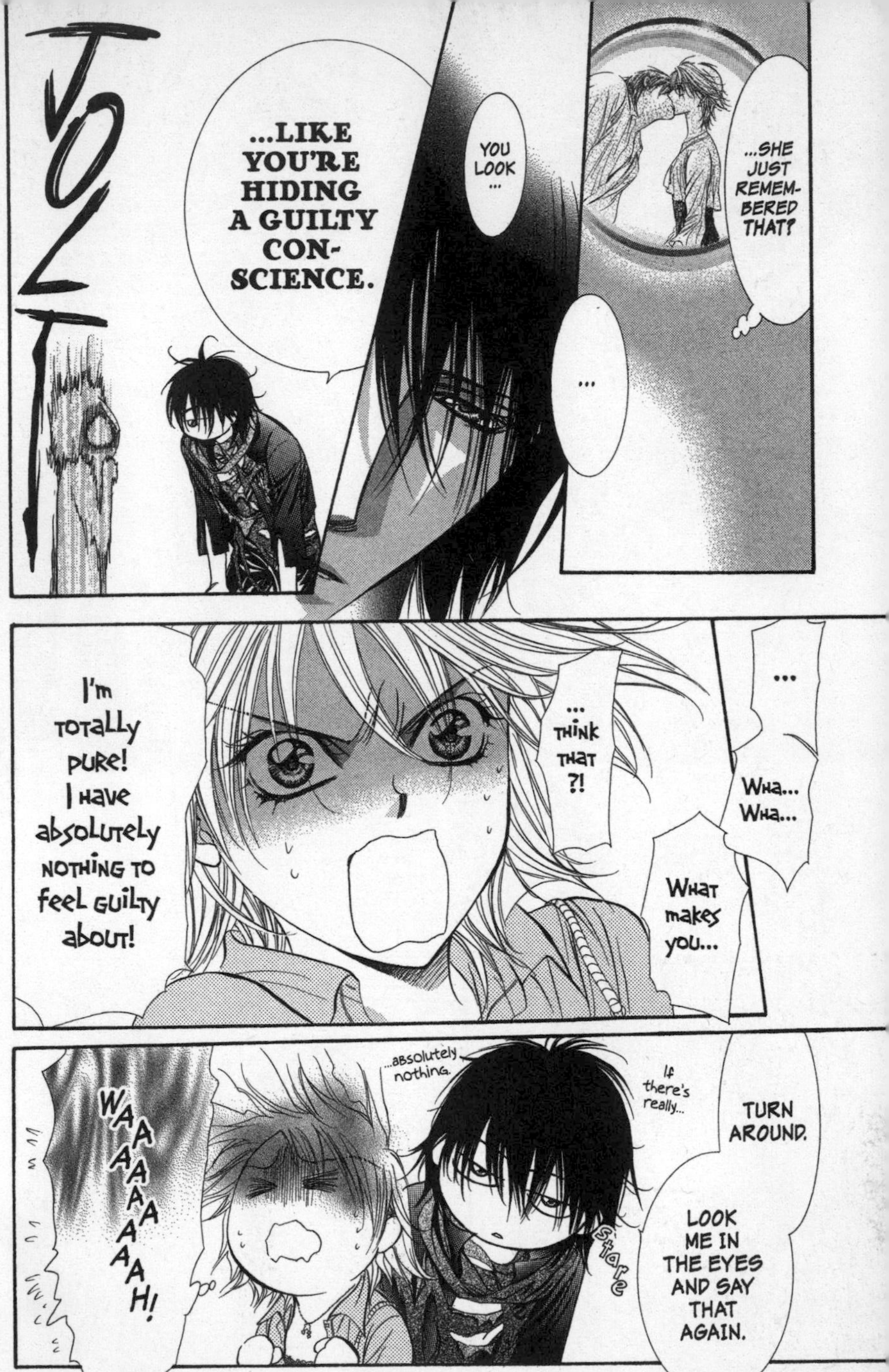
...SHE JUST REMEMBERED THAT?
...
YOU LOOK ...
...LIKE YOU'RE HIDING A GUILTY CONSCIENCE.
JOLT
...
Wha... Wha...
What makes you...
...think that?!
I'm totally pure! I have absolutely nothing to feel guilty about!
TURN AROUND.
LOOK ME IN THE EYES AND SAY THAT AGAIN.
If there's really...
...absolutely nothing.
Stare
WAAAAAAAAAH!

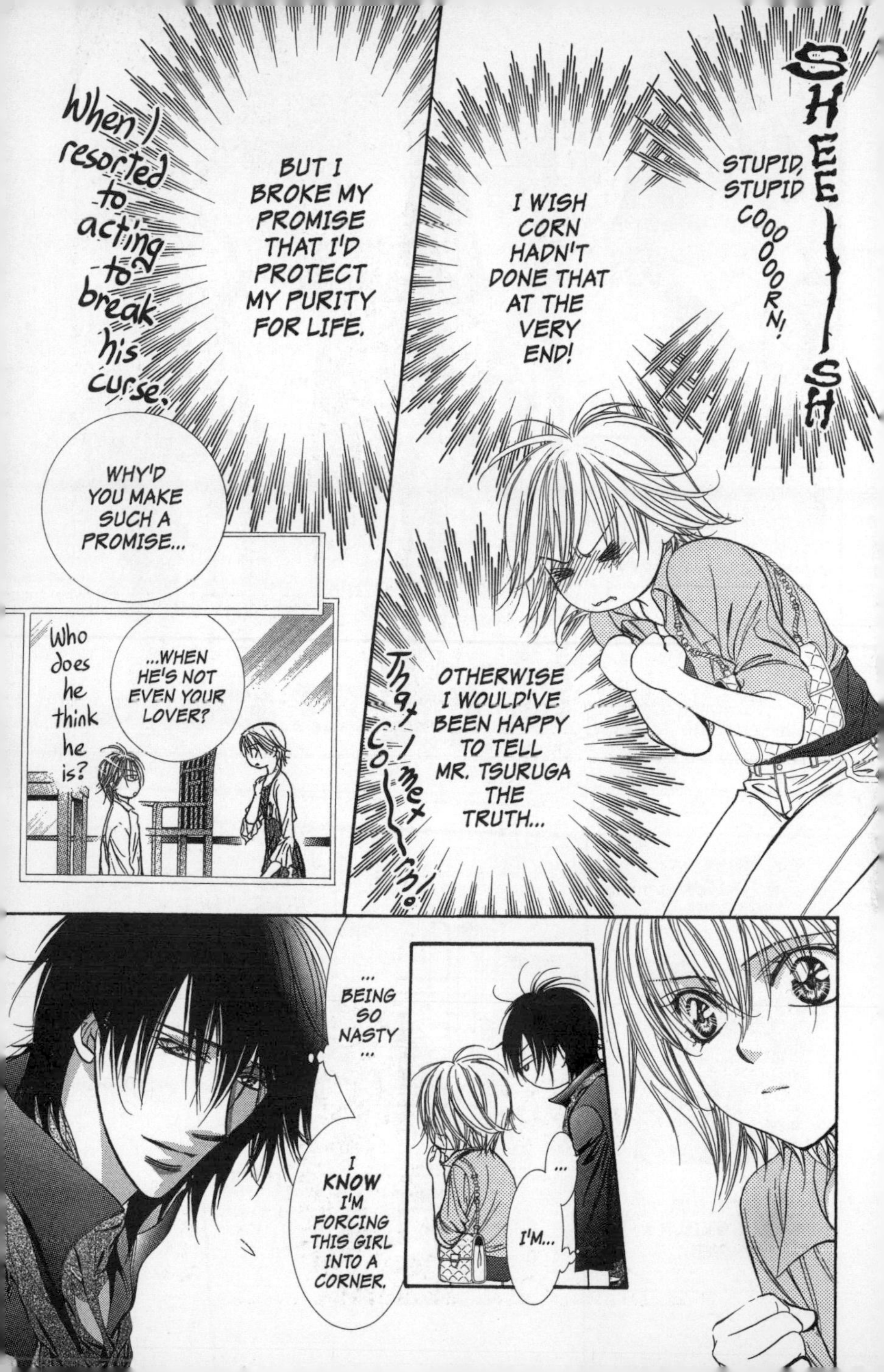
SHEE—SH
STUPID, STUPID COOOOOOORN!
I WISH CORN HADN'T DONE THAT AT THE VERY END!
OTHERWISE I WOULD'VE BEEN HAPPY TO TELL MR. TSURUGA THE TRUTH...
That I met Co——rn!
When I resorted to acting to break his curse,
BUT I BROKE MY PROMISE THAT I'D PROTECT MY PURITY FOR LIFE.
WHY'D YOU MAKE SUCH A PROMISE...
...WHEN HE'S NOT EVEN YOUR LOVER?
Who does he think he is?
...
I'M...
... BEING SO NASTY ...
I KNOW I'M FORCING THIS GIRL INTO A CORNER.

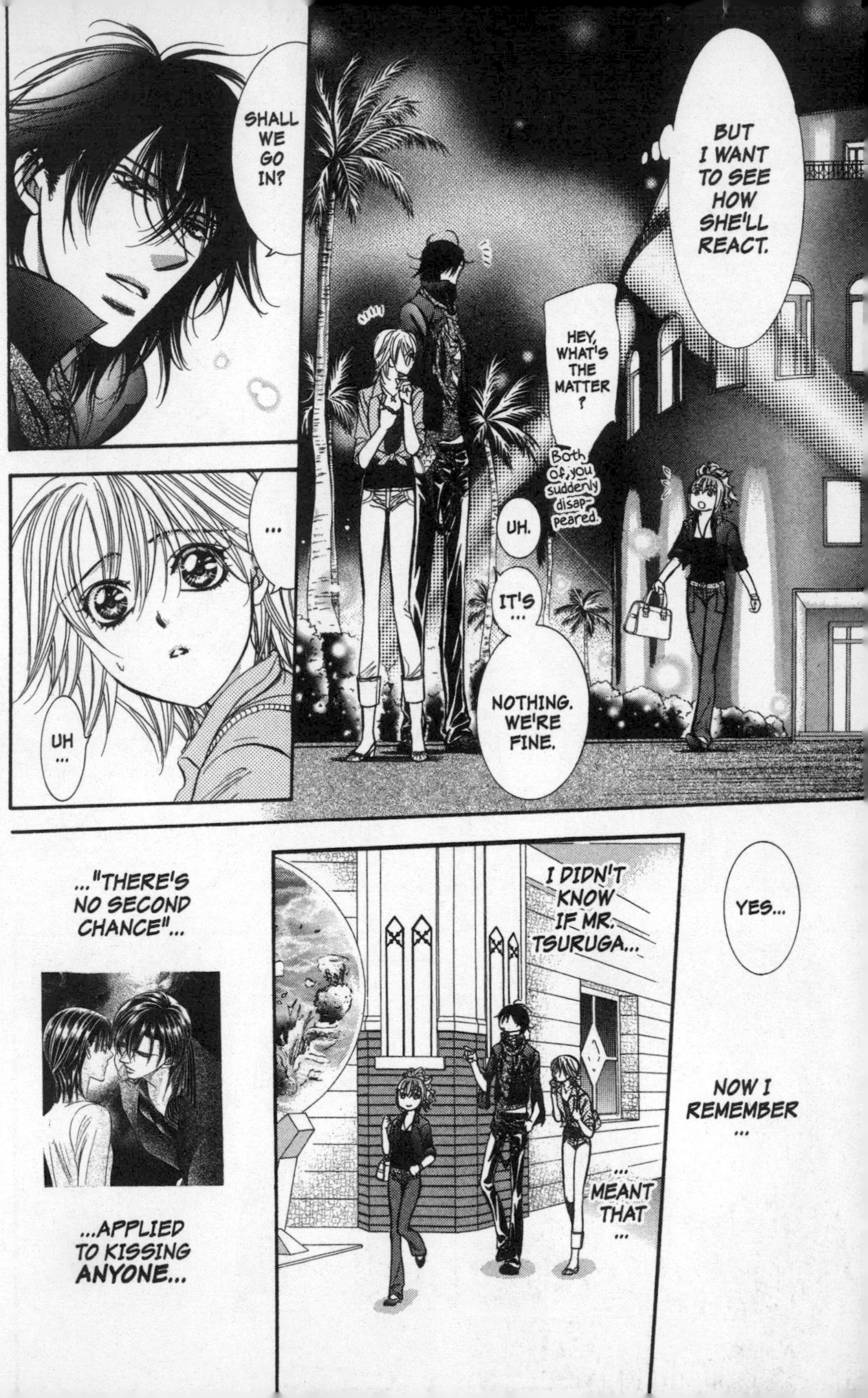
BUT I WANT TO SEE HOW SHE'LL REACT.
HEY, WHAT'S THE MATTER?
Both of you suddenly disappeared.
UH.
IT'S ...
NOTHING. WE'RE FINE.
SHALL WE GO IN?
...
UH ...
YES...
I DIDN'T KNOW IF MR. TSURUGA...
NOW I REMEMBER ...
... MEANT THAT ...
..."THERE'S NO SECOND CHANCE"...
...APPLIED TO KISSING ANYONE...

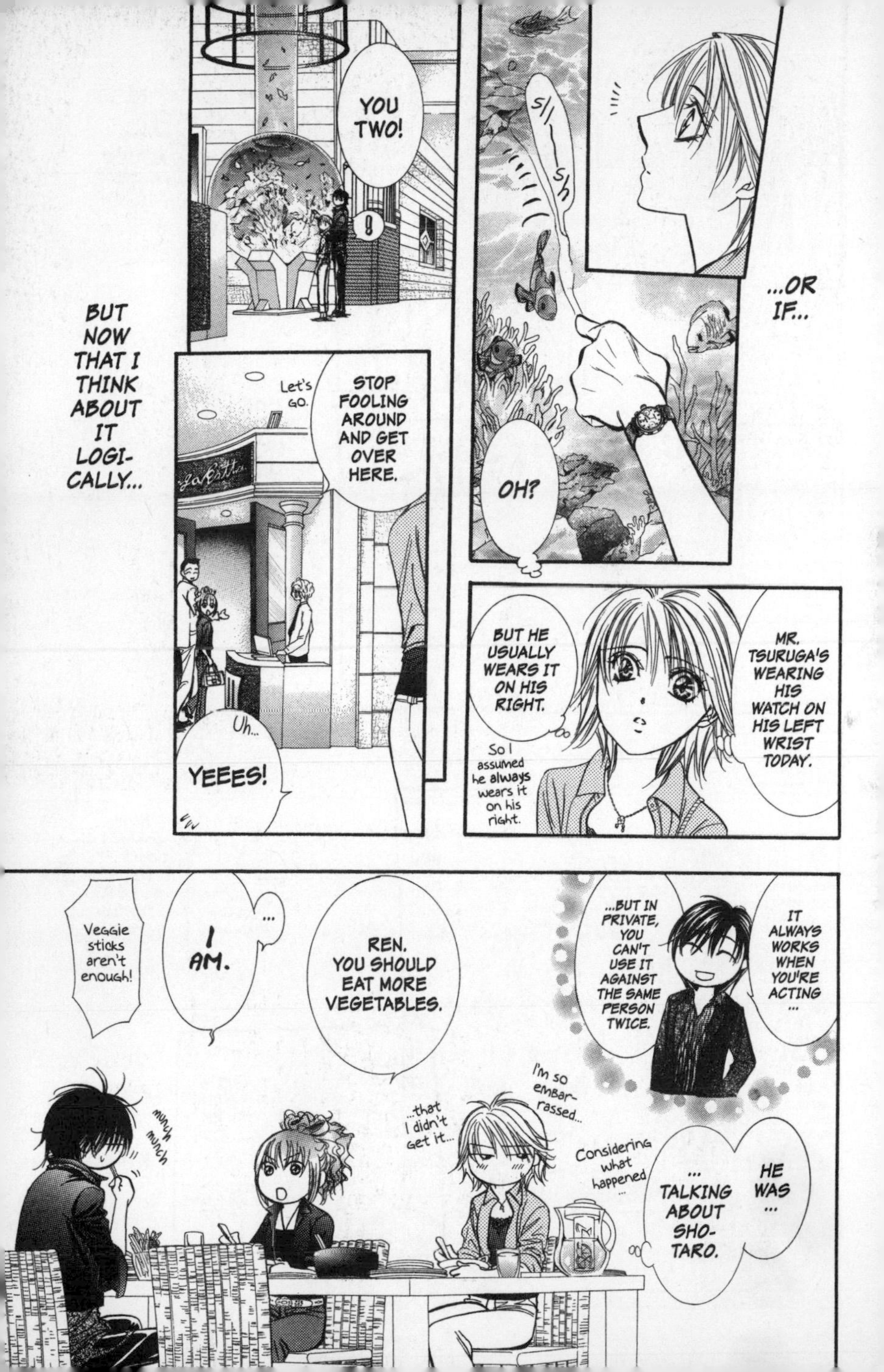

OH?
...OR IF...
MR. TSURUGA'S WEARING HIS WATCH ON HIS LEFT WRIST TODAY.
BUT HE USUALLY WEARS IT ON HIS RIGHT.
So I assumed he always wears it on his right.
YOU TWO!
!
STOP FOOLING AROUND AND GET OVER HERE.
Let's GO.
Uh...
YEEES!
BUT NOW THAT I THINK ABOUT IT LOGICALLY...
HE WAS...
...TALKING ABOUT SHO-TARO.
Considering what happened...
IT ALWAYS WORKS WHEN YOU'RE ACTING...
...BUT IN PRIVATE, YOU CAN'T USE IT AGAINST THE SAME PERSON TWICE.
I'm so embarrassed...
...that I didn't get it...
REN. YOU SHOULD EAT MORE VEGETABLES.
...
I AM.
Veggie sticks aren't enough!
munch munch

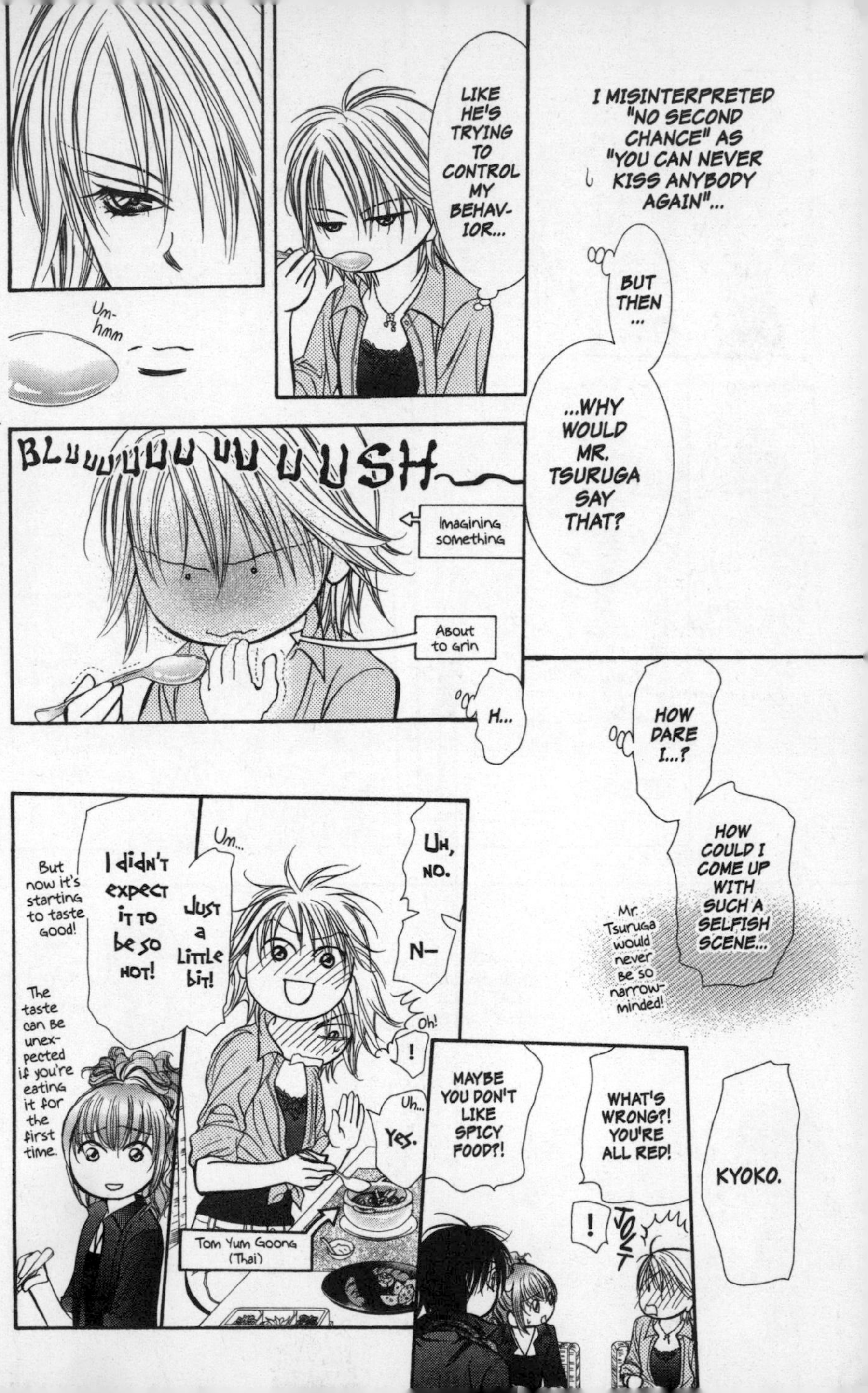
I MISINTERPRETED "NO SECOND CHANCE" AS "YOU CAN NEVER KISS ANYBODY AGAIN"...
LIKE HE'S TRYING TO CONTROL MY BEHAVIOR...
Um-hmm
BUT THEN...
...WHY WOULD MR. TSURUGA SAY THAT?
BLUUUUUUUUUUUSH
Imagining something
About to grin
H...
HOW DARE I...?
HOW COULD I COME UP WITH SUCH A SELFISH SCENE...
Mr. Tsuruga would never be so narrow-minded!
KYOKO.
WHAT'S WRONG?! YOU'RE ALL RED!
!
JOLT
MAYBE YOU DON'T LIKE SPICY FOOD?!
UH, NO.
N–
Oh!
!
Uh... Yes.
Um...
Just a little bit!
I didn't expect it to be so hot!
But now it's starting to taste good!
The taste can be unexpected if you're eating it for the first time.
Tom Yum Goong (Thai)

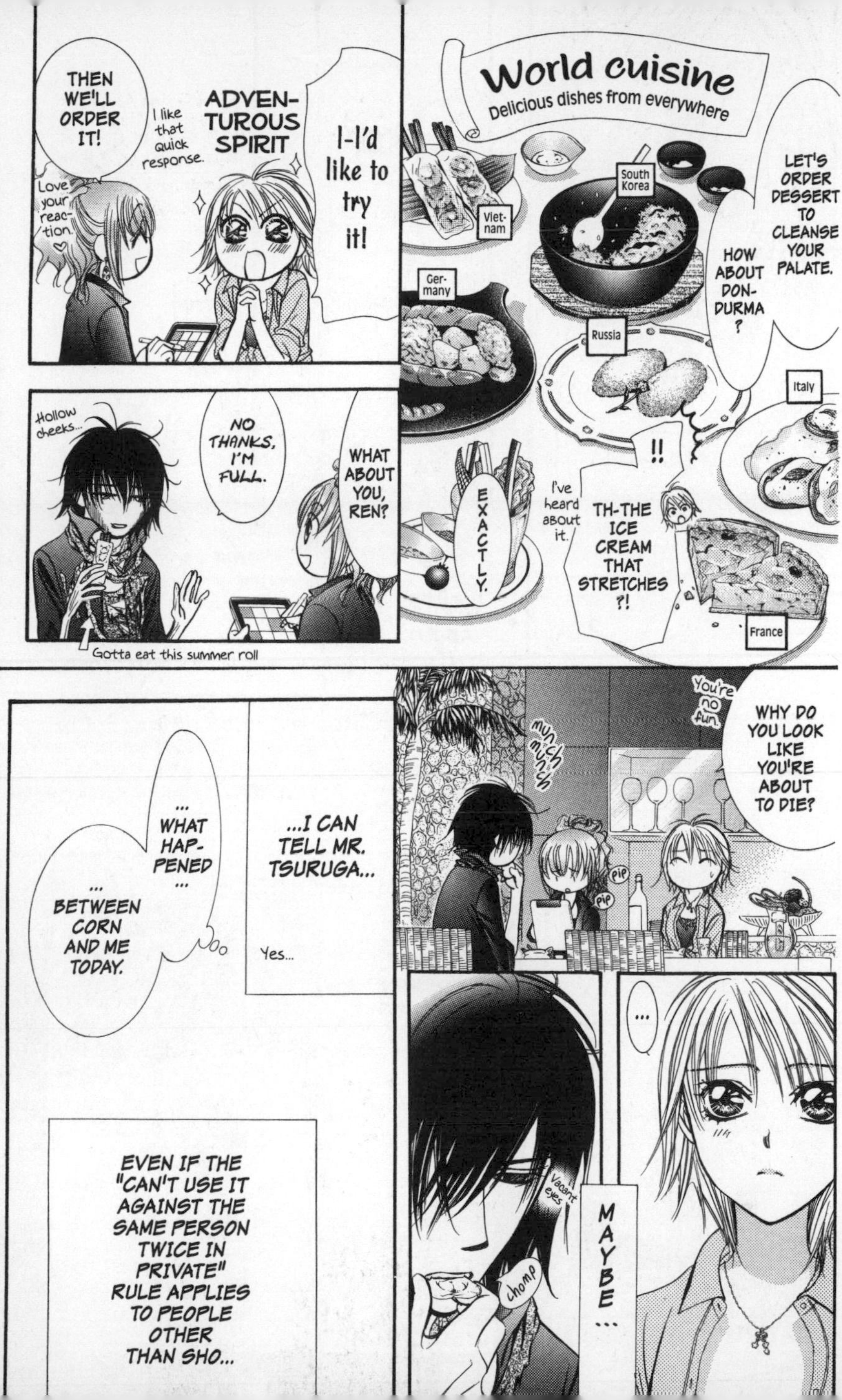
World cuisine
Delicious dishes from everywhere
South Korea
Viet-nam
Ger-many
Russia
Italy
France
LET'S ORDER DESSERT TO CLEANSE YOUR PALATE.
HOW ABOUT DON-DURMA?
!!
TH-THE ICE CREAM THAT STRETCHES?!
I've heard about it.
EXACTLY.
I-I'd like to try it!
ADVEN-TUROUS SPIRIT
I like that quick response.
THEN WE'LL ORDER IT!
Love your reac-tion. ♡
WHAT ABOUT YOU, REN?
NO THANKS, I'M FULL.
Hollow cheeks...
Gotta eat this summer roll
You're no fun.
WHY DO YOU LOOK LIKE YOU'RE ABOUT TO DIE?
munch munch
pip
pip
...
MAYBE...
Vacant eyes
chomp
...I CAN TELL MR. TSURUGA...
Yes...
...WHAT HAP-PENED... ...BETWEEN CORN AND ME TODAY.
EVEN IF THE "CAN'T USE IT AGAINST THE SAME PERSON TWICE IN PRIVATE" RULE APPLIES TO PEOPLE OTHER THAN SHO...

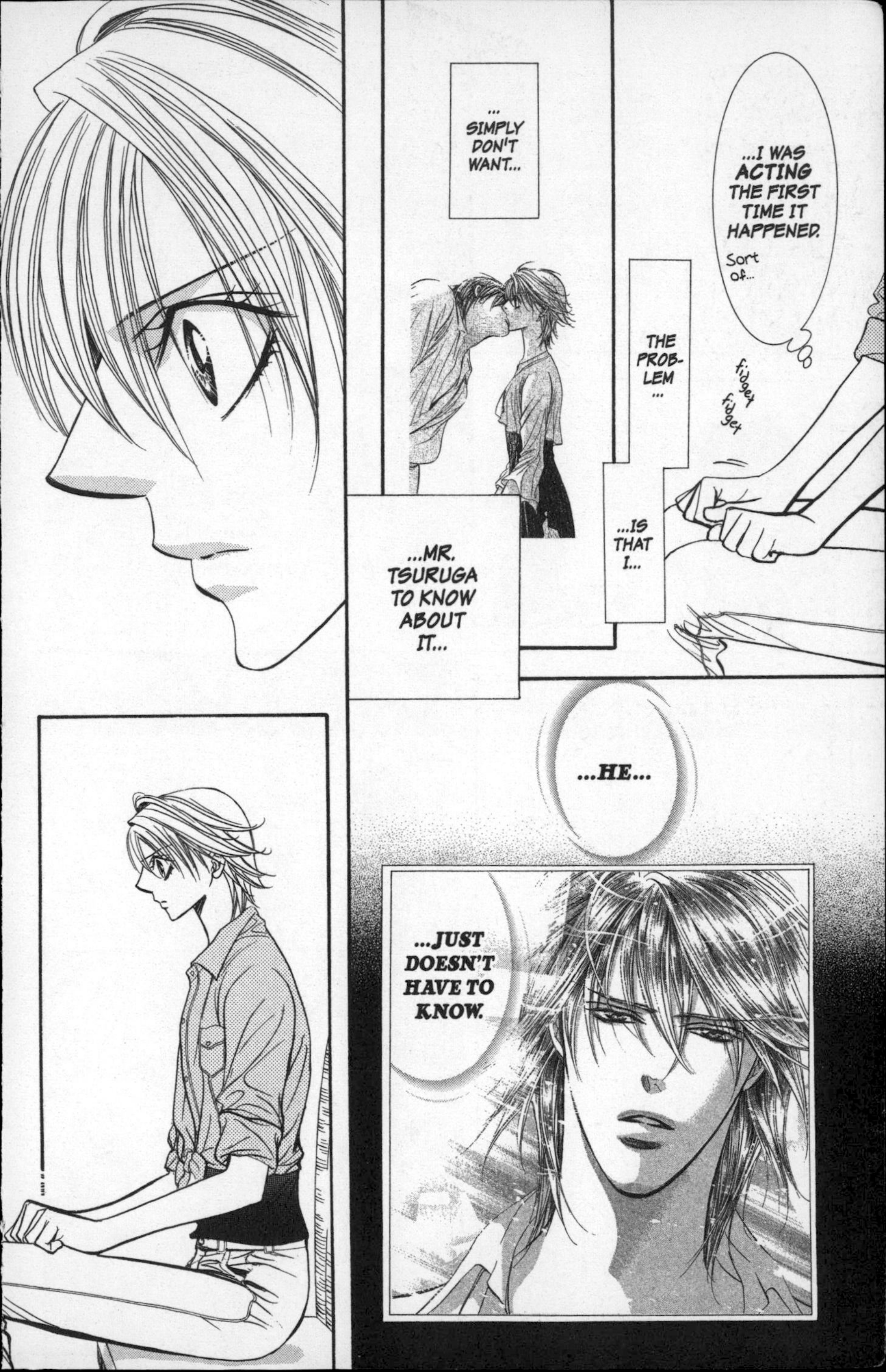
...I WAS ACTING THE FIRST TIME IT HAPPENED.
Sort of...
fidget fidget
THE PROB-LEM...
...IS THAT I...
...SIMPLY DON'T WANT...
...MR. TSURUGA TO KNOW ABOUT IT...
...HE...
...JUST DOESN'T HAVE TO KNOW.

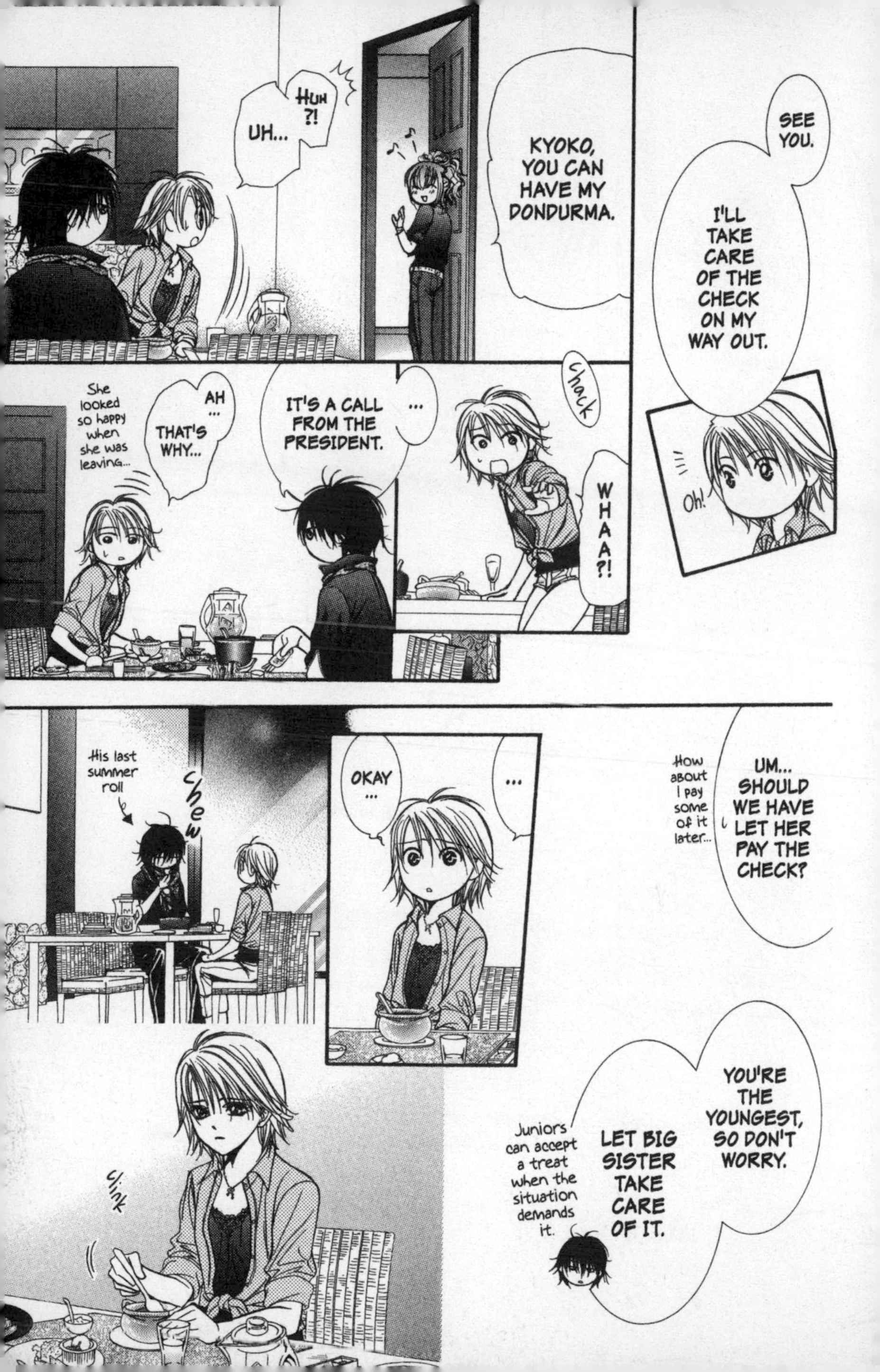
SEE YOU.
I'LL TAKE CARE OF THE CHECK ON MY WAY OUT.
KYOKO, YOU CAN HAVE MY DONDURMA.
HUH ?!
UH...
Oh!
chack
WHAA?!
...
IT'S A CALL FROM THE PRESIDENT.
AH ... THAT'S WHY...
She looked so happy when she was leaving...
UM... SHOULD WE HAVE LET HER PAY THE CHECK?
How about I pay some of it later...
...
OKAY ...
His last summer roll
chew
YOU'RE THE YOUNGEST, SO DON'T WORRY.
LET BIG SISTER TAKE CARE OF IT.
Juniors can accept a treat when the situation demands it.
clink

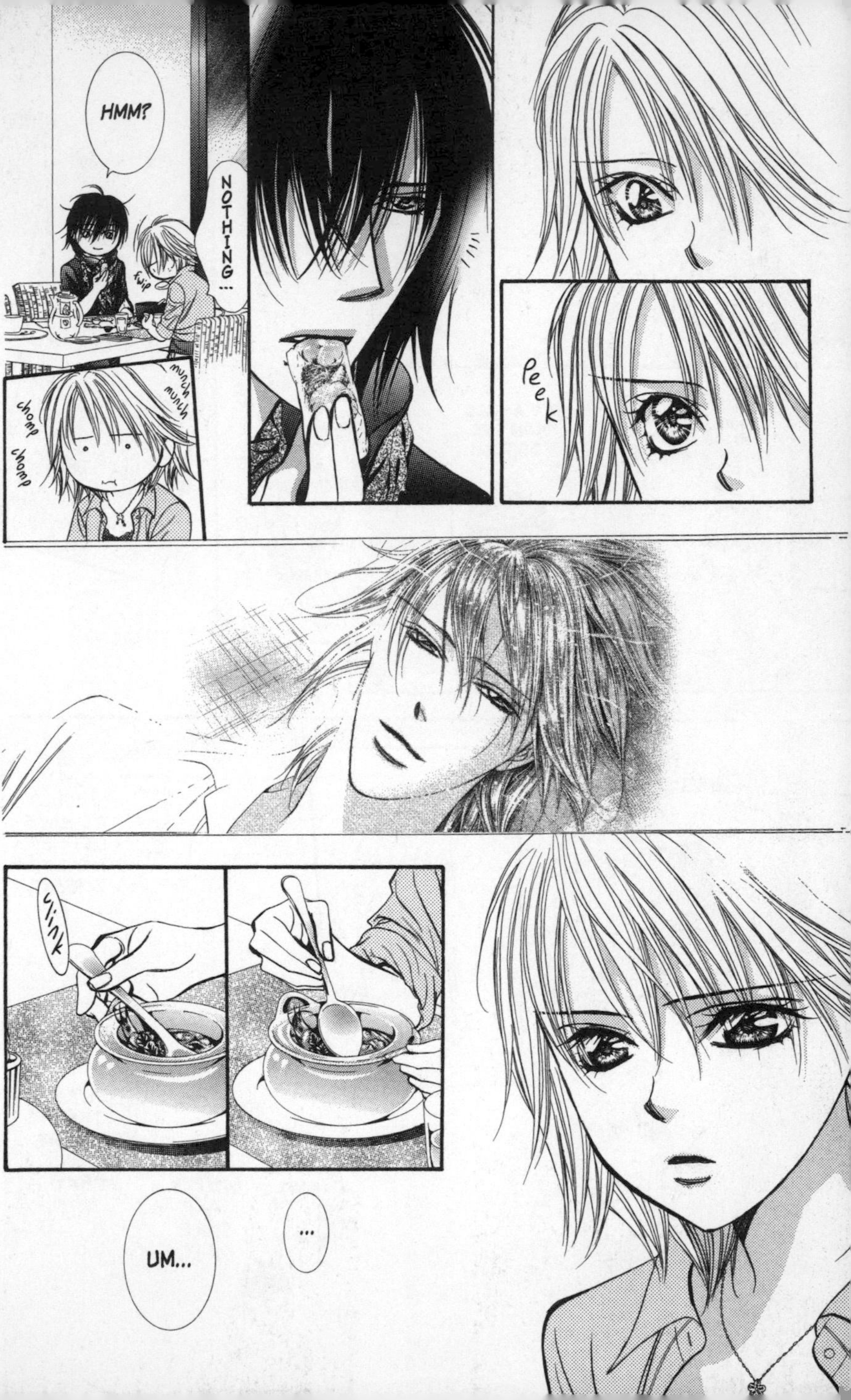
Peek
HMM?
NOTHING...
fwip
munch munch
chomp chomp
clink
...
UM...

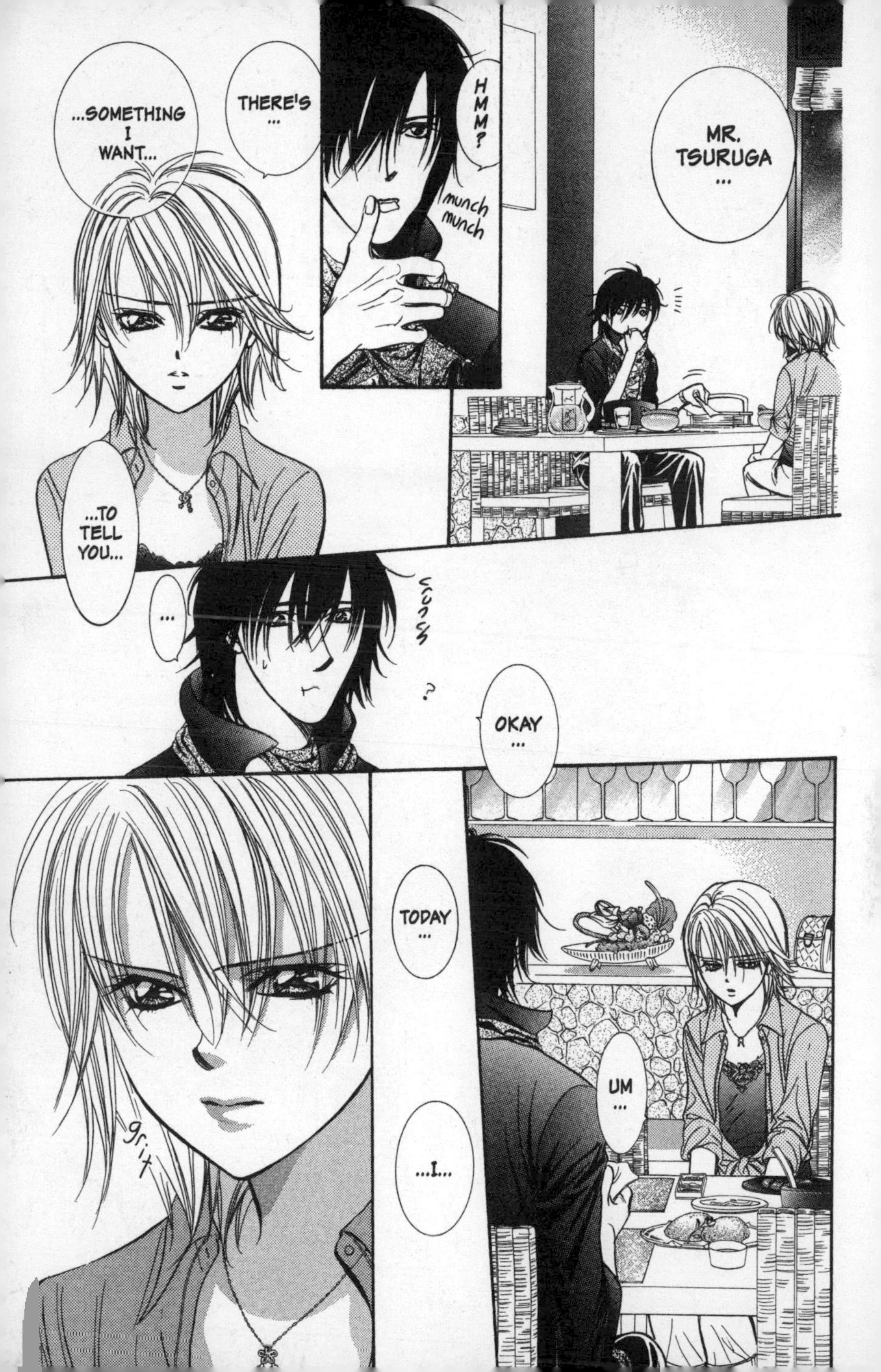
MR. TSURUGA ...
HMM?
munch munch
THERE'S ...
...SOMETHING I WANT...
...TO TELL YOU...
...
crunch
?
OKAY ...
UM ...
...I...
TODAY ...
grit

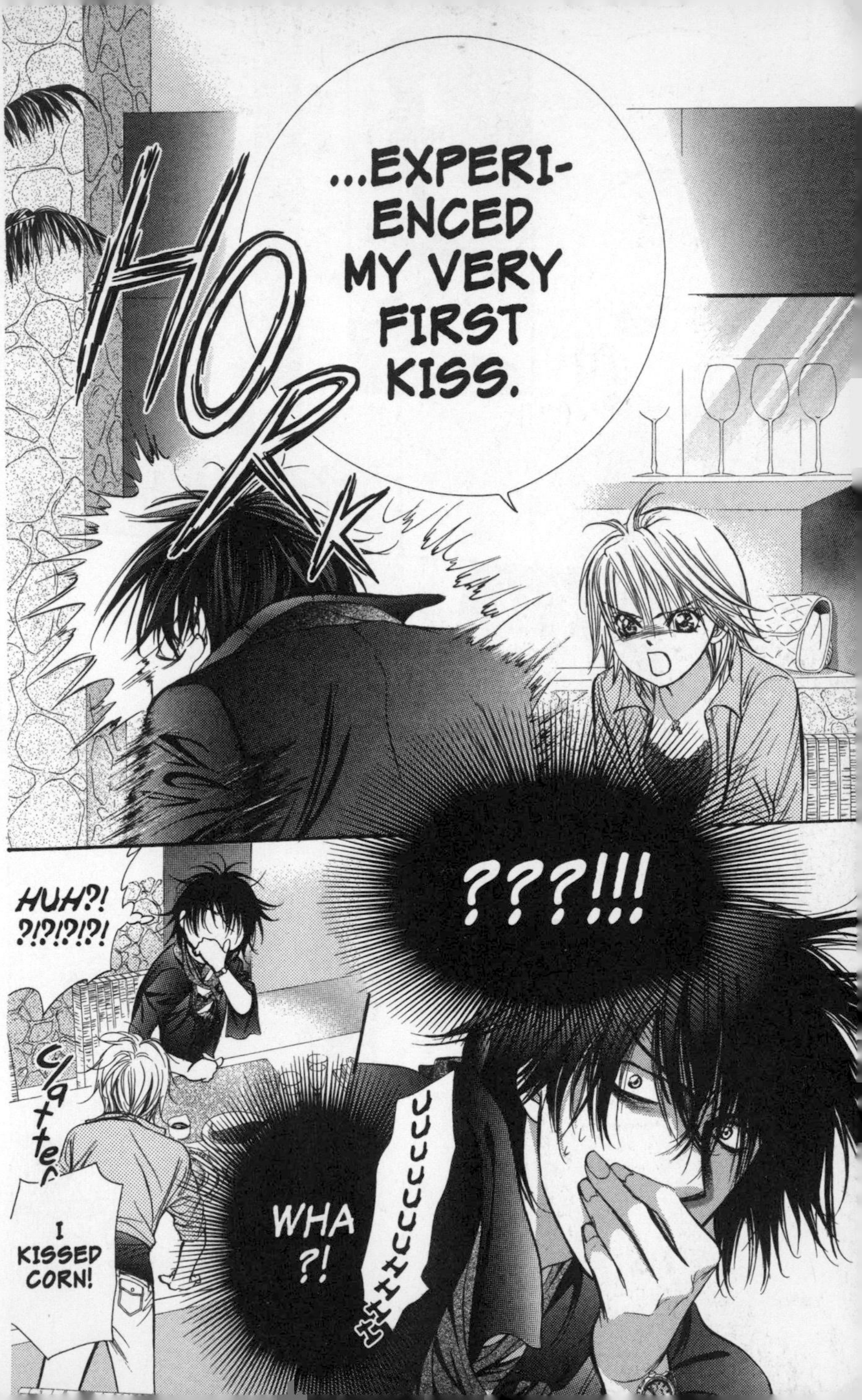
...EXPERIENCED MY VERY FIRST KISS.
HORK
???!!!
UUUUUUUUHHHH
WHA ?!
HUH?! ?!?!?!?!
clatter
I KISSED CORN!

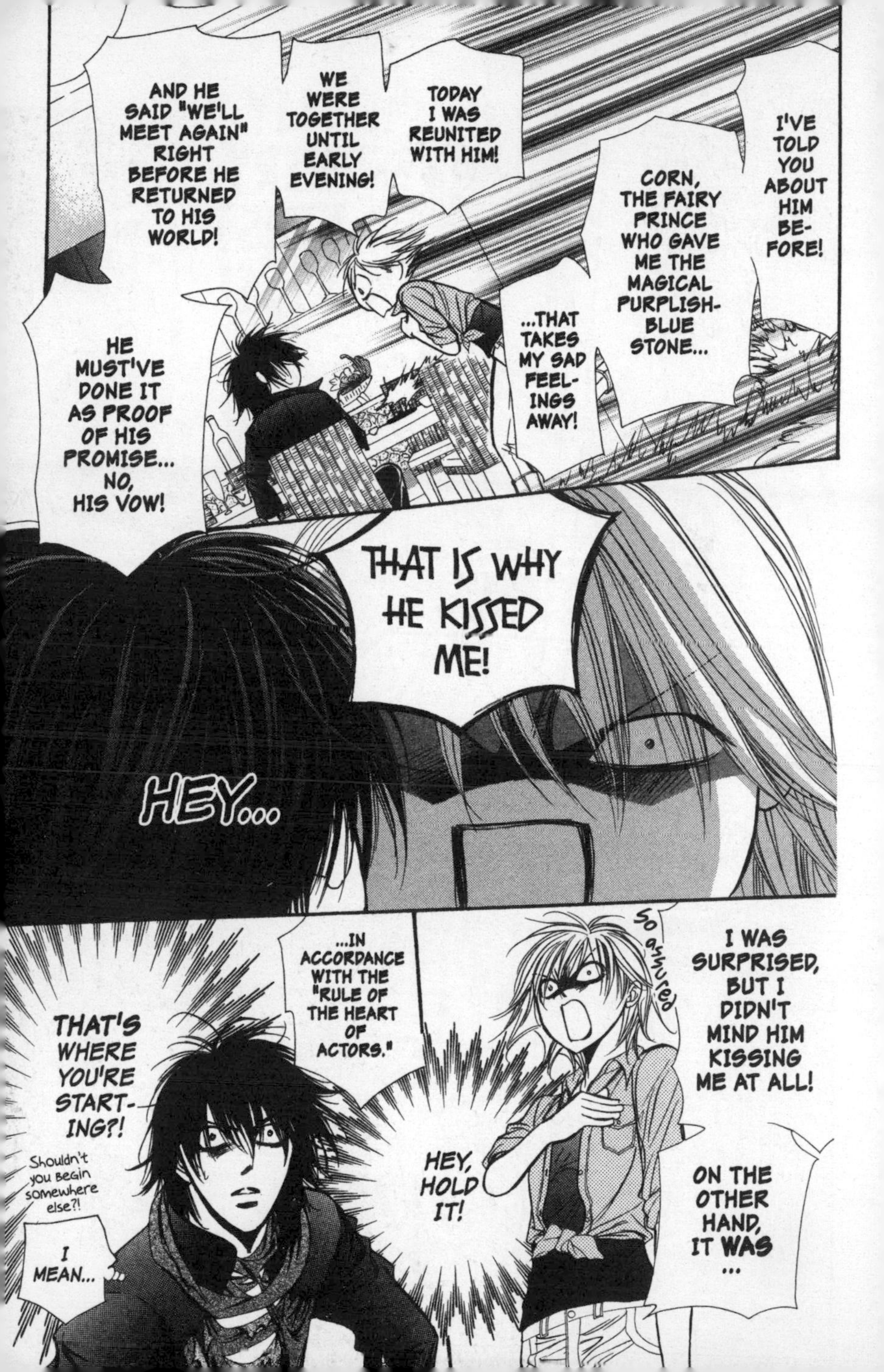
I'VE TOLD YOU ABOUT HIM BEFORE!
CORN, THE FAIRY PRINCE WHO GAVE ME THE MAGICAL PURPLISH-BLUE STONE...
...THAT TAKES MY SAD FEELINGS AWAY!
TODAY I WAS REUNITED WITH HIM!
WE WERE TOGETHER UNTIL EARLY EVENING!
AND HE SAID "WE'LL MEET AGAIN" RIGHT BEFORE HE RETURNED TO HIS WORLD!
HE MUST'VE DONE IT AS PROOF OF HIS PROMISE... NO, HIS VOW!
THAT IS WHY HE KISSED ME!
HEY...
So assured
I WAS SURPRISED, BUT I DIDN'T MIND HIM KISSING ME AT ALL!
ON THE OTHER HAND, IT WAS ...
...IN ACCORDANCE WITH THE "RULE OF THE HEART OF ACTORS."
HEY, HOLD IT!
THAT'S WHERE YOU'RE STARTING?!
Shouldn't you begin somewhere else?!
I MEAN...

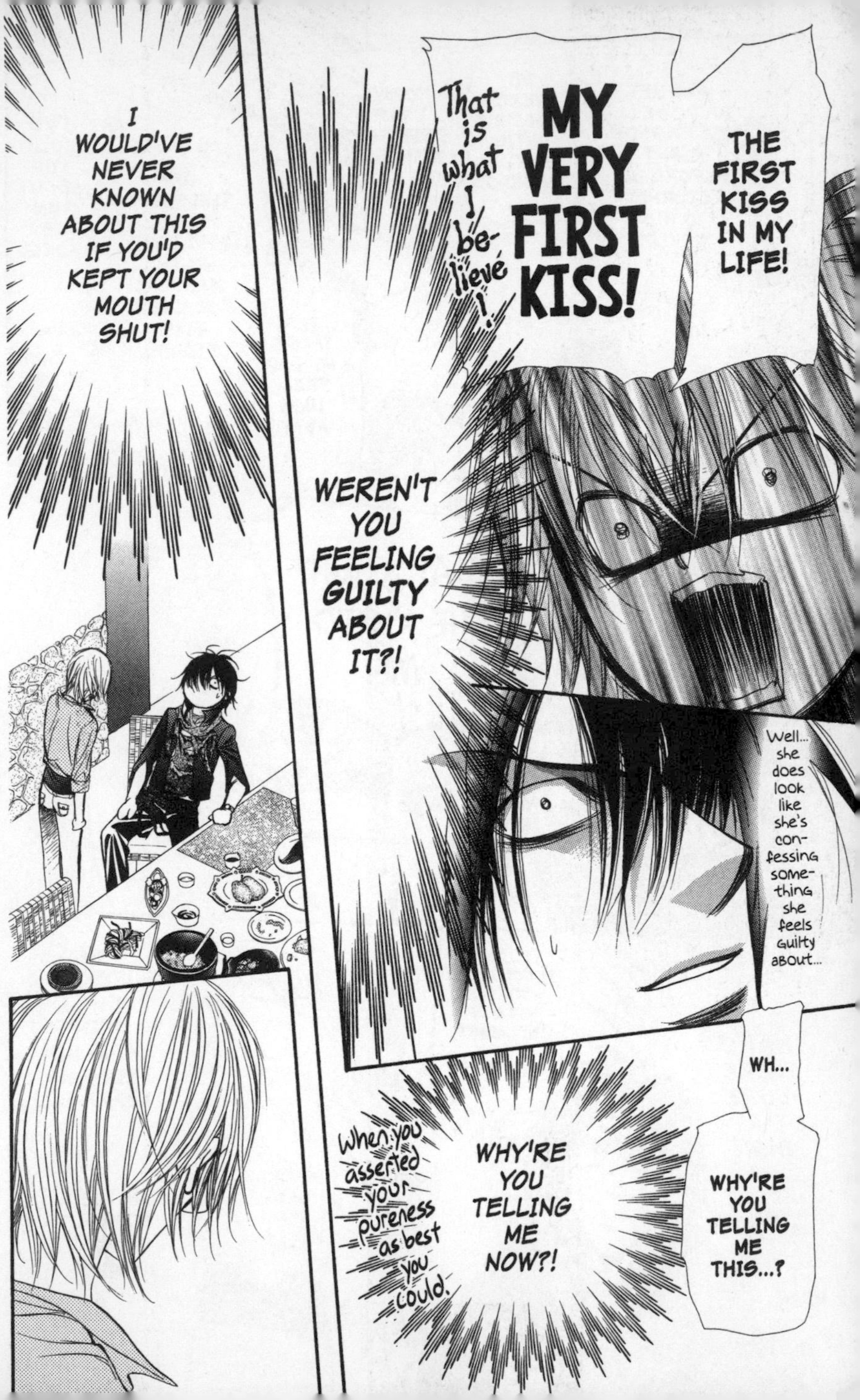
THE FIRST KISS IN MY LIFE!
MY VERY FIRST KISS!
That is what I be-lieve!
WEREN'T YOU FEELING GUILTY ABOUT IT?!
Well... she does look like she's con-fessing some-thing she feels guilty about...
WH...
WHY'RE YOU TELLING ME THIS...?
WHY'RE YOU TELLING ME NOW?!
When you asserted your pureness as best you could.
I WOULD'VE NEVER KNOWN ABOUT THIS IF YOU'D KEPT YOUR MOUTH SHUT!

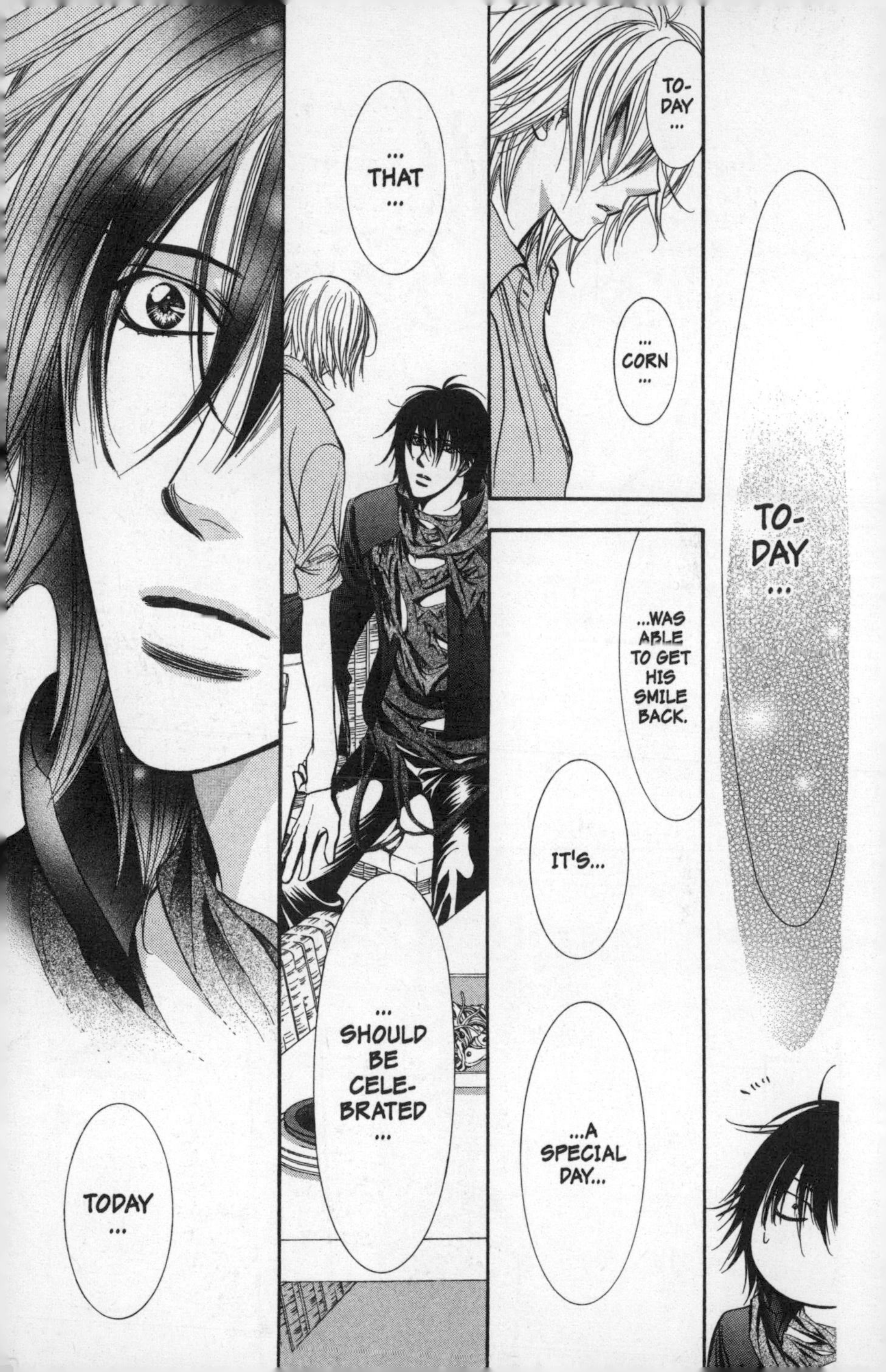
TO-DAY...
TO-DAY...
...CORN...
...WAS ABLE TO GET HIS SMILE BACK.
IT'S...
...A SPECIAL DAY...
...THAT...
...SHOULD BE CELE-BRATED...
TODAY...

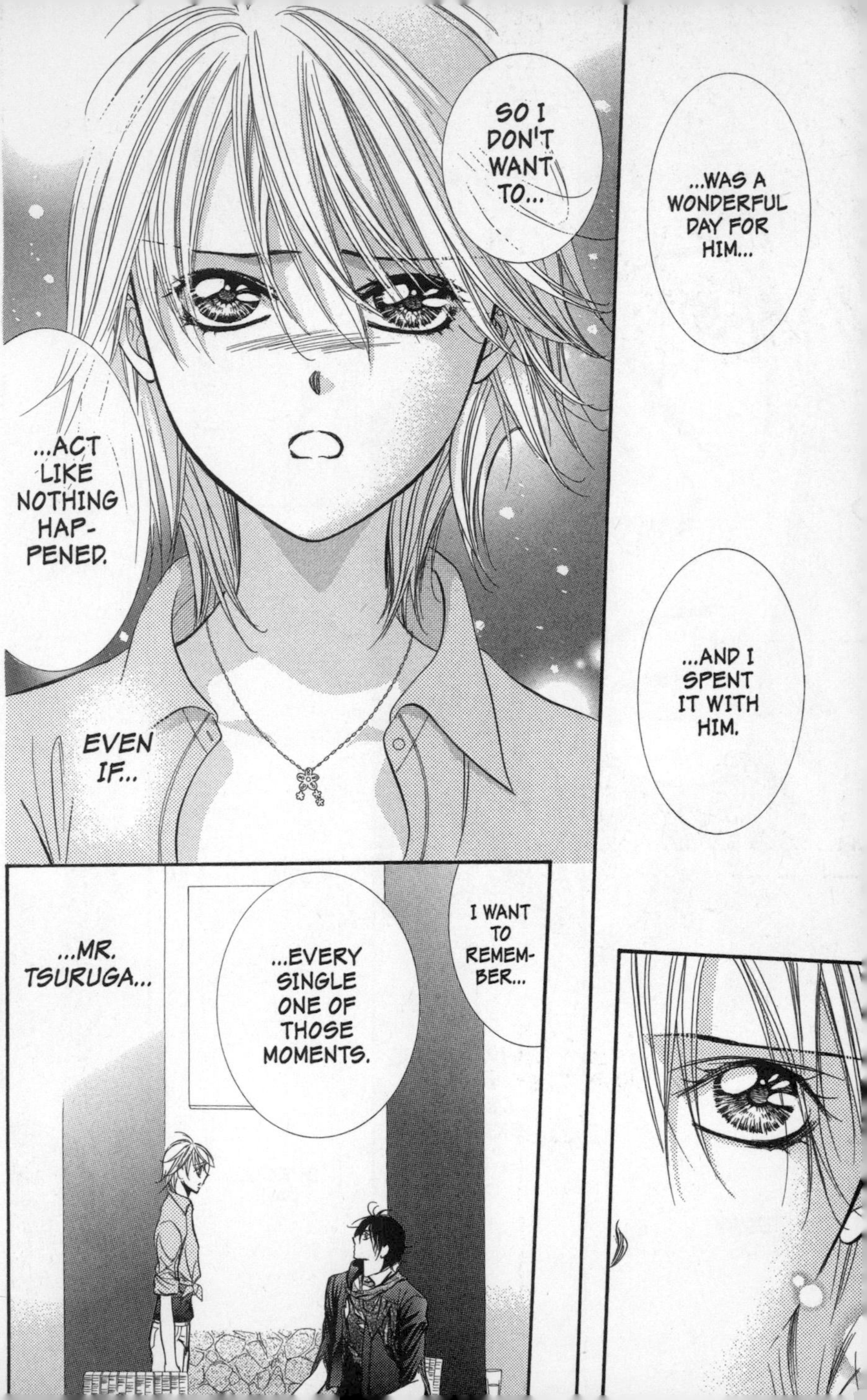
...WAS A WONDERFUL DAY FOR HIM...
...AND I SPENT IT WITH HIM.
SO I DON'T WANT TO...
...ACT LIKE NOTHING HAP-PENED.
EVEN IF...
I WANT TO REMEMBER...
...EVERY SINGLE ONE OF THOSE MOMENTS.
...MR. TSURUGA...

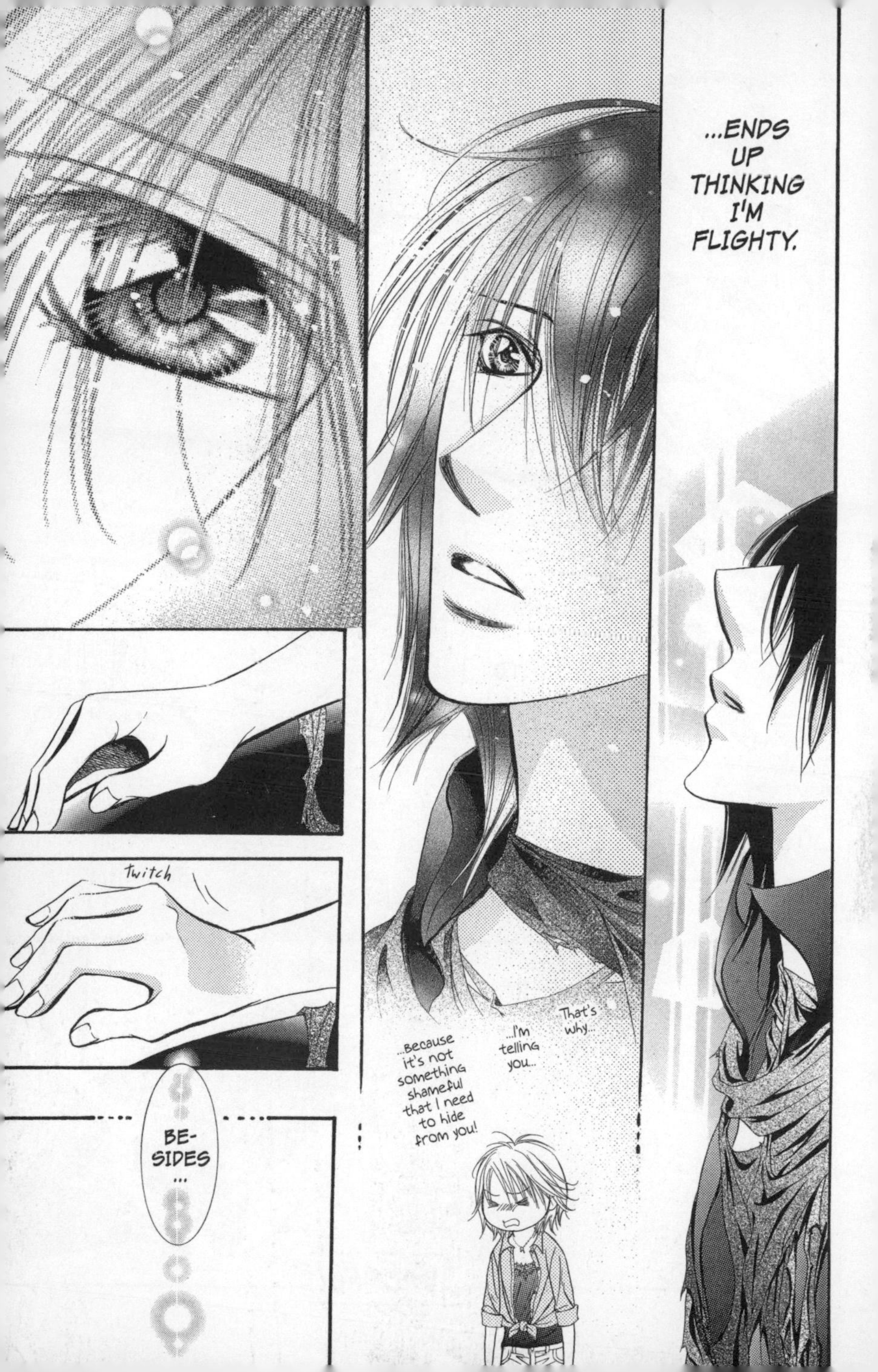
...ENDS UP THINKING I'M FLIGHTY.
That's why...
...I'm telling you...
...Because it's not something shameful that I need to hide from you!
twitch
BE-SIDES...

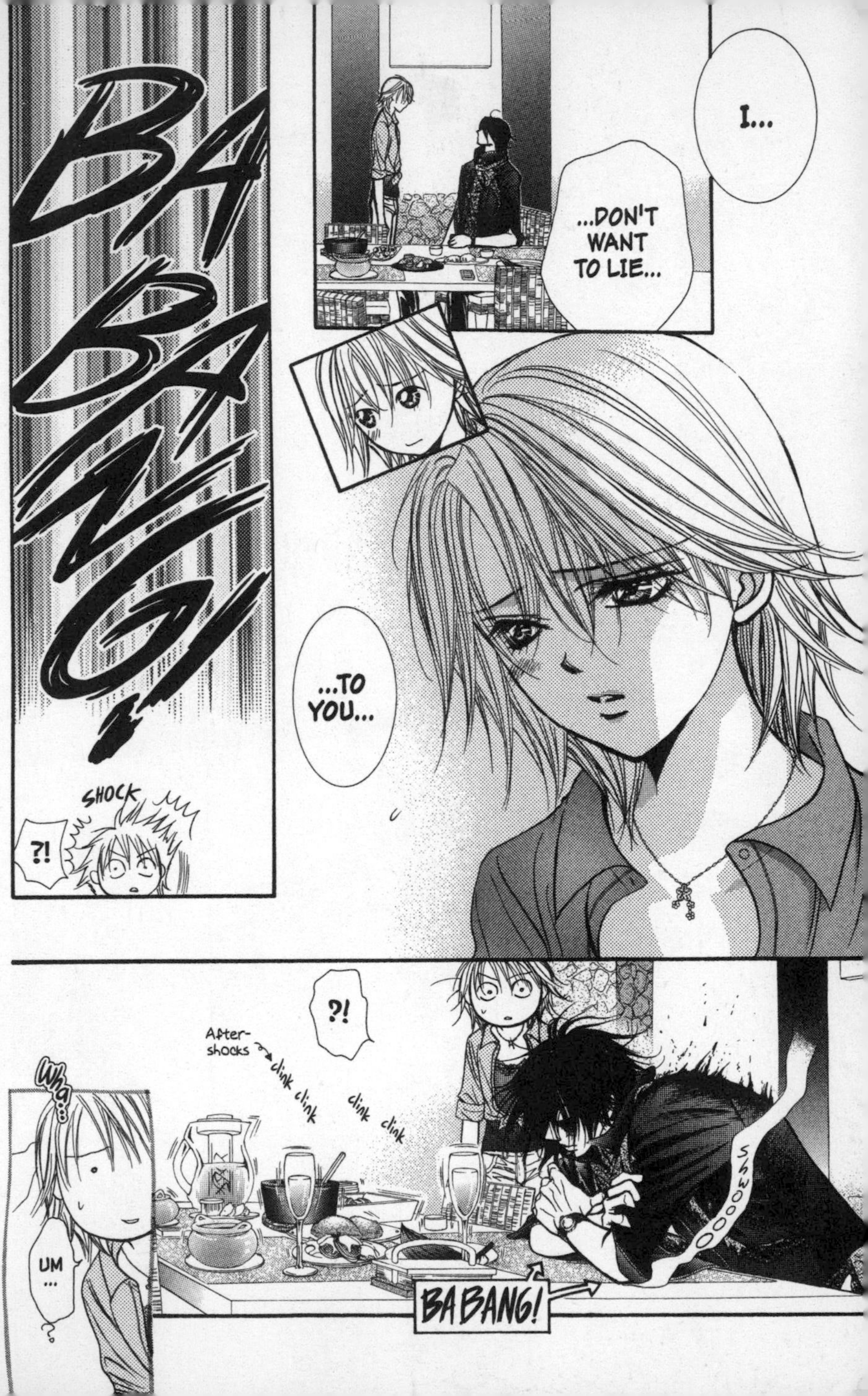
I...
...DON'T WANT TO LIE...
...TO YOU...
BA BA BANG!
SHOCK
?!
?!
After-shocks
clink clink
clink clink
Shwoooo
BA BANG!
Wha...
UM ...

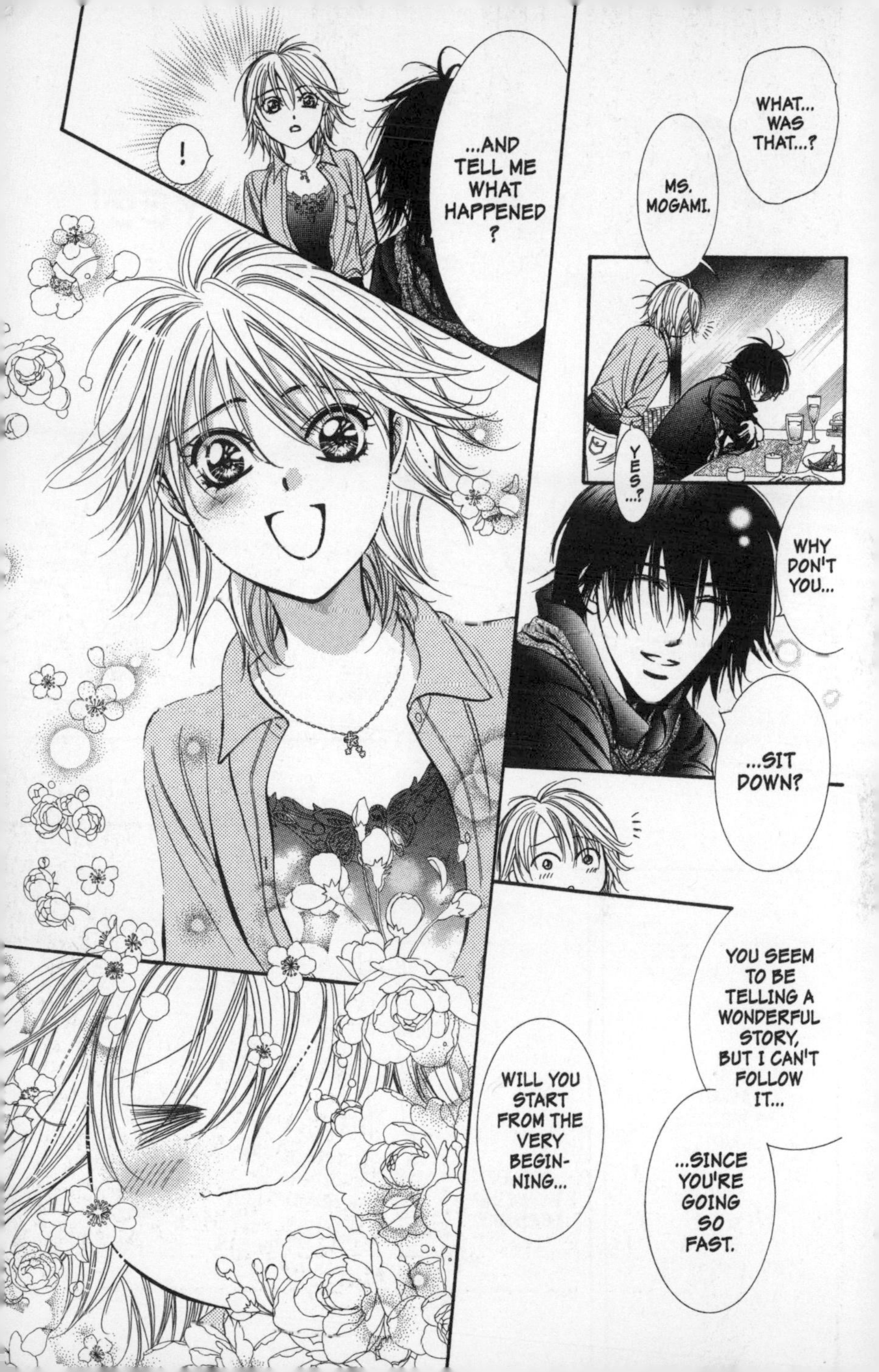
WHAT... WAS THAT...?
MS. MOGAMI.
YES...?
WHY DON'T YOU...
...SIT DOWN?
...AND TELL ME WHAT HAPPENED?
!
YOU SEEM TO BE TELLING A WONDERFUL STORY, BUT I CAN'T FOLLOW IT...
...SINCE YOU'RE GOING SO FAST.
WILL YOU START FROM THE VERY BEGIN-NING...

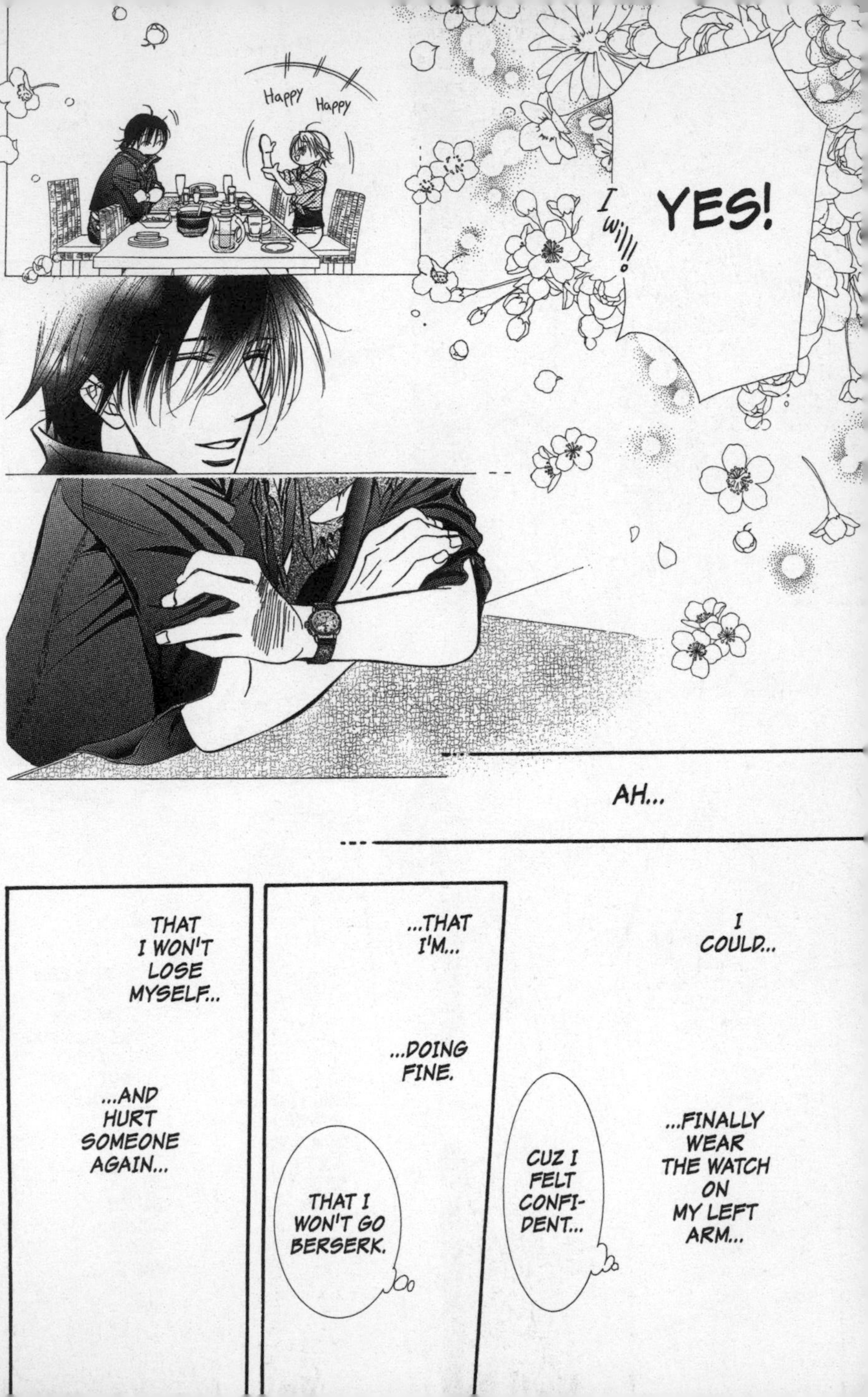
YES!
I will!!
Happy Happy
AH...
I COULD...
...FINALLY WEAR THE WATCH ON MY LEFT ARM...
CUZ I FELT CONFIDENT...
...THAT I'M...
...DOING FINE.
THAT I WON'T GO BERSERK.
THAT I WON'T LOSE MYSELF...
...AND HURT SOMEONE AGAIN...

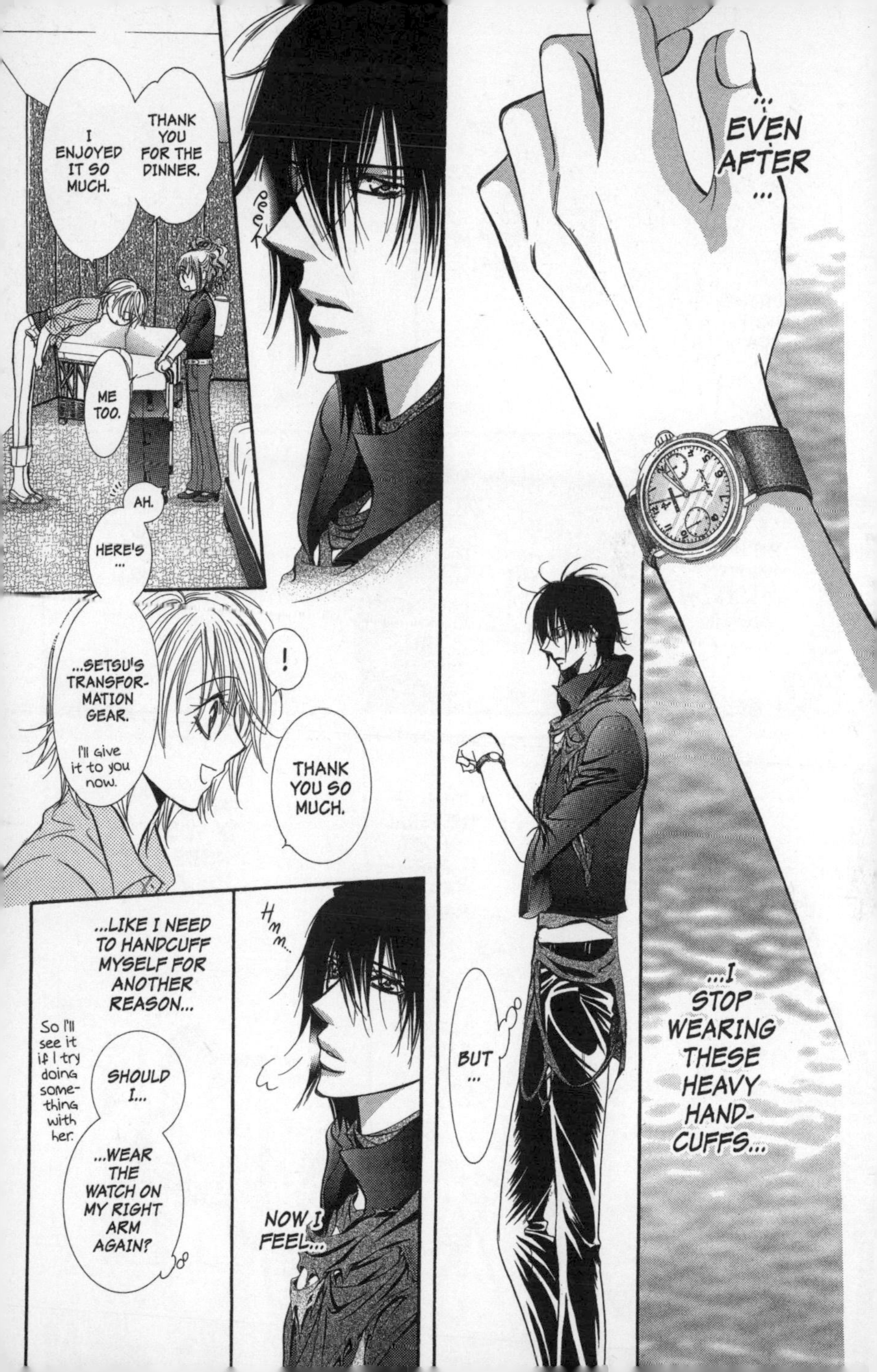
...EVEN AFTER ...
...I STOP WEARING THESE HEAVY HAND-CUFFS...
BUT ...
PEEK
THANK YOU FOR THE DINNER.
I ENJOYED IT SO MUCH.
ME TOO.
AH.
HERE'S ...
...SETSU'S TRANSFORMATION GEAR.
I'll give it to you now.
!
THANK YOU SO MUCH.
Hmm...
NOW I FEEL...
...LIKE I NEED TO HANDCUFF MYSELF FOR ANOTHER REASON...
SHOULD I...
...WEAR THE WATCH ON MY RIGHT ARM AGAIN?
So I'll see it if I try doing something with her.

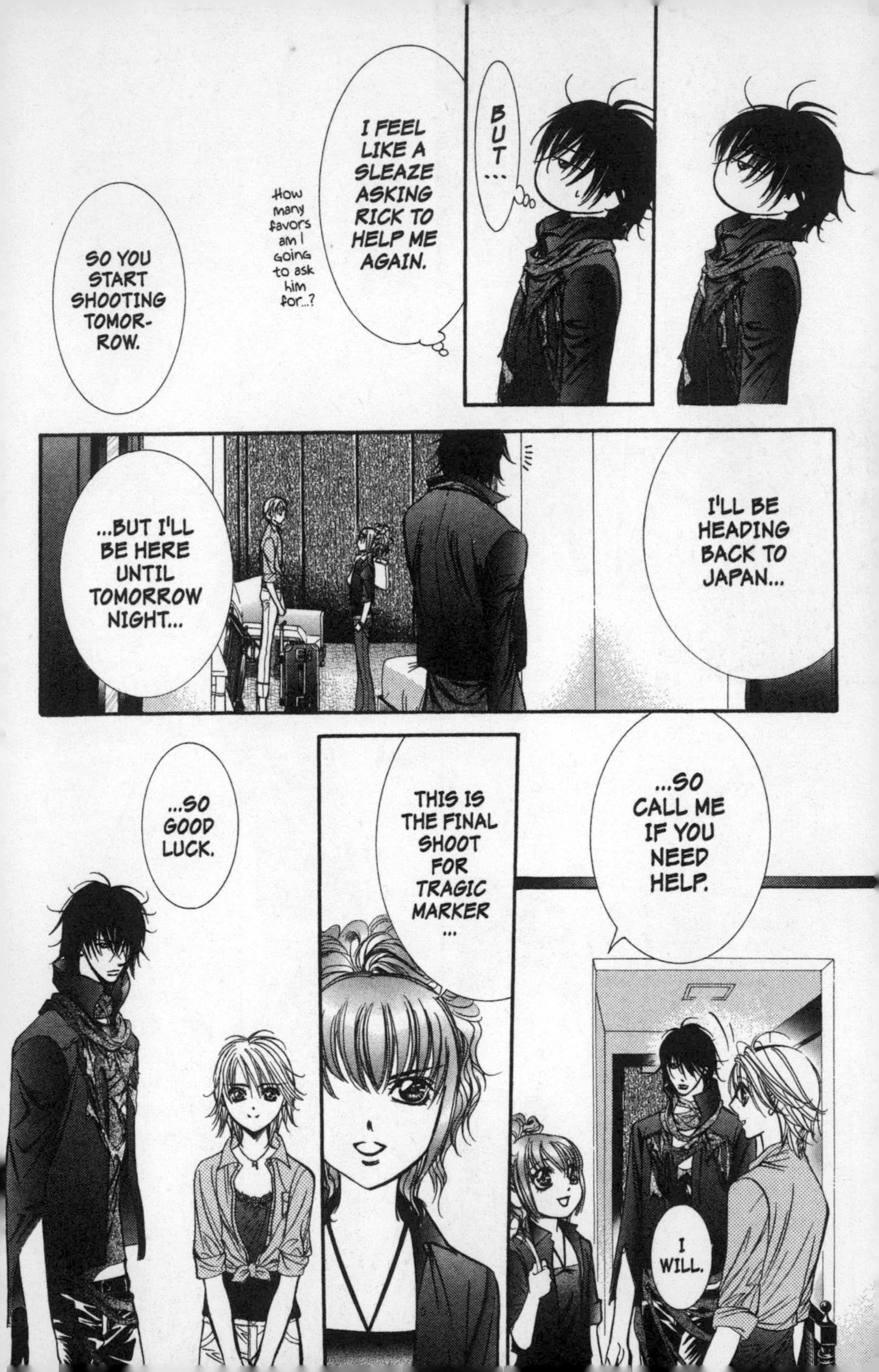
BUT...
I FEEL LIKE A SLEAZE ASKING RICK TO HELP ME AGAIN.
How many favors am I going to ask him for...?
SO YOU START SHOOTING TOMOR-ROW.
I'LL BE HEADING BACK TO JAPAN...
...BUT I'LL BE HERE UNTIL TOMORROW NIGHT...
...SO CALL ME IF YOU NEED HELP.
I WILL.
THIS IS THE FINAL SHOOT FOR TRAGIC MARKER...
...SO GOOD LUCK.

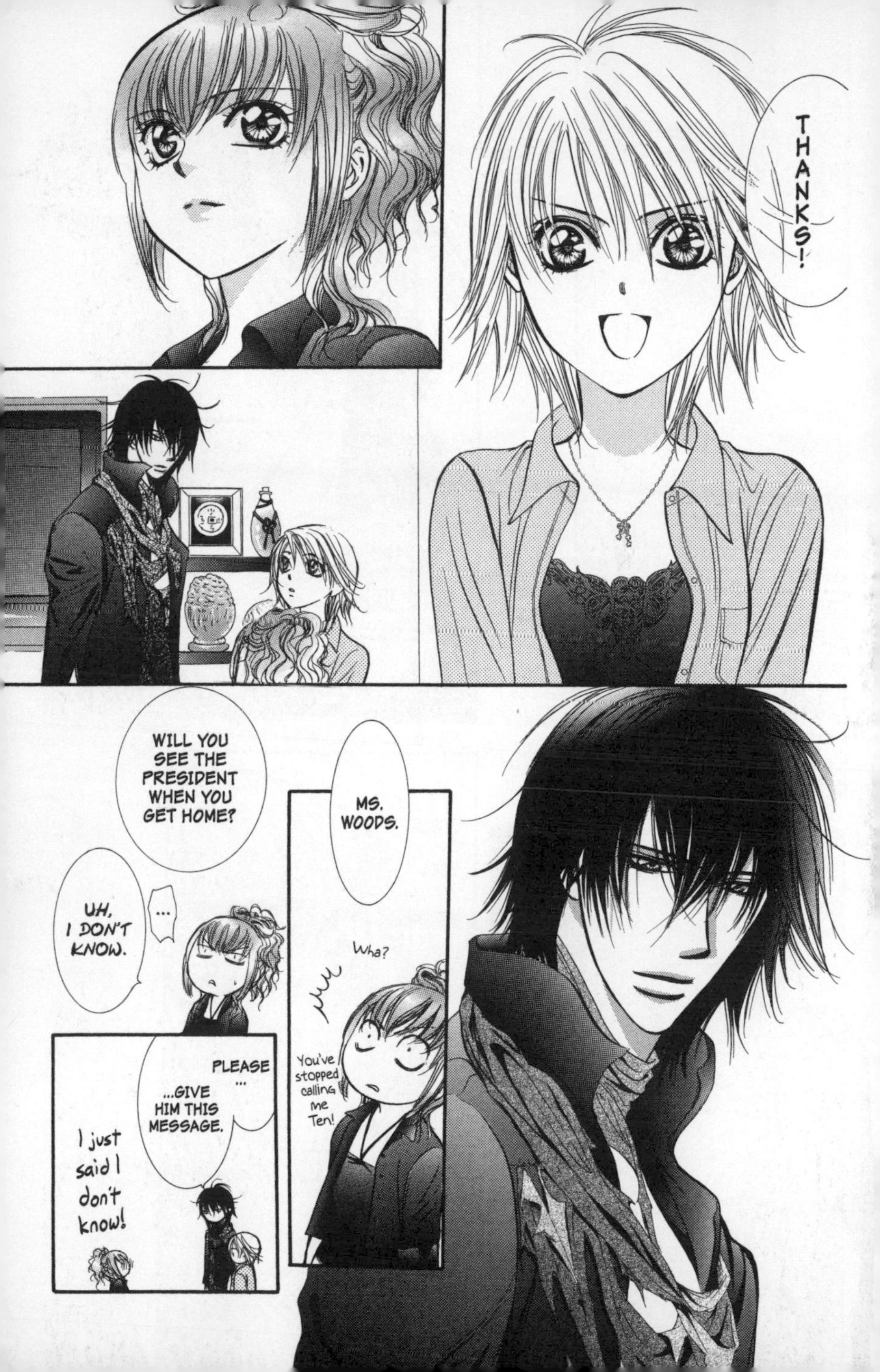
THANKS!
WILL YOU SEE THE PRESIDENT WHEN YOU GET HOME?
...
UH, I DON'T KNOW.
MS. WOODS.
Wha?
You've stopped calling me Ten!
PLEASE ...
...GIVE HIM THIS MESSAGE.
I just said I don't know!

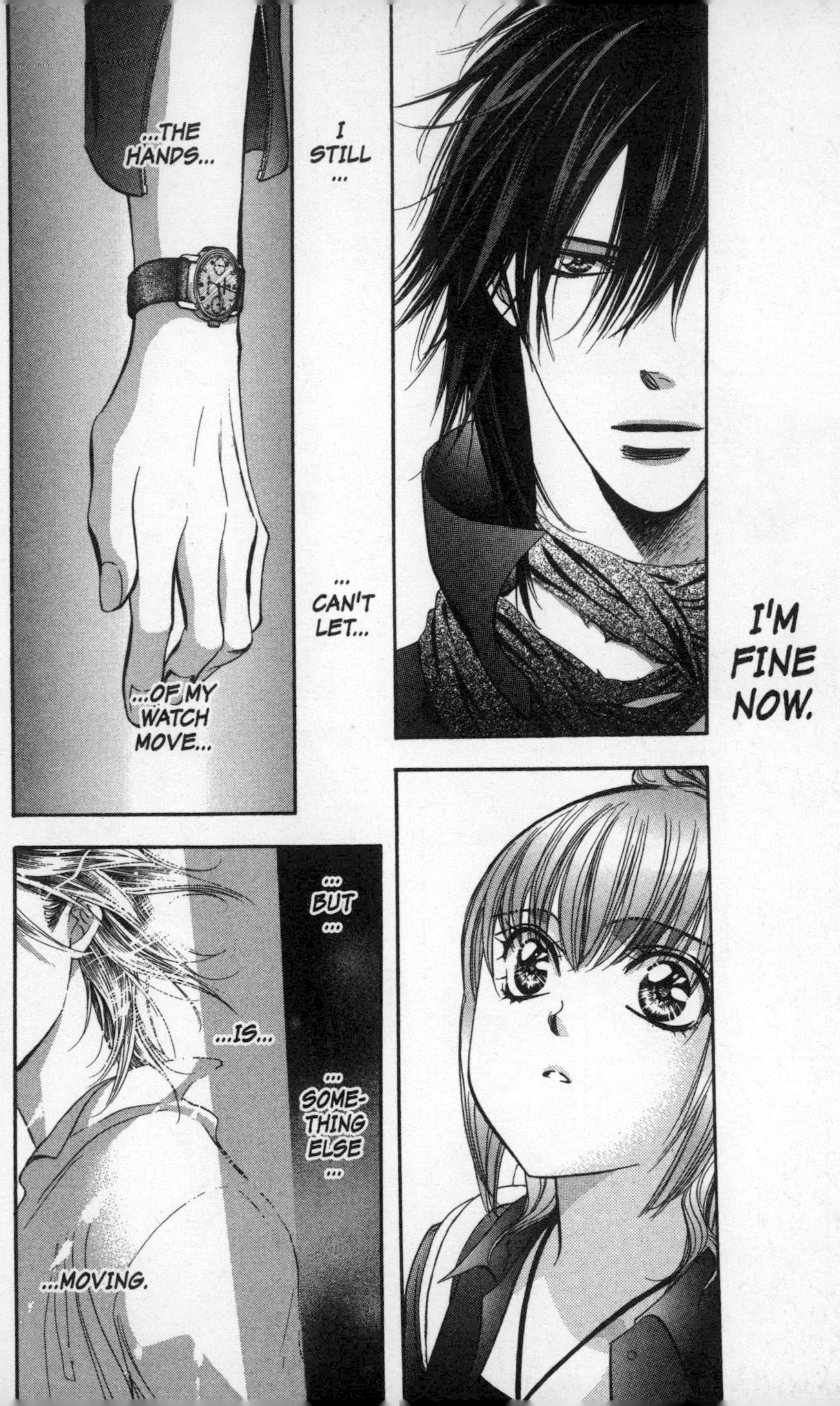
I'M FINE NOW.
I STILL ...
... CAN'T LET...
...THE HANDS...
...OF MY WATCH MOVE...
... BUT ...
... SOME-THING ELSE ...
...IS...
...MOVING.

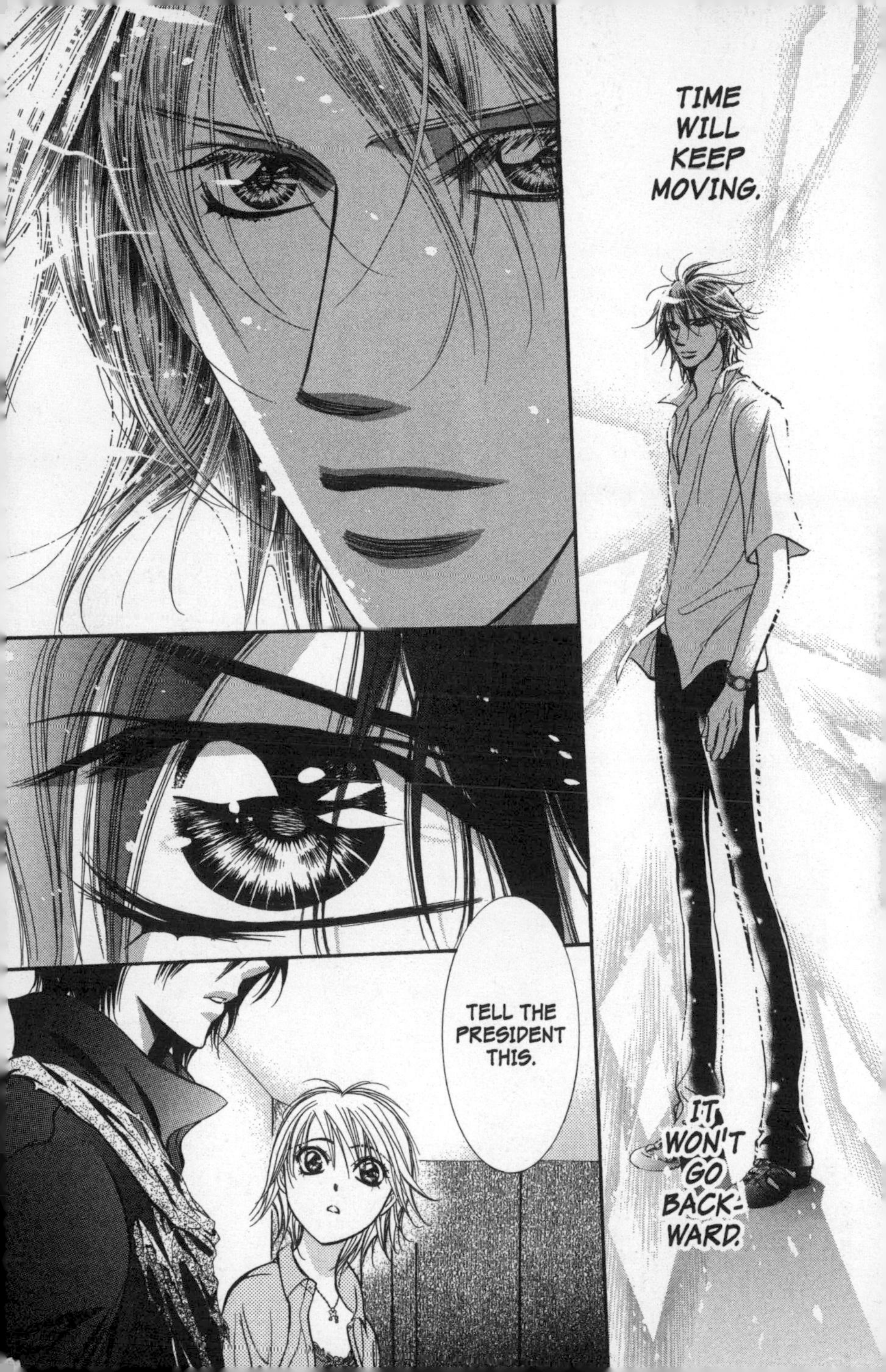
TIME WILL KEEP MOVING.
IT WON'T GO BACK-WARD.
TELL THE PRESIDENT THIS.

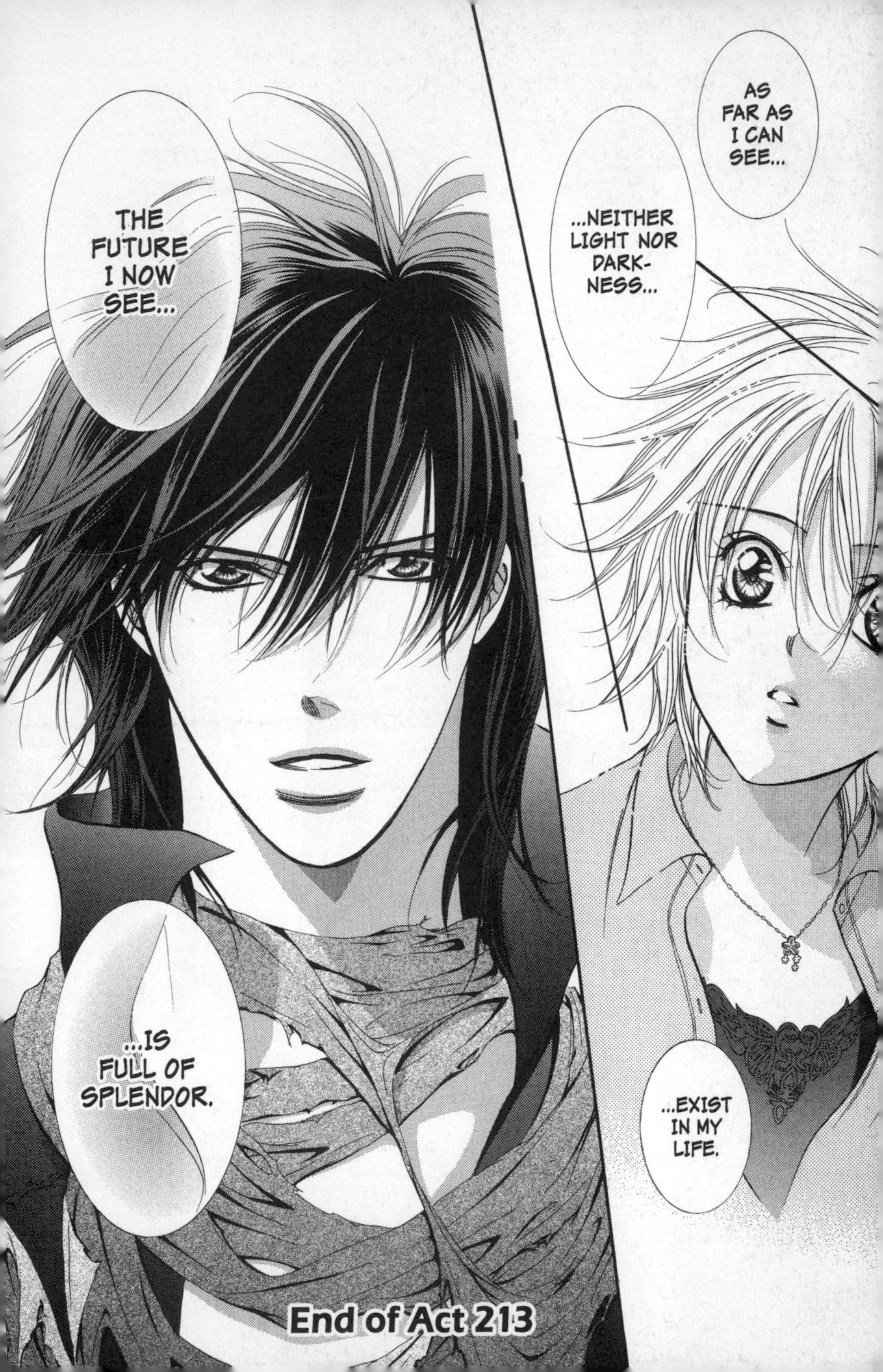
AS FAR AS I CAN SEE...
...NEITHER LIGHT NOR DARK-NESS...
...EXIST IN MY LIFE.
THE FUTURE I NOW SEE...
...IS FULL OF SPLENDOR.
End of Act 213

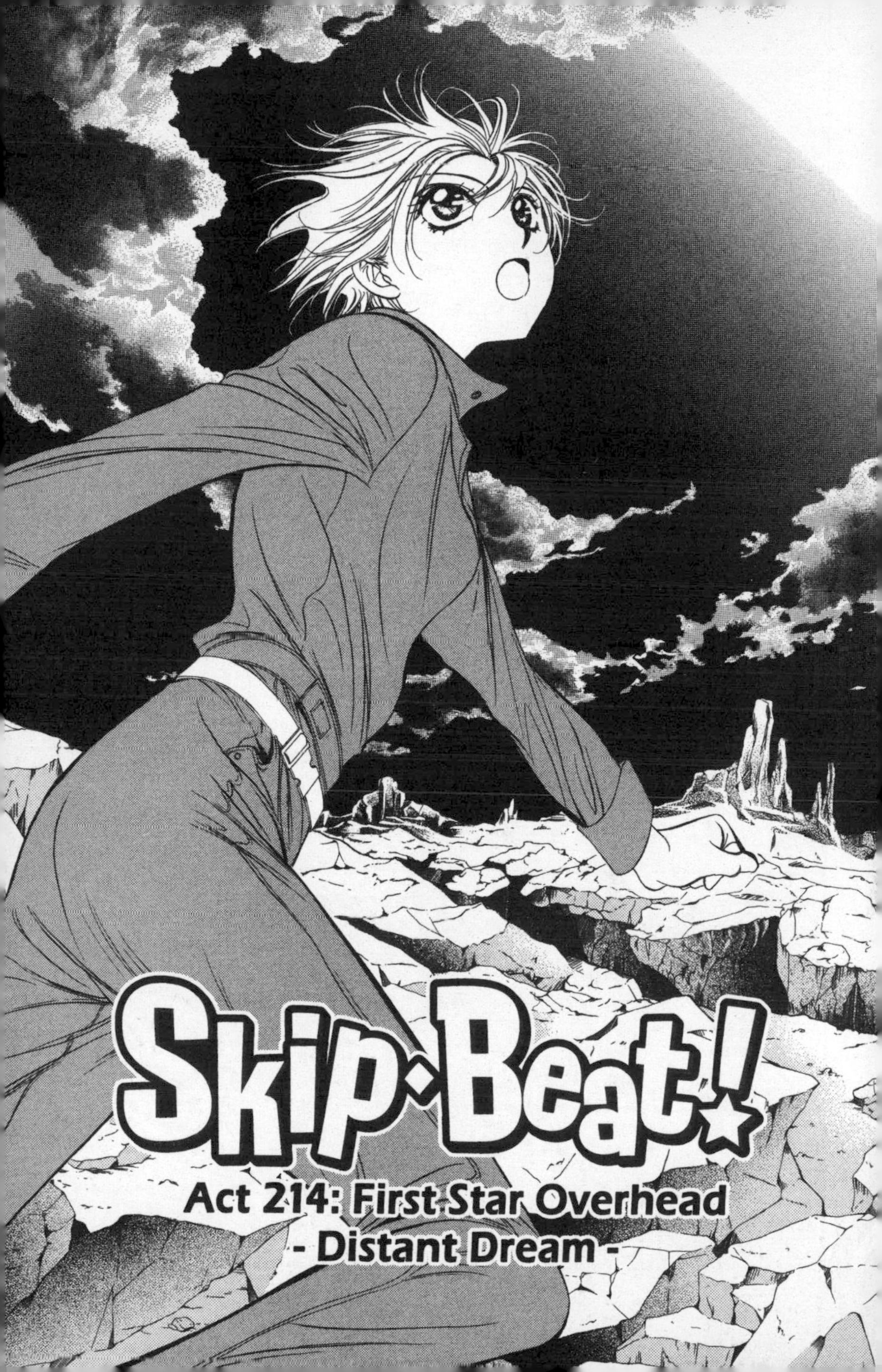
Skip·Beat!
Act 214: First Star Overhead
- Distant Dream -

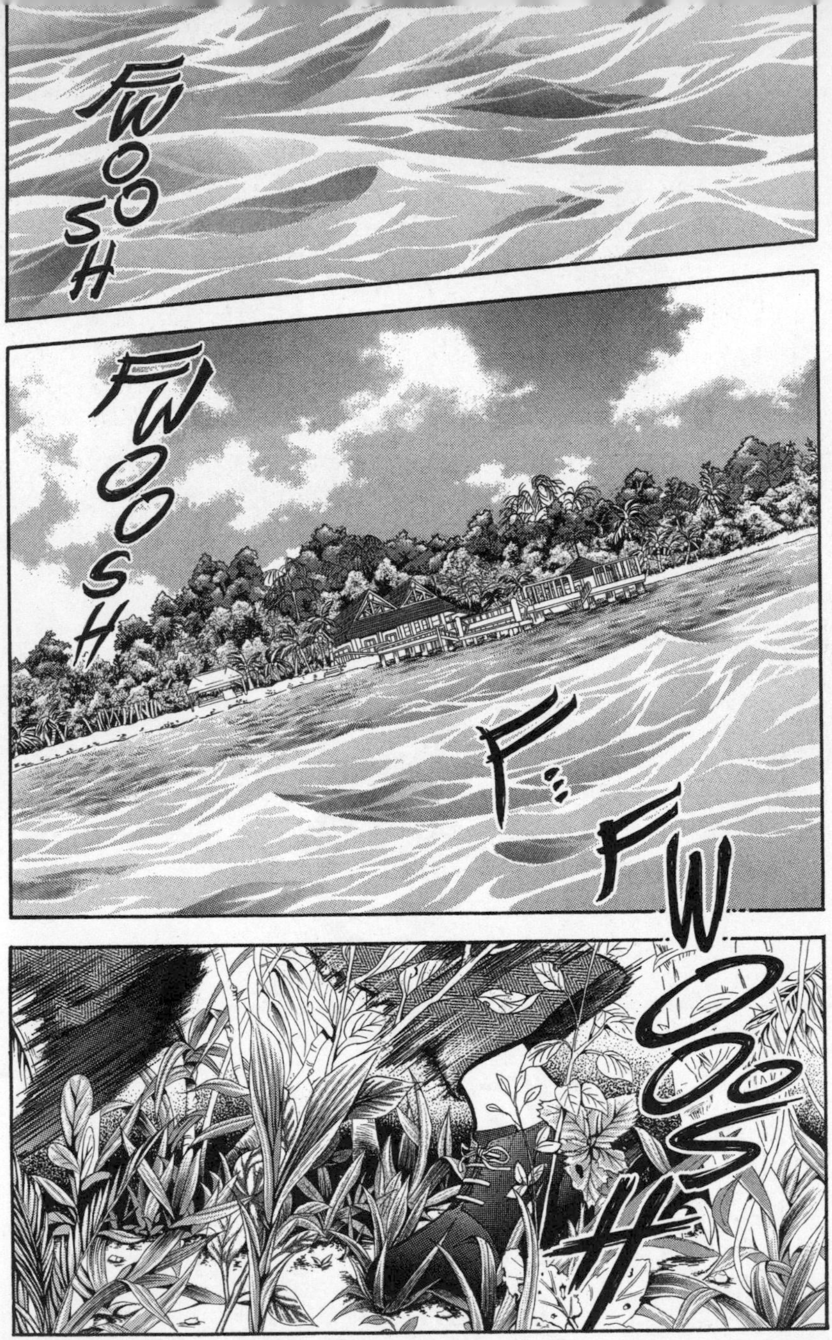
FWOOSH
FWOOOSH
F... FWOOOSH

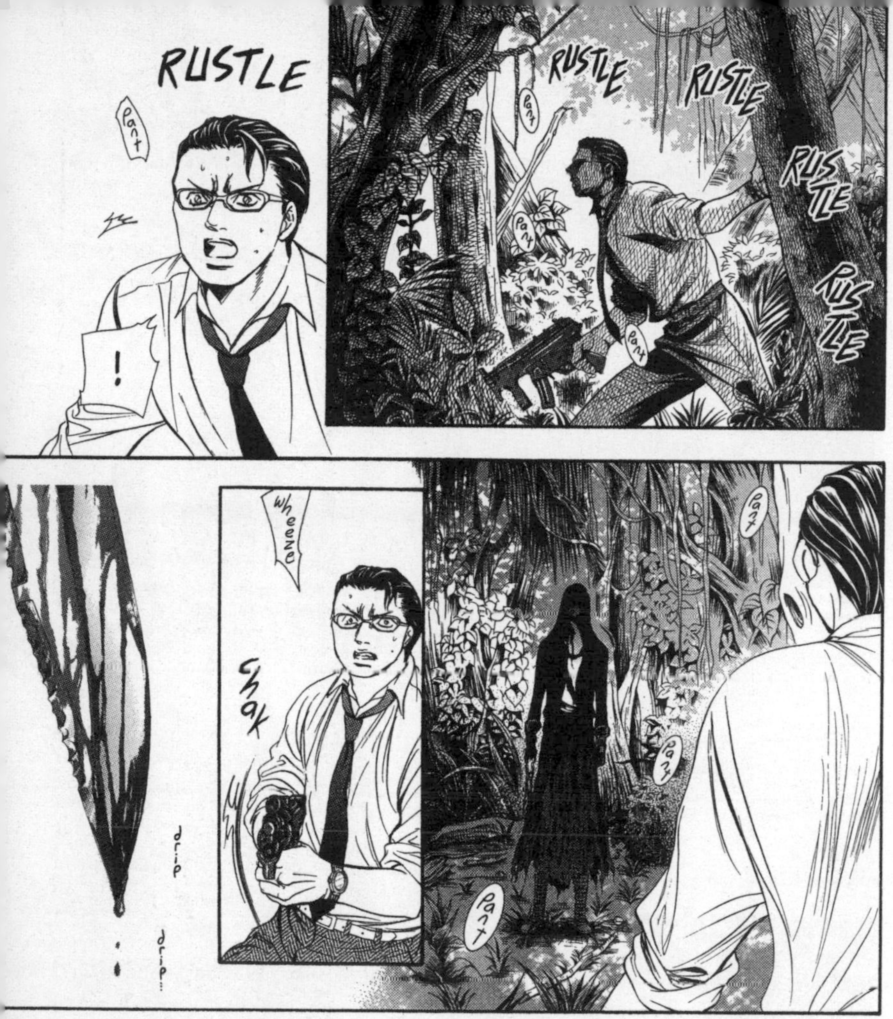
RUSTLE
Pant
RUSTLE
Pant
RUSTLE
RUSTLE
Pant
RUSTLE
Pant
!
Pant
Pant
Pant
wheeze
Chak
drip
drip...
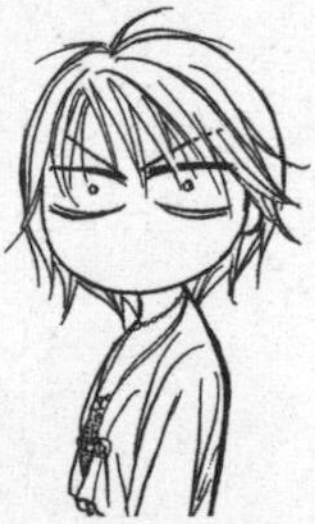

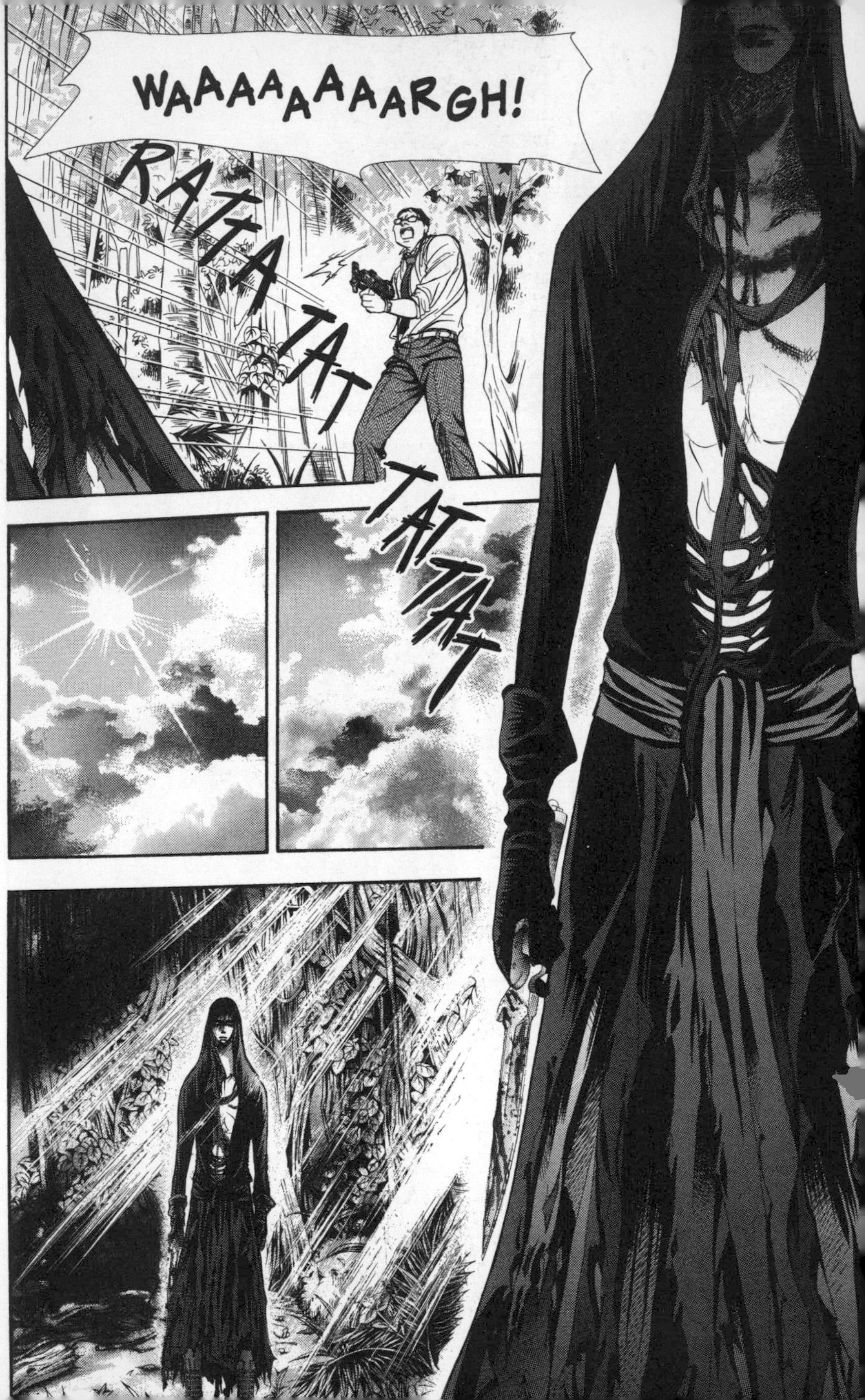
WAAAAAAAARGH!
RATTA TAT TAT TAT TAT

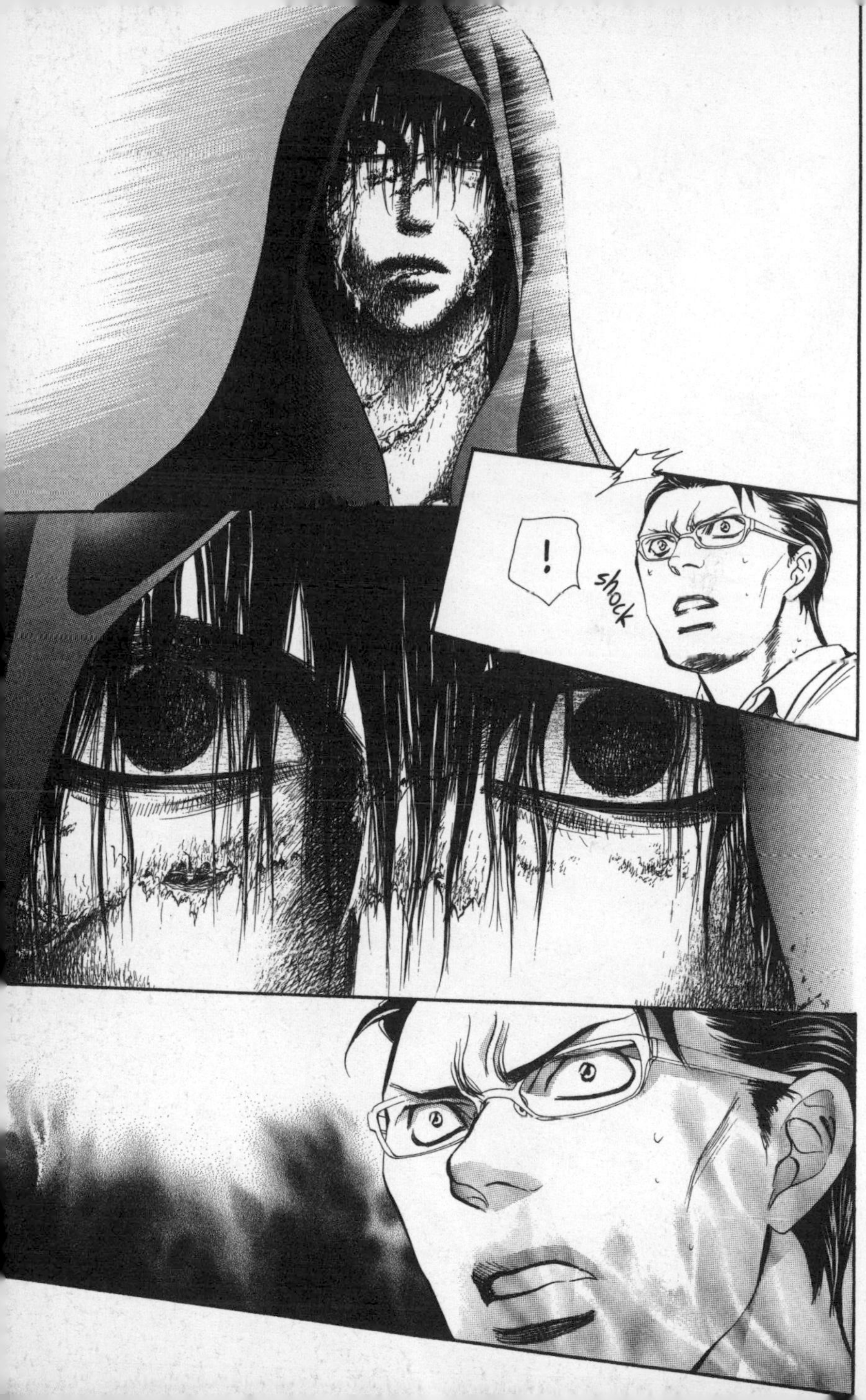
!
shock

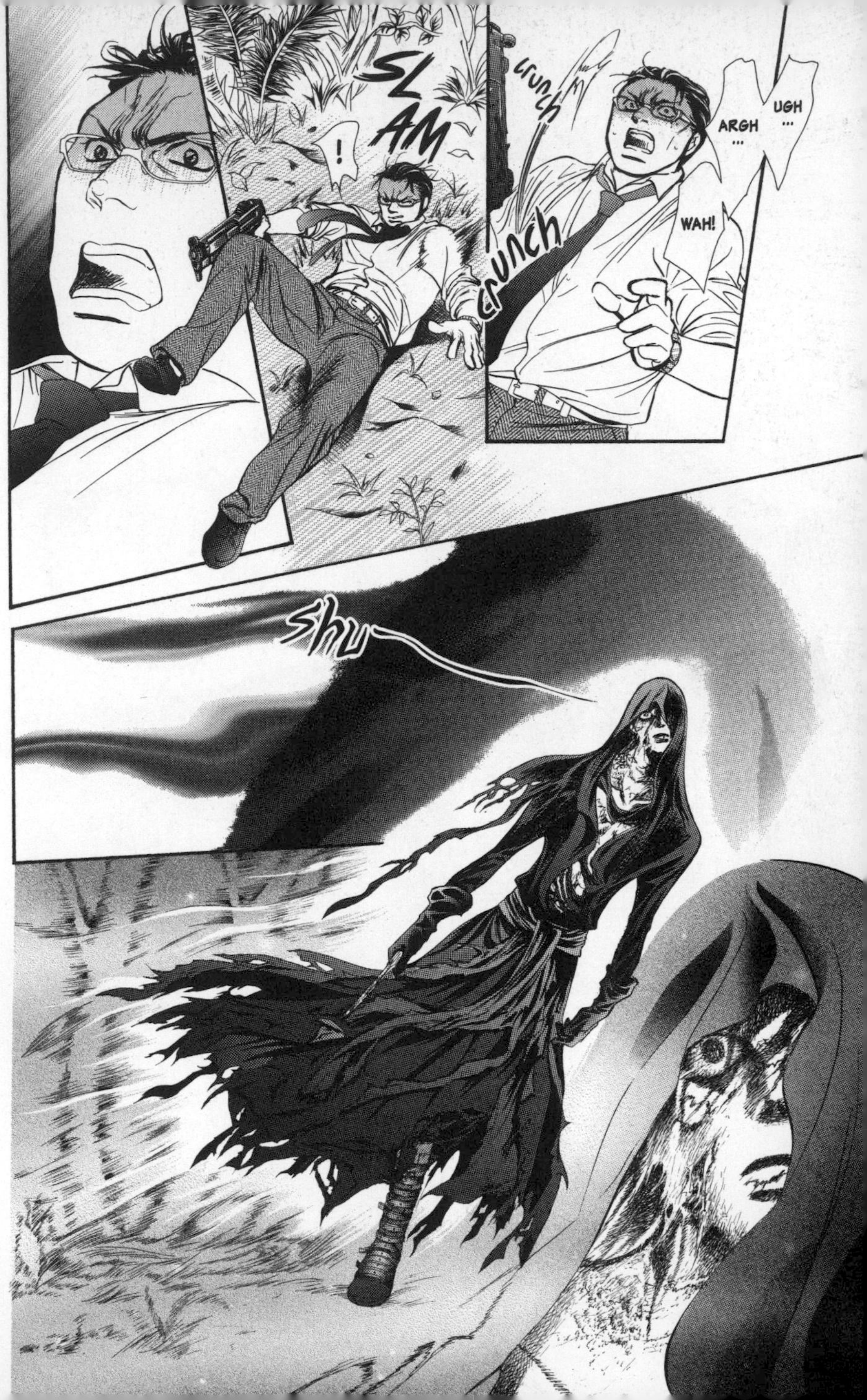
UGH ...
ARGH ...
crunch
WAH!
crunch
SLAM
!
shu

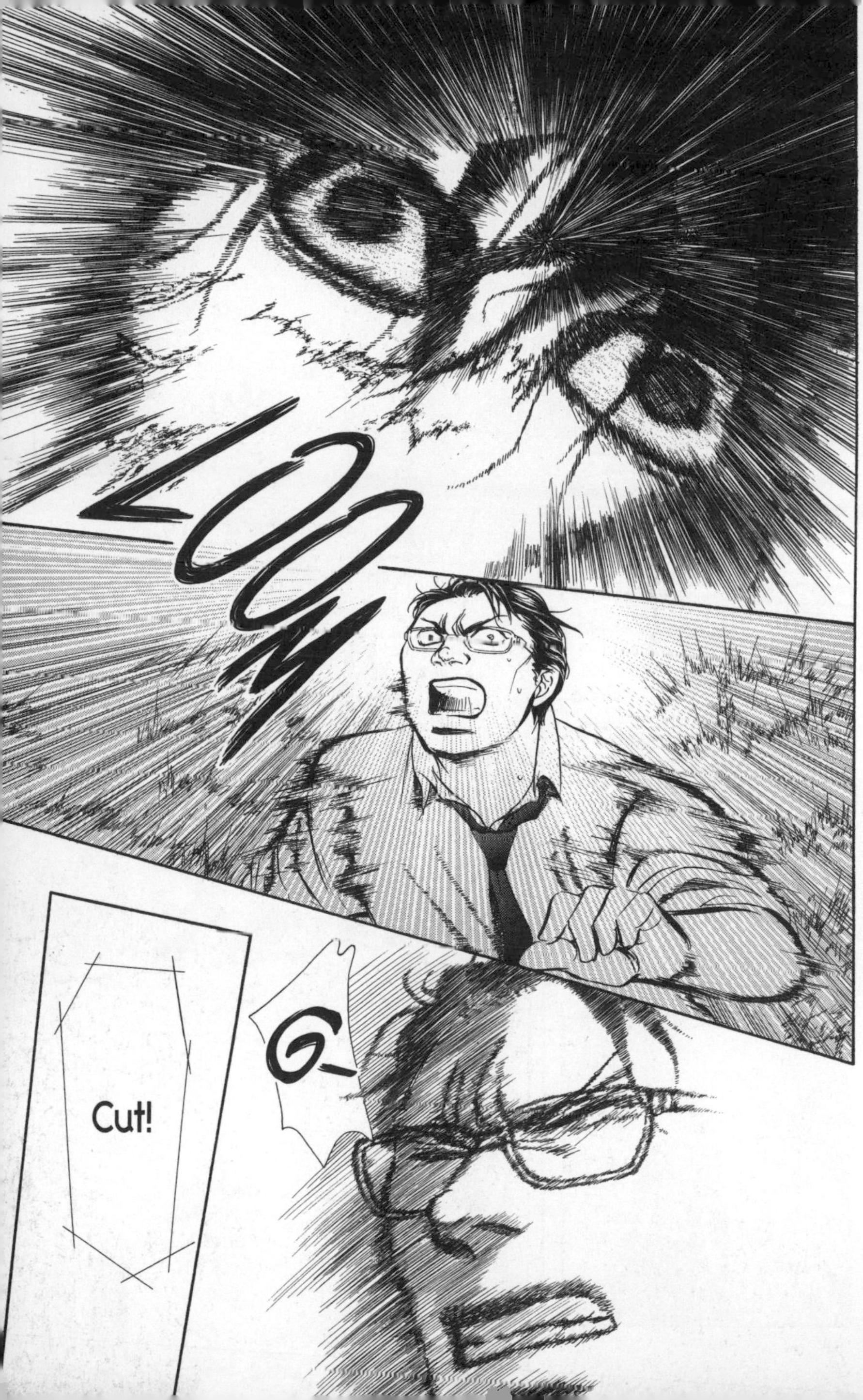
ZOOM
G-
Cut!

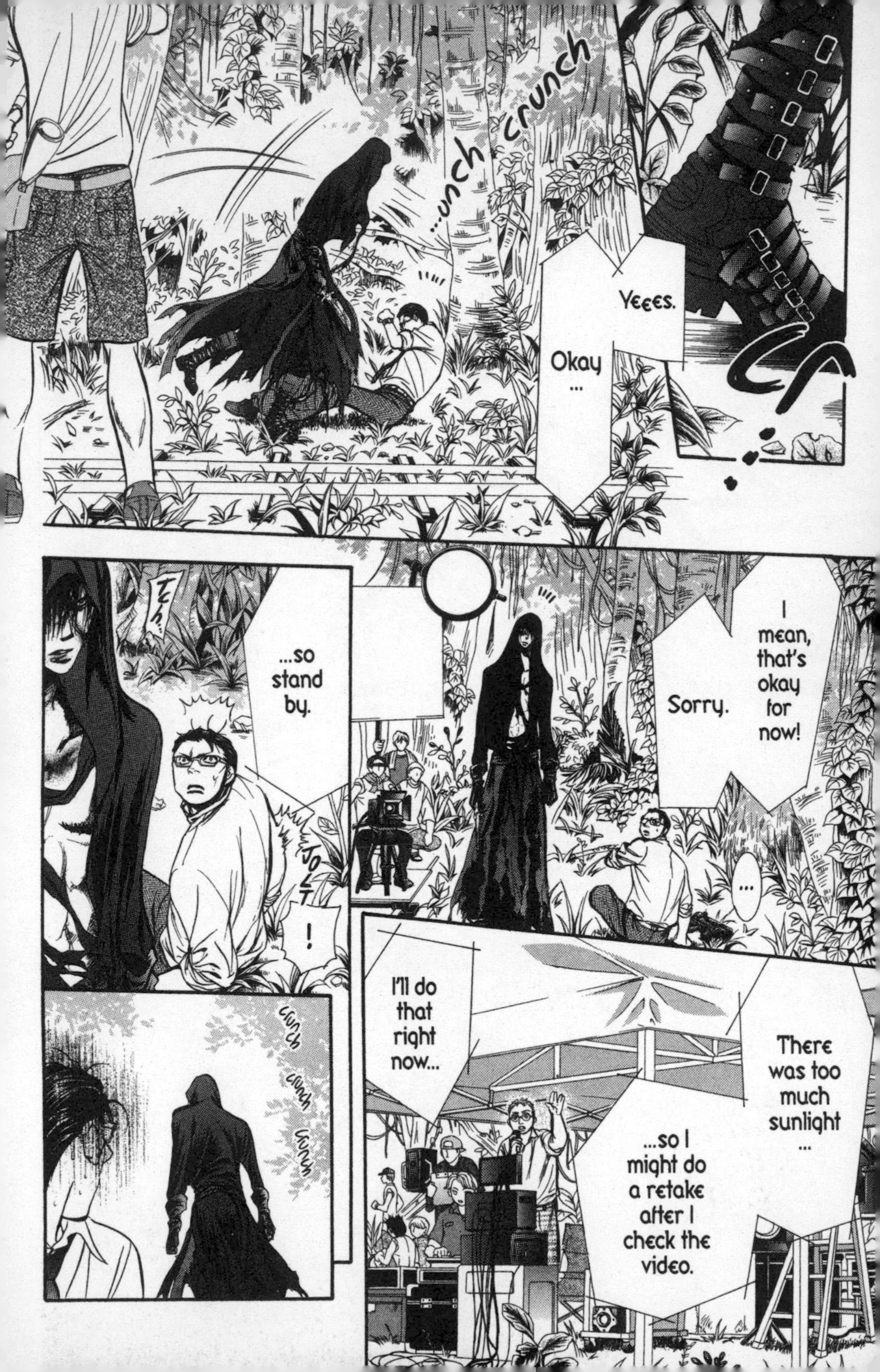
...unch crunch
Yeeees.
Okay ...
I mean, that's okay for now!
Sorry.
...
There was too much sunlight ...
...so I might do a retake after I check the video.
I'll do that right now...
Tch...
...so stand by.
JOLT
!
crunch
crunch
crunch

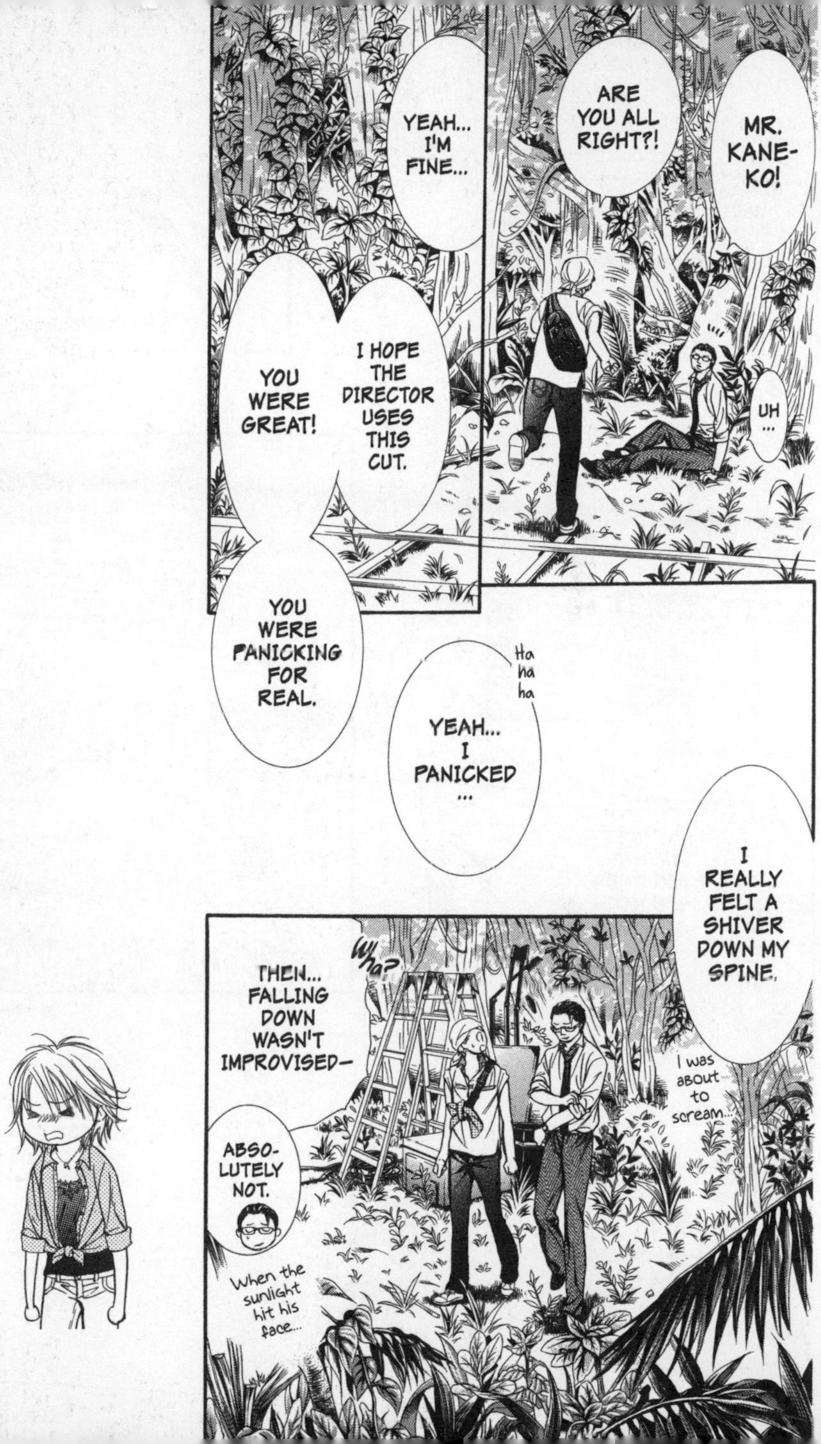
MR. KANEKO!
ARE YOU ALL RIGHT?!
UH...
YEAH... I'M FINE...
I HOPE THE DIRECTOR USES THIS CUT.
YOU WERE GREAT!
YOU WERE PANICKING FOR REAL.
Ha ha ha
YEAH... I PANICKED...
I REALLY FELT A SHIVER DOWN MY SPINE.
I was about to scream...
Wha?
THEN... FALLING DOWN WASN'T IMPROVISED—
ABSOLUTELY NOT.
When the sunlight hit his face...

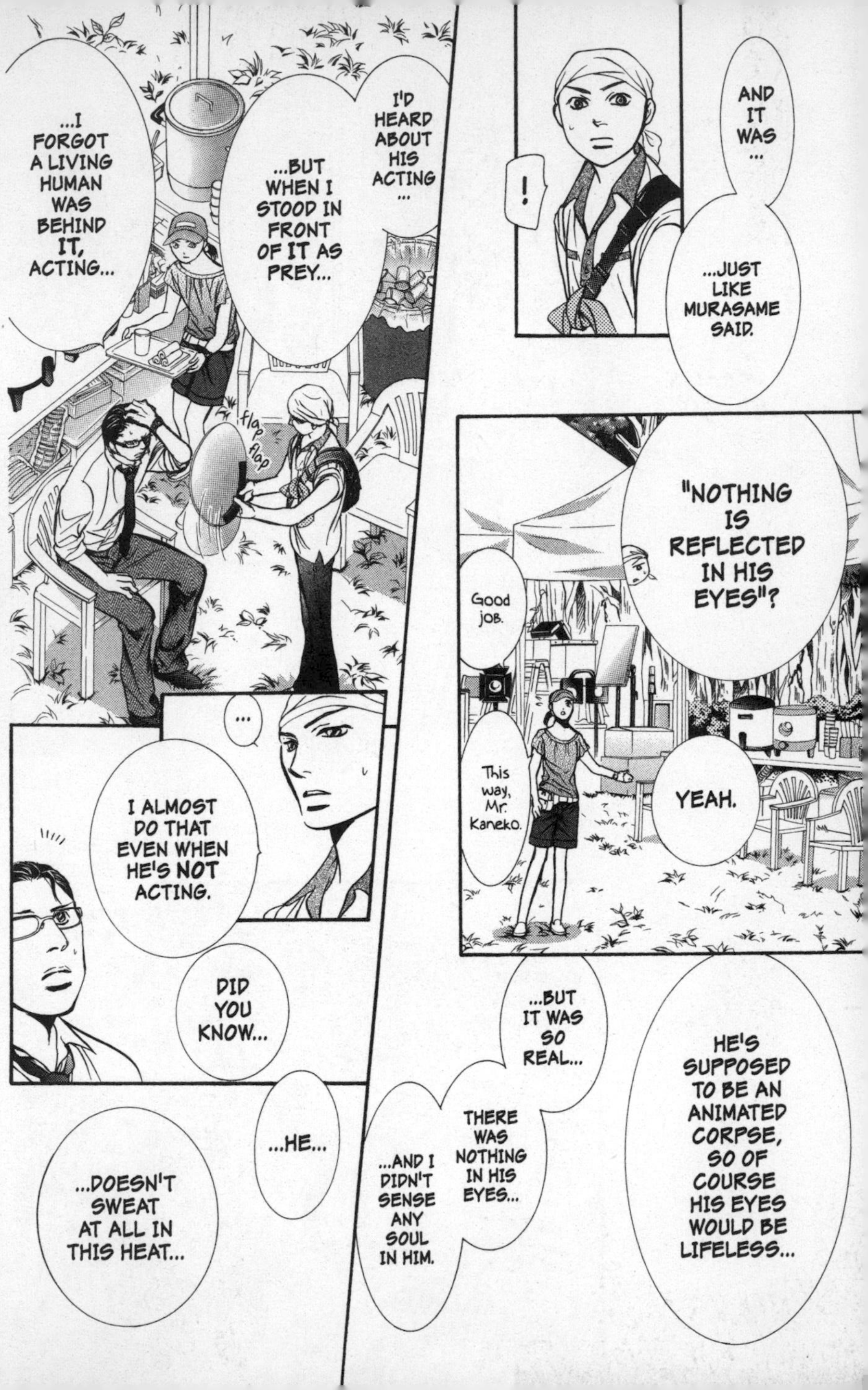

!
AND IT WAS...
...JUST LIKE MURASAME SAID.
"NOTHING IS REFLECTED IN HIS EYES"?
YEAH.
Good job.
This way, Mr. Kaneko.
HE'S SUPPOSED TO BE AN ANIMATED CORPSE, SO OF COURSE HIS EYES WOULD BE LIFELESS...
...BUT IT WAS SO REAL...
THERE WAS NOTHING IN HIS EYES...
...AND I DIDN'T SENSE ANY SOUL IN HIM.
I'D HEARD ABOUT HIS ACTING...
...BUT WHEN I STOOD IN FRONT OF IT AS PREY...
...I FORGOT A LIVING HUMAN WAS BEHIND IT, ACTING...
flap flap
...
I ALMOST DO THAT EVEN WHEN HE'S NOT ACTING.
DID YOU KNOW...
...HE...
...DOESN'T SWEAT AT ALL IN THIS HEAT...

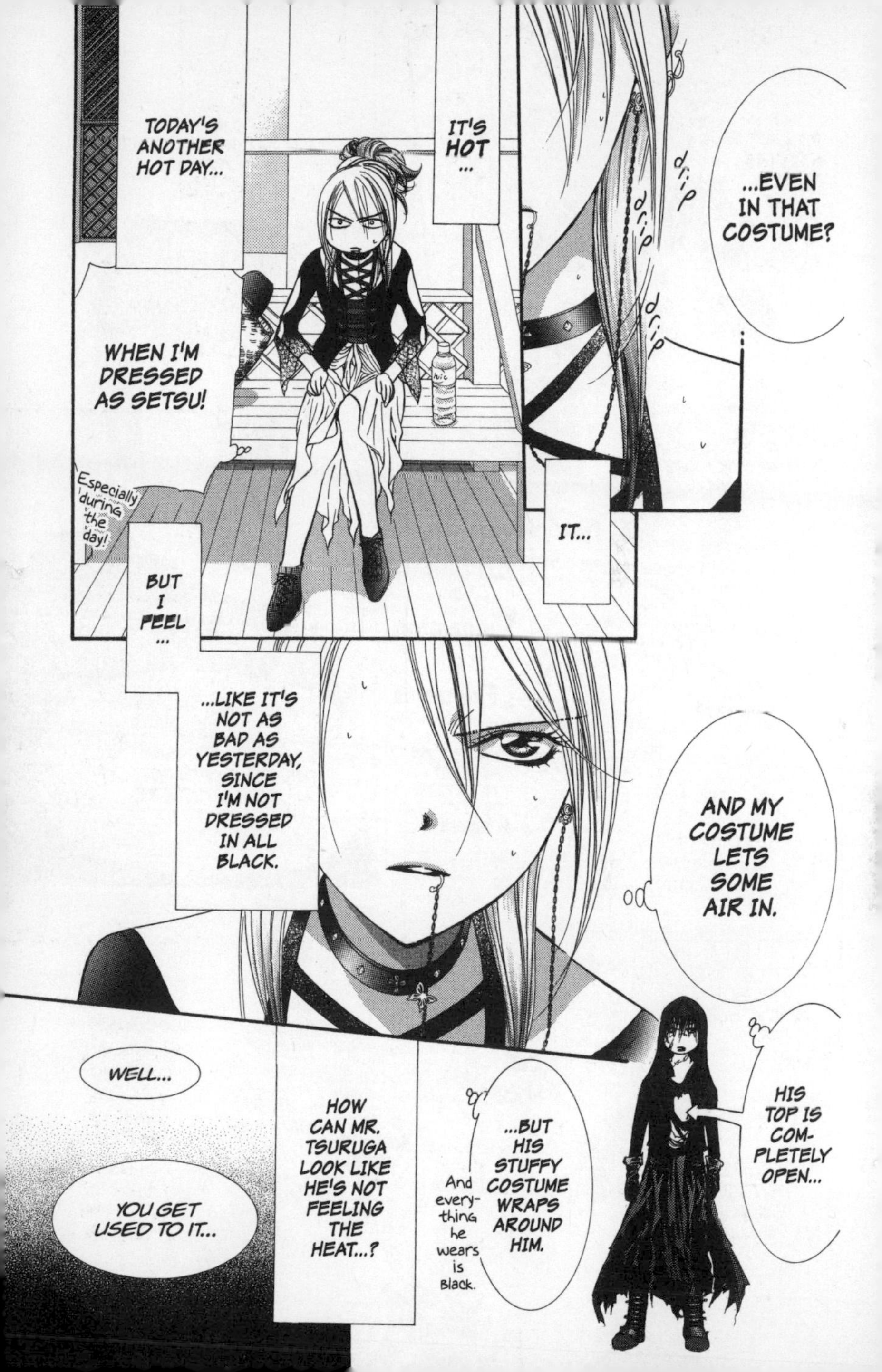
...EVEN IN THAT COSTUME?
drip drip drip drip
IT...
TODAY'S ANOTHER HOT DAY...
IT'S HOT...
WHEN I'M DRESSED AS SETSU!
Especially during the day!
BUT I FEEL...
...LIKE IT'S NOT AS BAD AS YESTERDAY, SINCE I'M NOT DRESSED IN ALL BLACK.
AND MY COSTUME LETS SOME AIR IN.
HIS TOP IS COMPLETELY OPEN...
...BUT HIS STUFFY COSTUME WRAPS AROUND HIM.
And everything he wears is black.
HOW CAN MR. TSURUGA LOOK LIKE HE'S NOT FEELING THE HEAT...?
WELL...
YOU GET USED TO IT...

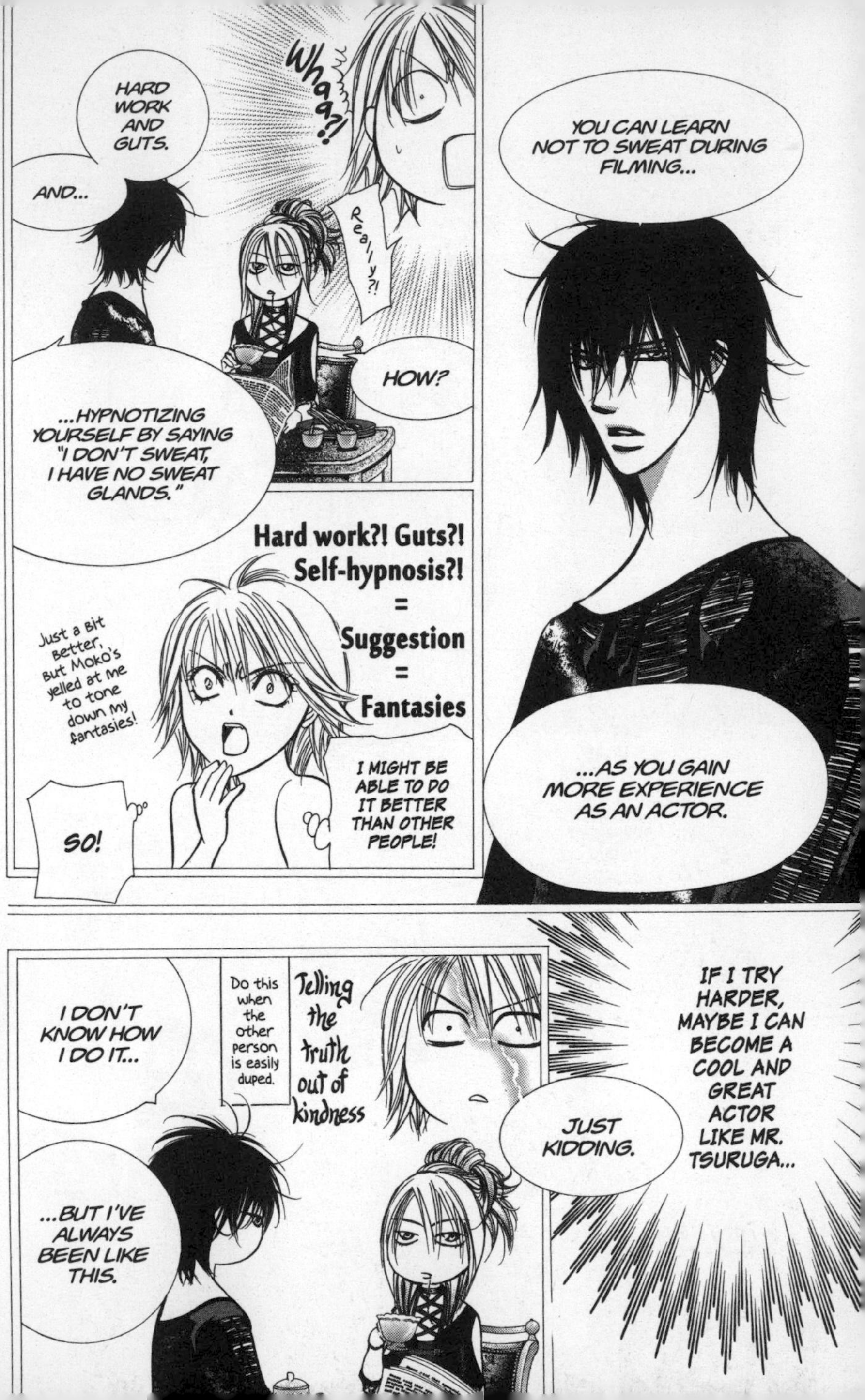

YOU CAN LEARN NOT TO SWEAT DURING FILMING...
...AS YOU GAIN MORE EXPERIENCE AS AN ACTOR.
Whaa?!
Really?!
HARD WORK AND GUTS.
AND...
HOW?
...HYPNOTIZING YOURSELF BY SAYING "I DON'T SWEAT, I HAVE NO SWEAT GLANDS."
Hard work?! Guts?! Self-hypnosis?! = Suggestion = Fantasies
I MIGHT BE ABLE TO DO IT BETTER THAN OTHER PEOPLE!
Just a bit better, but Moko's yelled at me to tone down my fantasies!
SO!
IF I TRY HARDER, MAYBE I CAN BECOME A COOL AND GREAT ACTOR LIKE MR. TSURUGA...
JUST KIDDING.
Telling the truth out of kindness
Do this when the other person is easily duped.
I DON'T KNOW HOW I DO IT...
...BUT I'VE ALWAYS BEEN LIKE THIS.

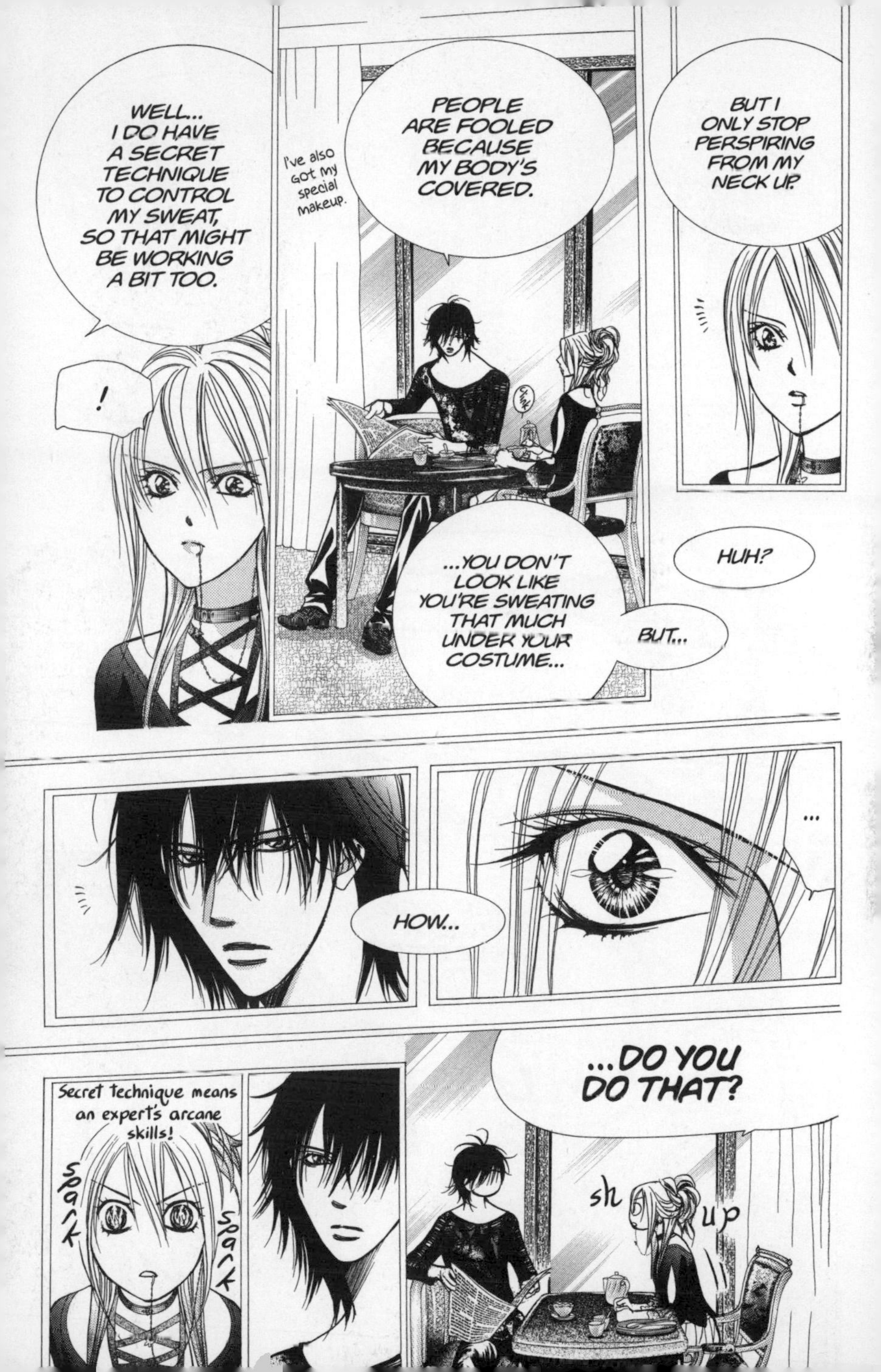
PEOPLE ARE FOOLED BECAUSE MY BODY'S COVERED.
I've also got my special makeup.
BUT I ONLY STOP PERSPIRING FROM MY NECK UP.
HUH?
BUT...
...YOU DON'T LOOK LIKE YOU'RE SWEATING THAT MUCH UNDER YOUR COSTUME...
WELL... I DO HAVE A SECRET TECHNIQUE TO CONTROL MY SWEAT, SO THAT MIGHT BE WORKING A BIT TOO.
!
...
HOW...
...DO YOU DO THAT?
sh
up
Secret technique means an expert's arcane skills!
spark
spark

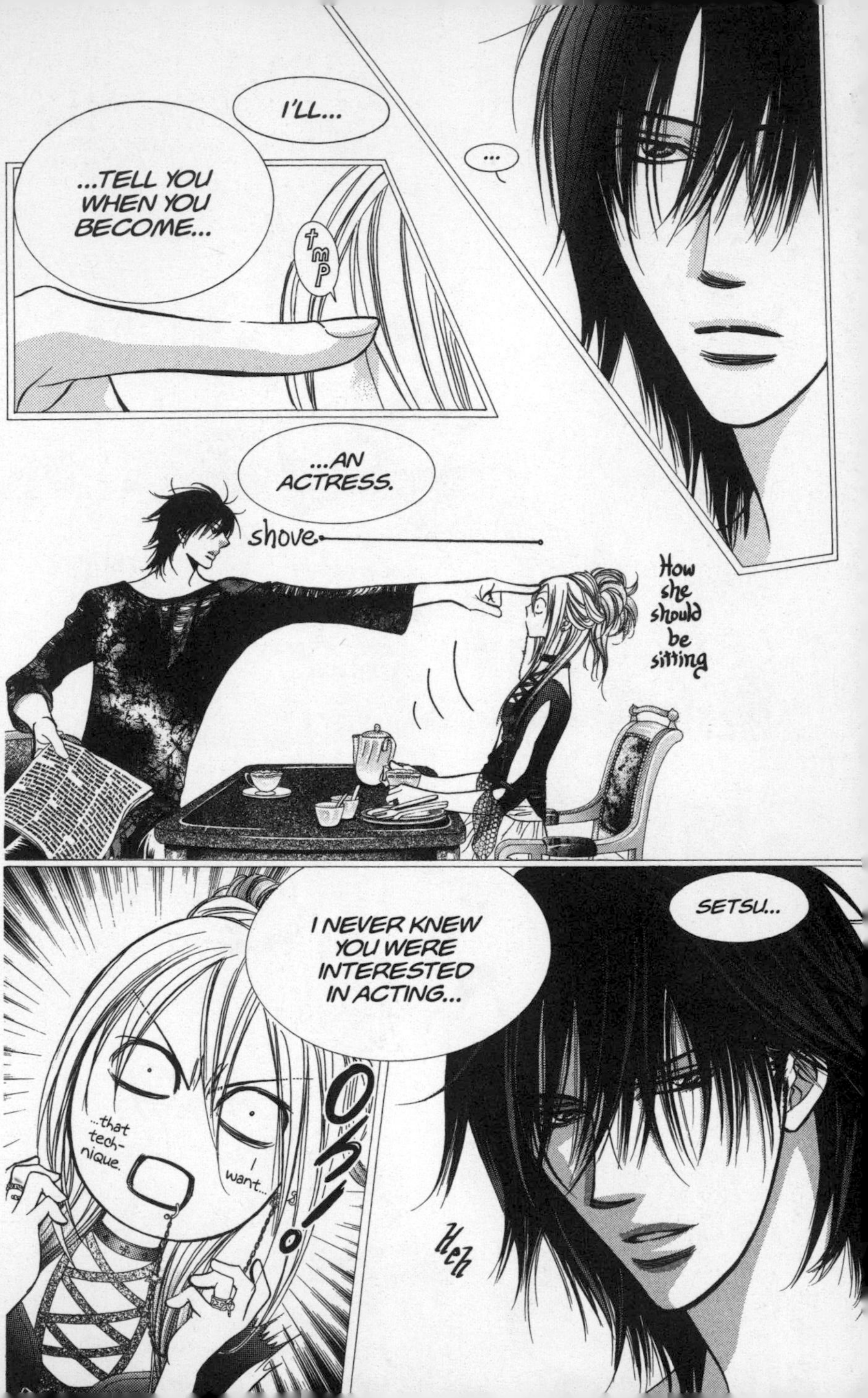
...
I'LL...
...TELL YOU WHEN YOU BECOME...
tmp
...AN ACTRESS.
shove
How she should be sitting
SETSU...
I NEVER KNEW YOU WERE INTERESTED IN ACTING...
Heh
I want...
...that tech-nique.

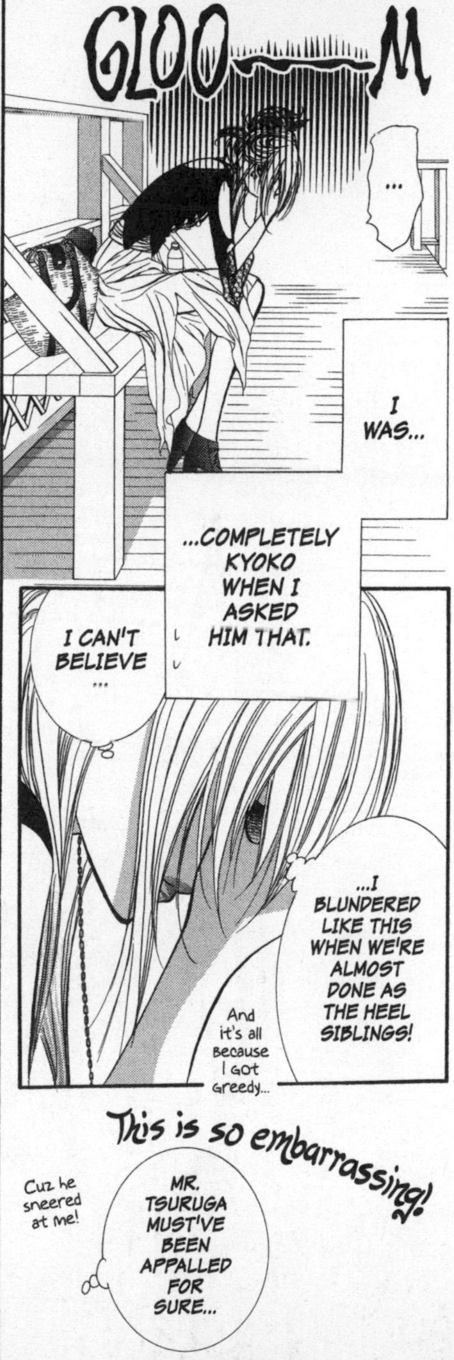
GLOO—M
...
I WAS...
...COMPLETELY KYOKO WHEN I ASKED HIM THAT.
I CAN'T BELIEVE...
...I BLUNDERED LIKE THIS WHEN WE'RE ALMOST DONE AS THE HEEL SIBLINGS!
And it's all because I got greedy...
This is so embarrassing!
MR. TSURUGA MUST'VE BEEN APPALLED FOR SURE...
Cuz he sneered at me!
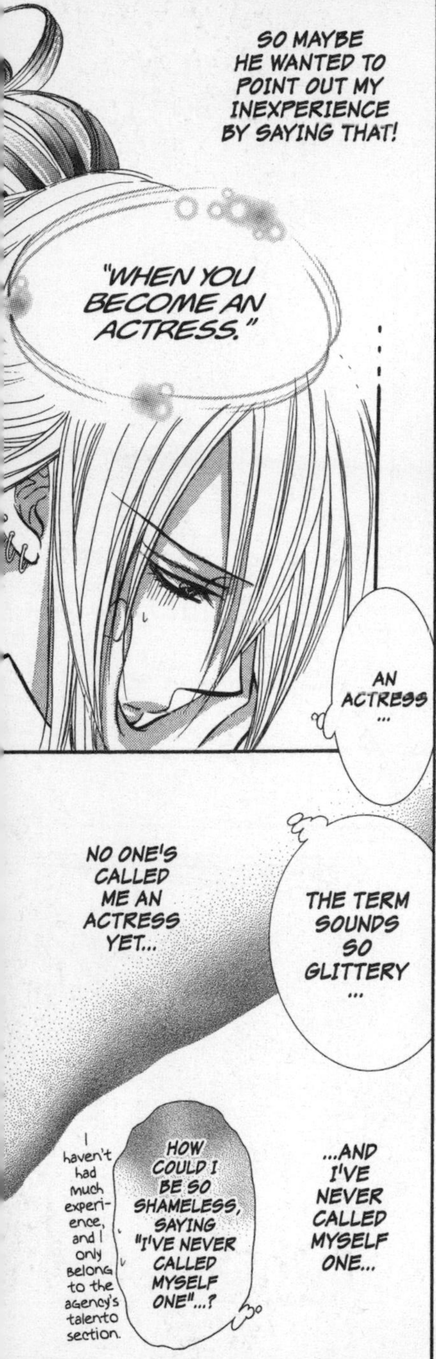
SO MAYBE HE WANTED TO POINT OUT MY INEXPERIENCE BY SAYING THAT!
"WHEN YOU BECOME AN ACTRESS."
AN ACTRESS...
THE TERM SOUNDS SO GLITTERY...
NO ONE'S CALLED ME AN ACTRESS YET...
...AND I'VE NEVER CALLED MYSELF ONE...
HOW COULD I BE SO SHAMELESS, SAYING "I'VE NEVER CALLED MYSELF ONE"...?
I haven't had much experience, and I only belong to the agency's talent section.

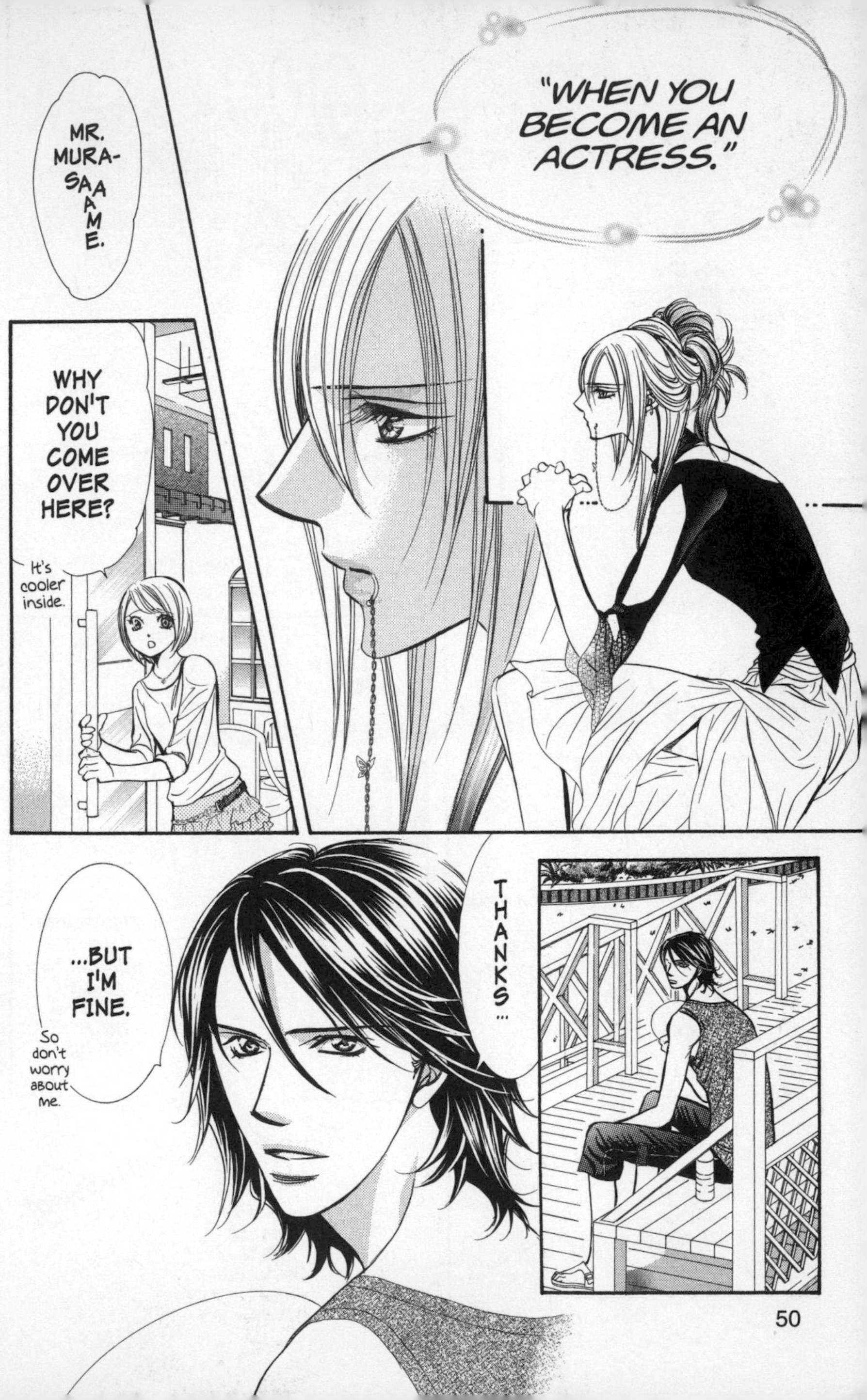
"WHEN YOU BECOME AN ACTRESS."
MR. MURA-SAAAME.
WHY DON'T YOU COME OVER HERE?
It's cooler inside.
THANKS...
...BUT I'M FINE.
So don't worry about me.

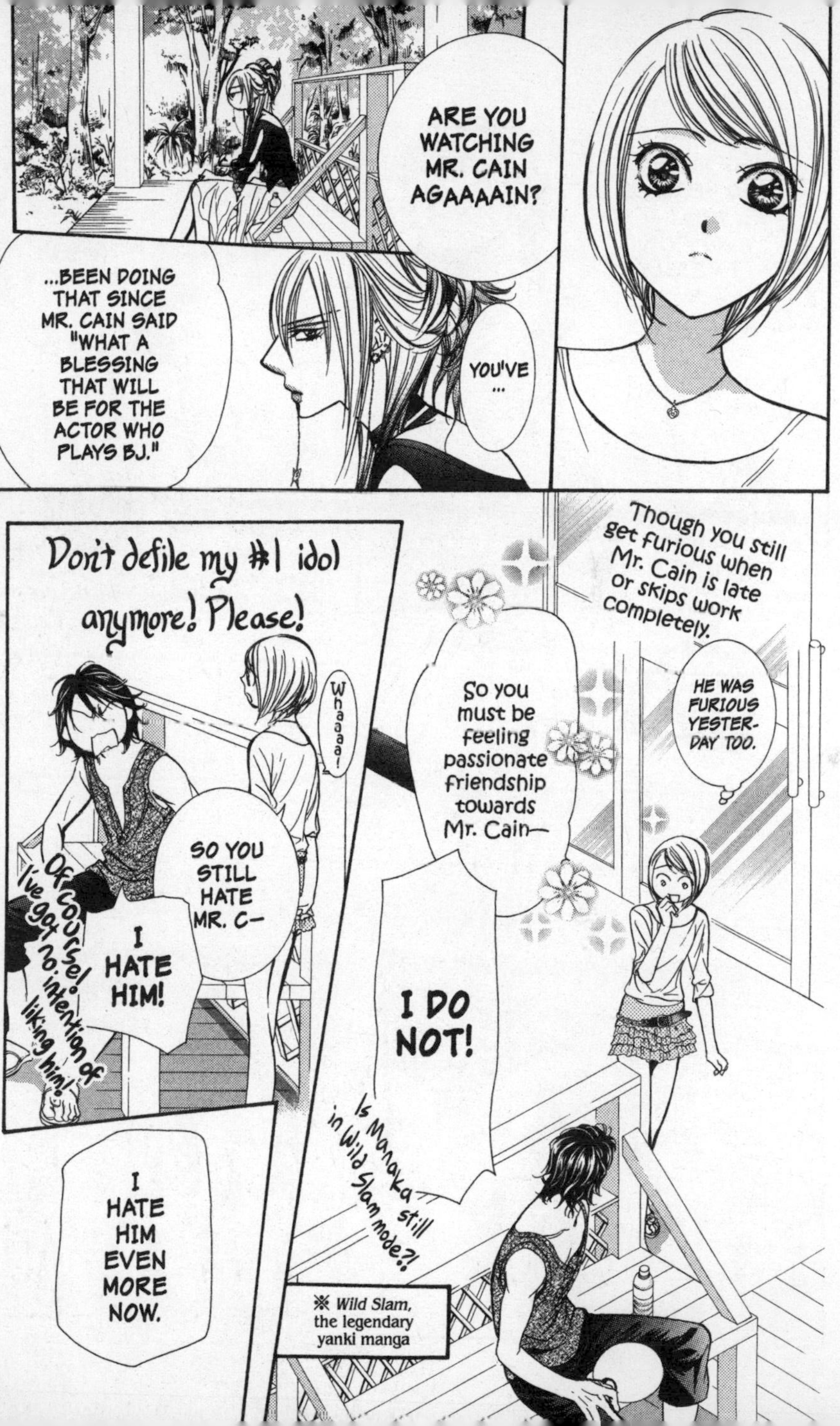
ARE YOU WATCHING MR. CAIN AGAAAAIN?
YOU'VE...
...BEEN DOING THAT SINCE MR. CAIN SAID "WHAT A BLESSING THAT WILL BE FOR THE ACTOR WHO PLAYS BJ."
Though you still get furious when Mr. Cain is late or skips work completely.
HE WAS FURIOUS YESTER-DAY TOO.
So you must be feeling passionate friendship towards Mr. Cain—
I DO NOT!
Is Manaka still in Wild Slam mode?!
※ Wild Slam, the legendary yanki manga
Don't defile my #1 idol anymore! Please!
Whaaaa!
SO YOU STILL HATE MR. C—
I HATE HIM!
Of course! I've got no intention of liking him!
I HATE HIM EVEN MORE NOW.

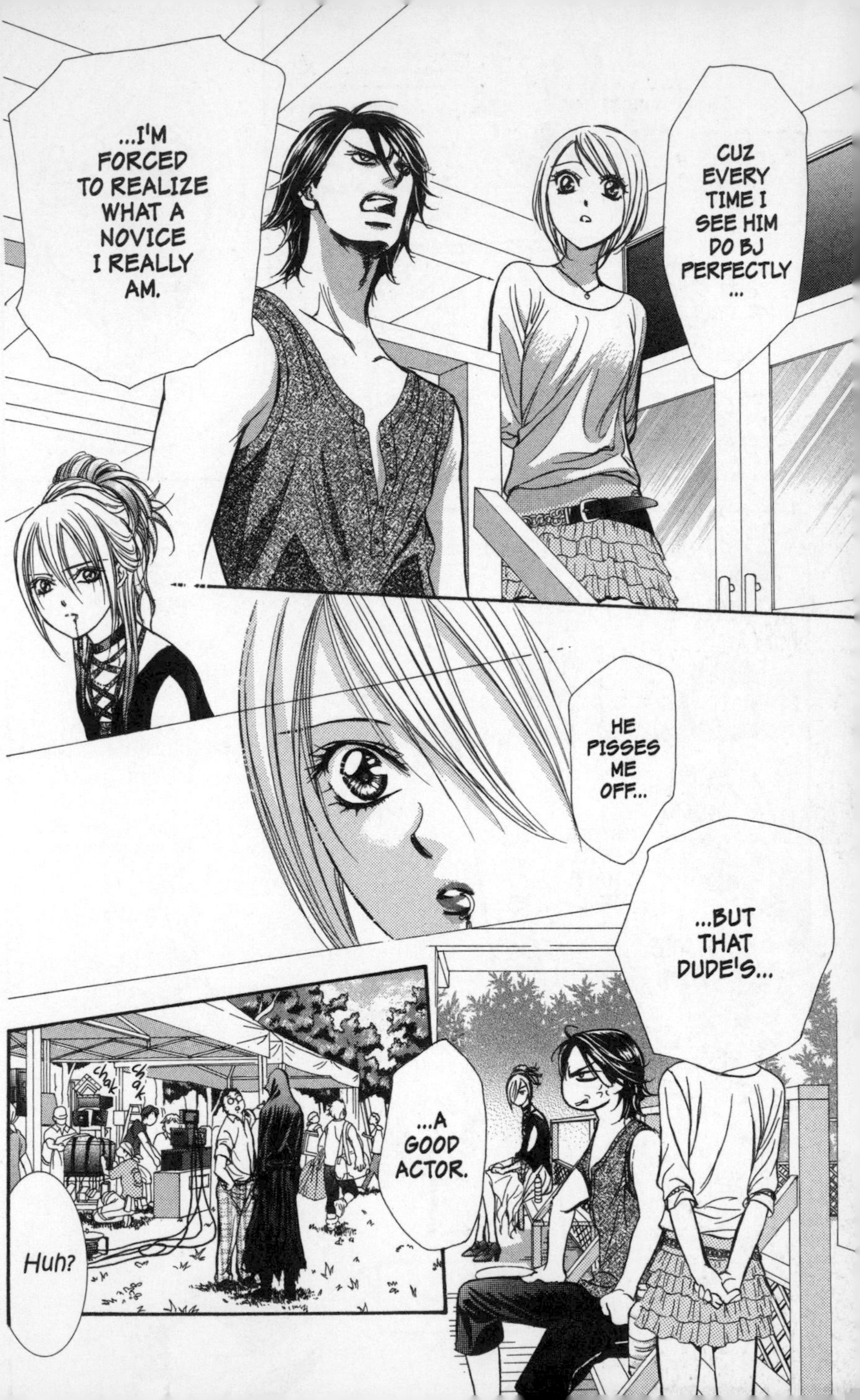
CUZ EVERY TIME I SEE HIM DO BJ PERFECTLY ...
...I'M FORCED TO REALIZE WHAT A NOVICE I REALLY AM.
HE PISSES ME OFF...
...BUT THAT DUDE'S...
...A GOOD ACTOR.
chak
chak
Huh?

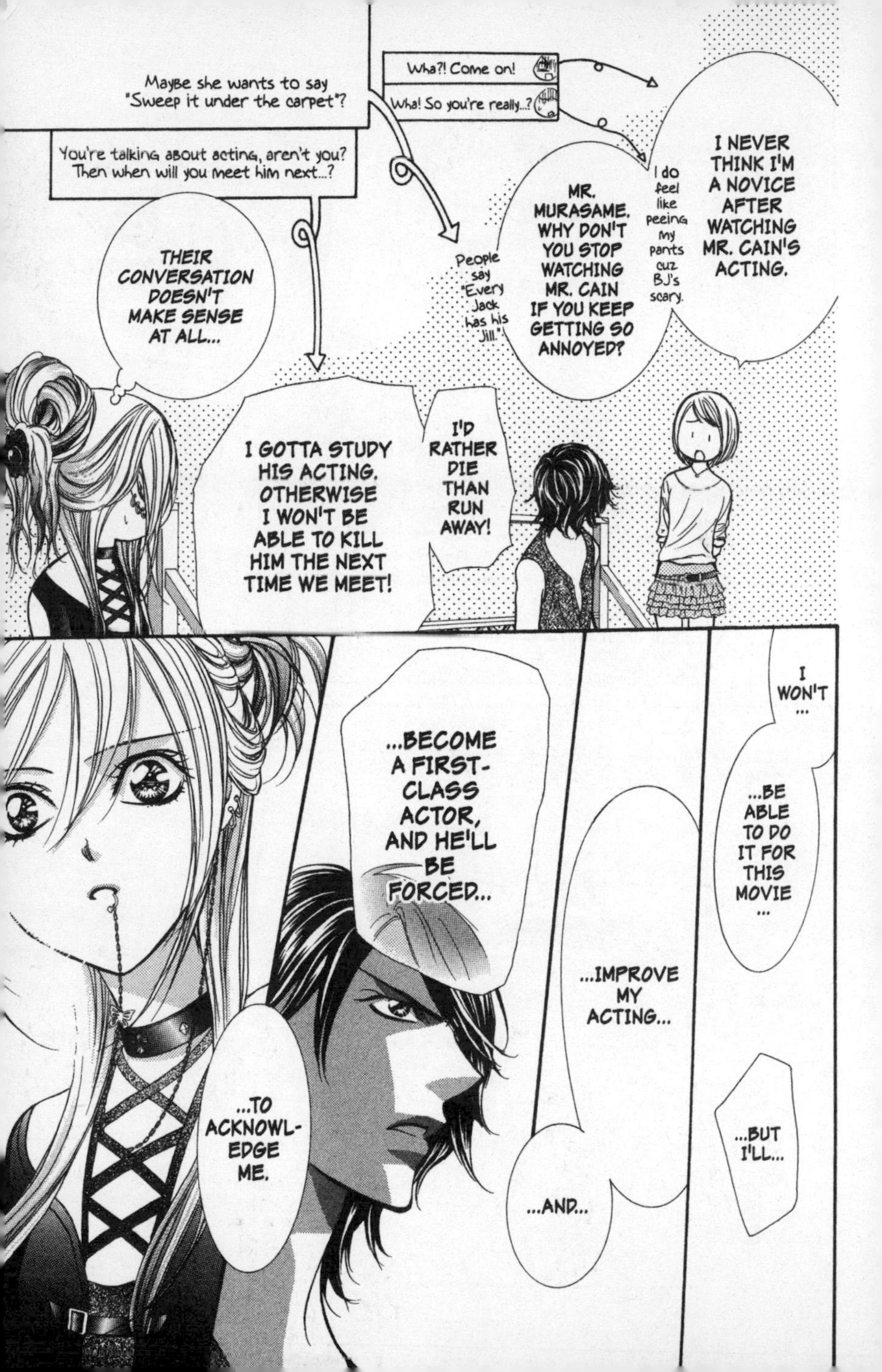
Wha?! Come on!
Wha! So you're really...?
Maybe she wants to say "Sweep it under the carpet"?
I NEVER THINK I'M A NOVICE AFTER WATCHING MR. CAIN'S ACTING.
I do feel like peeing my pants cuz BJ's scary.
MR. MURASAME. WHY DON'T YOU STOP WATCHING MR. CAIN IF YOU KEEP GETTING SO ANNOYED?
You're talking about acting, aren't you? Then when will you meet him next...?
People say "Every Jack has his Jill."
THEIR CONVERSATION DOESN'T MAKE SENSE AT ALL...
I'D RATHER DIE THAN RUN AWAY!
I GOTTA STUDY HIS ACTING. OTHERWISE I WON'T BE ABLE TO KILL HIM THE NEXT TIME WE MEET!
I WON'T...
...BE ABLE TO DO IT FOR THIS MOVIE...
...BUT I'LL...
...IMPROVE MY ACTING...
...AND...
...BECOME A FIRST-CLASS ACTOR, AND HE'LL BE FORCED...
...TO ACKNOWLEDGE ME.

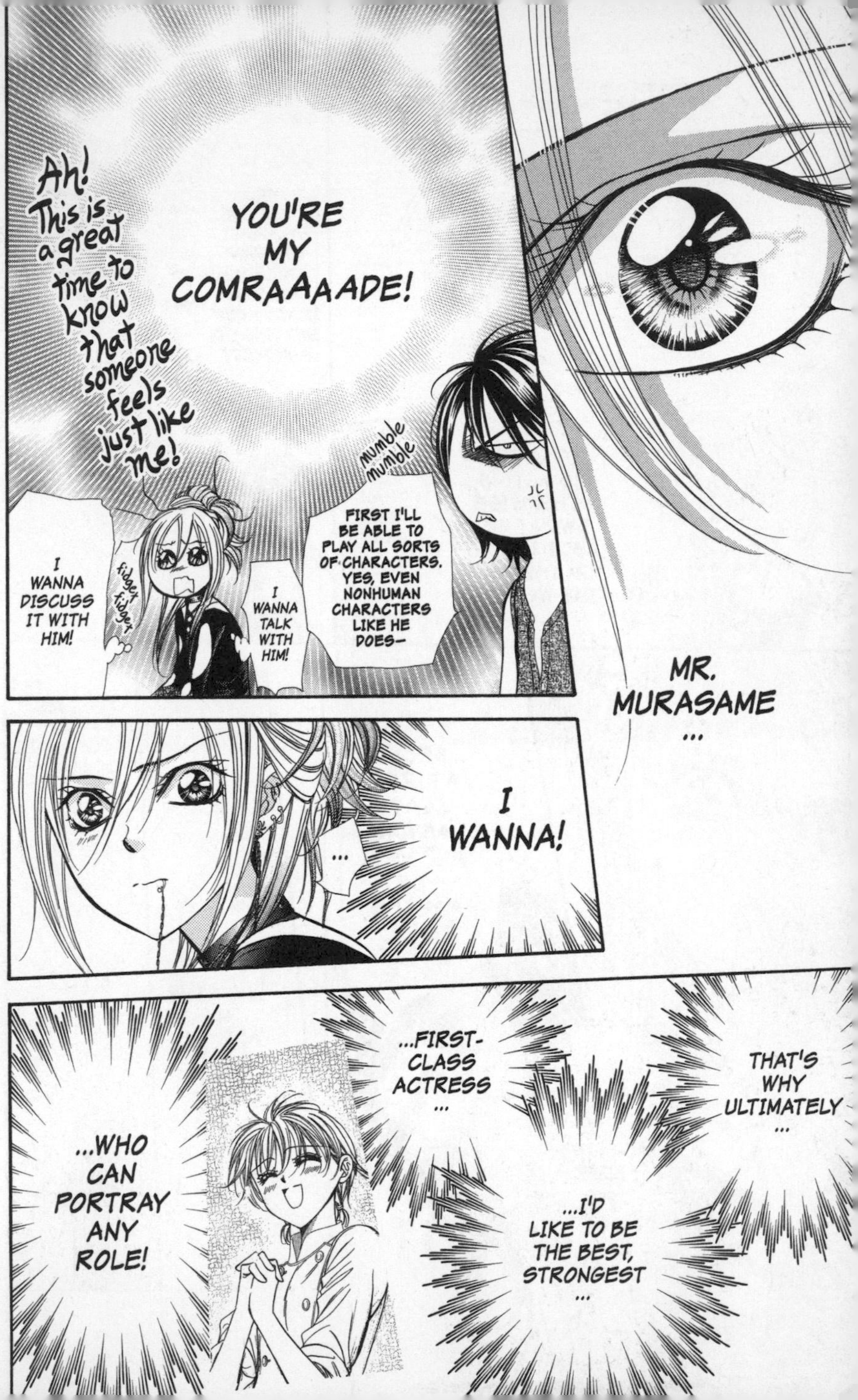
MR. MURASAME ...
YOU'RE MY COMRAAAADE!
Ah! This is a great time to know that someone feels just like me!
mumble mumble
FIRST I'LL BE ABLE TO PLAY ALL SORTS OF CHARACTERS. YES, EVEN NONHUMAN CHARACTERS LIKE HE DOES—
I WANNA TALK WITH HIM!
fidget fidget
I WANNA DISCUSS IT WITH HIM!
I WANNA!
...
THAT'S WHY ULTIMATELY ...
...I'D LIKE TO BE THE BEST, STRONGEST ...
...FIRST-CLASS ACTRESS ...
...WHO CAN PORTRAY ANY ROLE!

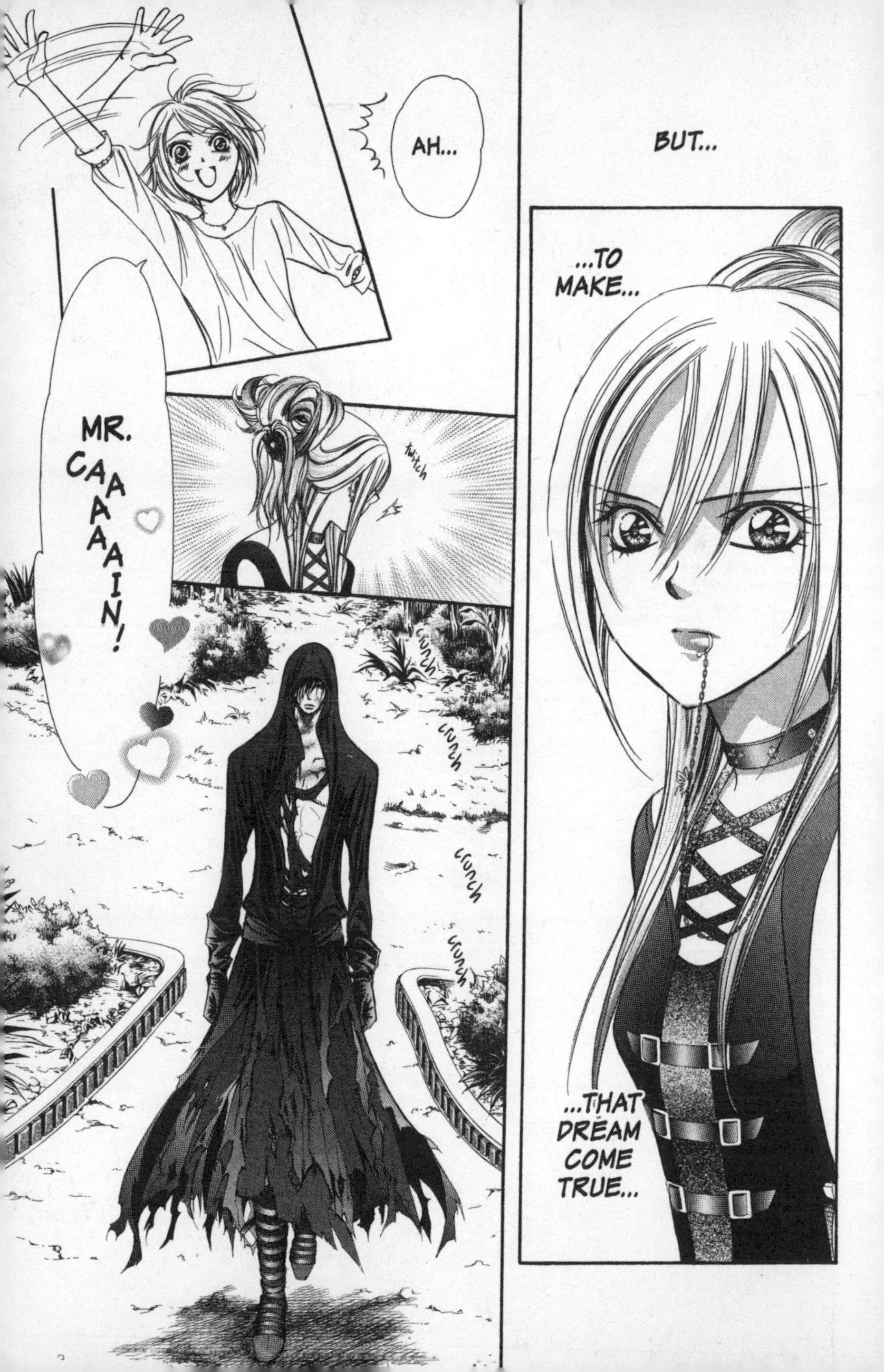
BUT...
...TO MAKE...
...THAT DREAM COME TRUE...
AH...
MR. CAAAAAIN!
twitch
crunch
crunch
crunch
crunch

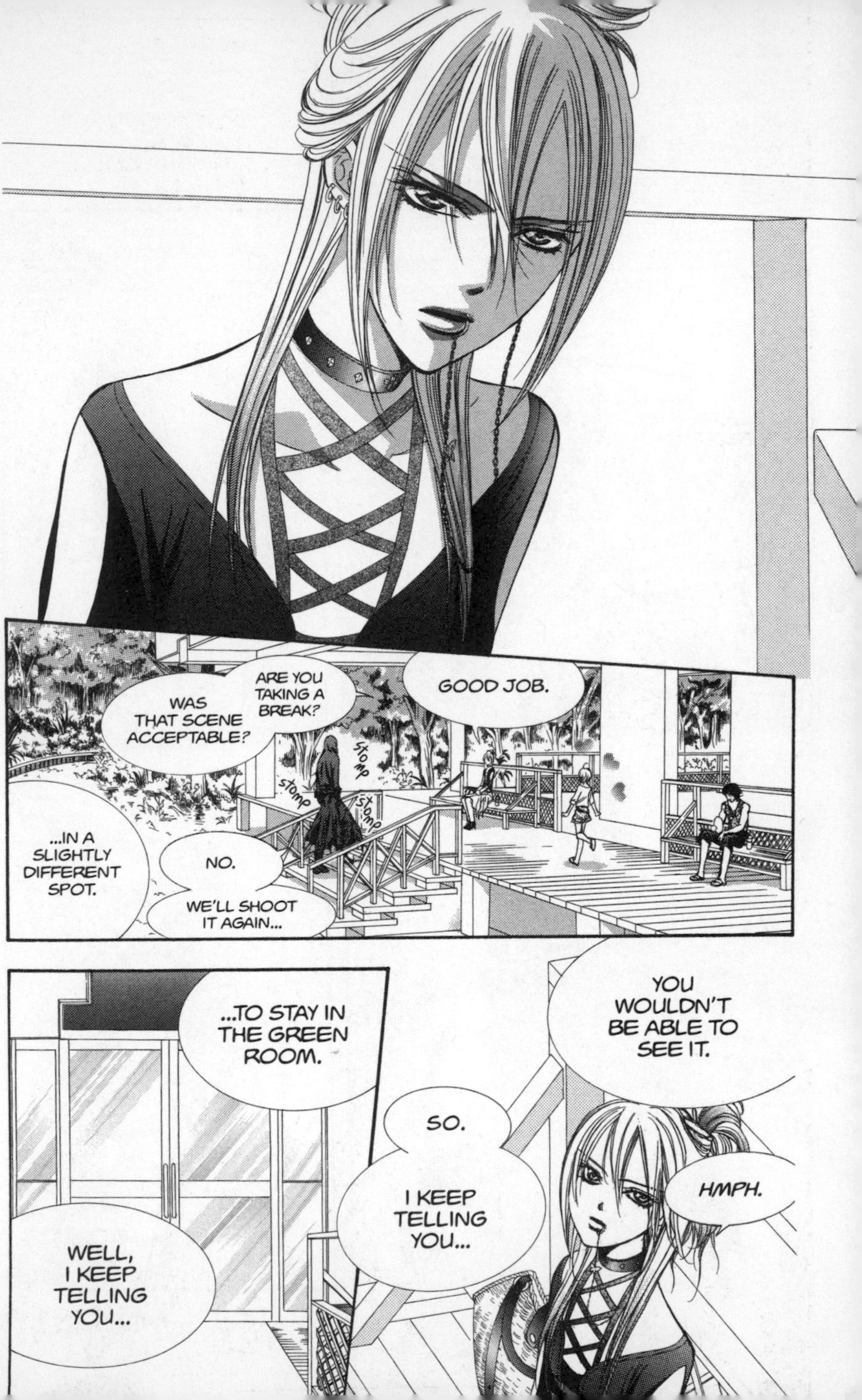
GOOD JOB.
ARE YOU TAKING A BREAK?
WAS THAT SCENE ACCEPTABLE?
stomp
stomp
stomp
NO.
WE'LL SHOOT IT AGAIN...
...IN A SLIGHTLY DIFFERENT SPOT.
YOU WOULDN'T BE ABLE TO SEE IT.
HMPH.
SO.
I KEEP TELLING YOU...
WELL, I KEEP TELLING YOU...
...TO STAY IN THE GREEN ROOM.

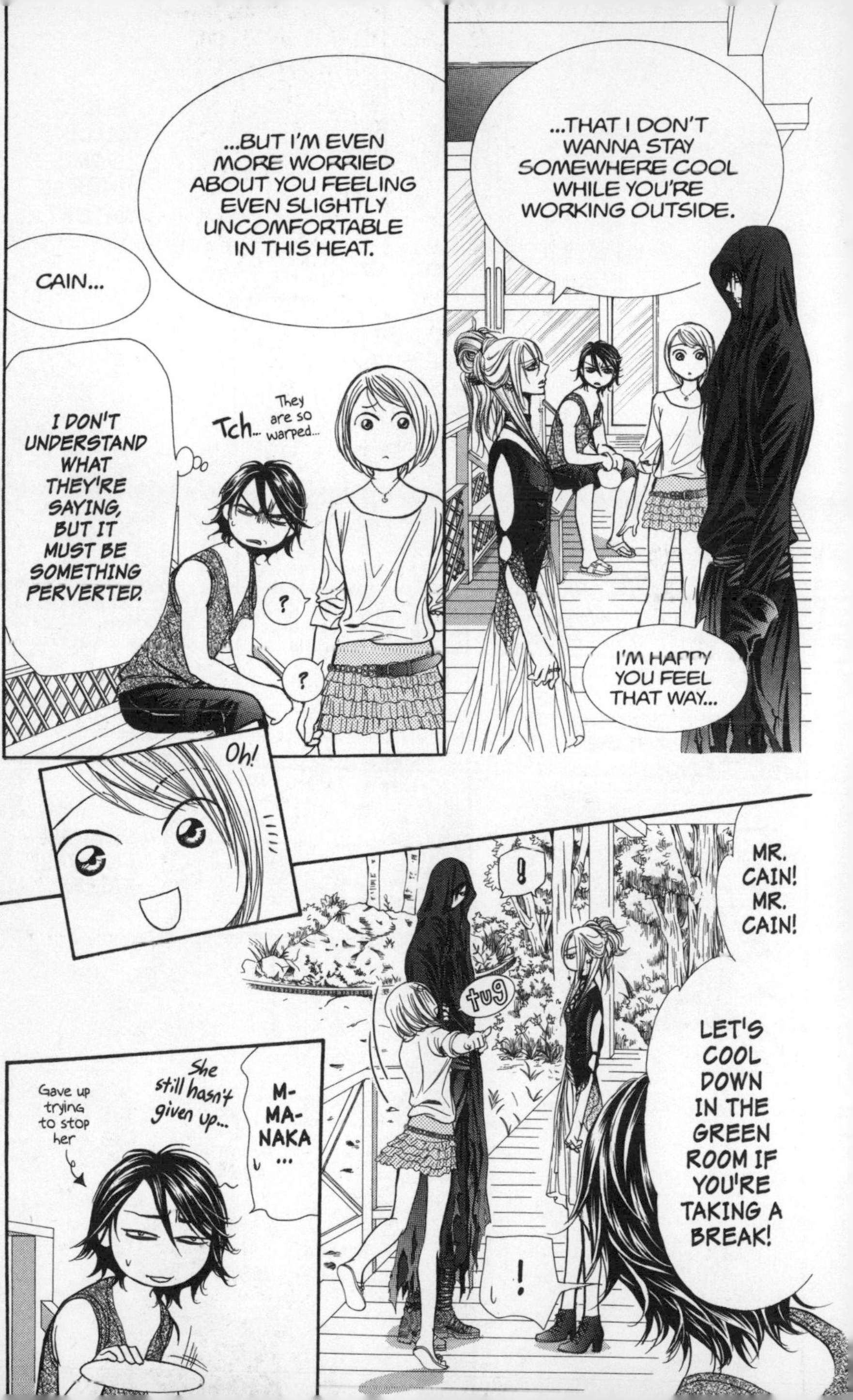
...THAT I DON'T WANNA STAY SOMEWHERE COOL WHILE YOU'RE WORKING OUTSIDE.
I'M HAPPY YOU FEEL THAT WAY...
...BUT I'M EVEN MORE WORRIED ABOUT YOU FEELING EVEN SLIGHTLY UNCOMFORTABLE IN THIS HEAT.
CAIN...
They are so warped...
Tch...
?
?
I DON'T UNDERSTAND WHAT THEY'RE SAYING, BUT IT MUST BE SOMETHING PERVERTED.
Oh!
MR. CAIN! MR. CAIN!
!
tug
LET'S COOL DOWN IN THE GREEN ROOM IF YOU'RE TAKING A BREAK!
!
M-MA-NAKA...
She still hasn't given up...
Gave up trying to stop her

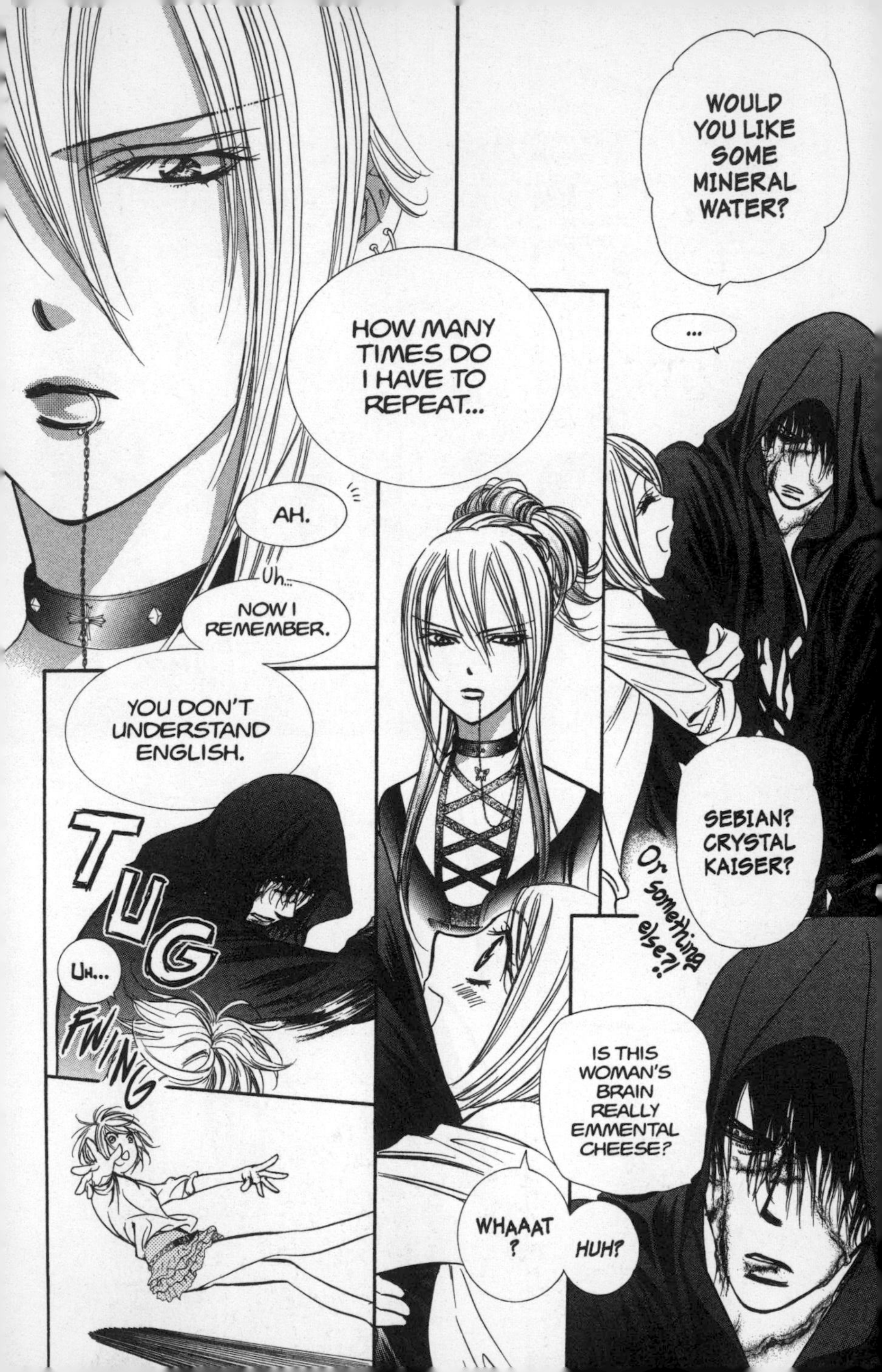
WOULD YOU LIKE SOME MINERAL WATER?
...
SEBIAN? CRYSTAL KAISER?
Or something else?!
HOW MANY TIMES DO I HAVE TO REPEAT...
AH.
Uh...
NOW I REMEMBER.
YOU DON'T UNDERSTAND ENGLISH.
IS THIS WOMAN'S BRAIN REALLY EMMENTAL CHEESE?
WHAAAT?
HUH?
TUG
UH...
FWING

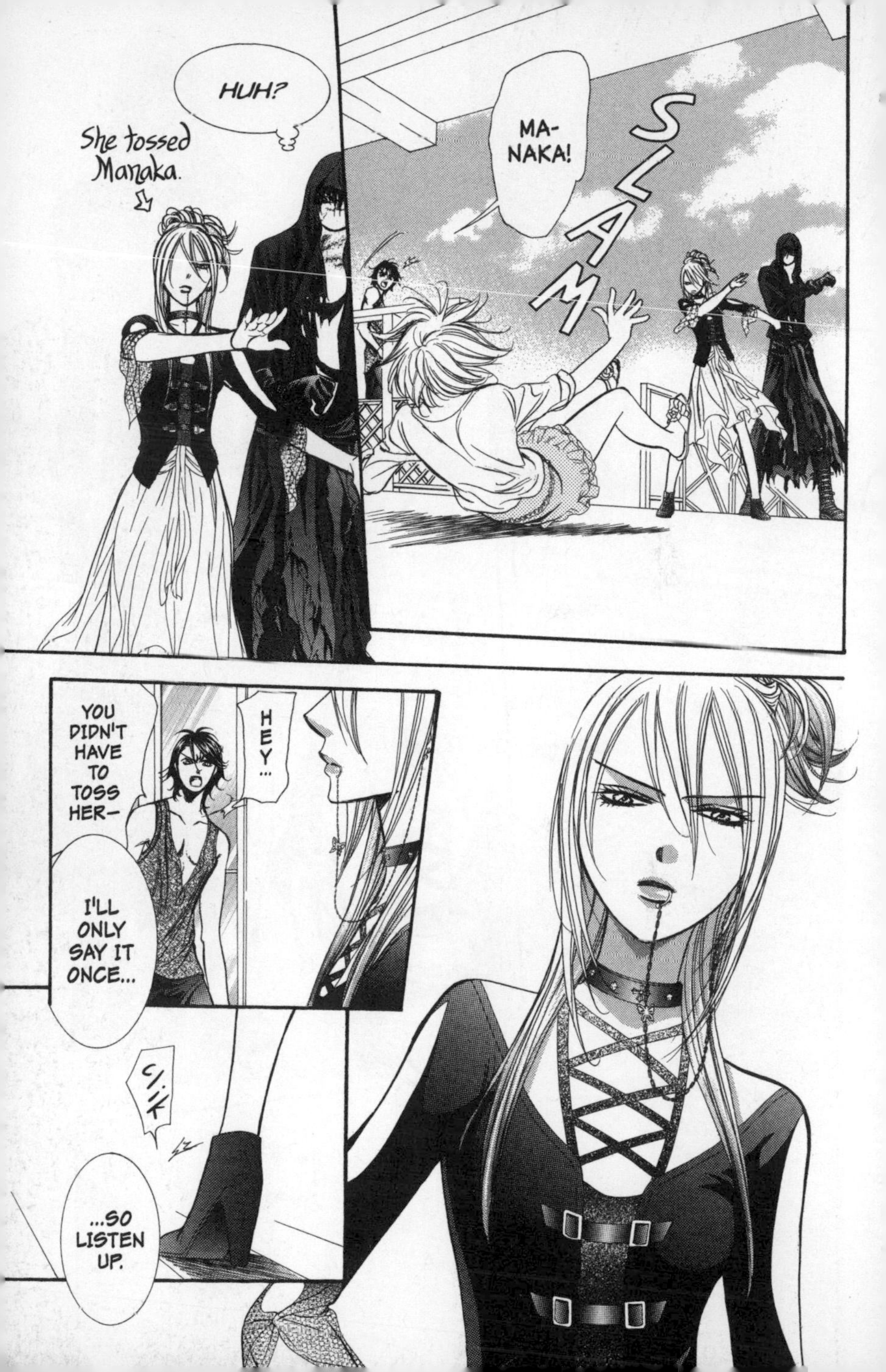
MA-
NAKA!
SLAM
HUH?
She tossed Manaka.
HEY...
YOU DIDN'T HAVE TO TOSS HER—
I'LL ONLY SAY IT ONCE...
CLIK
...SO LISTEN UP.

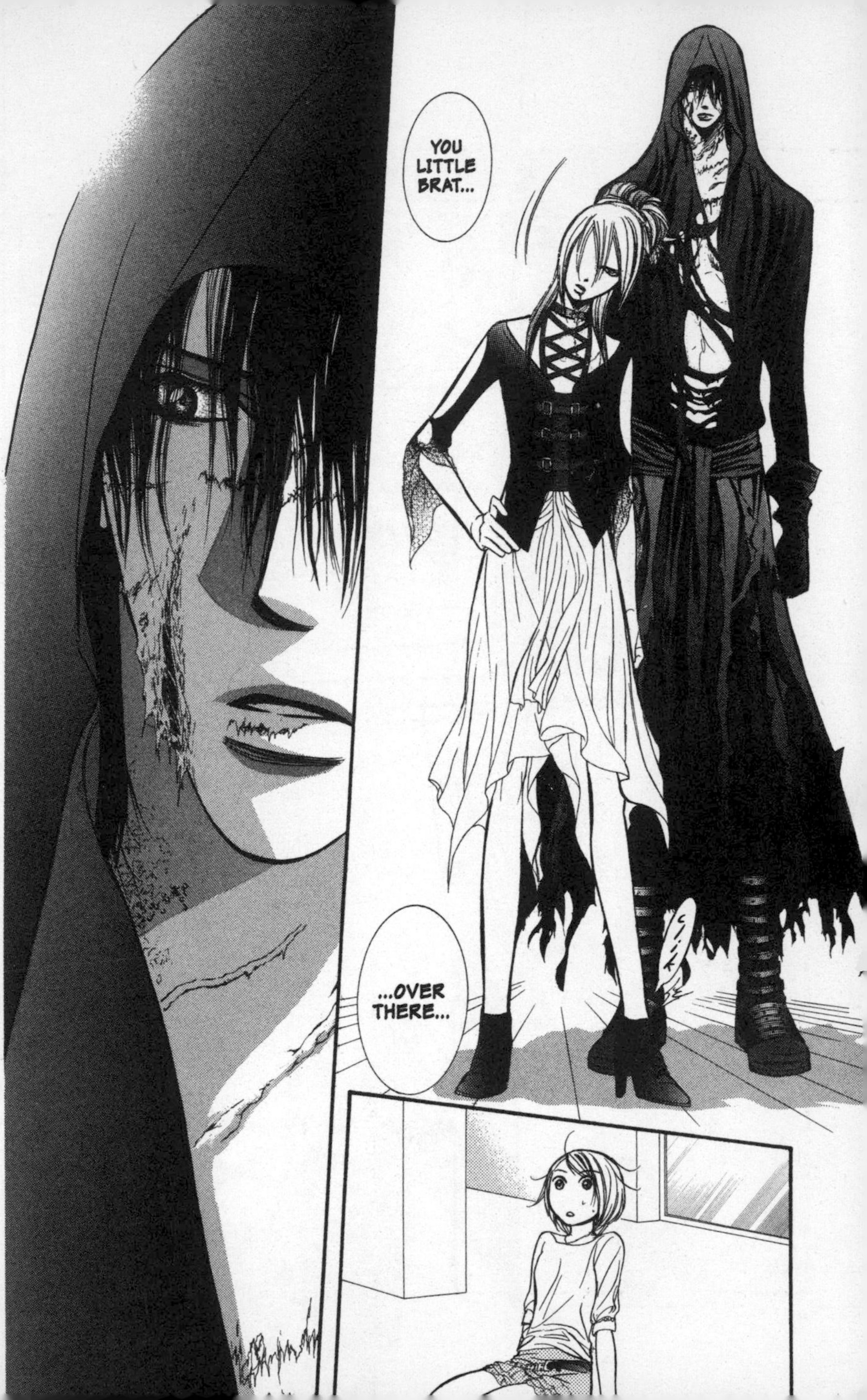
YOU LITTLE BRAT...
...OVER THERE...

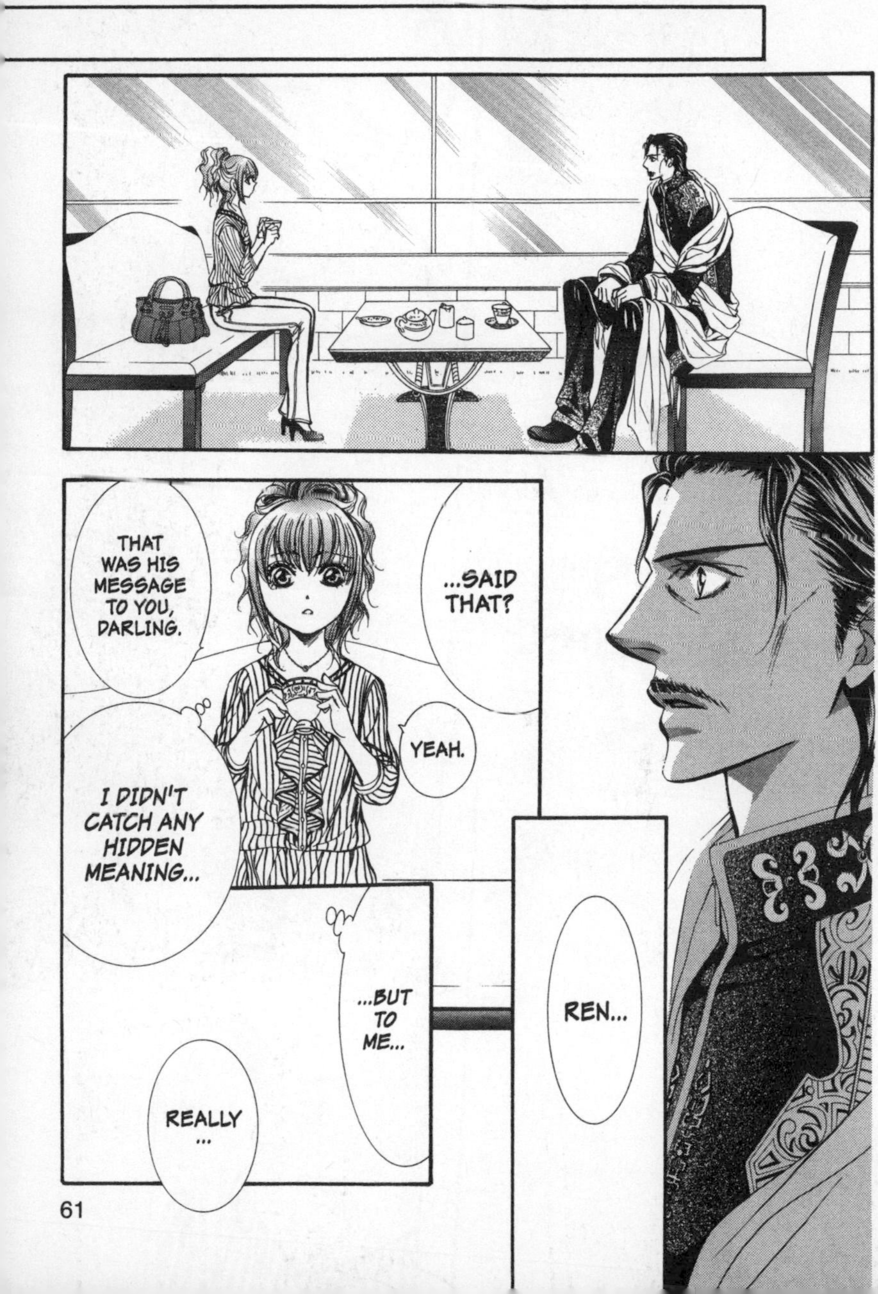
...SAID THAT?
THAT WAS HIS MESSAGE TO YOU, DARLING.
YEAH.
I DIDN'T CATCH ANY HIDDEN MEANING...
REN...
...BUT TO ME...
REALLY ...

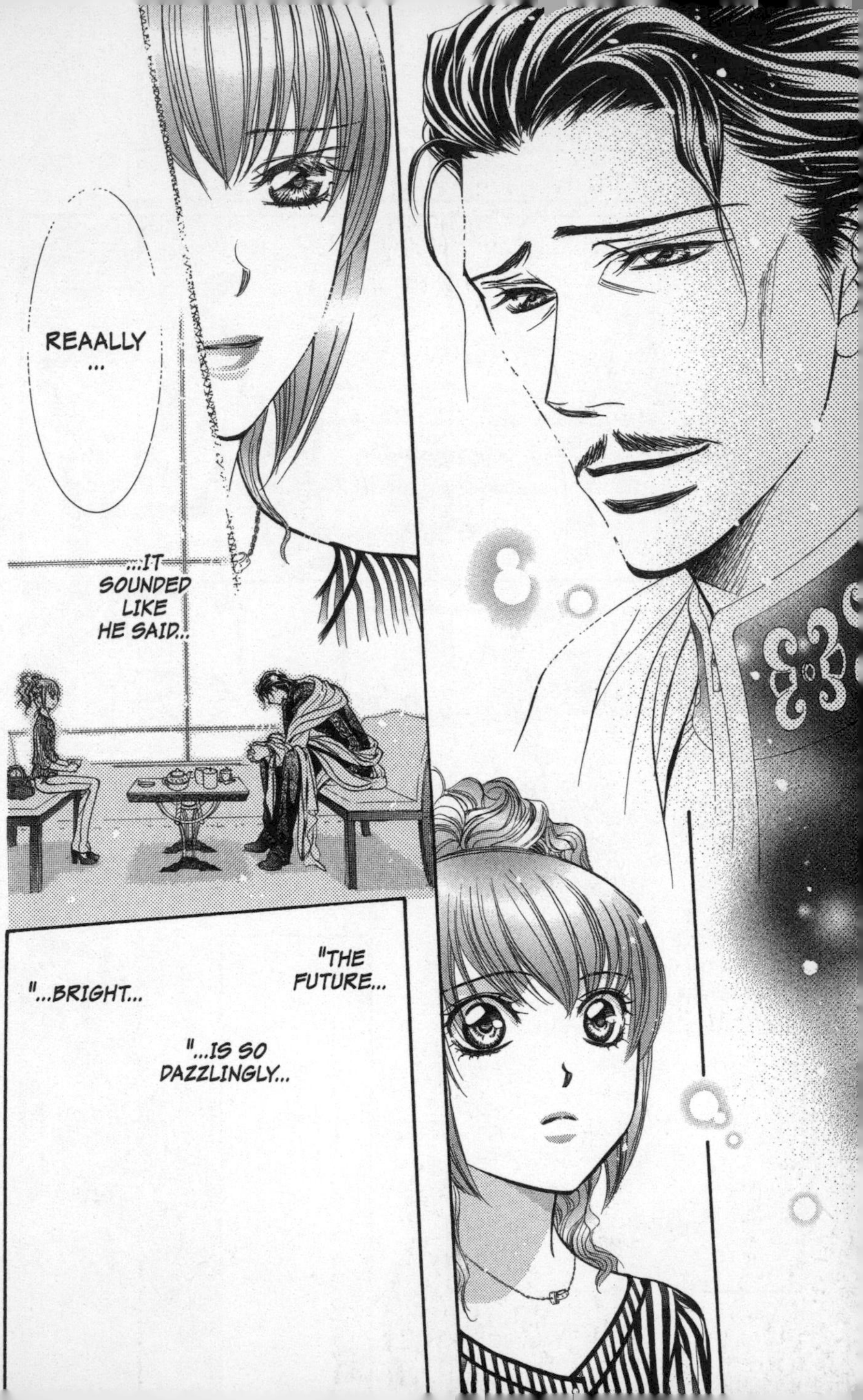
REAALLY ...
...IT SOUNDED LIKE HE SAID...
"THE FUTURE...
"...IS SO DAZZLINGLY...
"...BRIGHT...

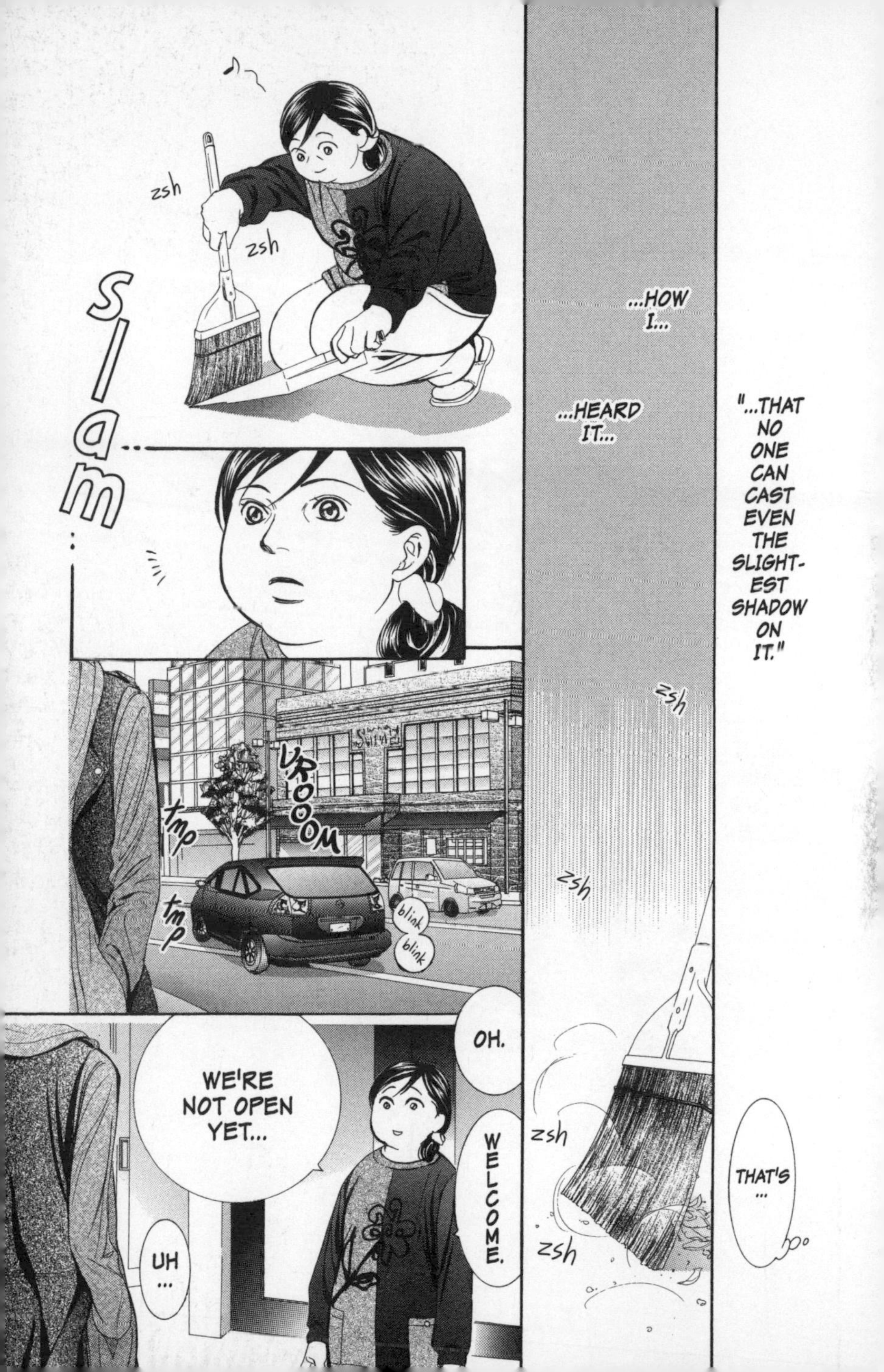
"...THAT NO ONE CAN CAST EVEN THE SLIGHTEST SHADOW ON IT."
...HOW I...
...HEARD IT...
zsh
zsh
zsh
zsh
THAT'S ...
♪
zsh
zsh
slam...
VROOOM
tmp
tmp
blink
blink
OH.
WELCOME.
WE'RE NOT OPEN YET...
UH ...

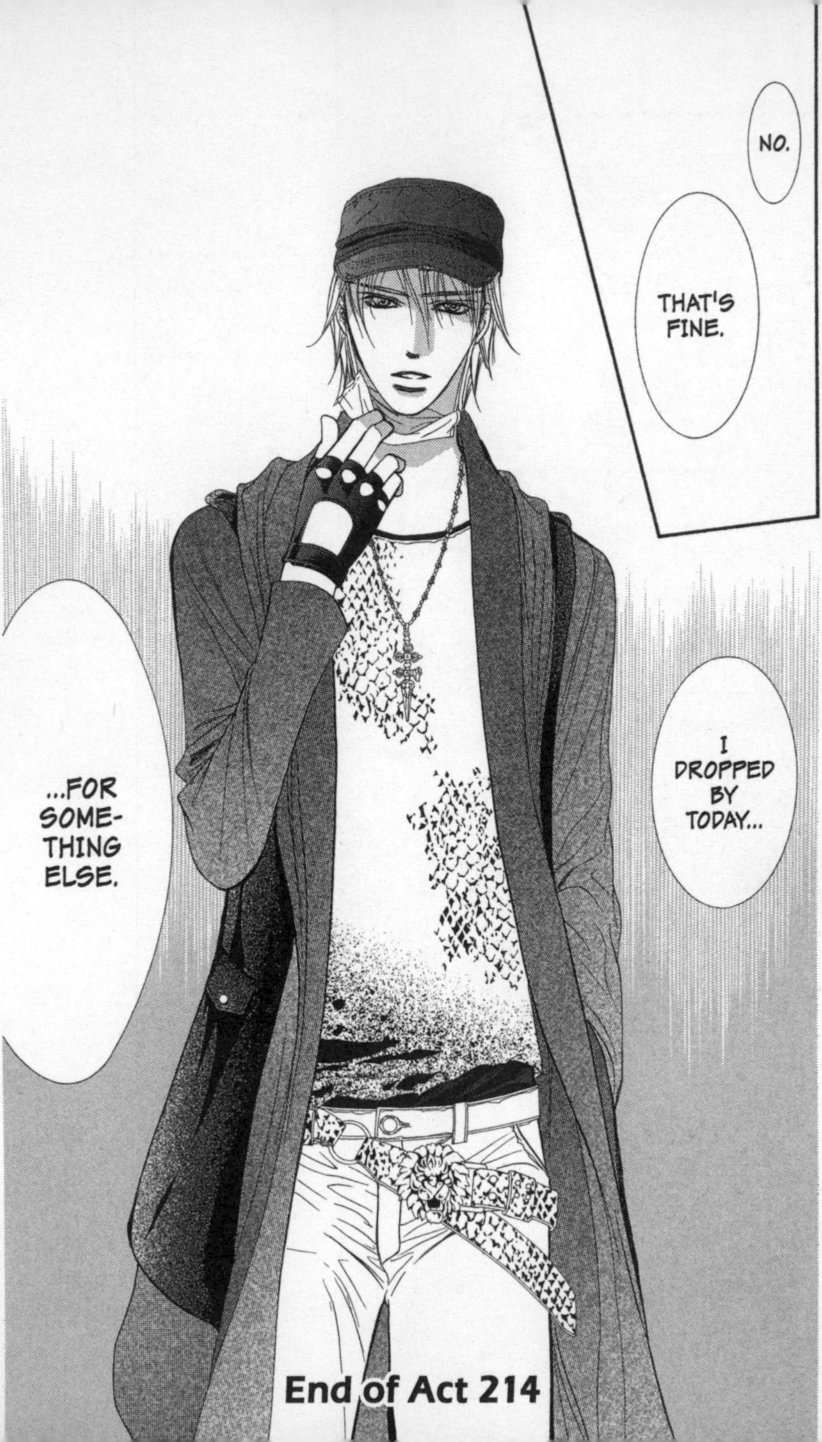
NO.
THAT'S FINE.
I DROPPED BY TODAY...
...FOR SOME-THING ELSE.

End of Act 214

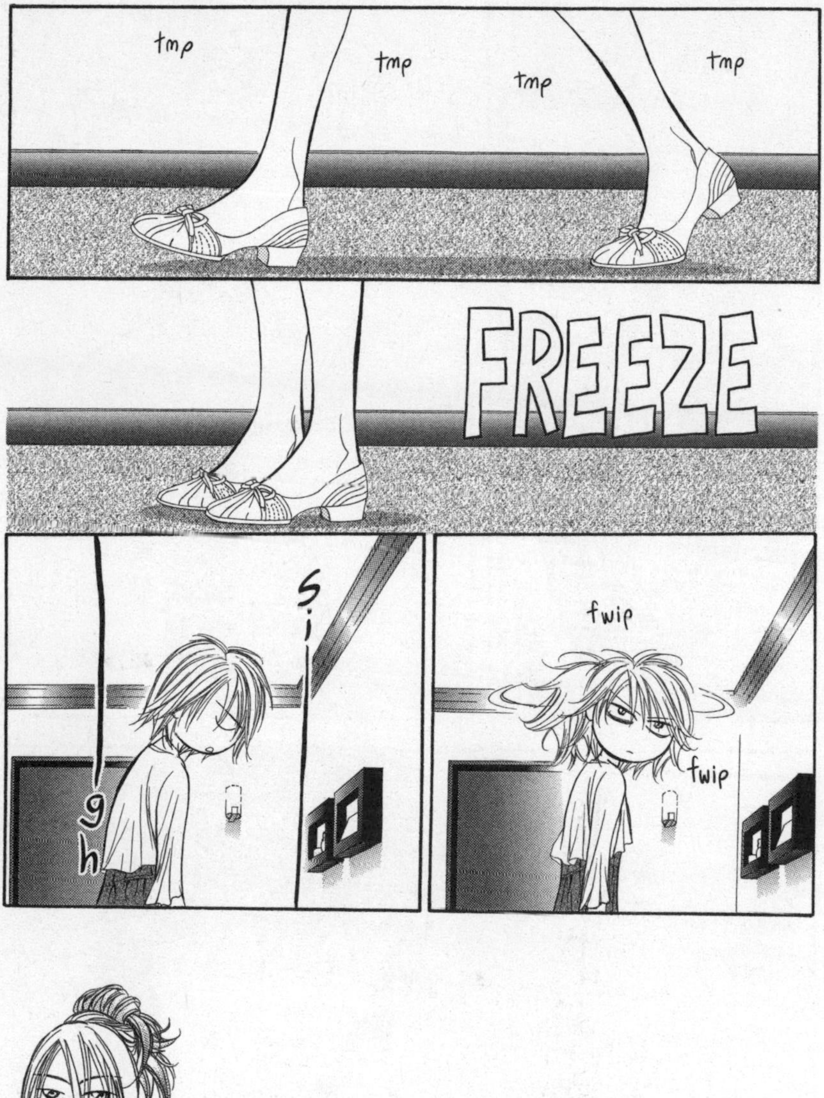
tmp
tmp
tmp
tmp
FREEZE
fwip
fwip
sigh

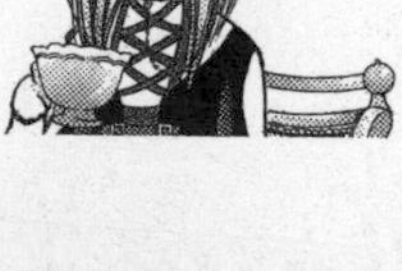

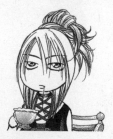

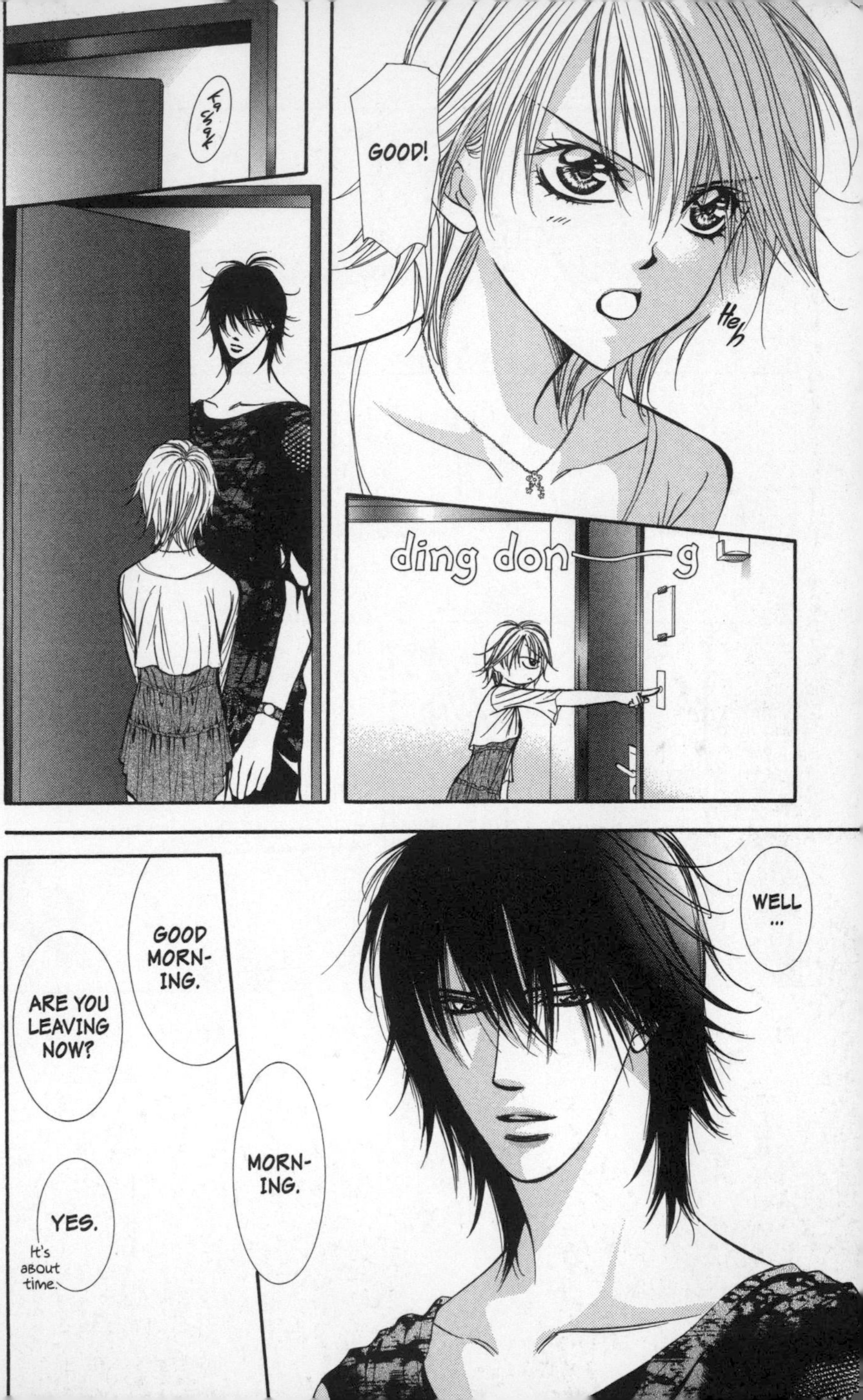
GOOD!
Heh
ding don——g
ka chak
WELL...
GOOD MORNING.
ARE YOU LEAVING NOW?
MORNING.
YES.
It's about time.

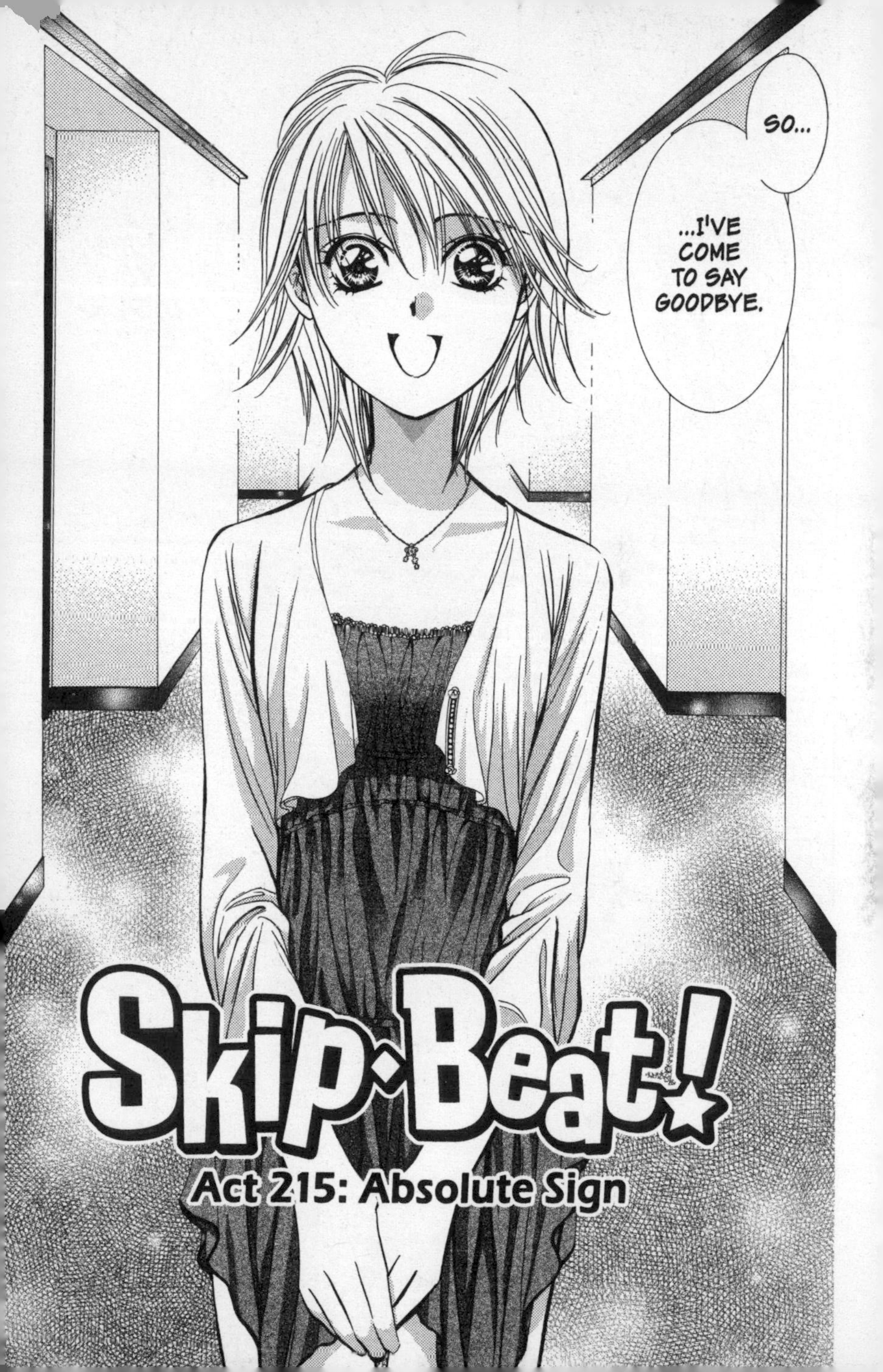
SO...
...I'VE COME TO SAY GOODBYE.
Skip·Beat!
Act 215: Absolute Sign

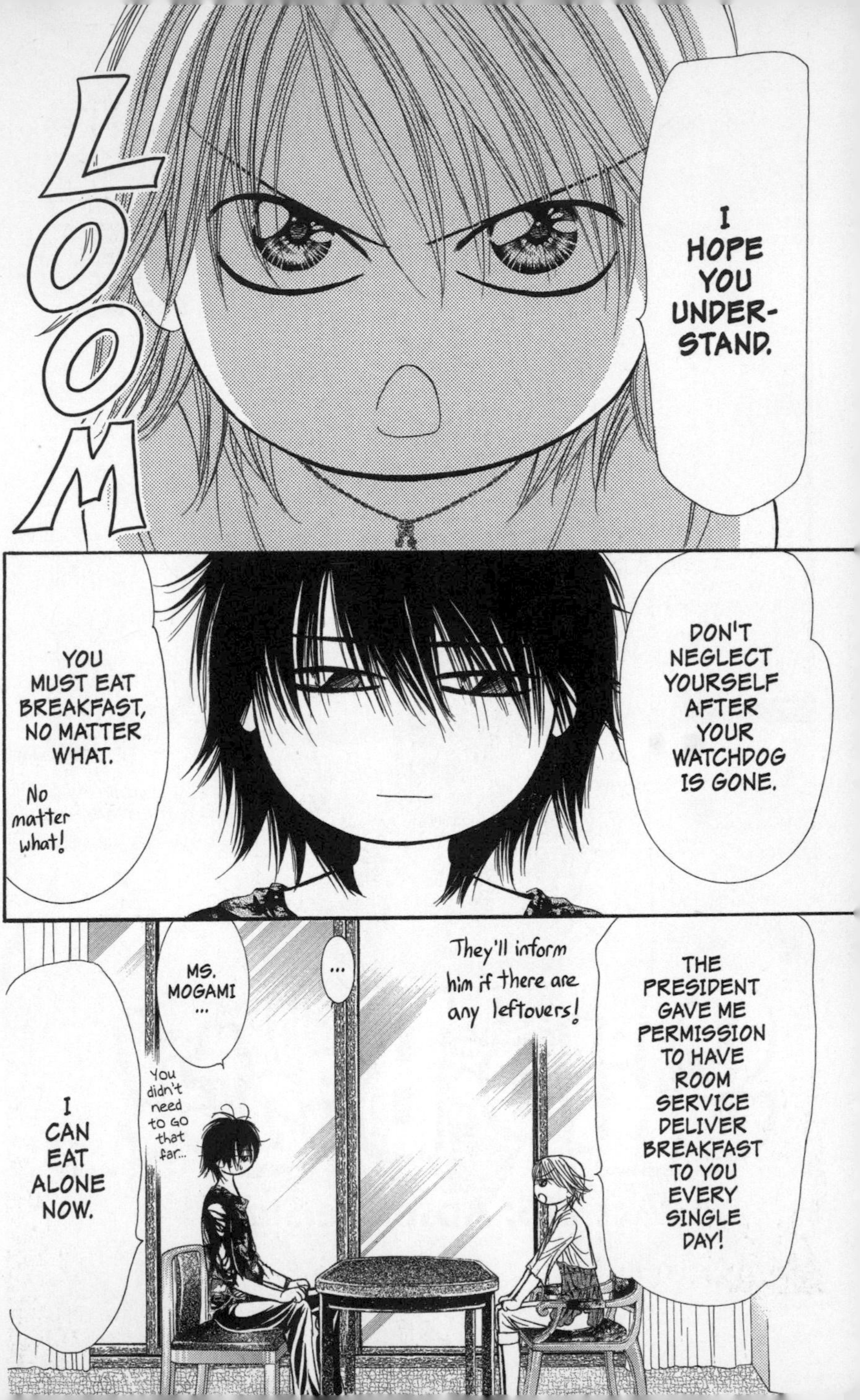
I HOPE YOU UNDERSTAND.
LOOOM
DON'T NEGLECT YOURSELF AFTER YOUR WATCHDOG IS GONE.
YOU MUST EAT BREAKFAST, NO MATTER WHAT.
No matter what!
THE PRESIDENT GAVE ME PERMISSION TO HAVE ROOM SERVICE DELIVER BREAKFAST TO YOU EVERY SINGLE DAY!
They'll inform him if there are any leftovers!
...
MS. MOGAMI ...
You didn't need to GO that far...
I CAN EAT ALONE NOW.

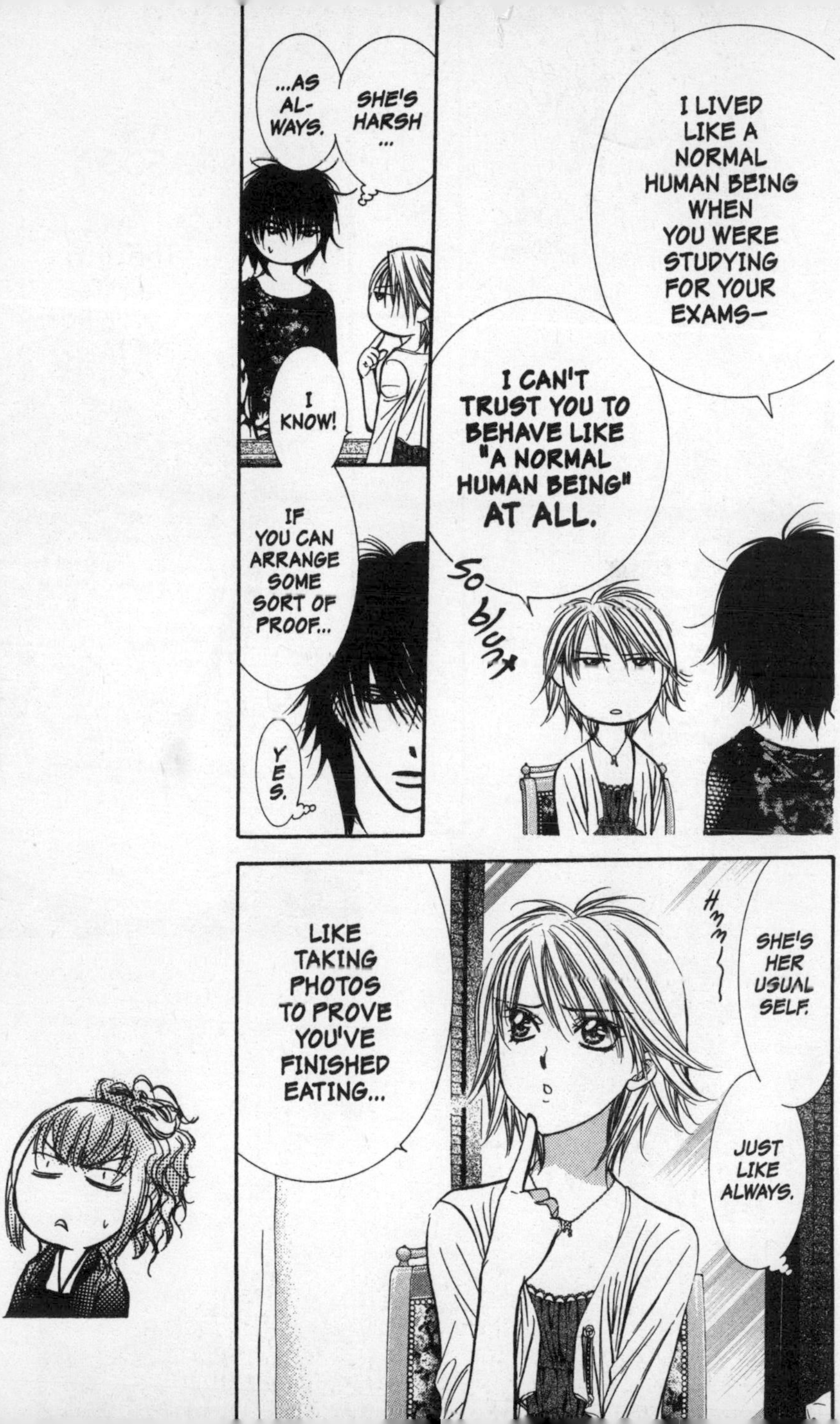
I LIVED LIKE A NORMAL HUMAN BEING WHEN YOU WERE STUDYING FOR YOUR EXAMS—
I CAN'T TRUST YOU TO BEHAVE LIKE "A NORMAL HUMAN BEING" AT ALL.
So blunt
SHE'S HARSH...
...AS AL-WAYS.
I KNOW!
IF YOU CAN ARRANGE SOME SORT OF PROOF...
YES.
Hmm—
SHE'S HER USUAL SELF.
LIKE TAKING PHOTOS TO PROVE YOU'VE FINISHED EATING...
JUST LIKE ALWAYS.

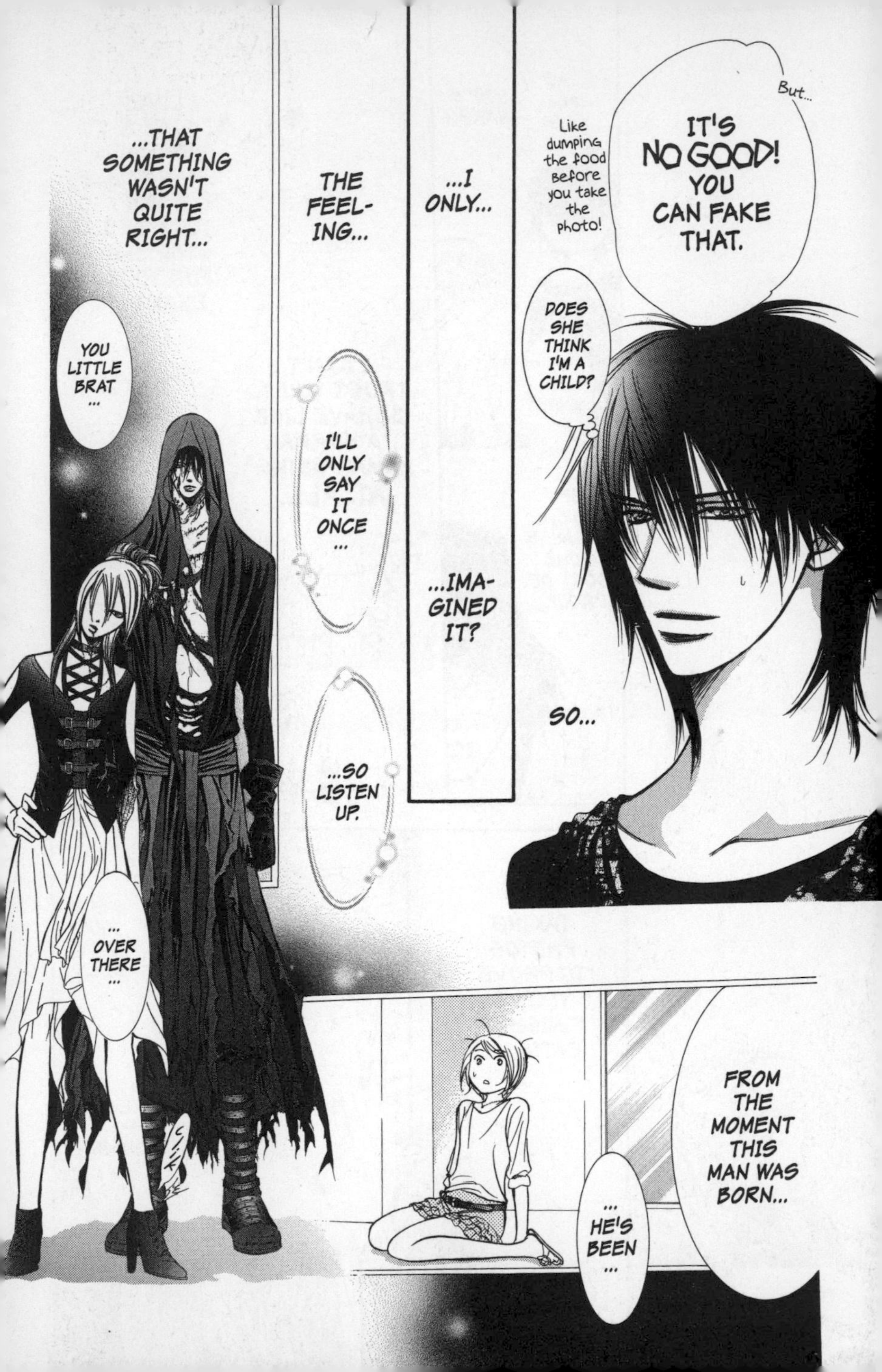
But...
IT'S NO GOOD! YOU CAN FAKE THAT.
Like dumping the food before you take the photo!
DOES SHE THINK I'M A CHILD?
SO...
...I ONLY...
...IMA-GINED IT?
THE FEEL-ING...
...THAT SOMETHING WASN'T QUITE RIGHT...
I'LL ONLY SAY IT ONCE...
...SO LISTEN UP.
YOU LITTLE BRAT...
...OVER THERE...
FROM THE MOMENT THIS MAN WAS BORN...
...HE'S BEEN...

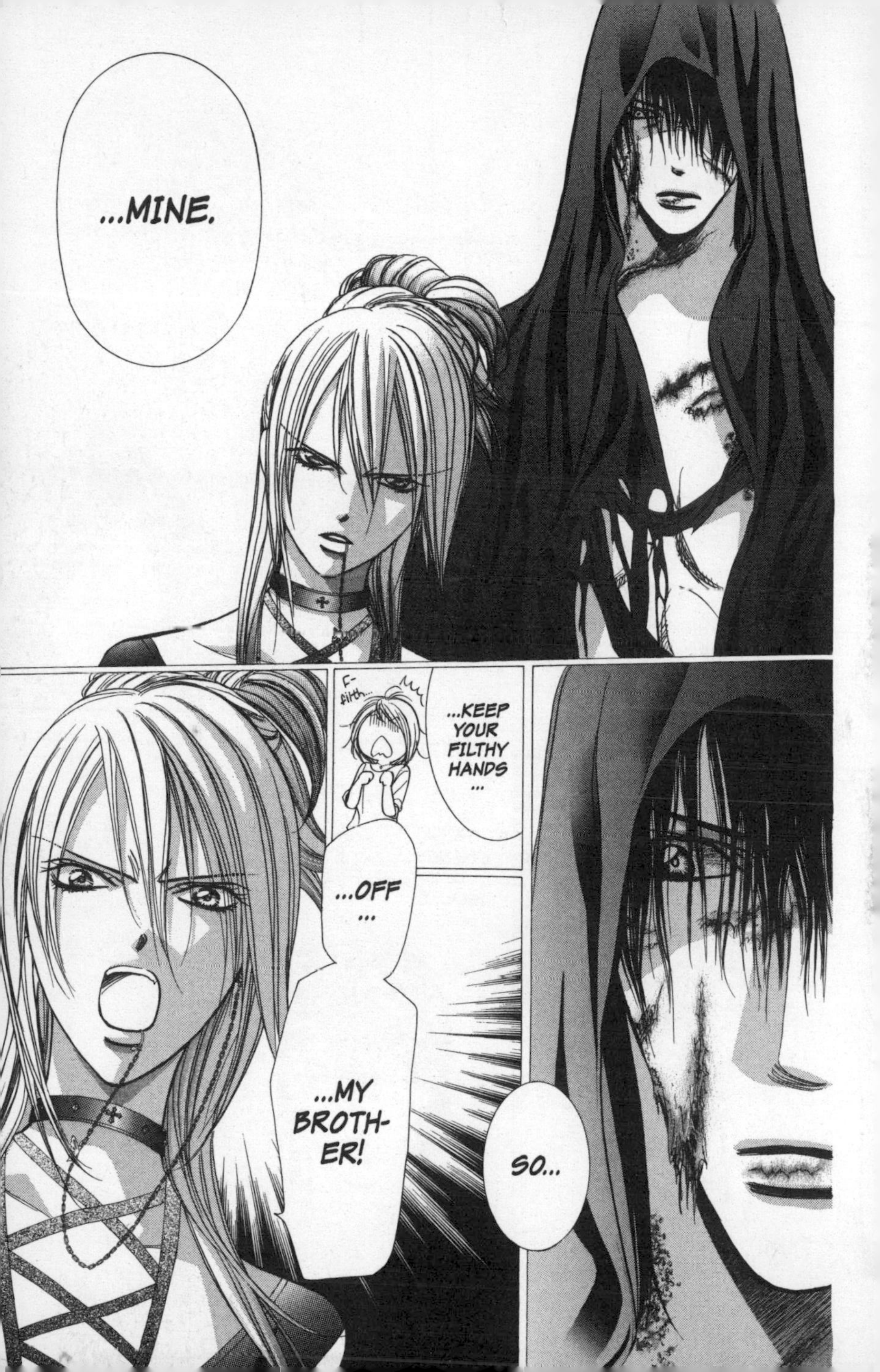
...MINE.
SO...
...KEEP YOUR FILTHY HANDS ...
F-filth...
...OFF ...
...MY BROTHER!

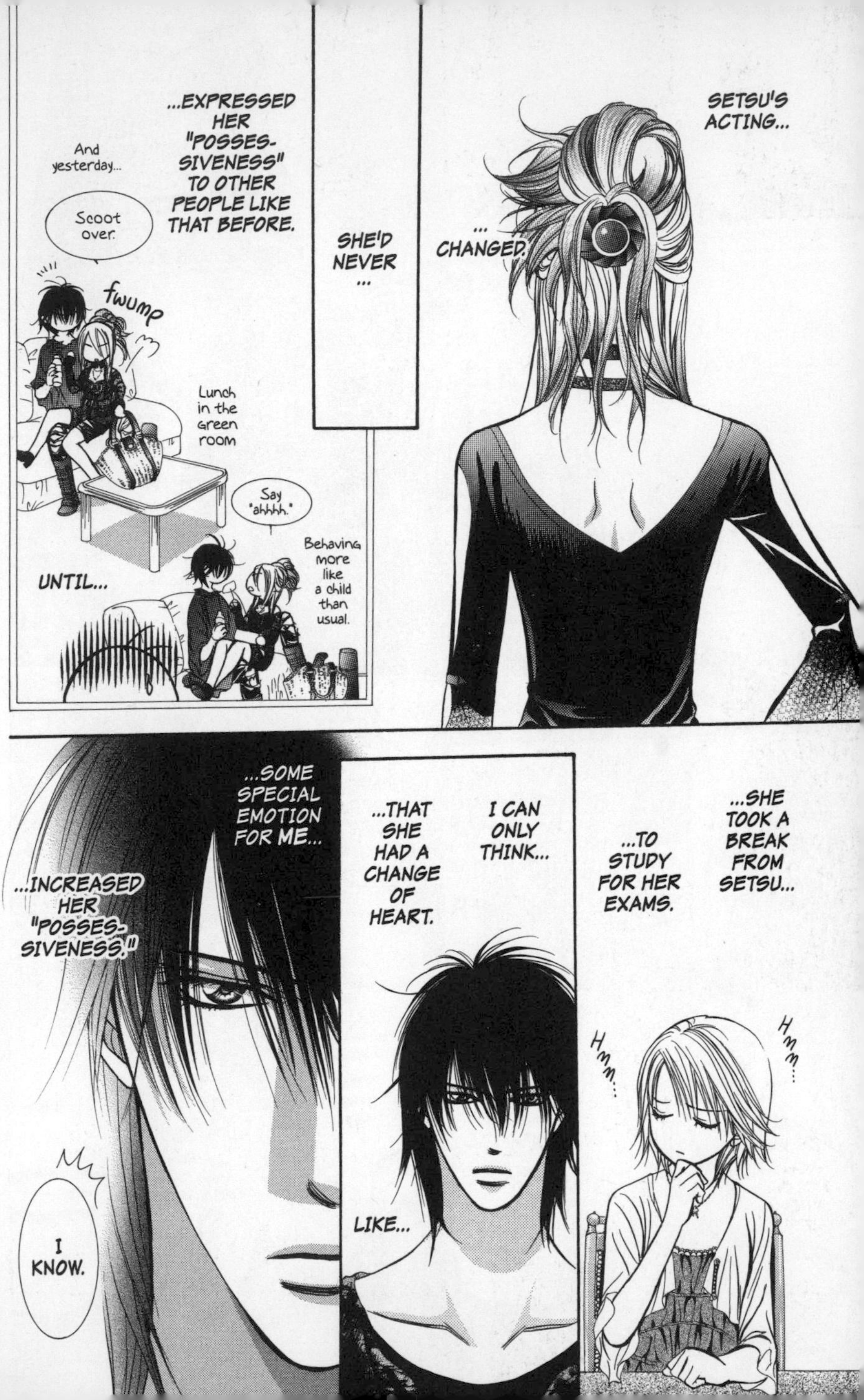
SETSU'S ACTING...
...CHANGED.
SHE'D NEVER ...
...EXPRESSED HER "POSSES-SIVENESS" TO OTHER PEOPLE LIKE THAT BEFORE.
And yesterday...
Scoot over.
fwump
Lunch in the Green room
Say "ahhhh."
Behaving more like a child than usual.
UNTIL...
...SHE TOOK A BREAK FROM SETSU...
...TO STUDY FOR HER EXAMS.
Hmm...
Hmm...
I CAN ONLY THINK...
...THAT SHE HAD A CHANGE OF HEART.
LIKE...
...SOME SPECIAL EMOTION FOR ME...
...INCREASED HER "POSSES-SIVENESS."
I KNOW.

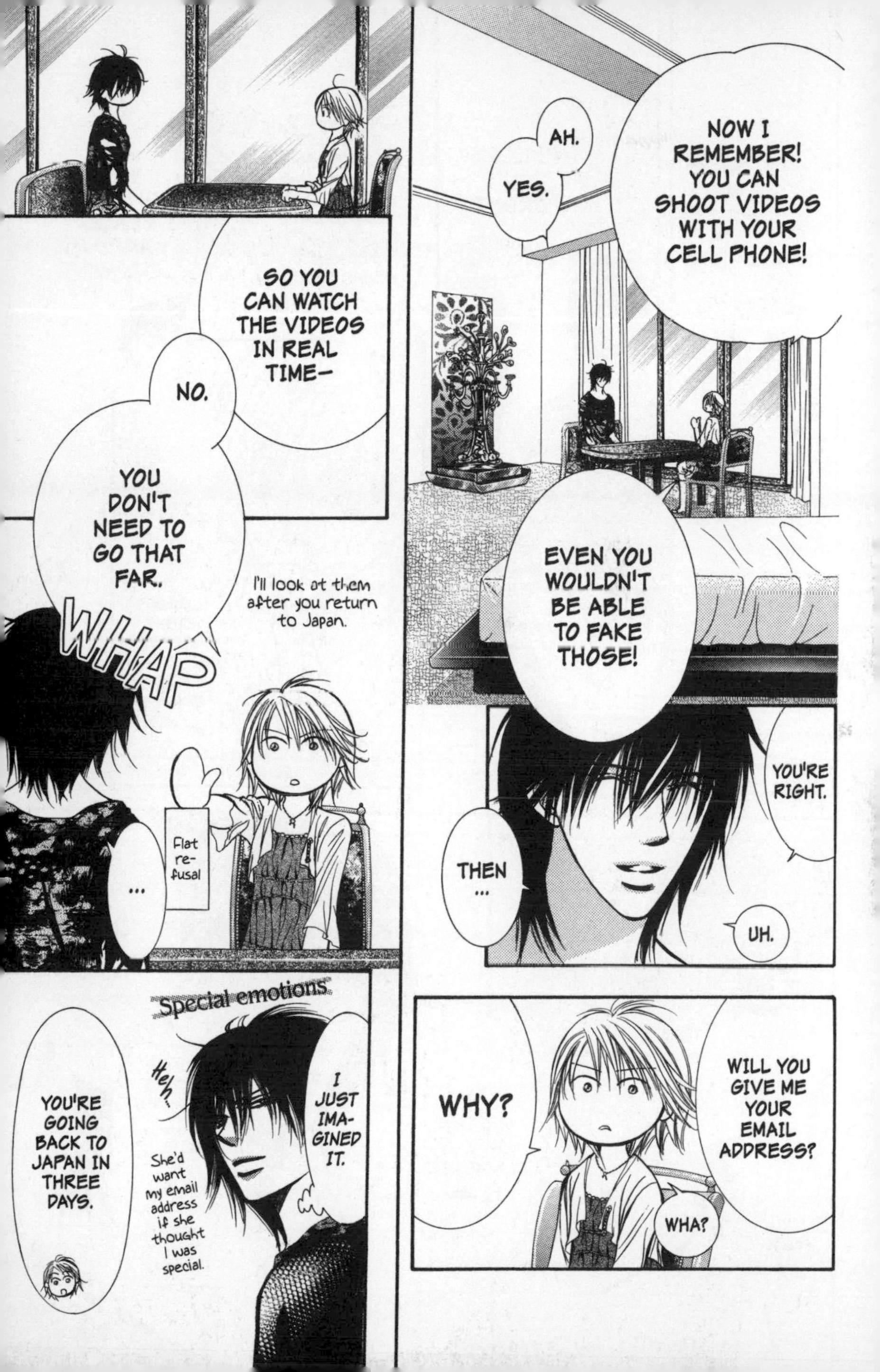

NOW I REMEMBER! YOU CAN SHOOT VIDEOS WITH YOUR CELL PHONE!
AH.
YES.
EVEN YOU WOULDN'T BE ABLE TO FAKE THOSE!
YOU'RE RIGHT.
THEN ...
UH.
WILL YOU GIVE ME YOUR EMAIL ADDRESS?
WHY?
WHA?
SO YOU CAN WATCH THE VIDEOS IN REAL TIME—
NO.
YOU DON'T NEED TO GO THAT FAR.
I'll look at them after you return to Japan.
WHAP
Flat re-fusal
...
I JUST IMAGINED IT.
Heh...
Special emotions
She'd want my email address if she thought I was special.
YOU'RE GOING BACK TO JAPAN IN THREE DAYS.

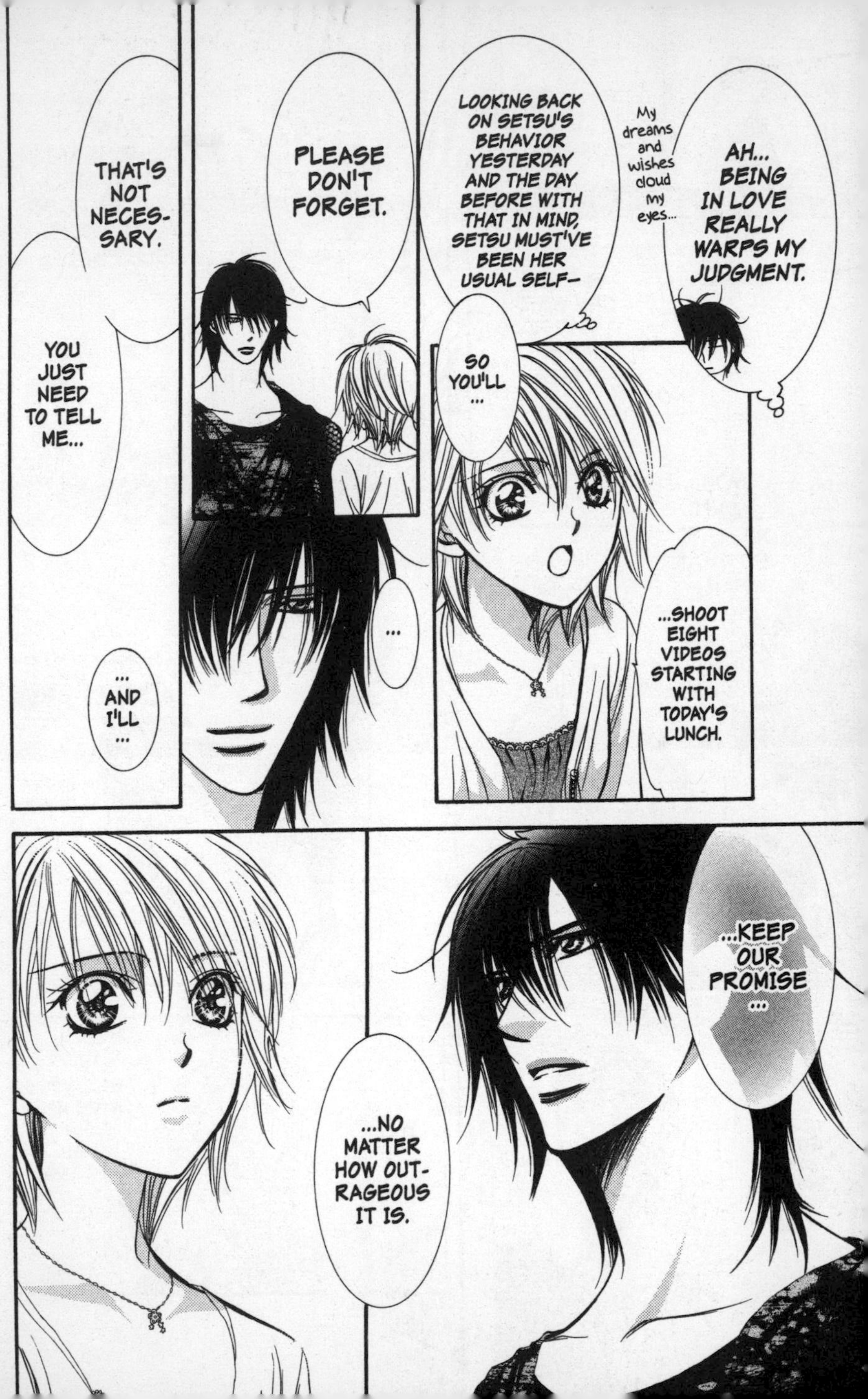
AH... BEING IN LOVE REALLY WARPS MY JUDGMENT.
My dreams and wishes cloud my eyes...
LOOKING BACK ON SETSU'S BEHAVIOR YESTERDAY AND THE DAY BEFORE WITH THAT IN MIND, SETSU MUST'VE BEEN HER USUAL SELF—
SO YOU'LL ...
...SHOOT EIGHT VIDEOS STARTING WITH TODAY'S LUNCH.
PLEASE DON'T FORGET.
...
THAT'S NOT NECES-SARY.
YOU JUST NEED TO TELL ME...
... AND I'LL ...
...KEEP OUR PROMISE ...
...NO MATTER HOW OUT-RAGEOUS IT IS.

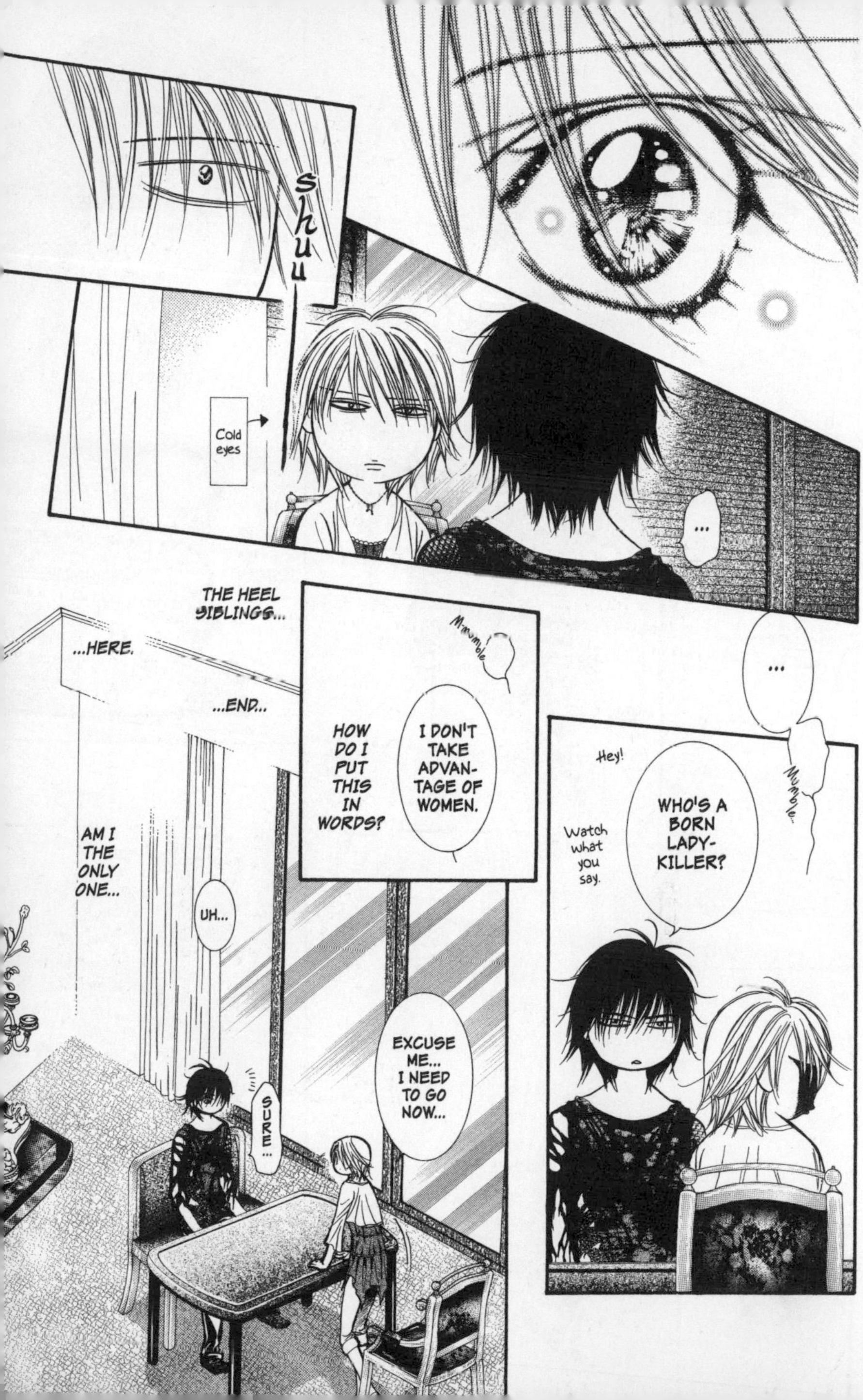

shuu
...
Cold eyes
...
Mumble
Hey!
WHO'S A BORN LADY-KILLER?
Watch what you say.
Mumble!
I DON'T TAKE ADVANTAGE OF WOMEN.
HOW DO I PUT THIS IN WORDS?
THE HEEL SIBLINGS...
...END...
...HERE.
AM I THE ONLY ONE...
UH...
EXCUSE ME... I NEED TO GO NOW...
SURE...

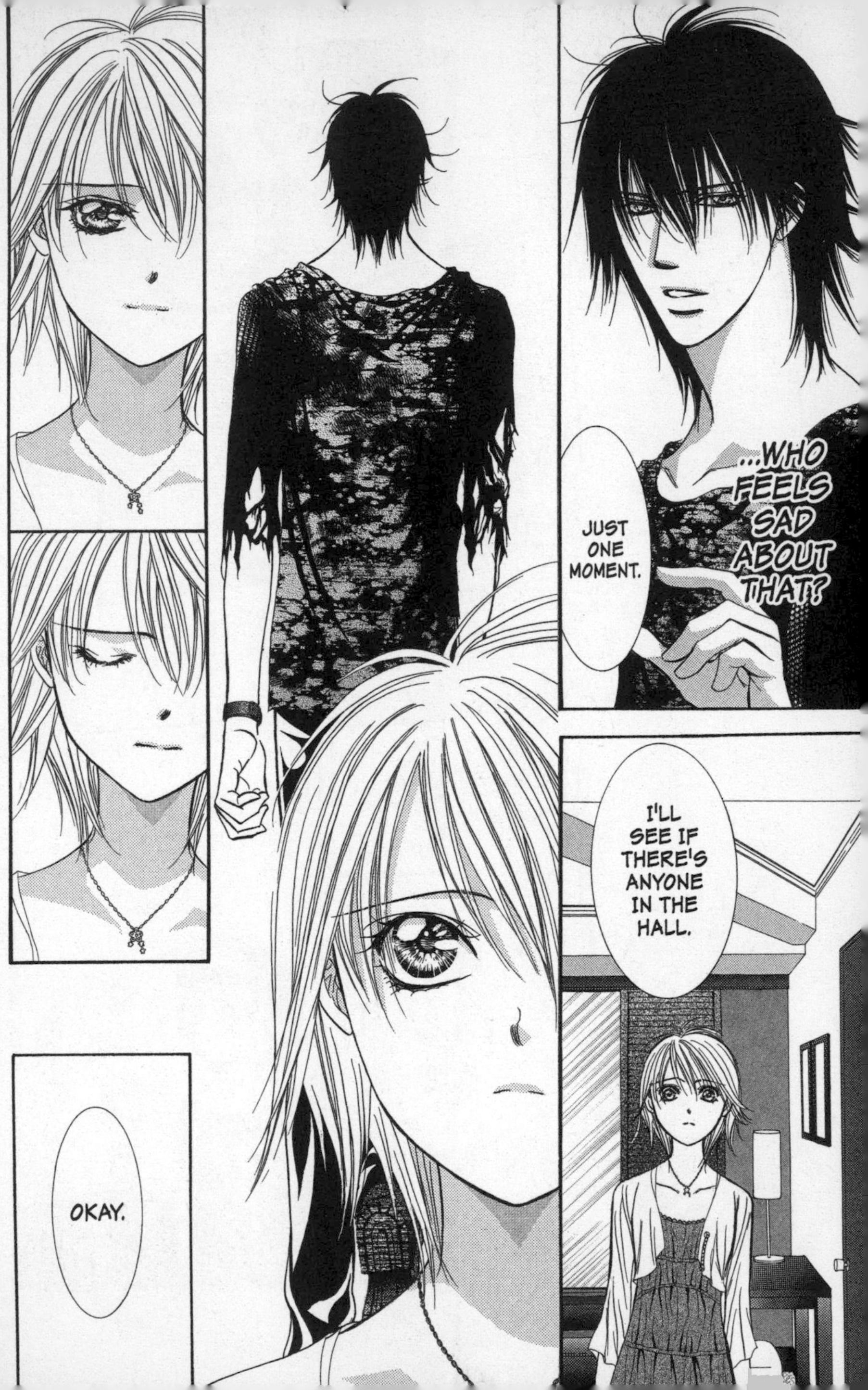
...WHO FEELS SAD ABOUT THAT?
JUST ONE MOMENT.
I'LL SEE IF THERE'S ANYONE IN THE HALL.
OKAY.

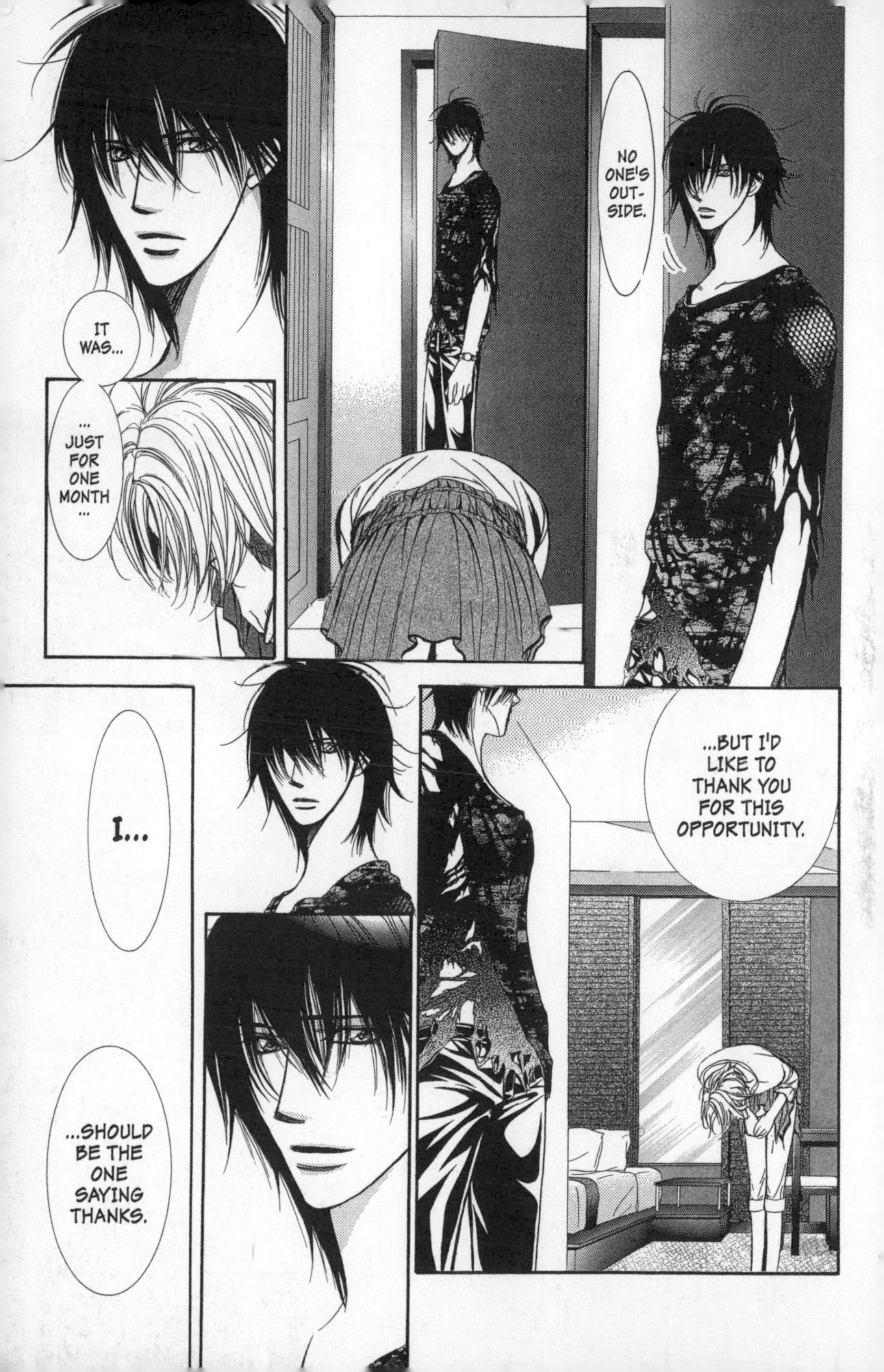
NO ONE'S OUT-SIDE.
IT WAS...
...JUST FOR ONE MONTH...
...BUT I'D LIKE TO THANK YOU FOR THIS OPPORTUNITY.
I...
...SHOULD BE THE ONE SAYING THANKS.

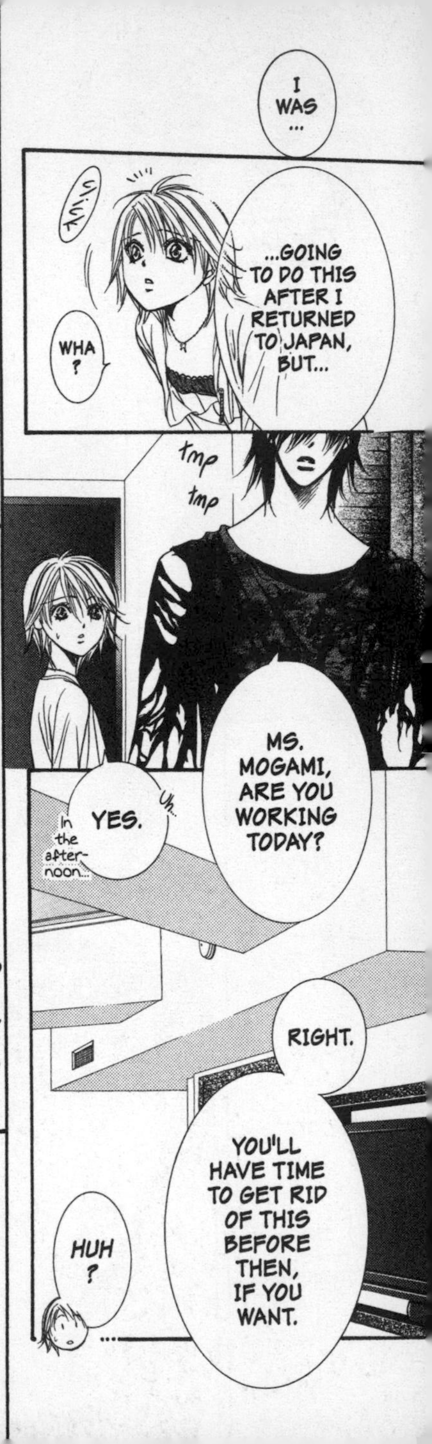
I WAS...
...GOING TO DO THIS AFTER I RETURNED TO JAPAN, BUT...
WHA?
tmp
tmp
MS. MOGAMI, ARE YOU WORKING TODAY?
Uh...
YES.
In the after-noon...
RIGHT.
YOU'LL HAVE TIME TO GET RID OF THIS BEFORE THEN, IF YOU WANT.
HUH?
...

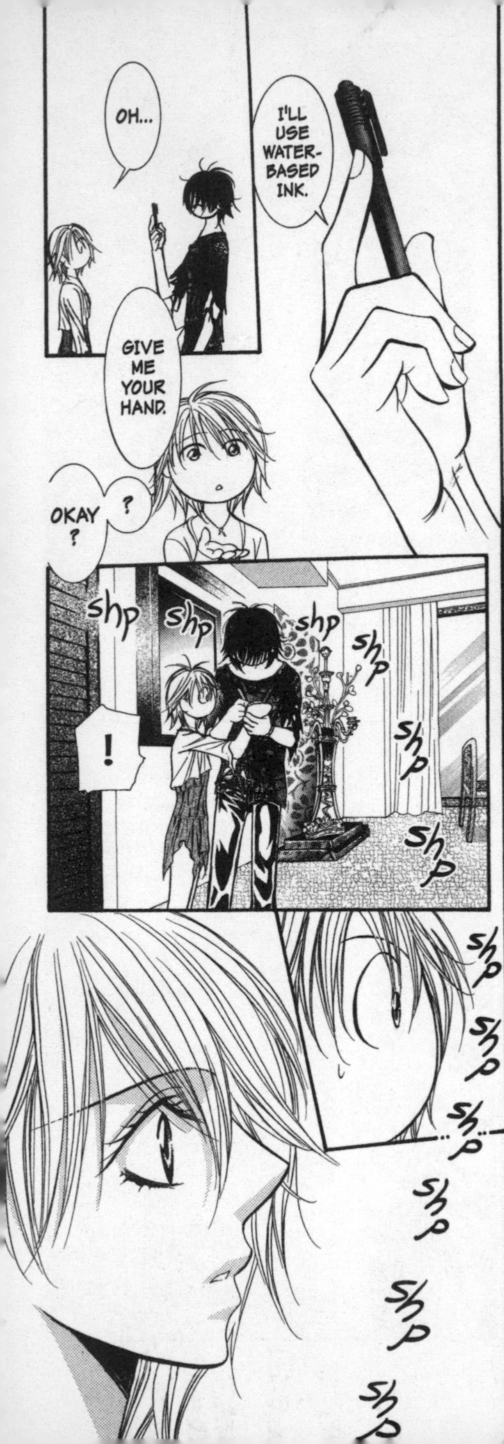
I'LL USE WATER-BASED INK.
OH...
GIVE ME YOUR HAND.
?
OKAY?
shp
shp
shp
shp
shp
shp
!
shp
shp
shp
shp
shp
shp

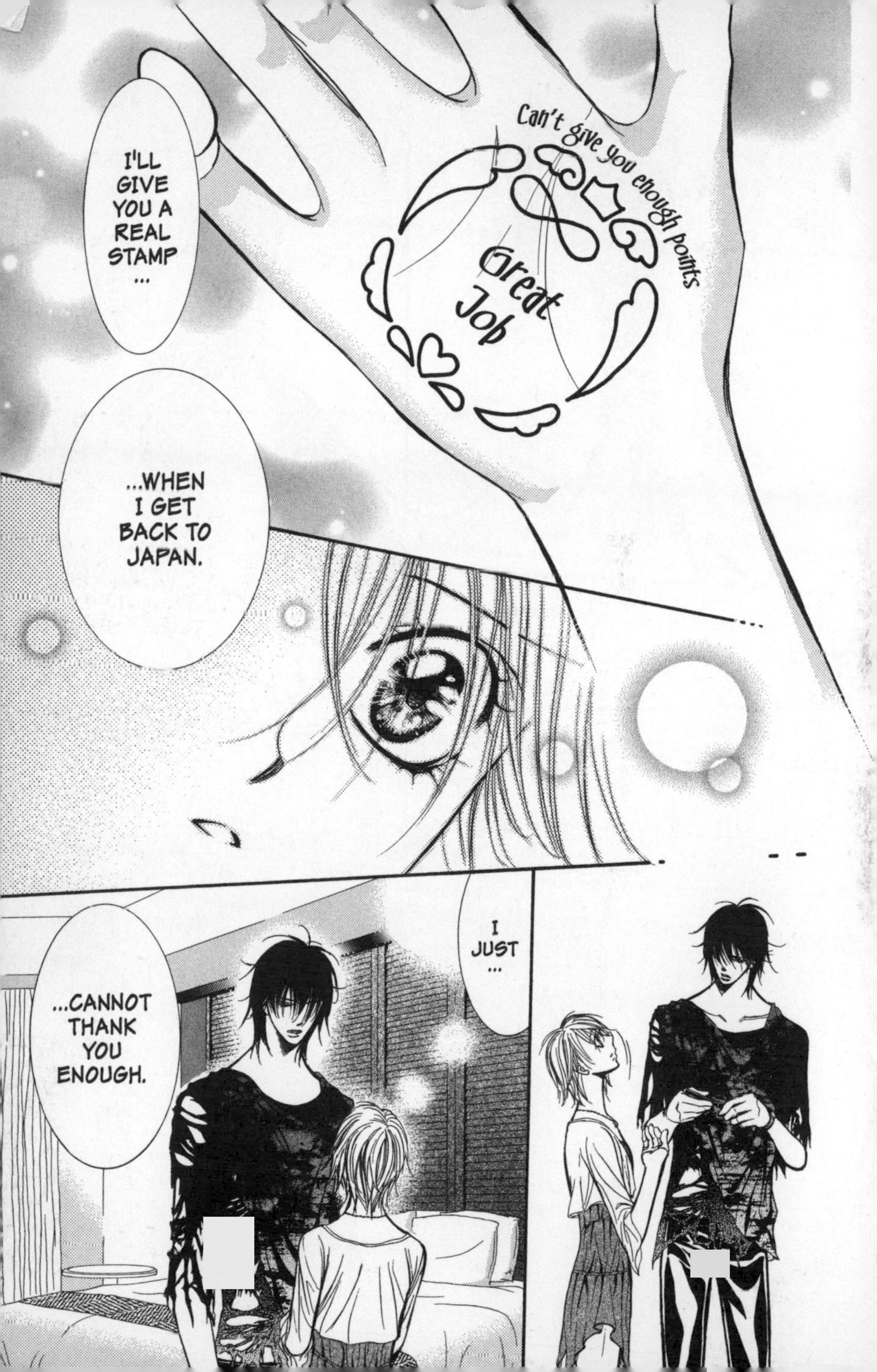
Can't give you enough points
Great Job
I'LL GIVE YOU A REAL STAMP ...
...WHEN I GET BACK TO JAPAN.
I JUST ...
...CANNOT THANK YOU ENOUGH.

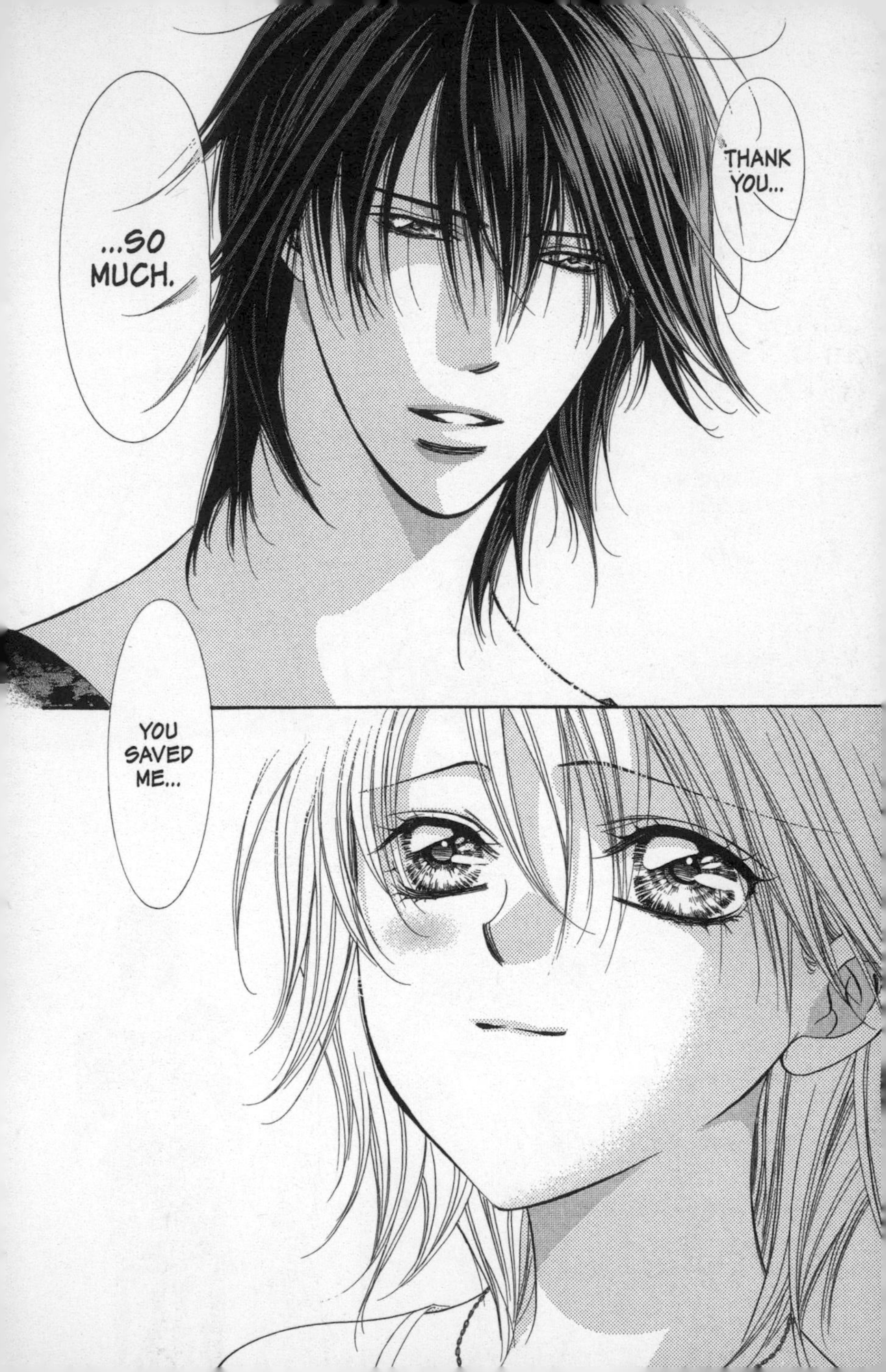
THANK YOU...
...SO MUCH.
YOU SAVED ME...

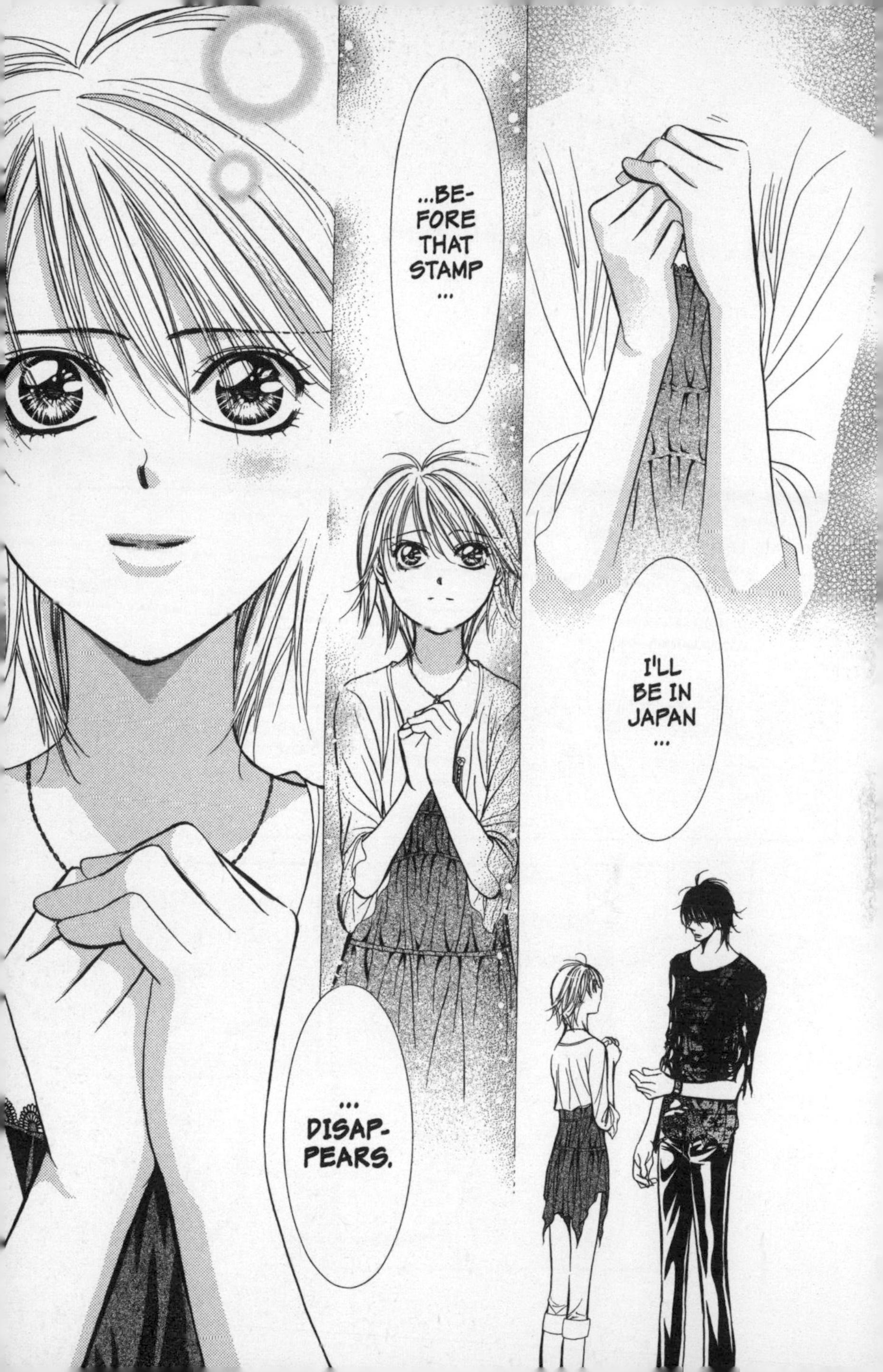
I'LL BE IN JAPAN ...
...BEFORE THAT STAMP ...
... DISAPPEARS.

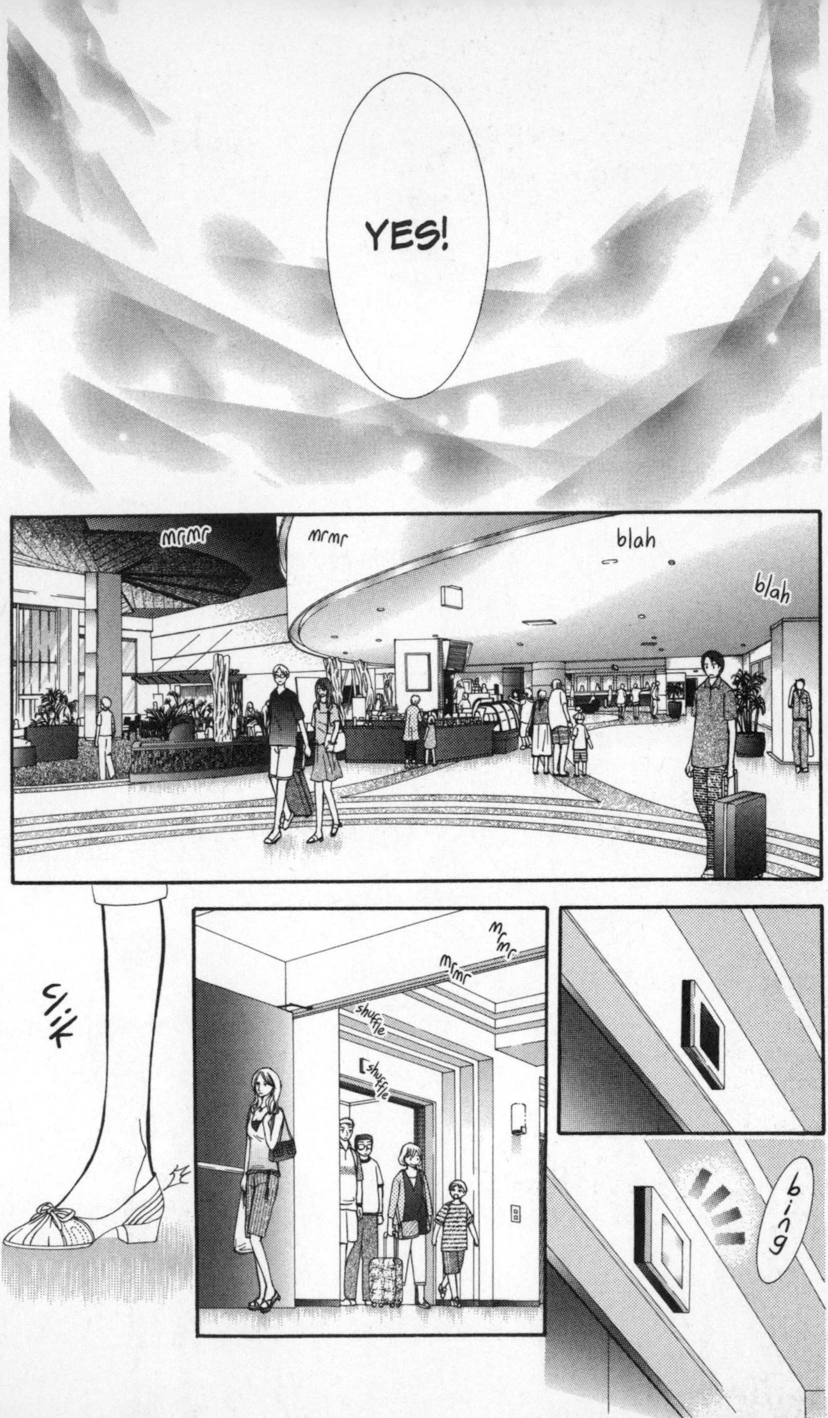
YES!
blah
blah
mrmr
mrmr
bing
mrmr
mrmr
shuffle
shuffle
clik

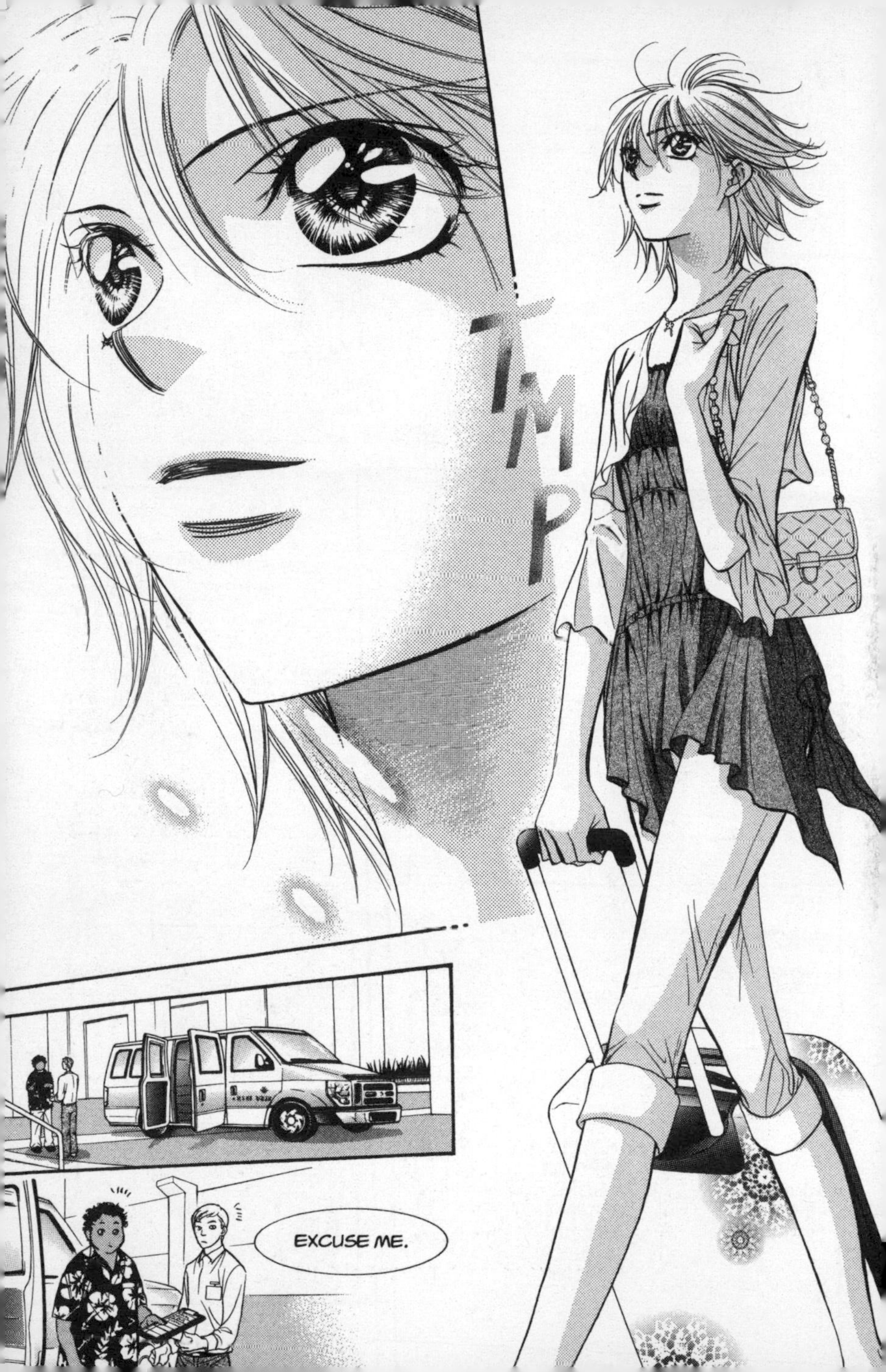
TMP
EXCUSE ME.

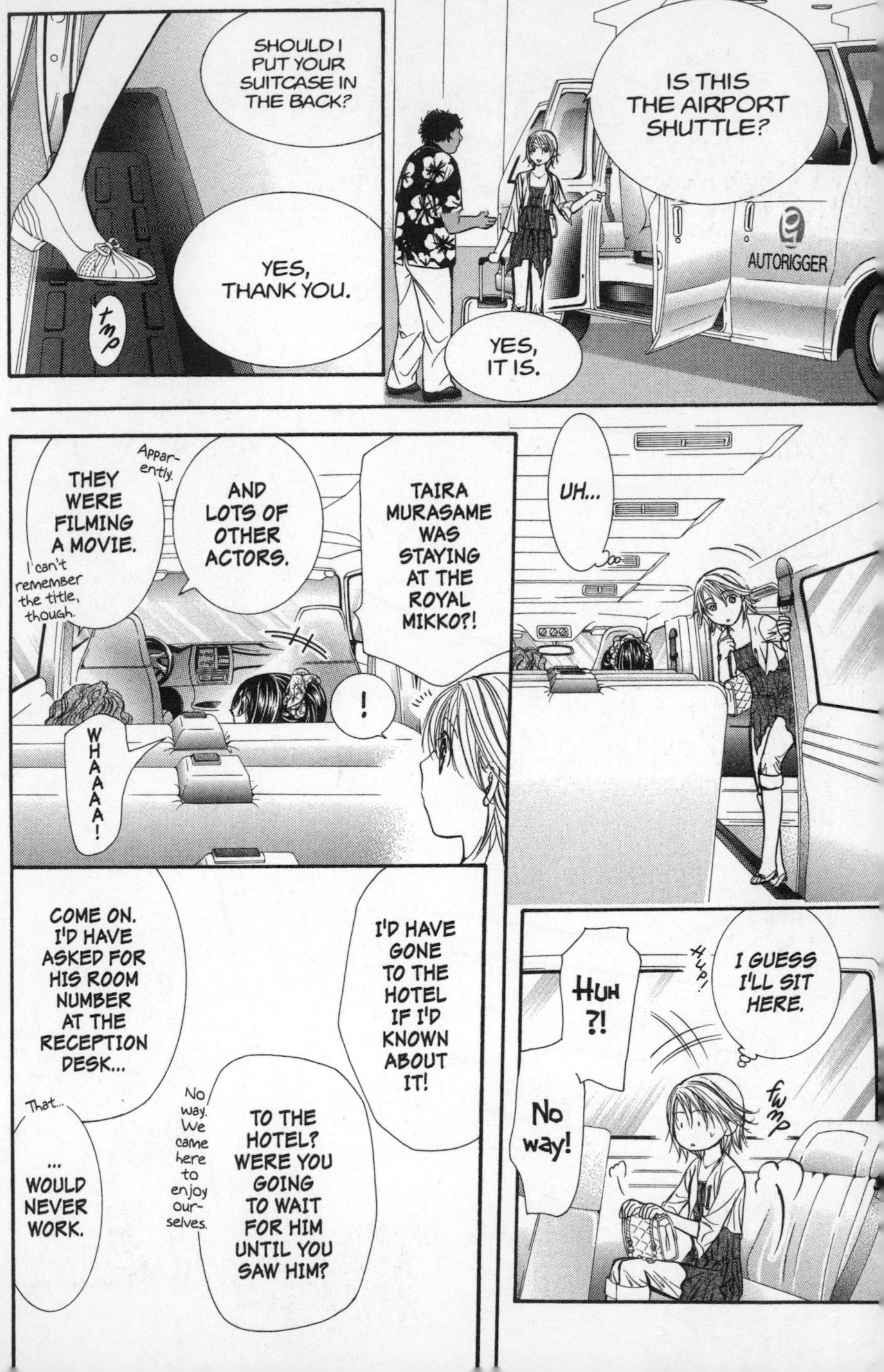

IS THIS THE AIRPORT SHUTTLE?
AUTORIGGER
YES, IT IS.
SHOULD I PUT YOUR SUITCASE IN THE BACK?
YES, THANK YOU.
tmp
UH...
I GUESS I'LL SIT HERE.
HUP!
HUH ?!
No way!
fwmp
TAIRA MURASAME WAS STAYING AT THE ROYAL MIKKO?!
!
AND LOTS OF OTHER ACTORS.
Apparently.
THEY WERE FILMING A MOVIE.
I can't remember the title, though.
WHAAAAA!
I'D HAVE GONE TO THE HOTEL IF I'D KNOWN ABOUT IT!
COME ON. I'D HAVE ASKED FOR HIS ROOM NUMBER AT THE RECEPTION DESK...
TO THE HOTEL? WERE YOU GOING TO WAIT FOR HIM UNTIL YOU SAW HIM?
No way. We came here to enjoy ourselves.
That...
...WOULD NEVER WORK.

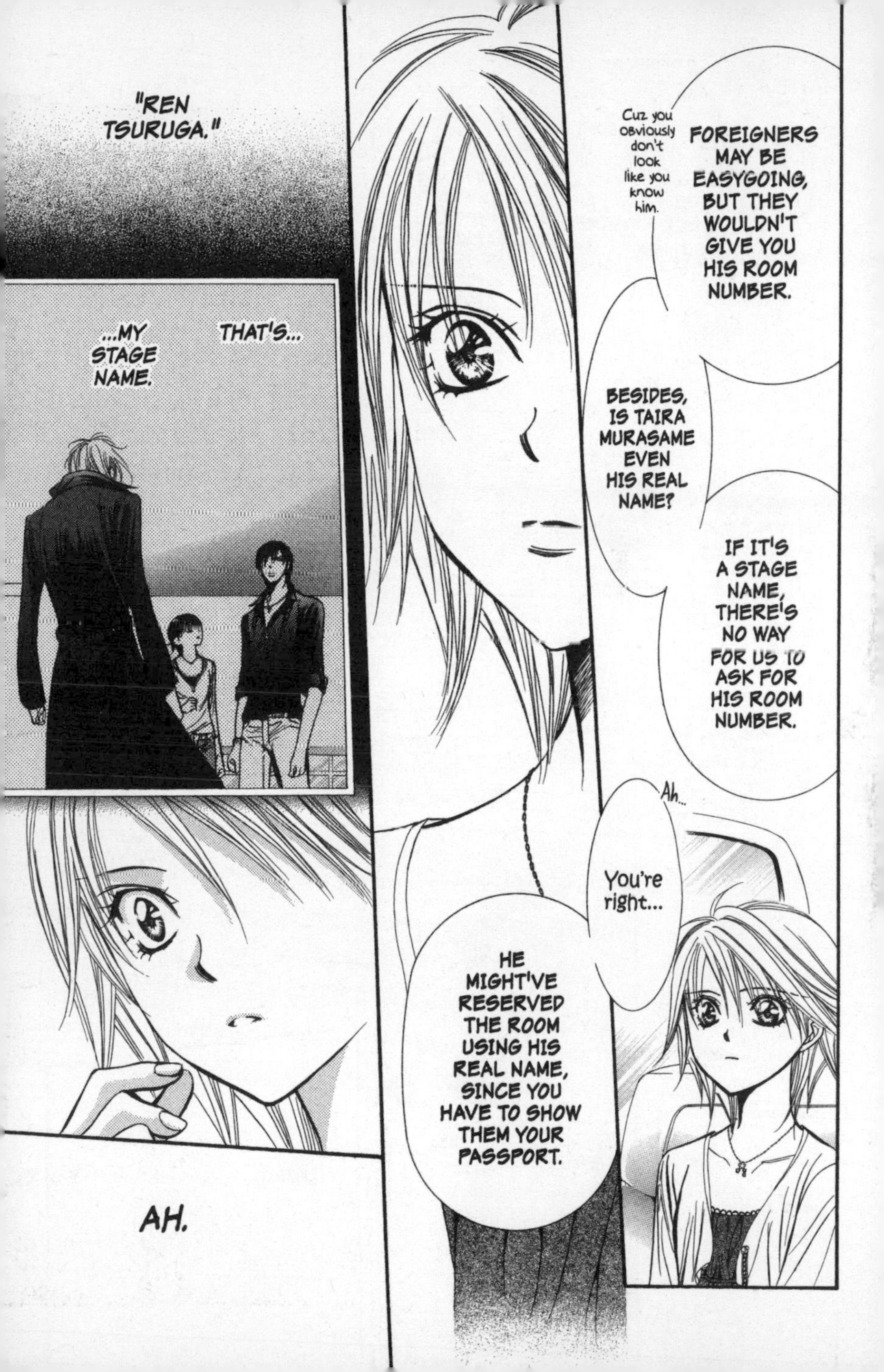

FOREIGNERS MAY BE EASYGOING, BUT THEY WOULDN'T GIVE YOU HIS ROOM NUMBER.
Cuz you obviously don't look like you know him.
BESIDES, IS TAIRA MURASAME EVEN HIS REAL NAME?
IF IT'S A STAGE NAME, THERE'S NO WAY FOR US TO ASK FOR HIS ROOM NUMBER.
Ah...
You're right...
HE MIGHT'VE RESERVED THE ROOM USING HIS REAL NAME, SINCE YOU HAVE TO SHOW THEM YOUR PASSPORT.
"REN TSURUGA."
THAT'S...
...MY STAGE NAME.
AH.

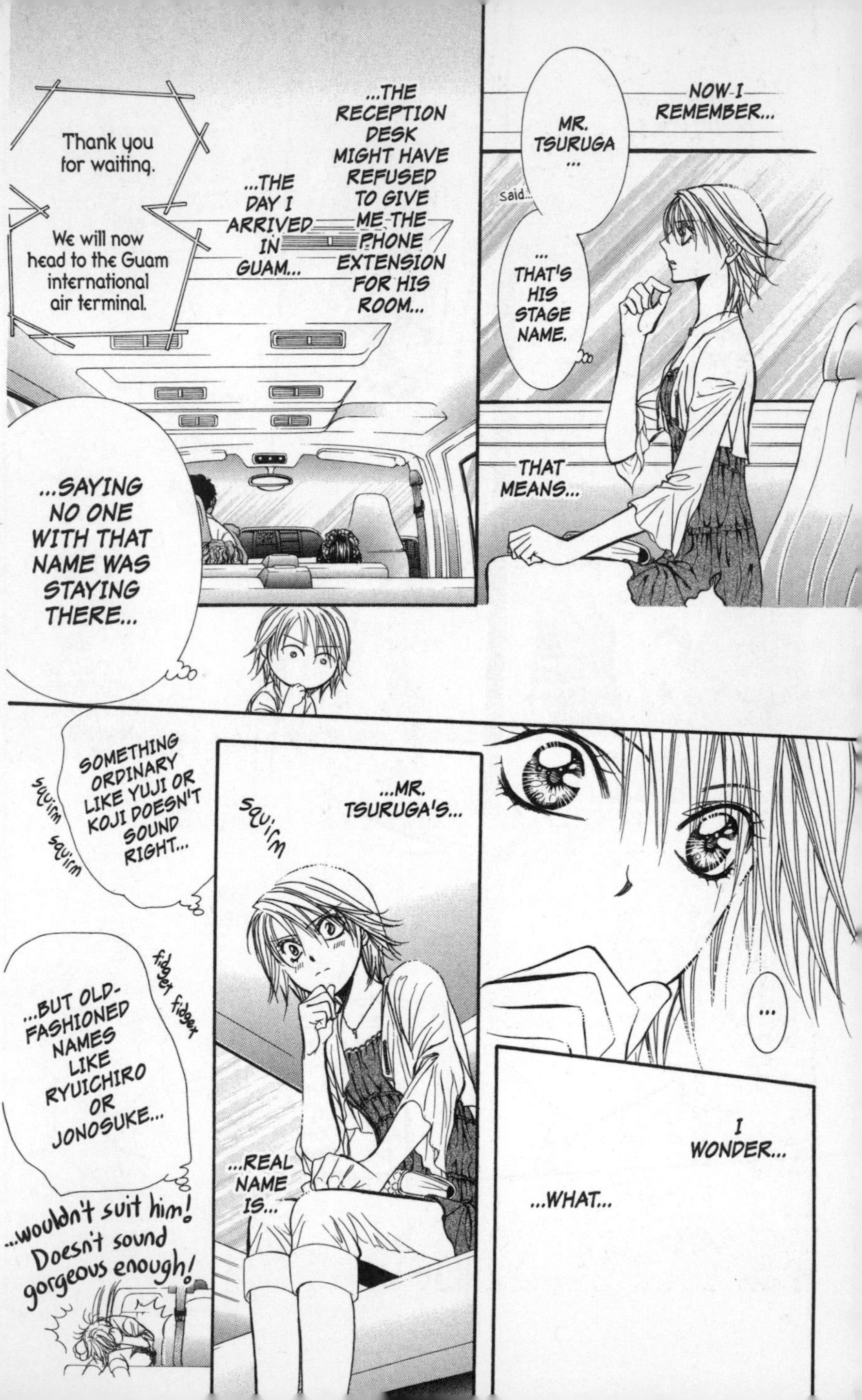
NOW I REMEMBER...
MR. TSURUGA ...
Said...
... THAT'S HIS STAGE NAME.
THAT MEANS...
...THE DAY I ARRIVED IN GUAM...
...THE RECEPTION DESK MIGHT HAVE REFUSED TO GIVE ME THE PHONE EXTENSION FOR HIS ROOM...
Thank you for waiting.
We will now head to the Guam international air terminal.
...SAYING NO ONE WITH THAT NAME WAS STAYING THERE...
...
I WONDER...
...WHAT...
...MR. TSURUGA'S...
squirm
...REAL NAME IS...
SOMETHING ORDINARY LIKE YUJI OR KOJI DOESN'T SOUND RIGHT...
squirm squirm
fidget fidget
...BUT OLD-FASHIONED NAMES LIKE RYUICHIRO OR JONOSUKE...
...wouldn't suit him! Doesn't sound gorgeous enough!

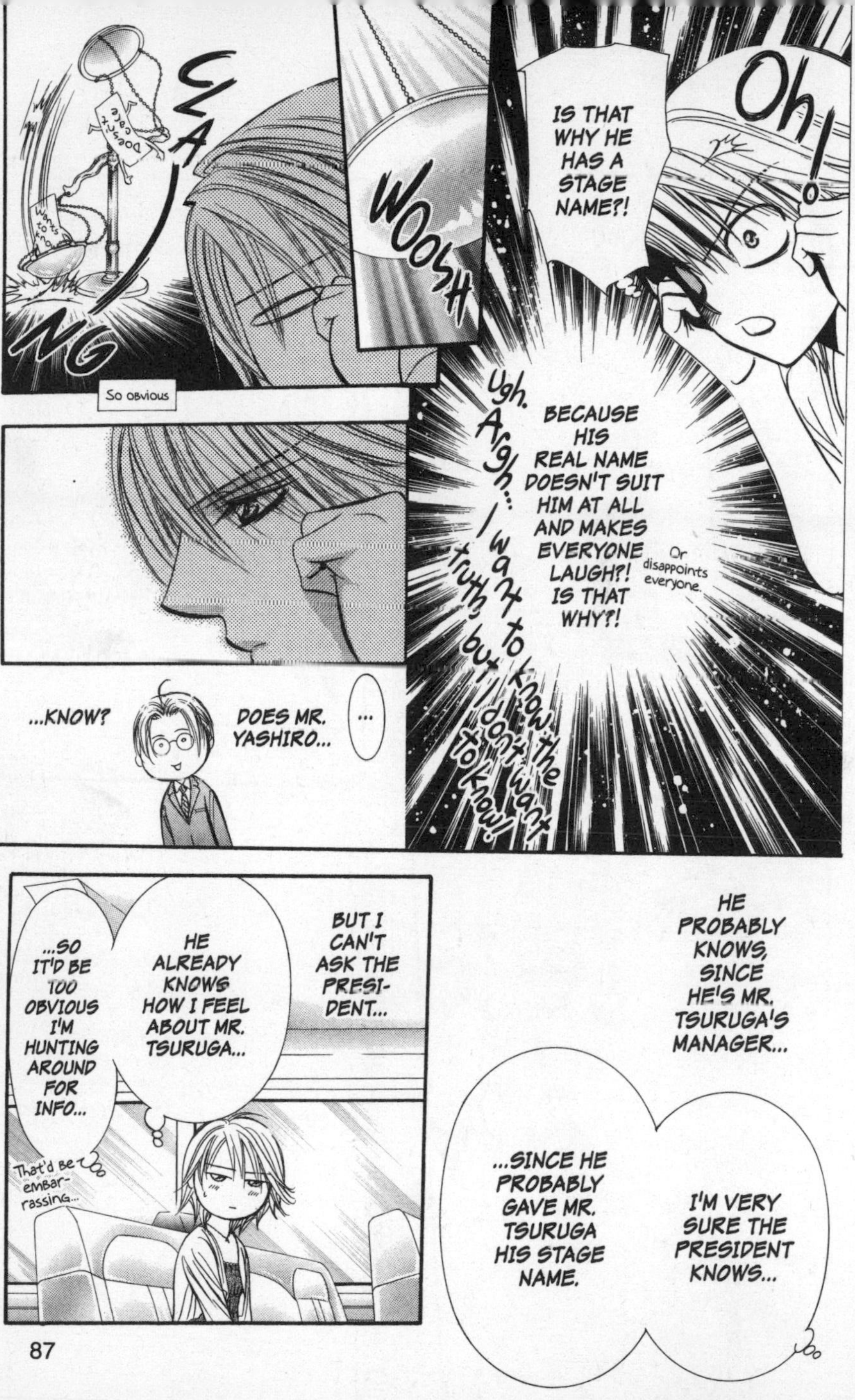

Oh!
IS THAT WHY HE HAS A STAGE NAME?!
BECAUSE HIS REAL NAME DOESN'T SUIT HIM AT ALL AND MAKES EVERYONE LAUGH?! IS THAT WHY?!
Or disappoints everyone.
Ugh. Argh... I want to know the truth, but I don't want to know!
WOOSH
CLANG
Doesn't care
Wants to know
So obvious
...
DOES MR. YASHIRO...
...KNOW?
HE PROBABLY KNOWS, SINCE HE'S MR. TSURUGA'S MANAGER...
I'M VERY SURE THE PRESIDENT KNOWS...
...SINCE HE PROBABLY GAVE MR. TSURUGA HIS STAGE NAME.
BUT I CAN'T ASK THE PRESI-DENT...
HE ALREADY KNOWS HOW I FEEL ABOUT MR. TSURUGA...
...SO IT'D BE TOO OBVIOUS I'M HUNTING AROUND FOR INFO...
That'd be embar-rassing...

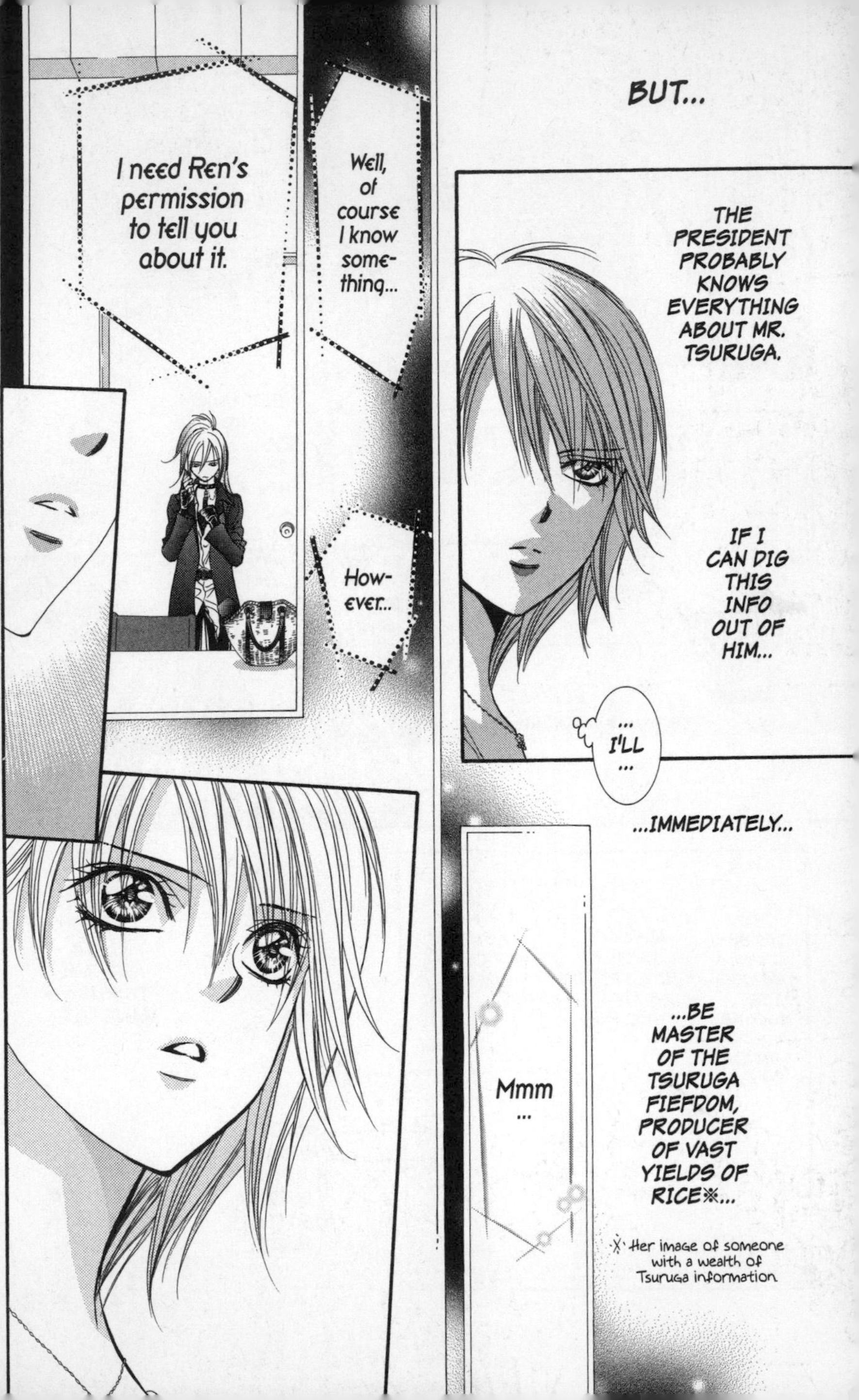
BUT...
THE PRESIDENT PROBABLY KNOWS EVERYTHING ABOUT MR. TSURUGA.
IF I CAN DIG THIS INFO OUT OF HIM...
... I'LL ...
...IMMEDIATELY...
...BE MASTER OF THE TSURUGA FIEFDOM, PRODUCER OF VAST YIELDS OF RICE※...
Mmm ...
※ Her image of someone with a wealth of Tsuruga information.
Well, of course I know some-thing...
I need Ren's permission to tell you about it.
How-ever...

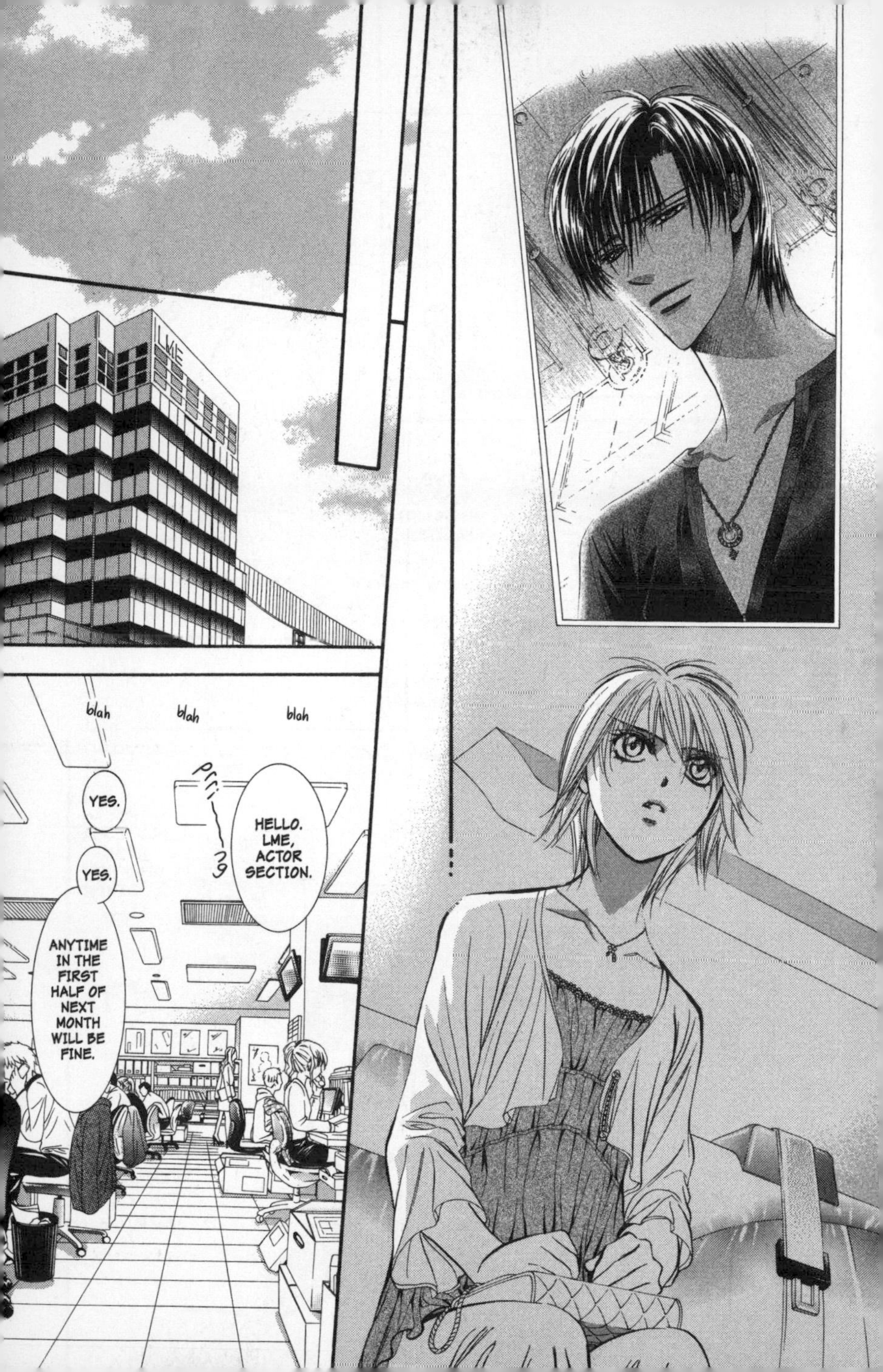
LME
blah
blah
blah
HELLO. LME, ACTOR SECTION.
YES.
YES.
ANYTIME IN THE FIRST HALF OF NEXT MONTH WILL BE FINE.

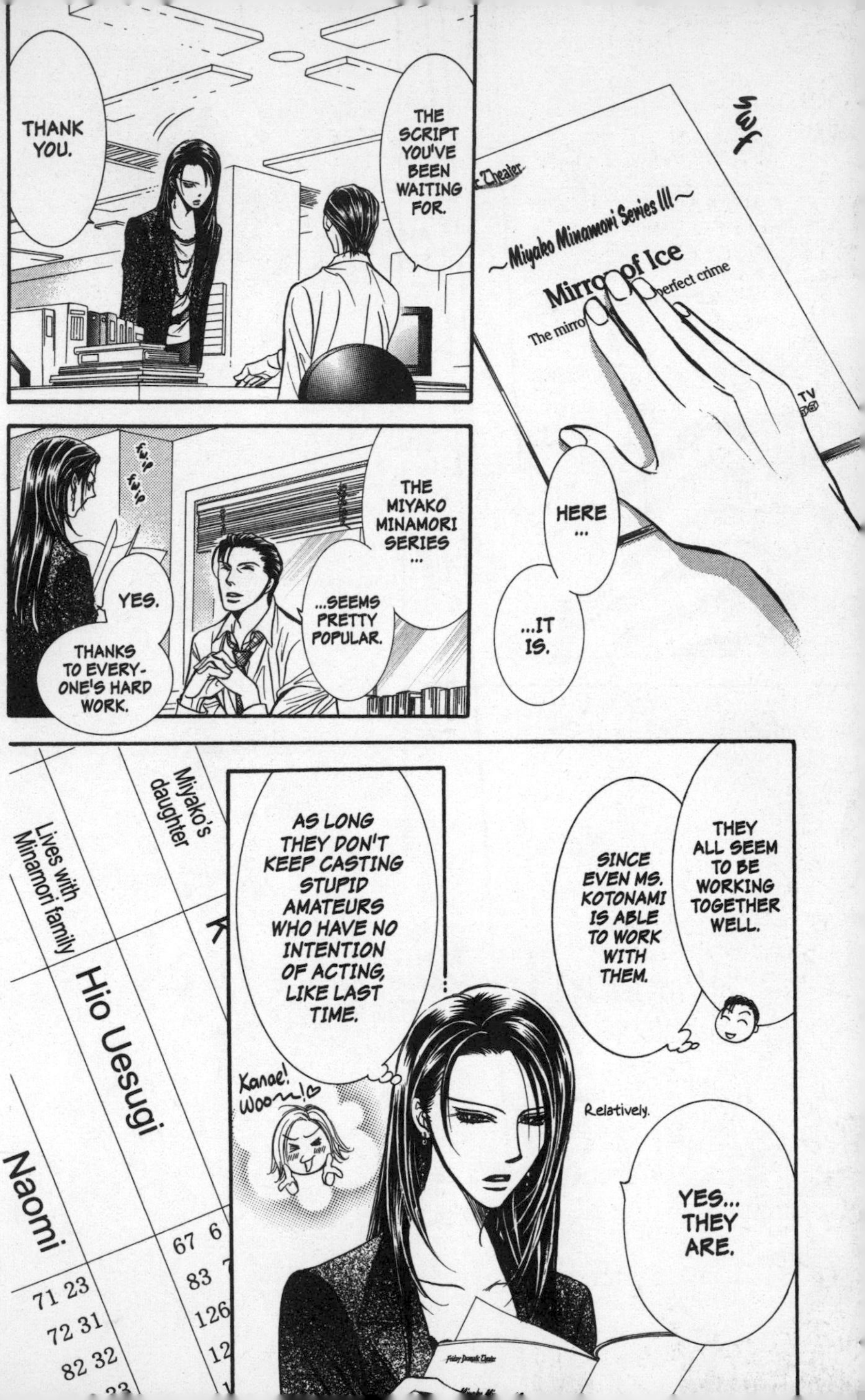

Theater
~Miyako Minamori Series III~
Mirro of Ice
The mirro perfect crime
TV
HERE...
...IT IS.
THE SCRIPT YOU'VE BEEN WAITING FOR.
THANK YOU.
THE MIYAKO MINAMORI SERIES...
...SEEMS PRETTY POPULAR.
YES.
THANKS TO EVERY-ONE'S HARD WORK.
THEY ALL SEEM TO BE WORKING TOGETHER WELL.
SINCE EVEN MS. KOTONAMI IS ABLE TO WORK WITH THEM.
YES... THEY ARE.
Relatively.
AS LONG THEY DON'T KEEP CASTING STUPID AMATEURS WHO HAVE NO INTENTION OF ACTING, LIKE LAST TIME.
Kanae! Woo~!♡
Miyako's daughter
Lives with Minamori family
Hio Uesugi
Naomi

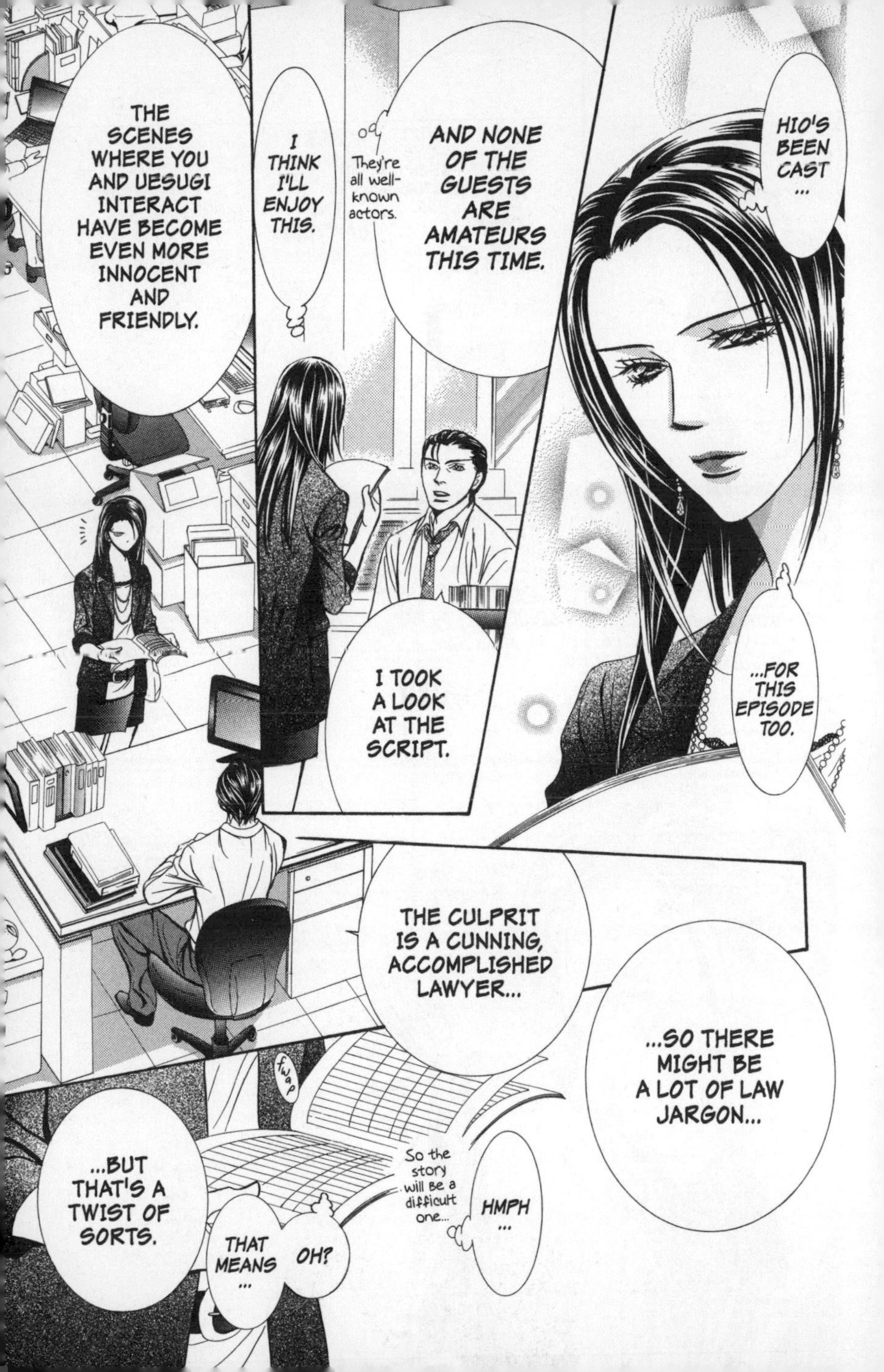
HIO'S BEEN CAST...
...FOR THIS EPISODE TOO.
AND NONE OF THE GUESTS ARE AMATEURS THIS TIME.
They're all well-known actors.
I THINK I'LL ENJOY THIS.
I TOOK A LOOK AT THE SCRIPT.
THE SCENES WHERE YOU AND UESUGI INTERACT HAVE BECOME EVEN MORE INNOCENT AND FRIENDLY.
THE CULPRIT IS A CUNNING, ACCOMPLISHED LAWYER...
...SO THERE MIGHT BE A LOT OF LAW JARGON...
HMPH...
So the story will be a difficult one...
OH?
...BUT THAT'S A TWIST OF SORTS.
THAT MEANS...
fwap

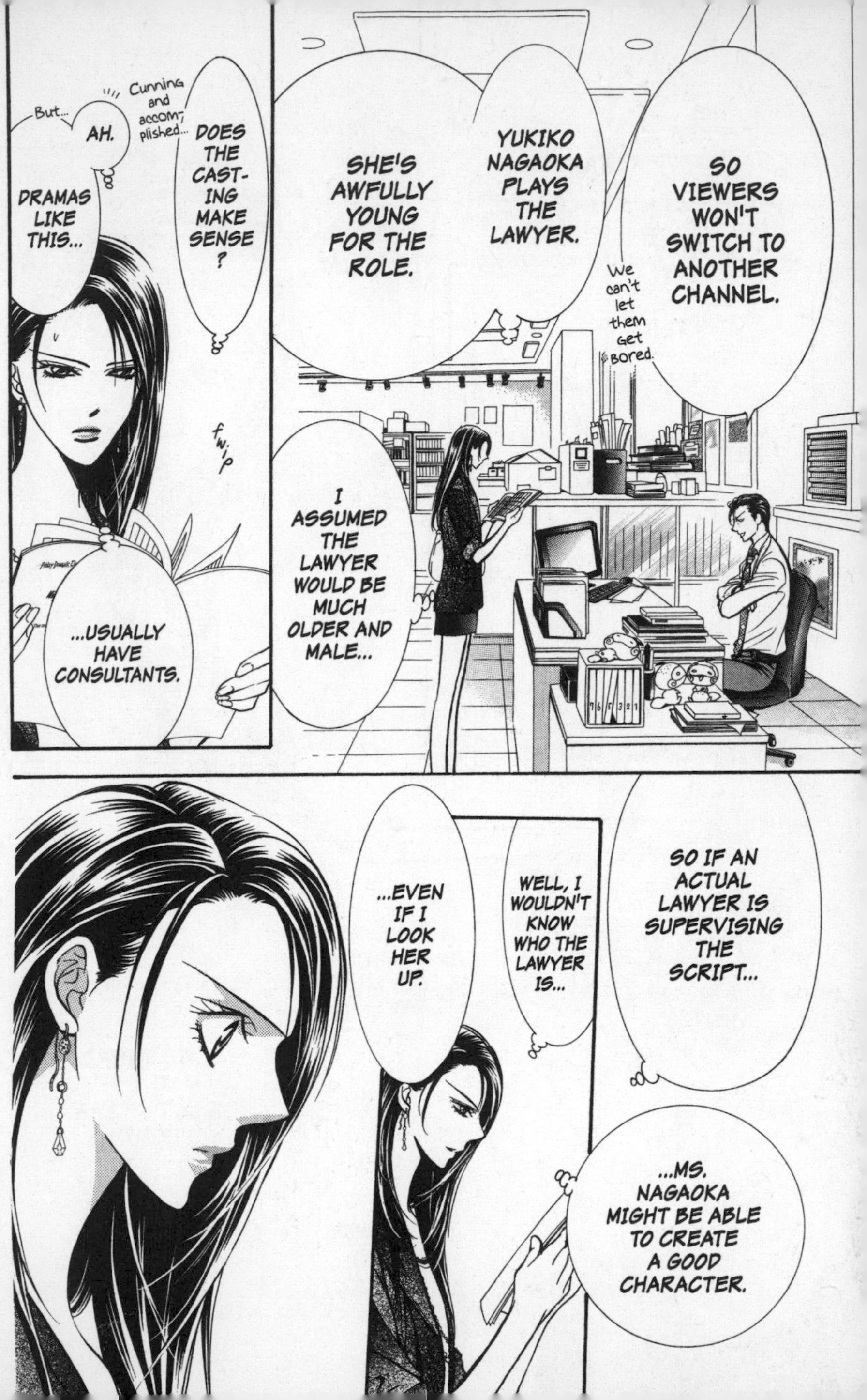
SO VIEWERS WON'T SWITCH TO ANOTHER CHANNEL.
We can't let them get bored.
YUKIKO NAGAOKA PLAYS THE LAWYER.
SHE'S AWFULLY YOUNG FOR THE ROLE.
I ASSUMED THE LAWYER WOULD BE MUCH OLDER AND MALE...
DOES THE CAST-ING MAKE SENSE?
Cunning and accom-plished...
AH.
But...
DRAMAS LIKE THIS...
fwip
...USUALLY HAVE CONSULTANTS.
SO IF AN ACTUAL LAWYER IS SUPERVISING THE SCRIPT...
...MS. NAGAOKA MIGHT BE ABLE TO CREATE A GOOD CHARACTER.
WELL, I WOULDN'T KNOW WHO THE LAWYER IS...
...EVEN IF I LOOK HER UP.

SO...

YOU AND UESUGI ADD SIMPLICITY AND REFINEMENT.

AN OASIS IN THE DESERT.

YOUR ROLES ARE VERY IMPORTANT.

YOU'LL GIVE THE VIEWERS...

...A VERY NECESSARY BREATHER!

Prrring

We'll call you later.

The supervisor isn't here right now.

HEEEEEEY...

You listening to me? MS. KOTO-NAAAMI.

DON'T IGNORE ME.

...

Friday Dramatic Theater

Mizuko Minamori Series III ~
Mirror of Ice
reflects the perfect crime

FINAL VERSION

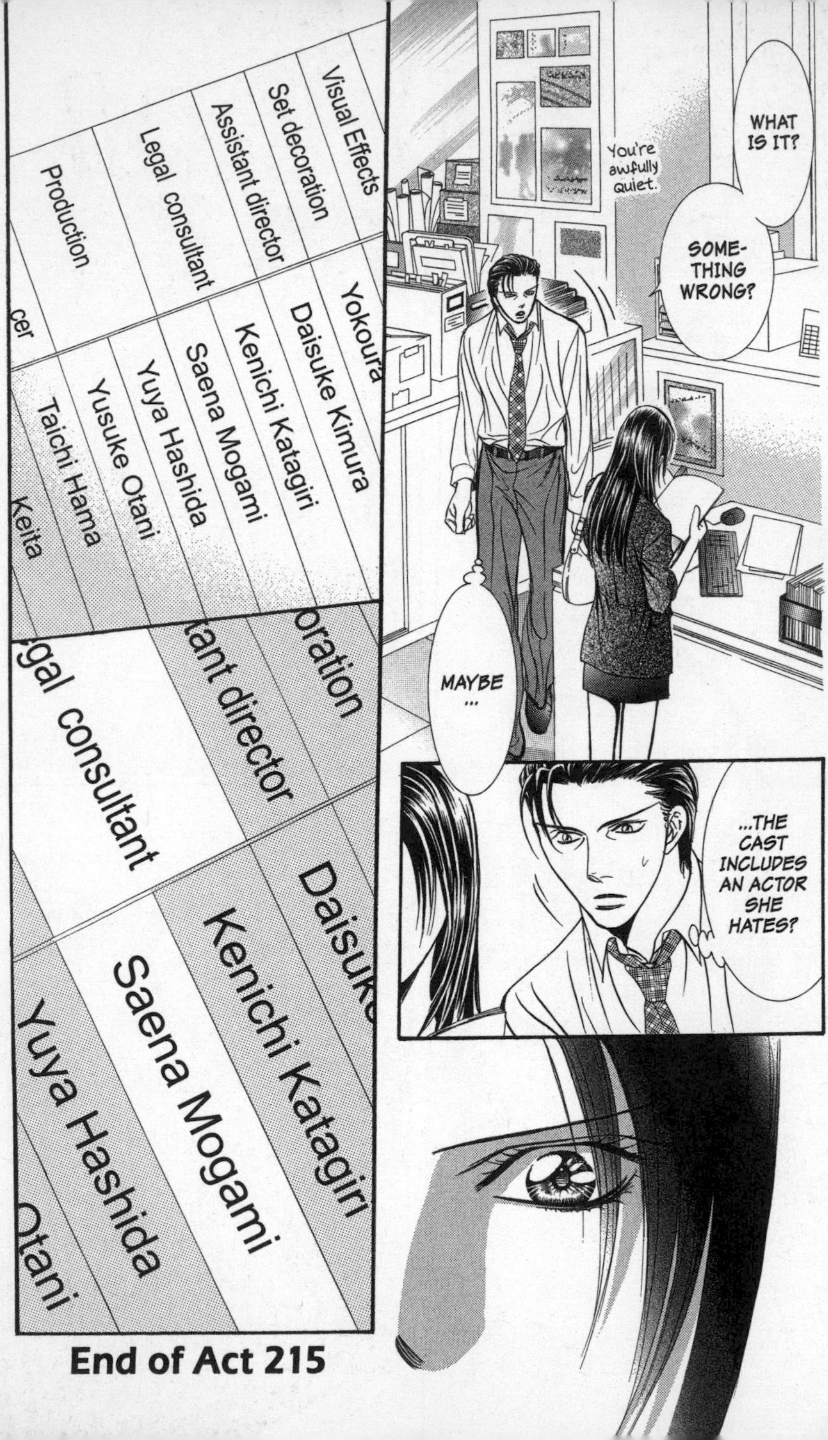
WHAT IS IT?
SOME-THING WRONG?
You're awfully quiet.
MAYBE ...
...THE CAST INCLUDES AN ACTOR SHE HATES?
Visual Effects
Set decoration
Assistant director
Legal consultant
Production
cer
Yokoura
Daisuke Kimura
Kenichi Katagiri
Saena Mogami
Yuya Hashida
Yusuke Otani
Taichi Hama
Keita
oration
tant director
egal consultant
Daisuke
Kenichi Katagiri
Saena Mogami
Yuya Hashida
Otani

End of Act 215

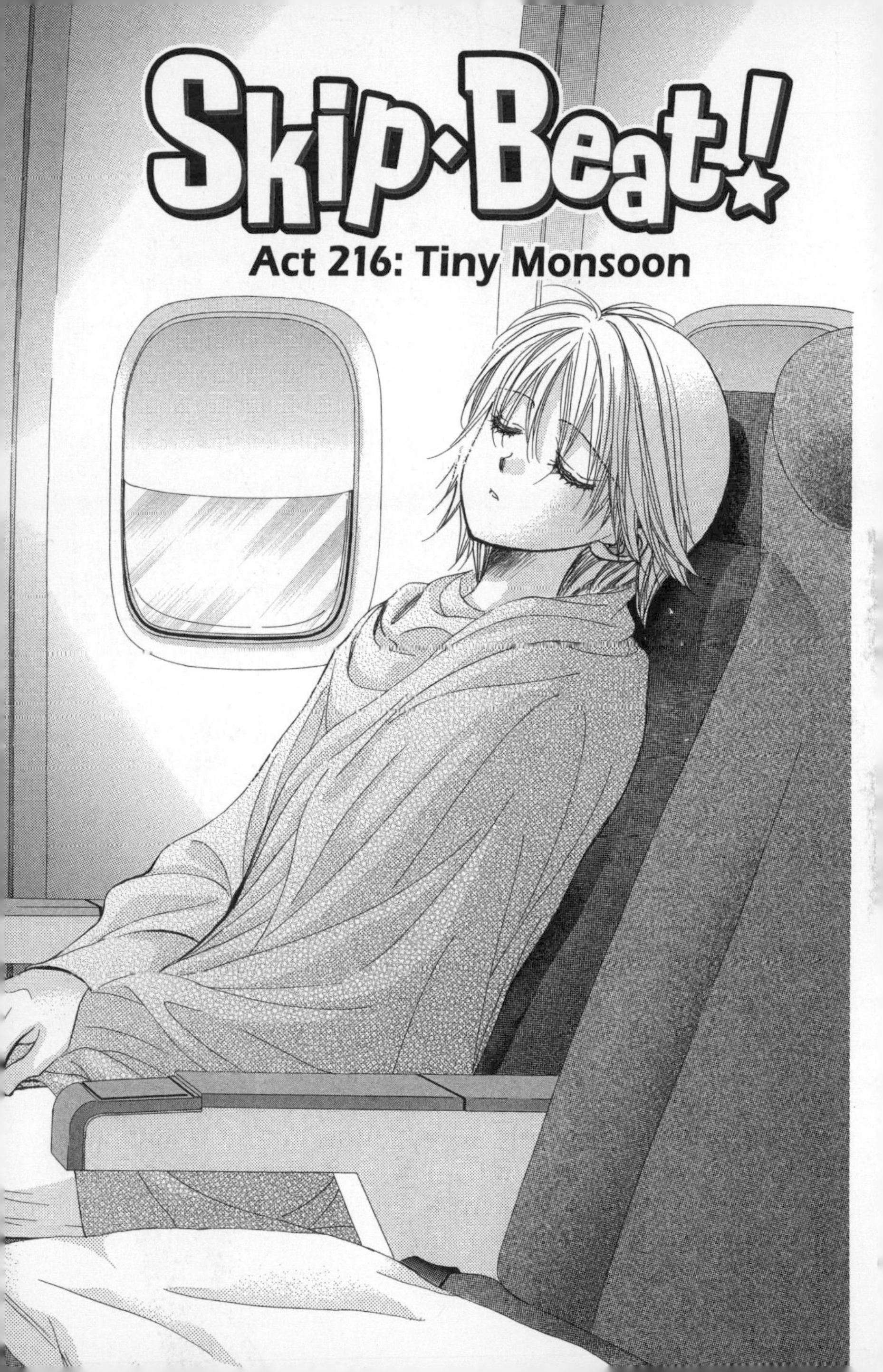
Skip·Beat!
Act 216: Tiny Monsoon

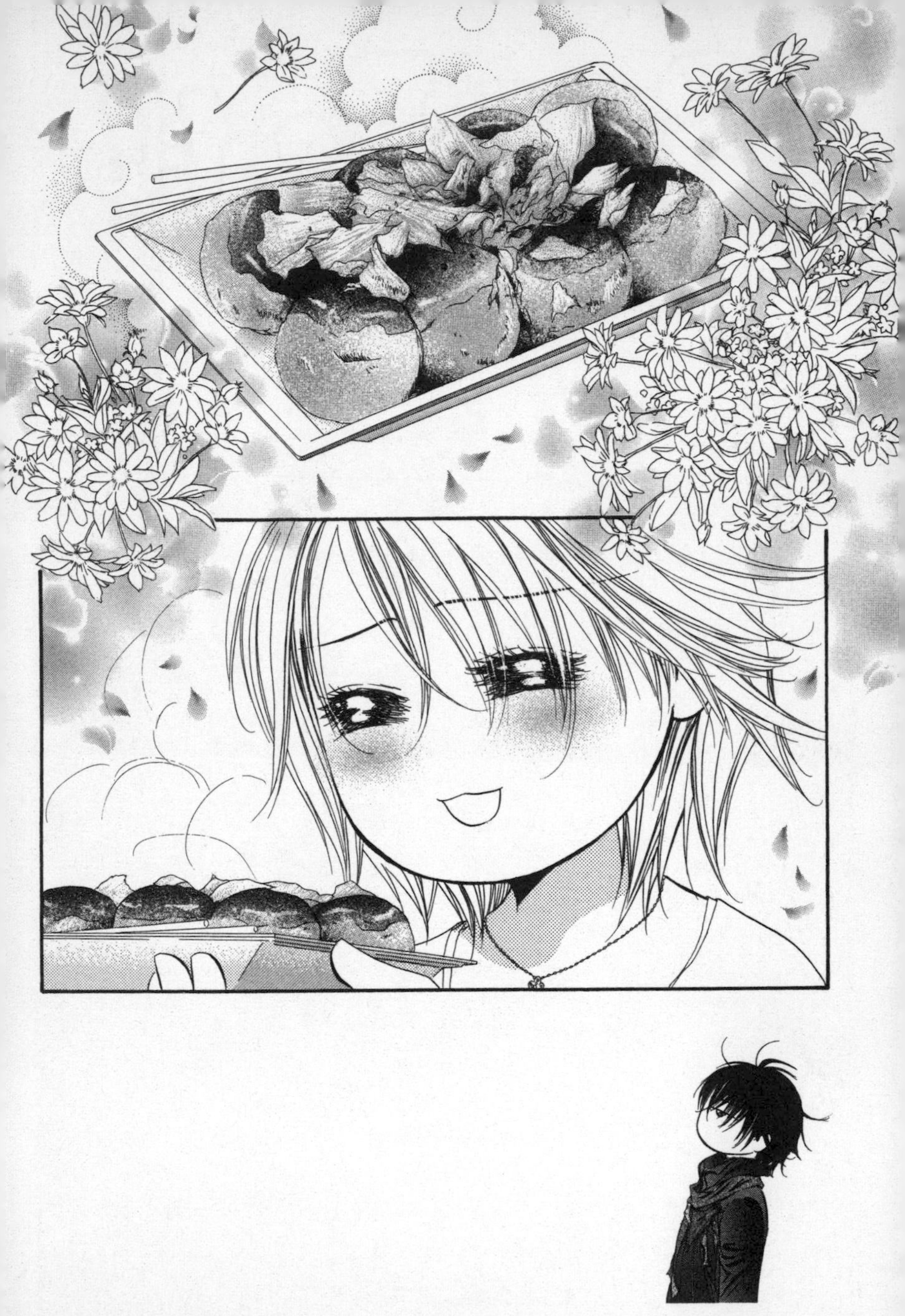

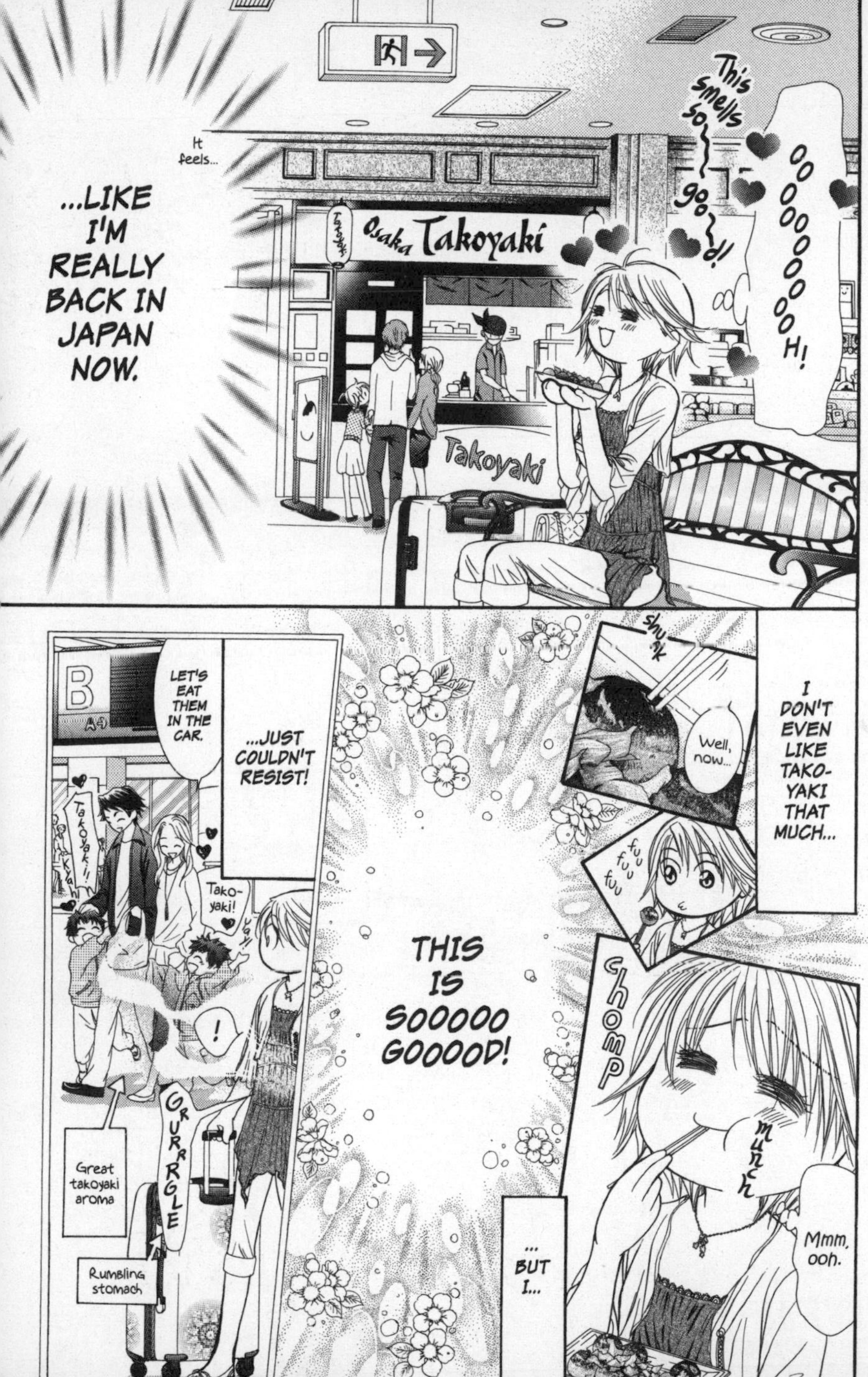
This smells so~~~go~~~d!
OOOOOOOOOOOOOH!
Osaka Takoyaki
Takoyaki
It feels...
...LIKE I'M REALLY BACK IN JAPAN NOW.
I DON'T EVEN LIKE TAKO-YAKI THAT MUCH...
shunk
Well, now...
fuu fuu fuu fuu
CHOMP
munch
Mmm, ooh.
...BUT I...
THIS IS SOOOOO GOOOOD!
...JUST COULDN'T RESIST!
LET'S EAT THEM IN THE CAR.
Takoyaki!
Kyah!
Tako-yaki!
!
GRURRRGLE
Great takoyaki aroma
Rumbling stomach

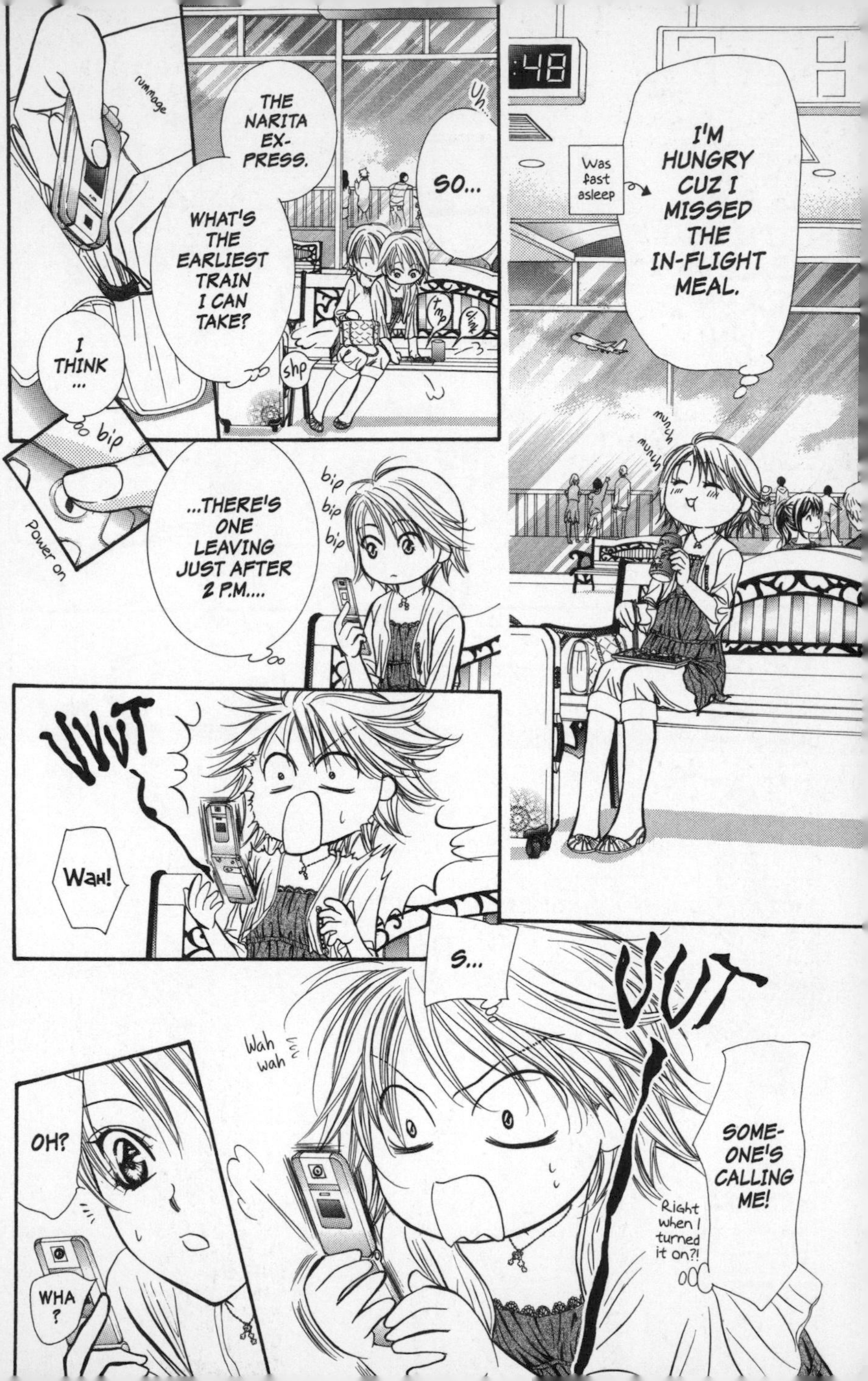

I'M HUNGRY CUZ I MISSED THE IN-FLIGHT MEAL.
Was fast asleep
munch munch
Uh...
SO...
THE NARITA EX-PRESS.
WHAT'S THE EARLIEST TRAIN I CAN TAKE?
tmp
clink
shp
rummage
I THINK...
bip
Power on
bip bip bip
...THERE'S ONE LEAVING JUST AFTER 2 P.M....
VVUT
Wah!
S...
VUT
SOME-ONE'S CALLING ME!
Right when I turned it on?!
Wah wah
OH?
WHA?

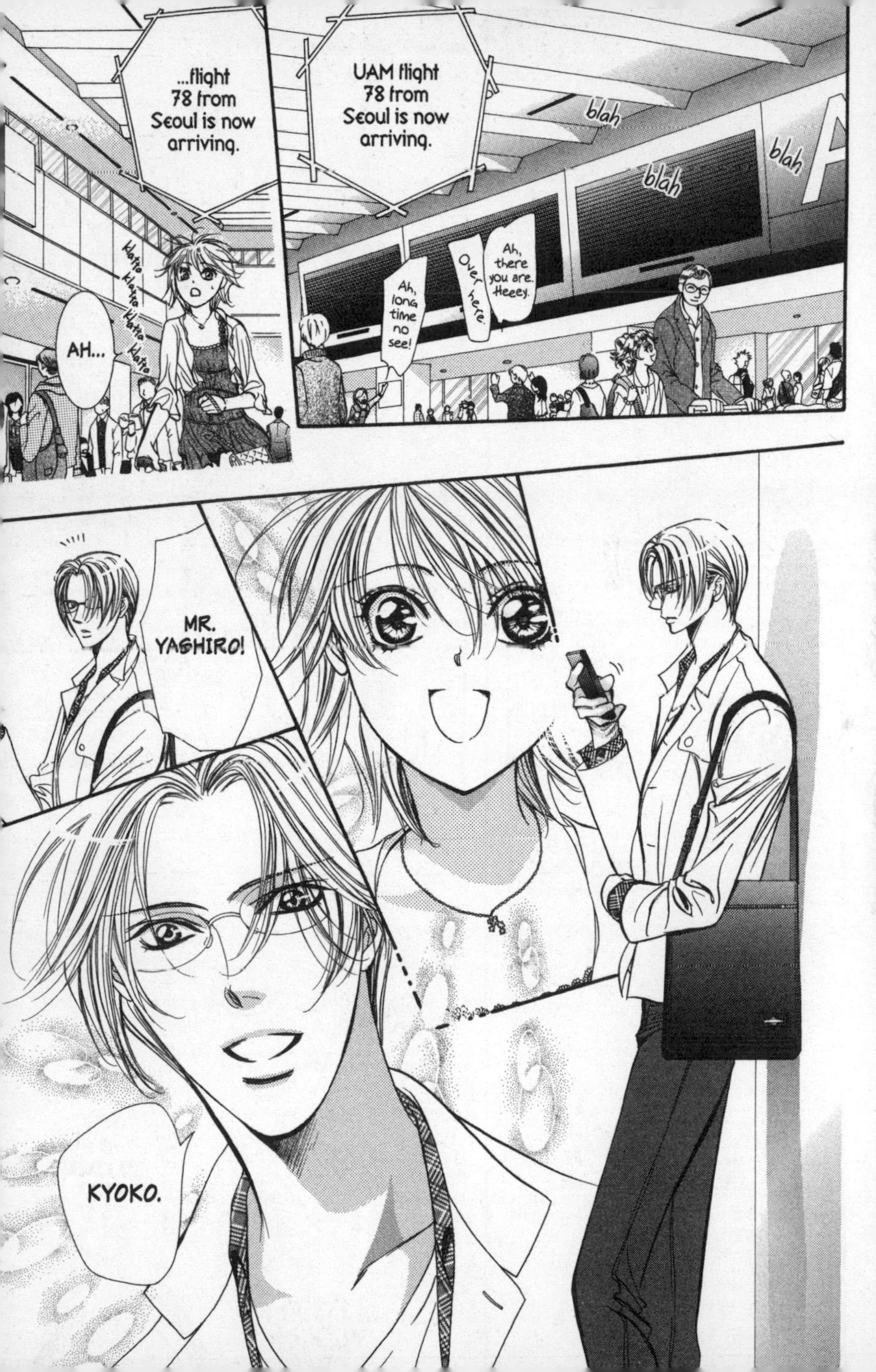
UAM flight 78 from Seoul is now arriving.
blah
blah
blah
Ah, there you are. Heeey.
Over here.
Ah, long time no see!
...flight 78 from Seoul is now arriving.
klatta klatta klatta klatta
AH...
MR. YAGHIRO!
KYOKO.

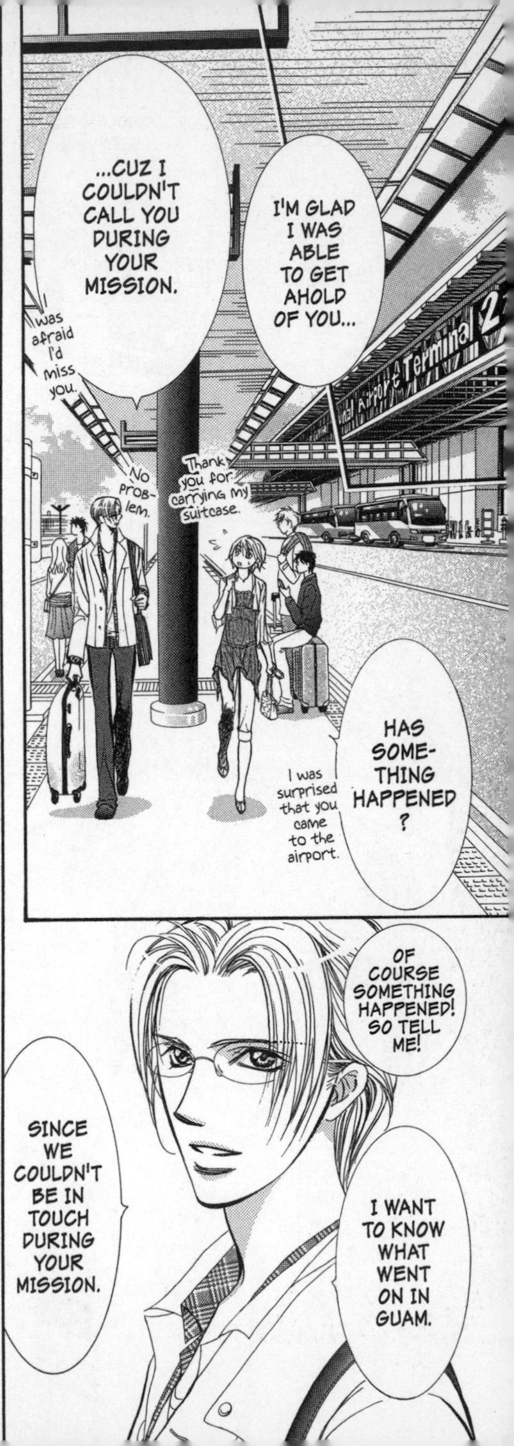
I'M GLAD I WAS ABLE TO GET AHOLD OF YOU...
...CUZ I COULDN'T CALL YOU DURING YOUR MISSION.
I was afraid I'd miss you.
Terminal 2
Thank you for carrying my suitcase.
No problem.
HAS SOMETHING HAPPENED?
I was surprised that you came to the airport.
OF COURSE SOMETHING HAPPENED! SO TELL ME!
I WANT TO KNOW WHAT WENT ON IN GUAM.
SINCE WE COULDN'T BE IN TOUCH DURING YOUR MISSION.

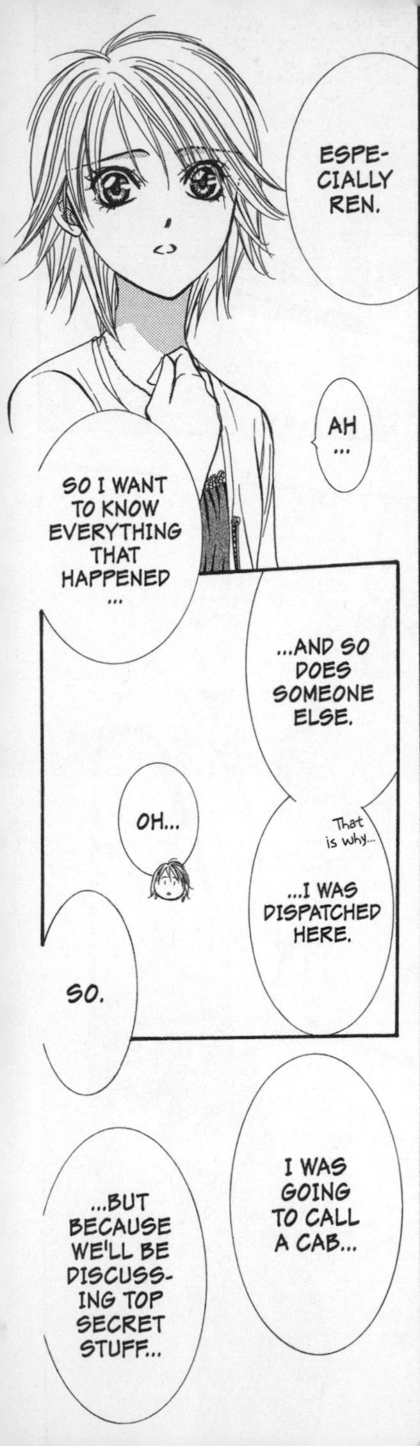
ESPE-CIALLY REN.
AH...
SO I WANT TO KNOW EVERYTHING THAT HAPPENED...
...AND SO DOES SOMEONE ELSE.
That is why...
...I WAS DISPATCHED HERE.
OH...
SO.
I WAS GOING TO CALL A CAB...
...BUT BECAUSE WE'LL BE DISCUSS-ING TOP SECRET STUFF...

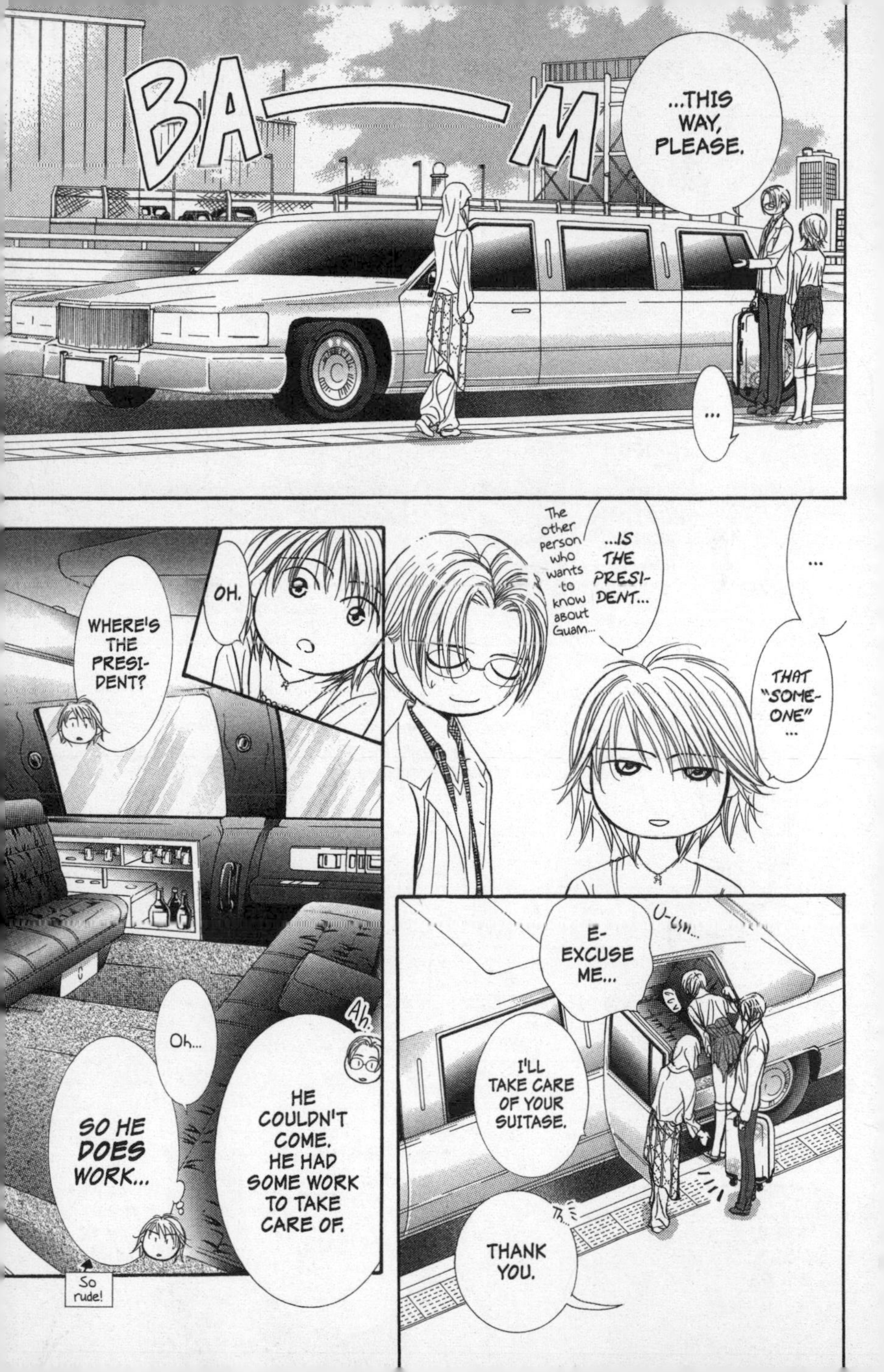
BA—M
...THIS WAY, PLEASE.
...
...
THAT "SOME-ONE"...
...IS THE PRESI-DENT...
The other person who wants to know about Guam...
U-ssh...
E-EXCUSE ME...
I'LL TAKE CARE OF YOUR SUITASE.
THANK YOU.
OH.
WHERE'S THE PRESI-DENT?
Ah.
HE COULDN'T COME. HE HAD SOME WORK TO TAKE CARE OF.
Oh...
SO HE DOES WORK...
So rude!

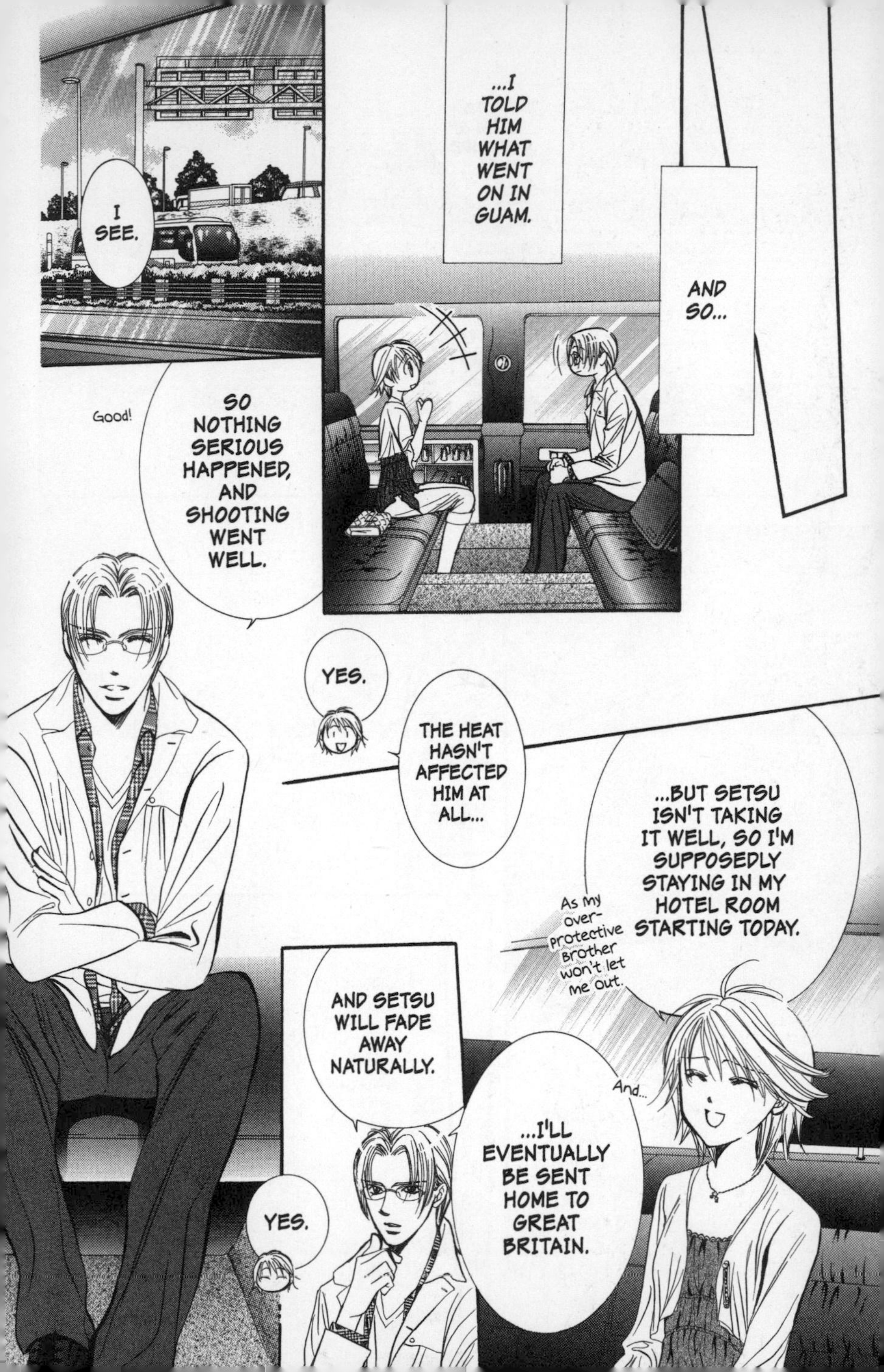
...I TOLD HIM WHAT WENT ON IN GUAM.
AND SO...
I SEE.
SO NOTHING SERIOUS HAPPENED, AND SHOOTING WENT WELL.
Good!
YES.
THE HEAT HASN'T AFFECTED HIM AT ALL...
...BUT SETSU ISN'T TAKING IT WELL, SO I'M SUPPOSEDLY STAYING IN MY HOTEL ROOM STARTING TODAY.
As my over-protective brother won't let me out.
AND SETSU WILL FADE AWAY NATURALLY.
And...
...I'LL EVENTUALLY BE SENT HOME TO GREAT BRITAIN.
YES.

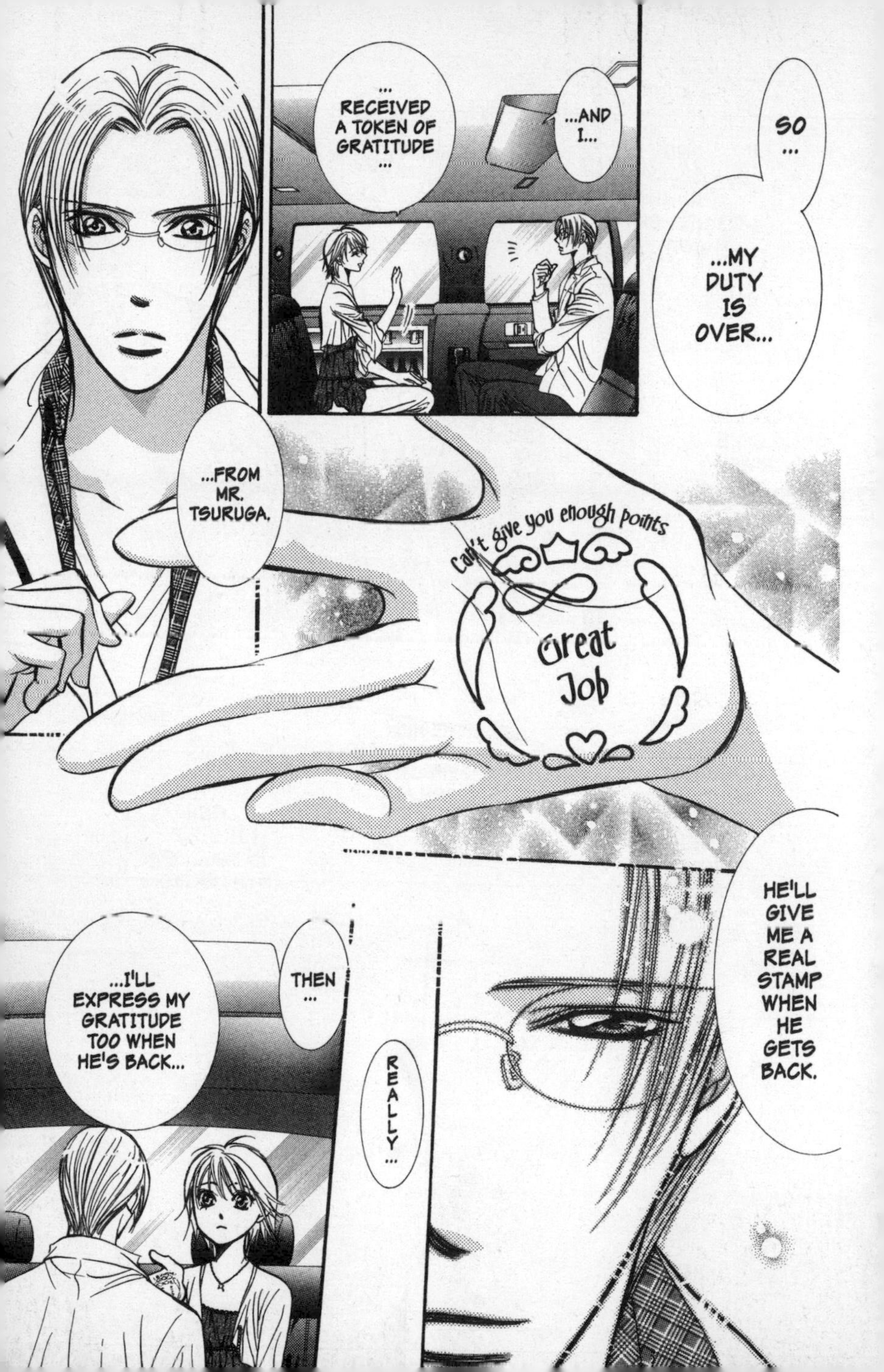
SO... ...MY DUTY IS OVER...
...AND I...
...RECEIVED A TOKEN OF GRATITUDE...
...FROM MR. TSURUGA.
Can't give you enough points
Great Job
HE'LL GIVE ME A REAL STAMP WHEN HE GETS BACK.
REALLY...
THEN...
...I'LL EXPRESS MY GRATITUDE TOO WHEN HE'S BACK...

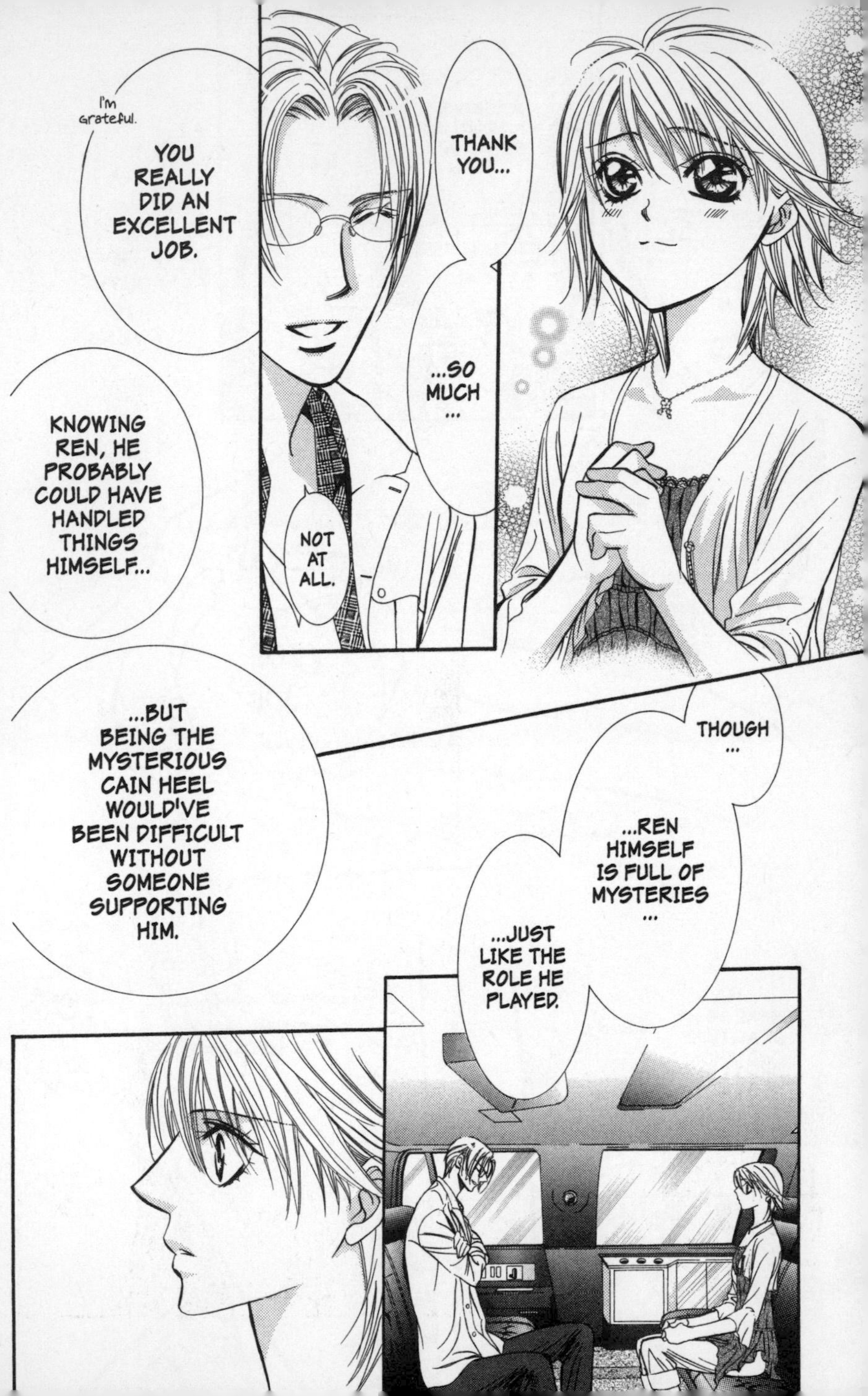
THANK YOU...
...SO MUCH...
NOT AT ALL.
I'm grateful.
YOU REALLY DID AN EXCELLENT JOB.
KNOWING REN, HE PROBABLY COULD HAVE HANDLED THINGS HIMSELF...
...BUT BEING THE MYSTERIOUS CAIN HEEL WOULD'VE BEEN DIFFICULT WITHOUT SOMEONE SUPPORTING HIM.
THOUGH...
...REN HIMSELF IS FULL OF MYSTERIES...
...JUST LIKE THE ROLE HE PLAYED.

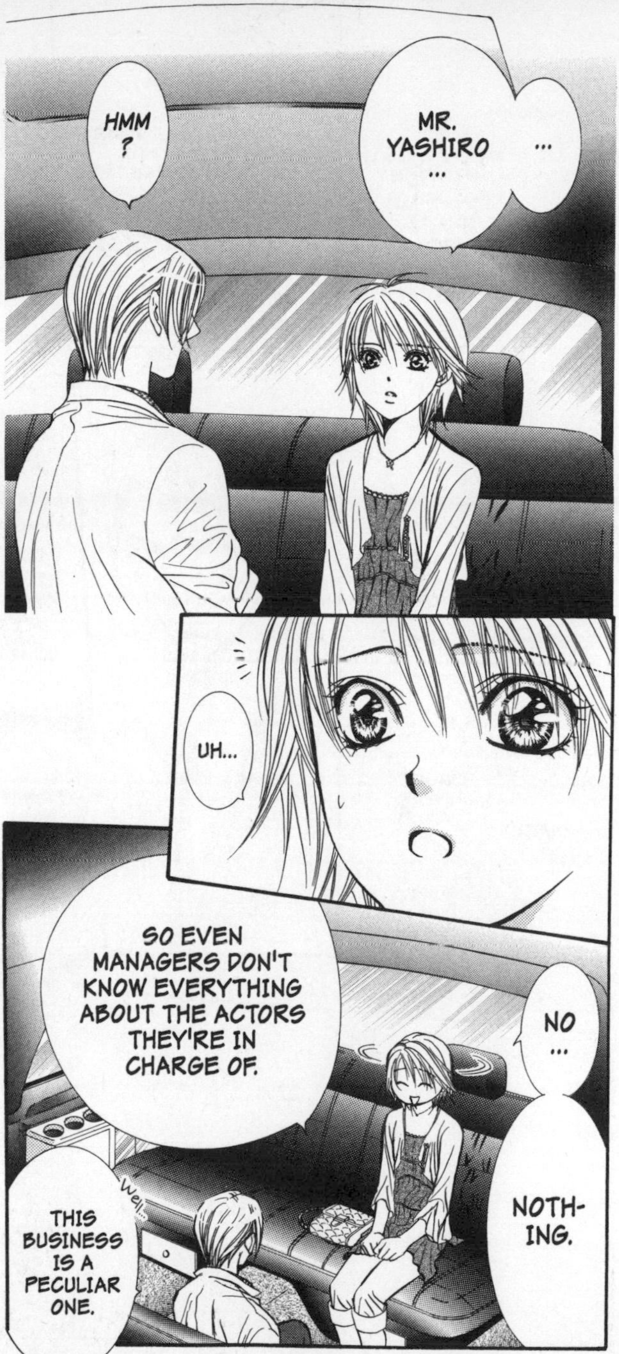
MR. YASHIRO ...
...
HMM ?
UH...
NO ...
NOTH-ING.
SO EVEN MANAGERS DON'T KNOW EVERYTHING ABOUT THE ACTORS THEY'RE IN CHARGE OF.
Well...
THIS BUSINESS IS A PECULIAR ONE.
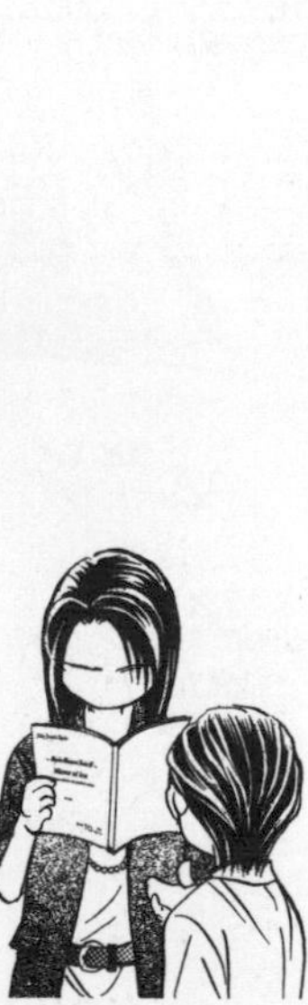

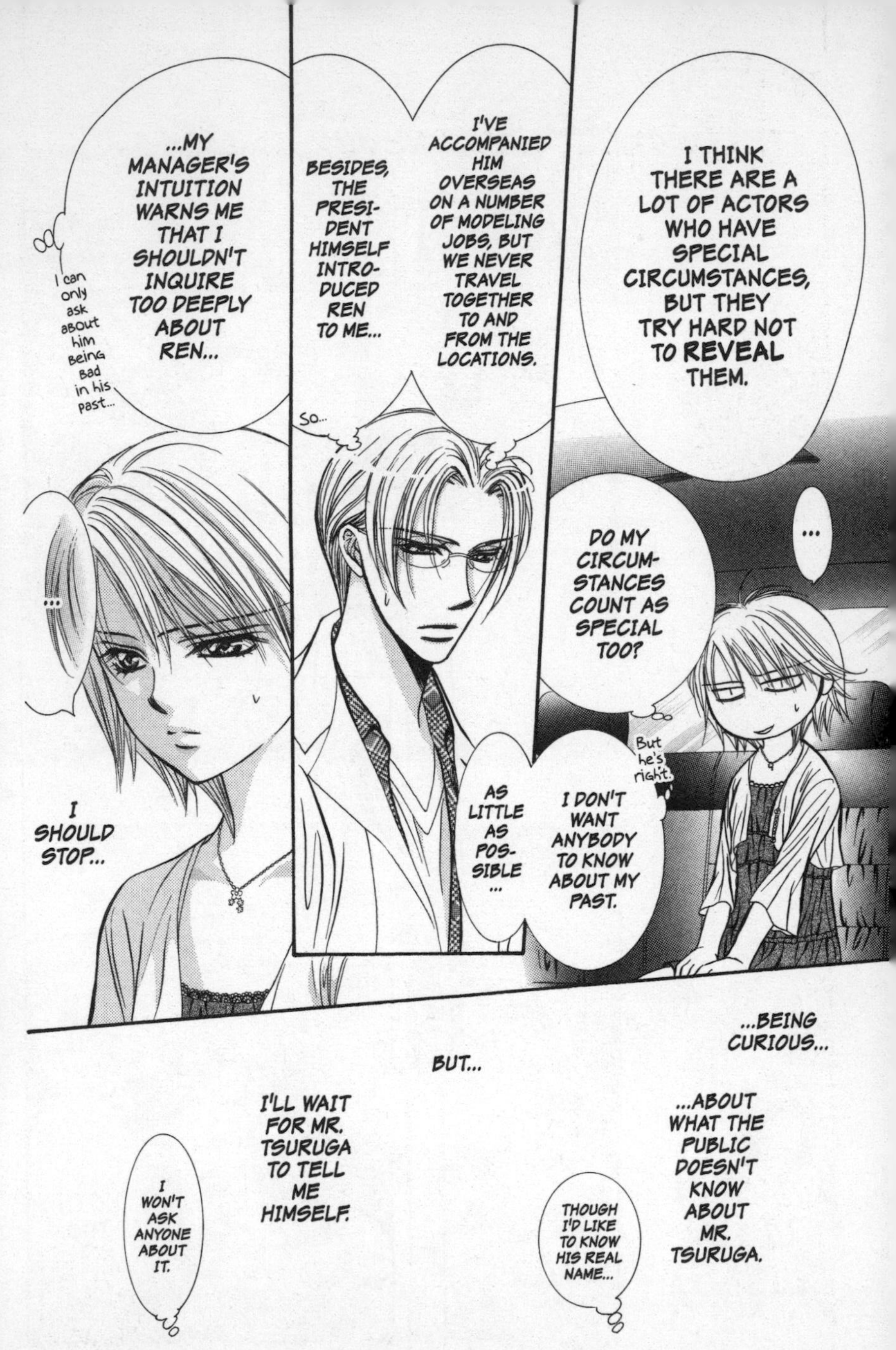
I THINK THERE ARE A LOT OF ACTORS WHO HAVE SPECIAL CIRCUMSTANCES, BUT THEY TRY HARD NOT TO REVEAL THEM.
...
DO MY CIRCUM-STANCES COUNT AS SPECIAL TOO?
But he's right.
I DON'T WANT ANYBODY TO KNOW ABOUT MY PAST.
I'VE ACCOMPANIED HIM OVERSEAS ON A NUMBER OF MODELING JOBS, BUT WE NEVER TRAVEL TOGETHER TO AND FROM THE LOCATIONS.
BESIDES, THE PRESI-DENT HIMSELF INTRO-DUCED REN TO ME...
So...
AS LITTLE AS POS-SIBLE...
...MY MANAGER'S INTUITION WARNS ME THAT I SHOULDN'T INQUIRE TOO DEEPLY ABOUT REN...
I can only ask about him being bad in his past...
...
I SHOULD STOP...
...BEING CURIOUS...
...ABOUT WHAT THE PUBLIC DOESN'T KNOW ABOUT MR. TSURUGA.
THOUGH I'D LIKE TO KNOW HIS REAL NAME...
BUT...
I'LL WAIT FOR MR. TSURUGA TO TELL ME HIMSELF.
I WON'T ASK ANYONE ABOUT IT.

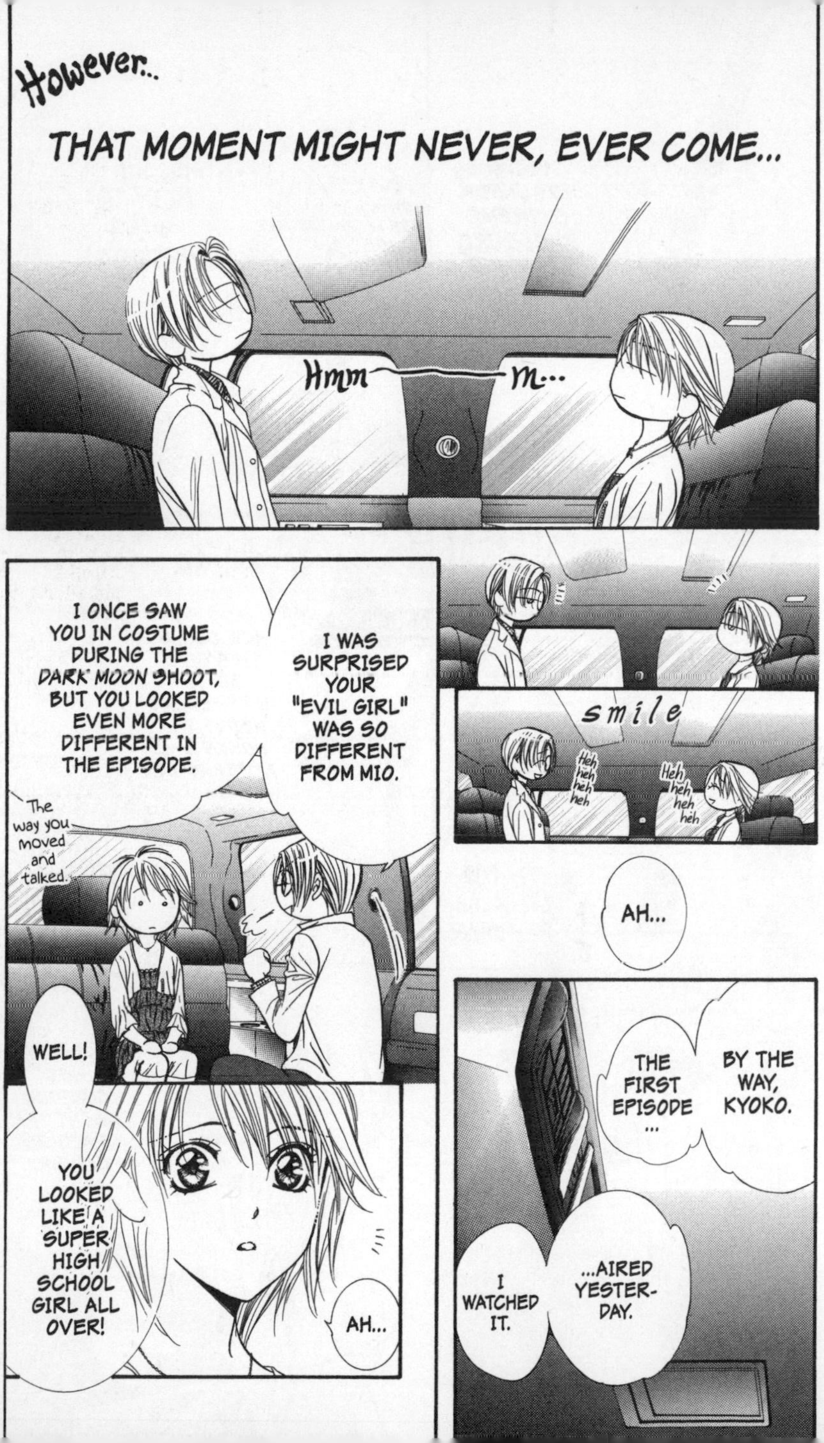
However...
THAT MOMENT MIGHT NEVER, EVER COME...
Hmm—m...
smile
Heh heh heh heh
Heh heh heh heh
AH...
BY THE WAY, KYOKO.
THE FIRST EPISODE...
...AIRED YESTERDAY.
I WATCHED IT.
I WAS SURPRISED YOUR "EVIL GIRL" WAS SO DIFFERENT FROM MIO.
I ONCE SAW YOU IN COSTUME DURING THE DARK MOON SHOOT, BUT YOU LOOKED EVEN MORE DIFFERENT IN THE EPISODE.
The way you moved and talked.
WELL!
YOU LOOKED LIKE A SUPER HIGH SCHOOL GIRL ALL OVER!
AH...

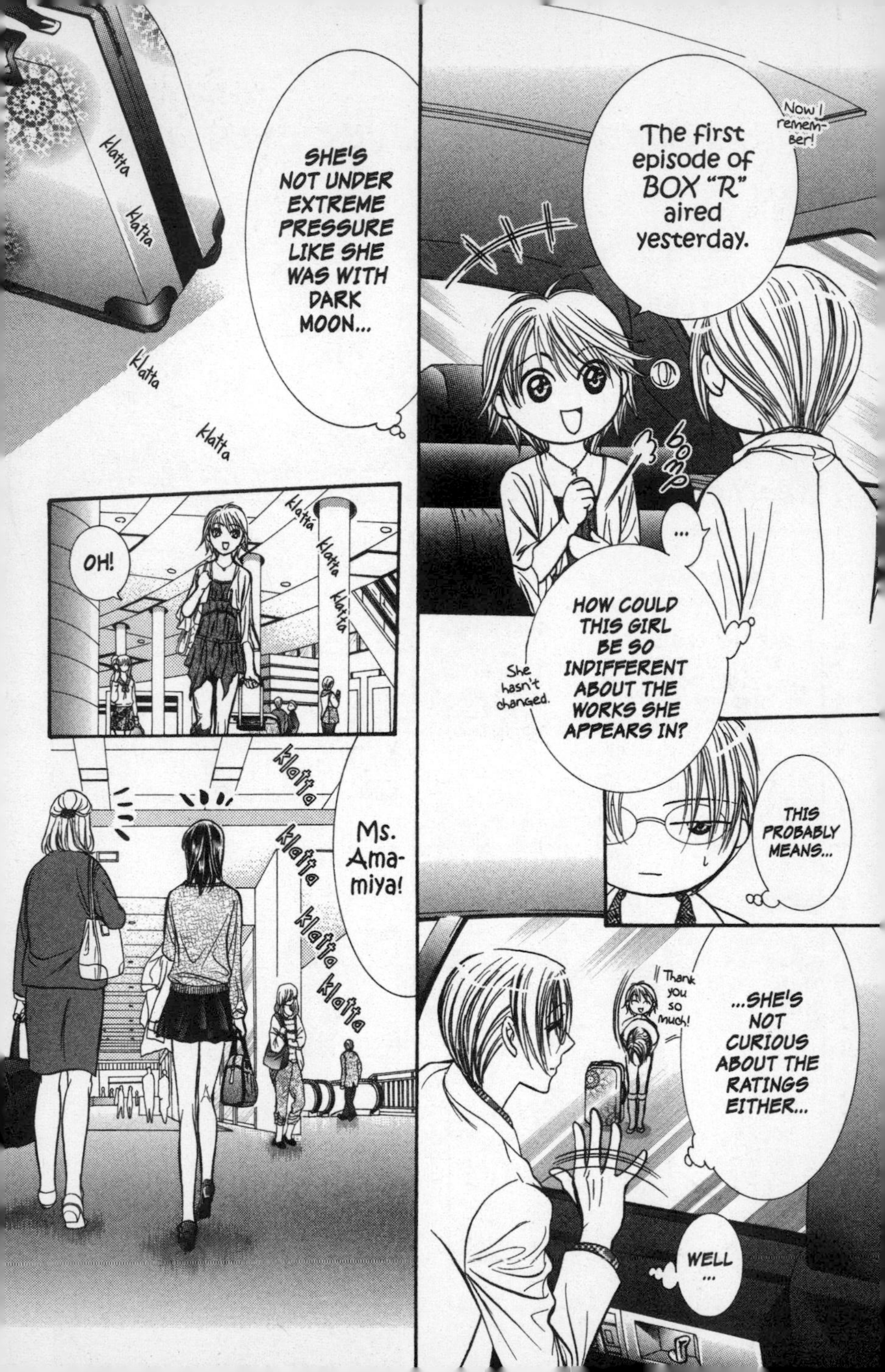

Now I remem-ber!
The first episode of BOX "R" aired yesterday.
bomp
...
HOW COULD THIS GIRL BE SO INDIFFERENT ABOUT THE WORKS SHE APPEARS IN?
She hasn't changed.
THIS PROBABLY MEANS...
...SHE'S NOT CURIOUS ABOUT THE RATINGS EITHER...
Thank you so much!
WELL ...
SHE'S NOT UNDER EXTREME PRESSURE LIKE SHE WAS WITH DARK MOON...
klatta
klatta
klatta
klatta
klatta
klatta
klatta
OH!
klatta
klatta
klatta
klatta
Ms. Ama-miya!

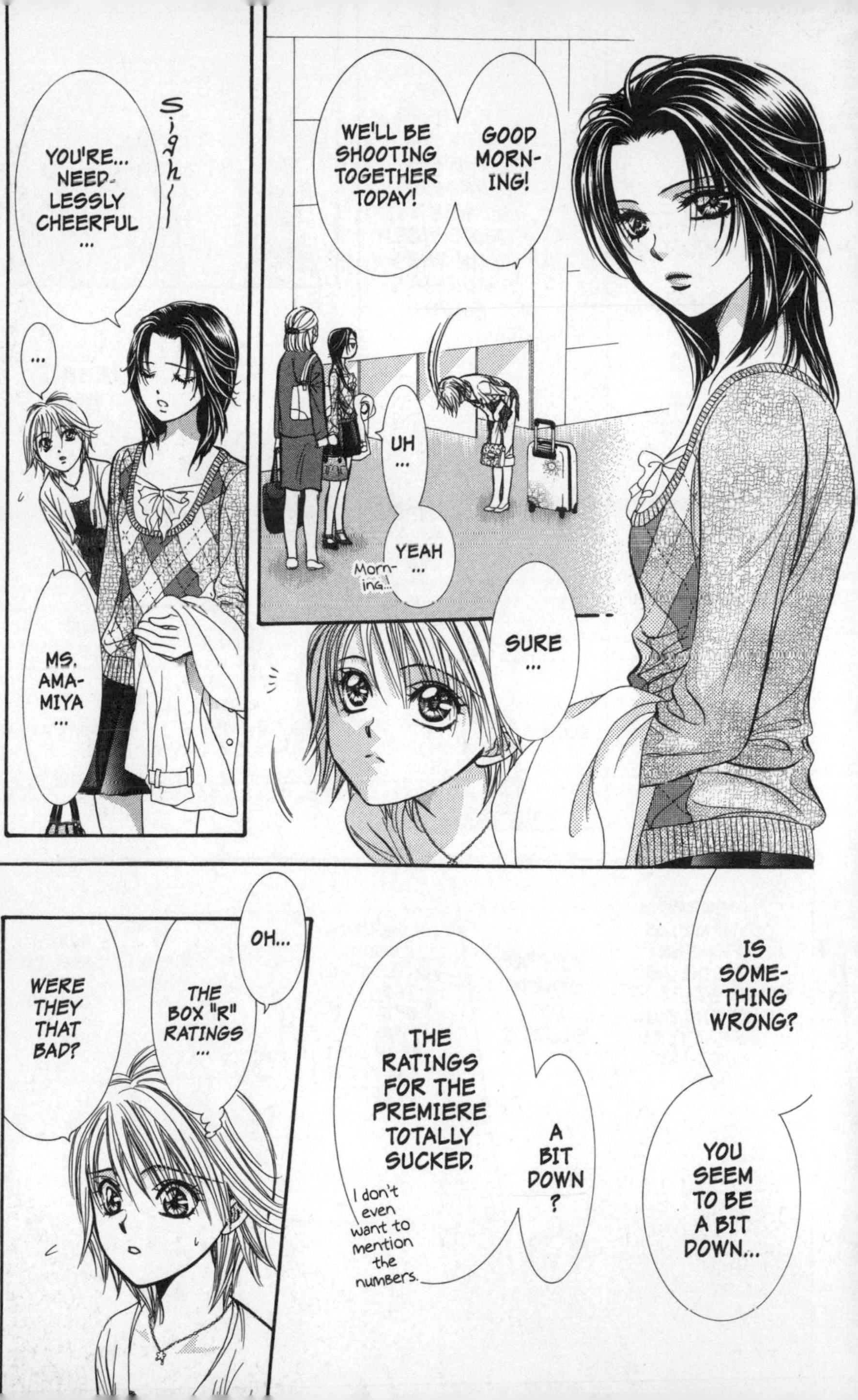
GOOD MORNING!
WE'LL BE SHOOTING TOGETHER TODAY!
UH...
YEAH...
Morning...
SURE...
Sigh~
YOU'RE... NEEDLESSLY CHEERFUL...
...
MS. AMAMIYA...
IS SOMETHING WRONG?
YOU SEEM TO BE A BIT DOWN...
A BIT DOWN?
THE RATINGS FOR THE PREMIERE TOTALLY SUCKED.
I don't even want to mention the numbers.
OH...
THE BOX "R" RATINGS...
WERE THEY THAT BAD?

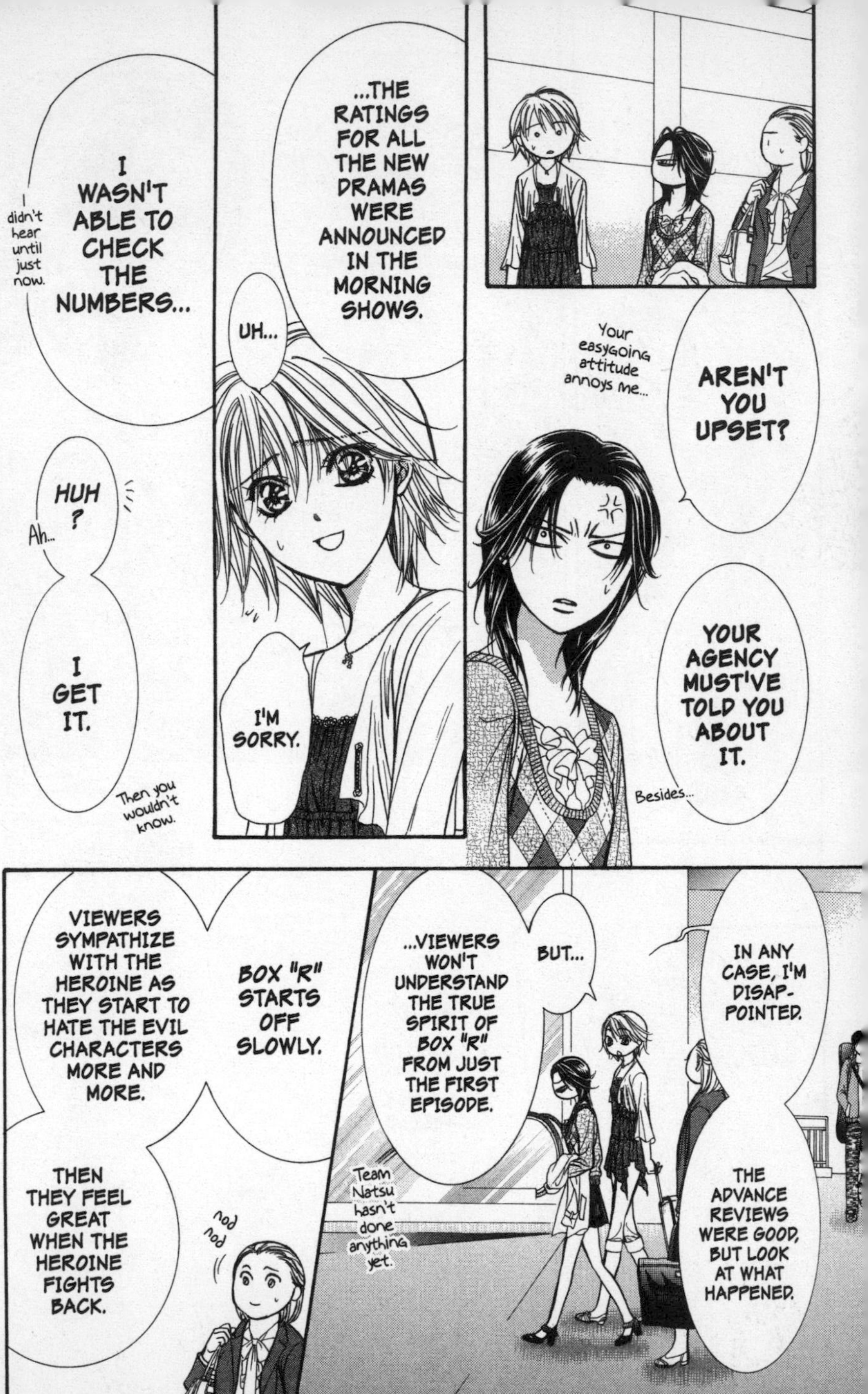

Your easygoing attitude annoys me...
AREN'T YOU UPSET?
YOUR AGENCY MUST'VE TOLD YOU ABOUT IT.
Besides...
...THE RATINGS FOR ALL THE NEW DRAMAS WERE ANNOUNCED IN THE MORNING SHOWS.
UH...
I'M SORRY.
I WASN'T ABLE TO CHECK THE NUMBERS...
I didn't hear until just now.
HUH?
Ah...
I GET IT.
Then you wouldn't know.
IN ANY CASE, I'M DISAP-POINTED.
THE ADVANCE REVIEWS WERE GOOD, BUT LOOK AT WHAT HAPPENED.
BUT...
...VIEWERS WON'T UNDERSTAND THE TRUE SPIRIT OF BOX "R" FROM JUST THE FIRST EPISODE.
Team Natsu hasn't done anything yet.
BOX "R" STARTS OFF SLOWLY.
VIEWERS SYMPATHIZE WITH THE HEROINE AS THEY START TO HATE THE EVIL CHARACTERS MORE AND MORE.
THEN THEY FEEL GREAT WHEN THE HEROINE FIGHTS BACK.
nod nod

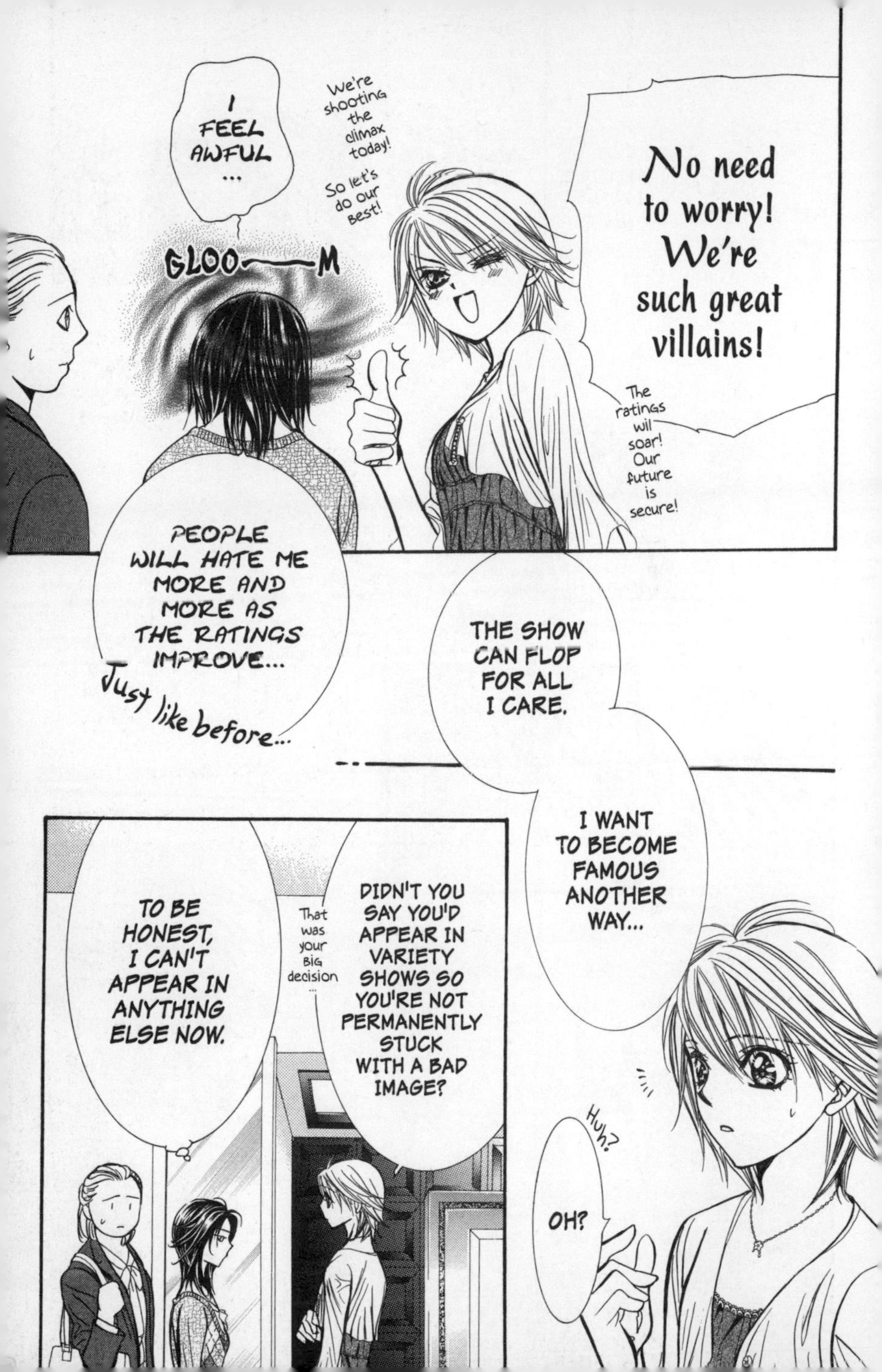
No need to worry! We're such great villains!
The ratings wil soar! Our future is secure!
We're shooting the climax today!
So let's do our best!
I FEEL AWFUL ...
GLOO——M
PEOPLE WILL HATE ME MORE AND MORE AS THE RATINGS IMPROVE...
Just like before...
THE SHOW CAN FLOP FOR ALL I CARE.
I WANT TO BECOME FAMOUS ANOTHER WAY...
Huh?
OH?
DIDN'T YOU SAY YOU'D APPEAR IN VARIETY SHOWS SO YOU'RE NOT PERMANENTLY STUCK WITH A BAD IMAGE?
That was your BIG decision ...
TO BE HONEST, I CAN'T APPEAR IN ANYTHING ELSE NOW.

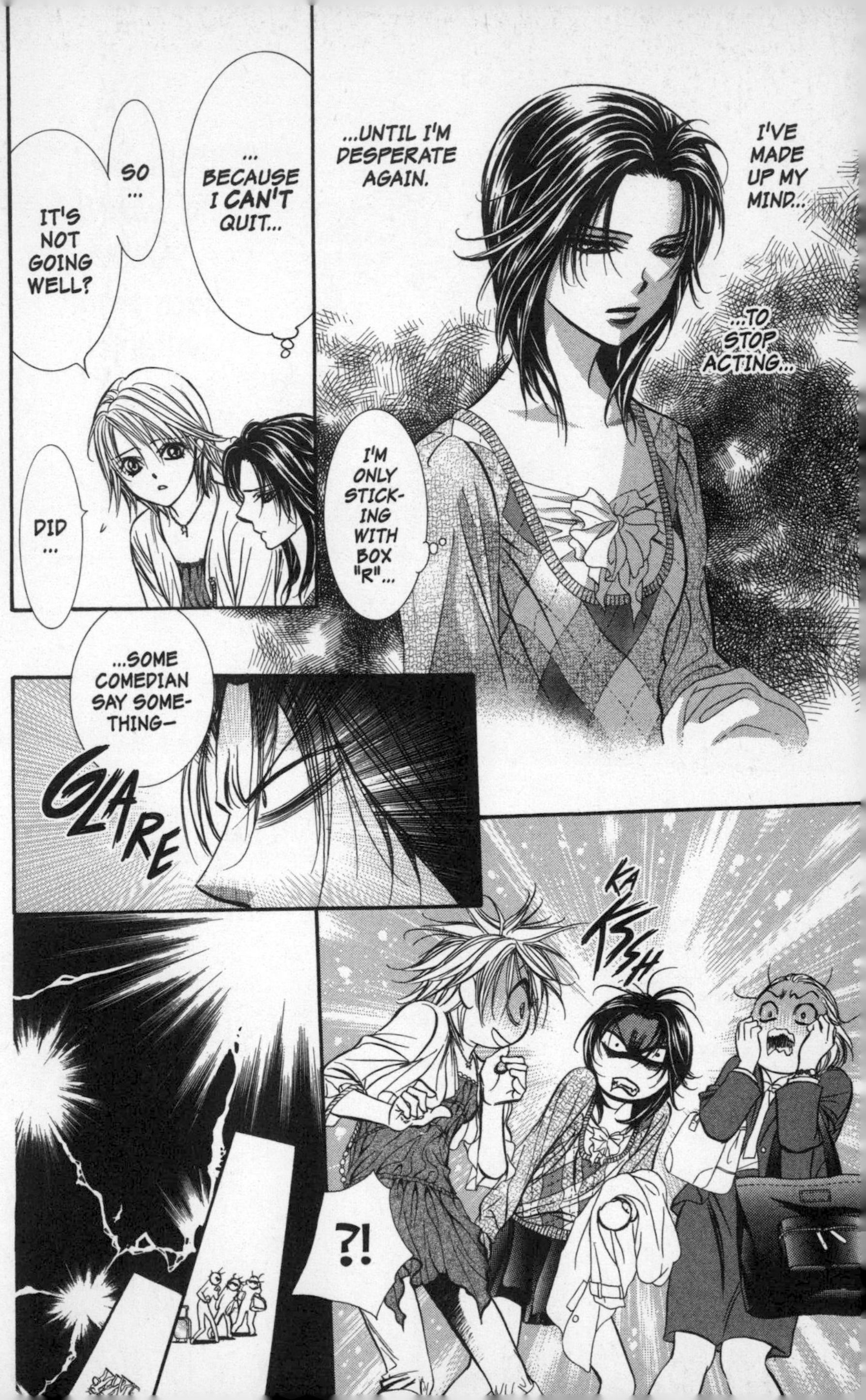
I'VE MADE UP MY MIND...
...TO STOP ACTING...
...UNTIL I'M DESPERATE AGAIN.
I'M ONLY STICKING WITH BOX "R"...
... BECAUSE I CAN'T QUIT...
SO ...
IT'S NOT GOING WELL?
DID ...
...SOME COMEDIAN SAY SOMETHING—
GLARE
KA KSH
?!

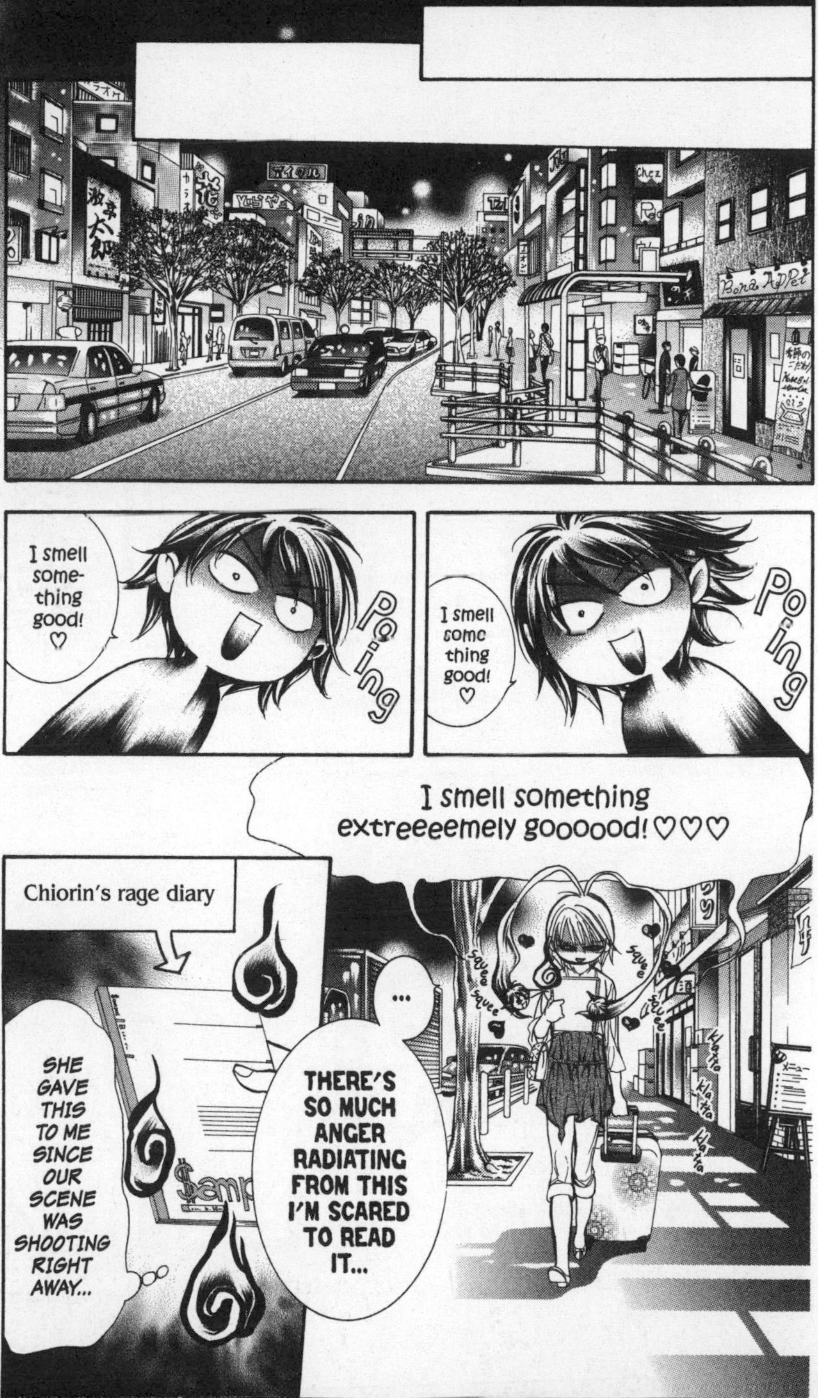

I smell some thing good! ♡
Poing
I smell some-thing good! ♡
Poing
I smell something extreeeemely goooood! ♡♡♡
squee squee squee squee
klatta klatta klatta
...
THERE'S SO MUCH ANGER RADIATING FROM THIS I'M SCARED TO READ IT...
Chiorin's rage diary
SHE GAVE THIS TO ME SINCE OUR SCENE WAS SHOOTING RIGHT AWAY...

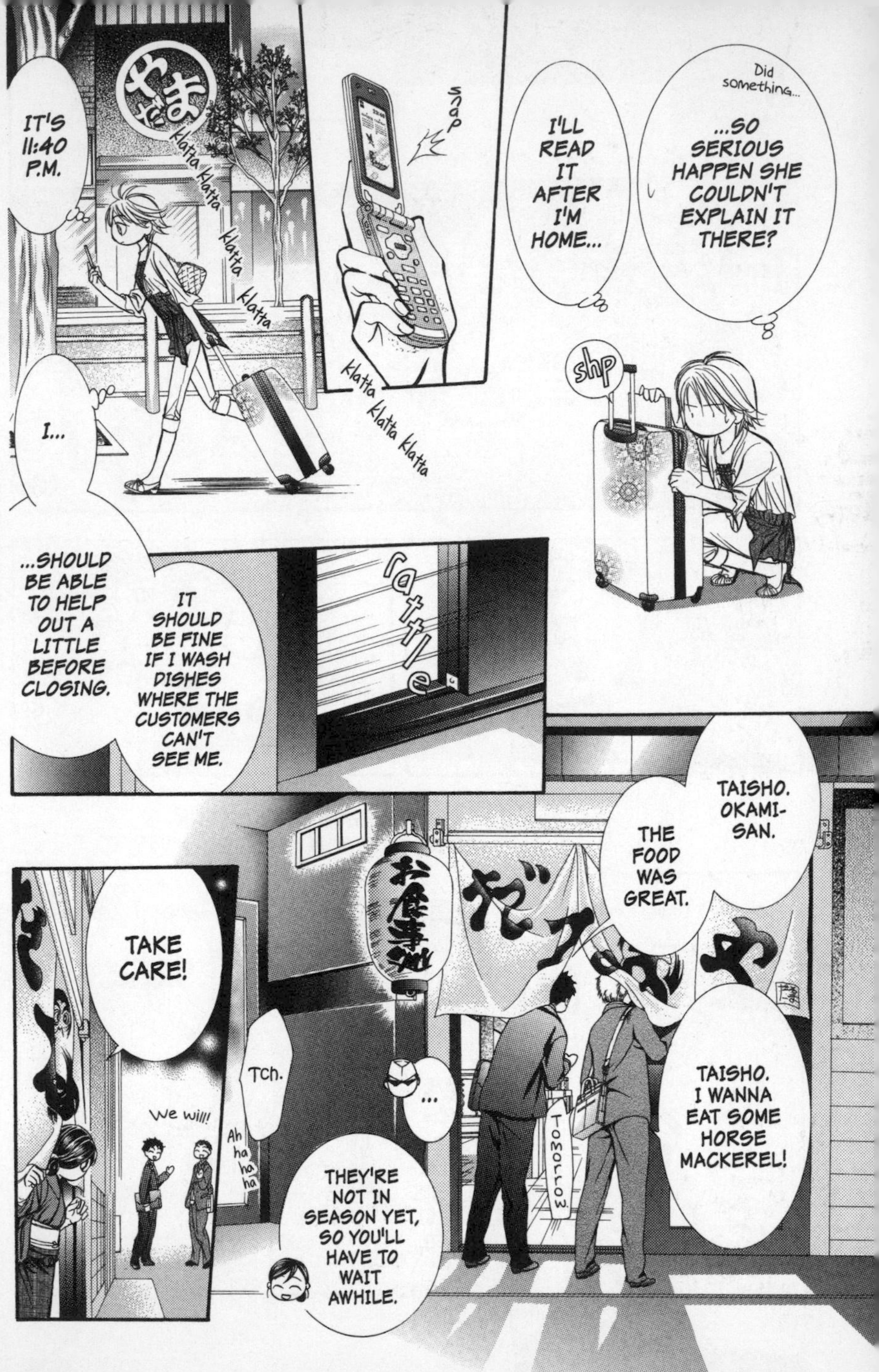
Did something...
...SO SERIOUS HAPPEN SHE COULDN'T EXPLAIN IT THERE?
I'LL READ IT AFTER I'M HOME...
shp
snap
IT'S 11:40 P.M.
klatta klatta klatta klatta klatta
klatta klatta klatta
I...
...SHOULD BE ABLE TO HELP OUT A LITTLE BEFORE CLOSING.
rattle
IT SHOULD BE FINE IF I WASH DISHES WHERE THE CUSTOMERS CAN'T SEE ME.
TAISHO. OKAMI-SAN.
THE FOOD WAS GREAT.
TAISHO. I WANNA EAT SOME HORSE MACKEREL!
Tomorrow.
...
THEY'RE NOT IN SEASON YET, SO YOU'LL HAVE TO WAIT AWHILE.
Tch.
Ah ha ha ha
We will!
TAKE CARE!

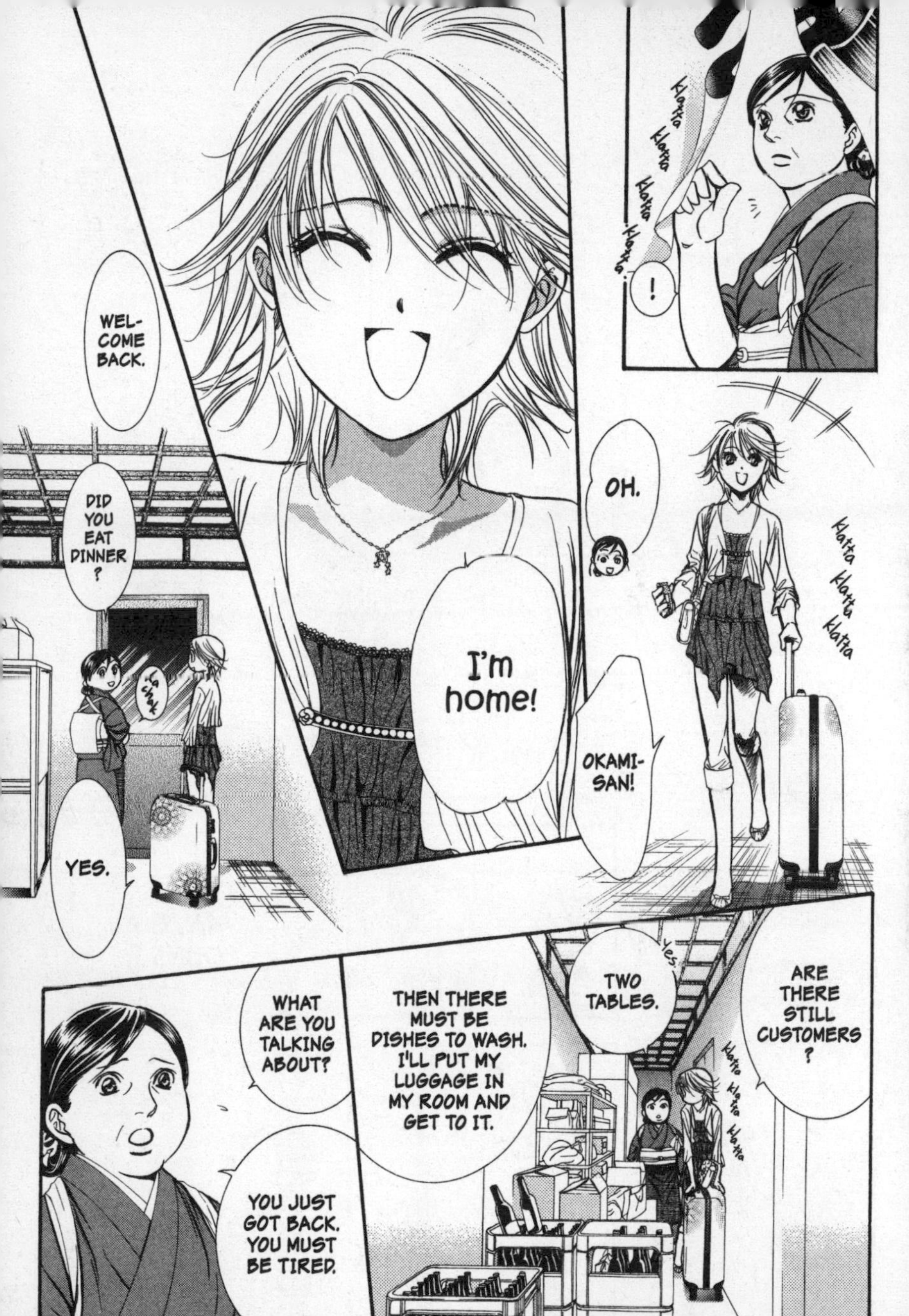
Klatta klatta klatta klatta
!
OH.
OKAMI-SAN!
Klatta klatta klatta
I'm home!
WEL-COME BACK.
DID YOU EAT DINNER?
YES.
ARE THERE STILL CUSTOMERS?
Klatta klatta klatta
Yes
TWO TABLES.
THEN THERE MUST BE DISHES TO WASH. I'LL PUT MY LUGGAGE IN MY ROOM AND GET TO IT.
WHAT ARE YOU TALKING ABOUT?
YOU JUST GOT BACK. YOU MUST BE TIRED.

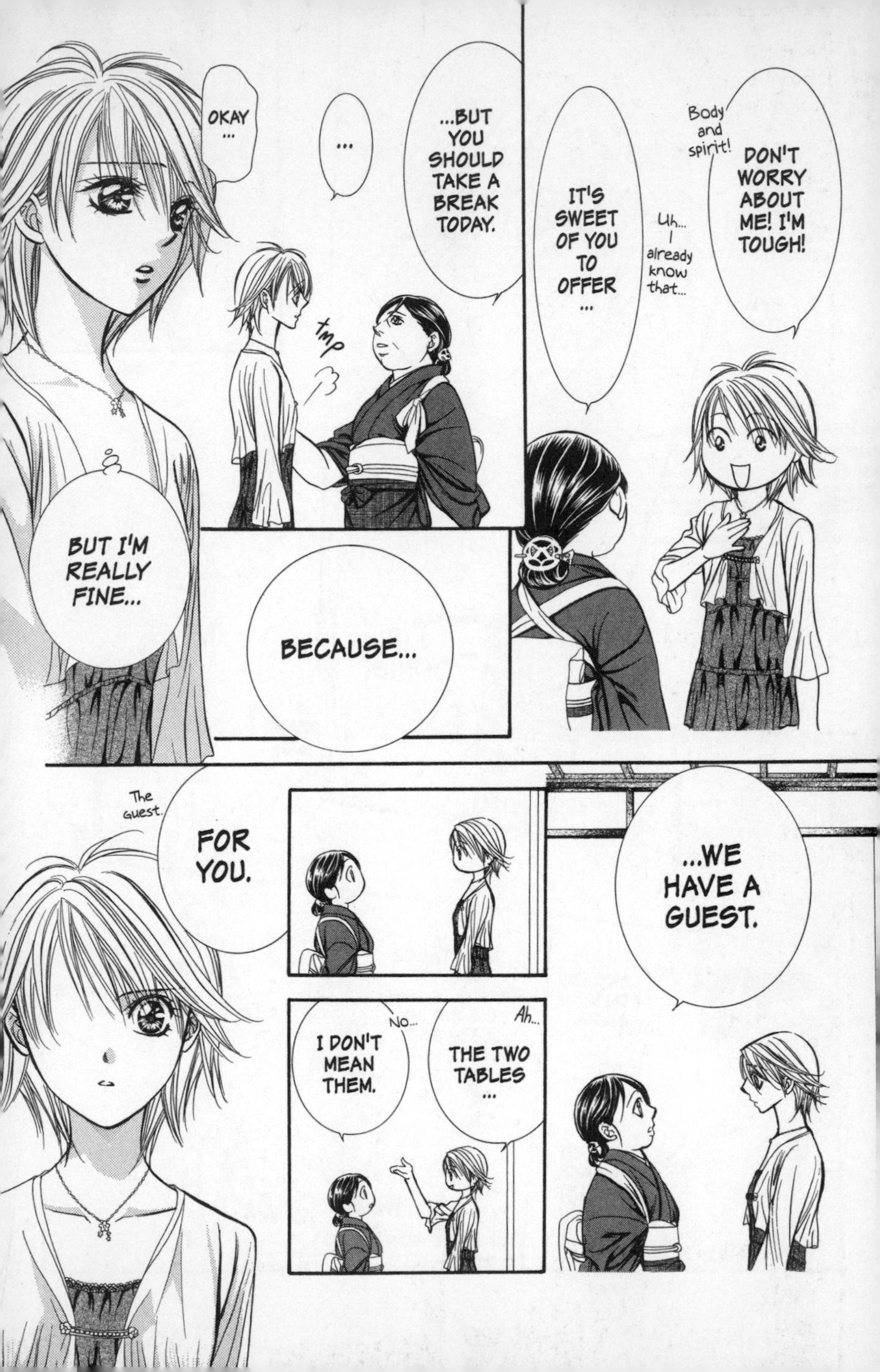
DON'T WORRY ABOUT ME! I'M TOUGH!
Body and spirit!
IT'S SWEET OF YOU TO OFFER...
Uh... I already know that...
...BUT YOU SHOULD TAKE A BREAK TODAY.
...
tmp
OKAY...
BUT I'M REALLY FINE...
BECAUSE...
...WE HAVE A GUEST.
Ah...
THE TWO TABLES...
No...
I DON'T MEAN THEM.
FOR YOU.
The guest.

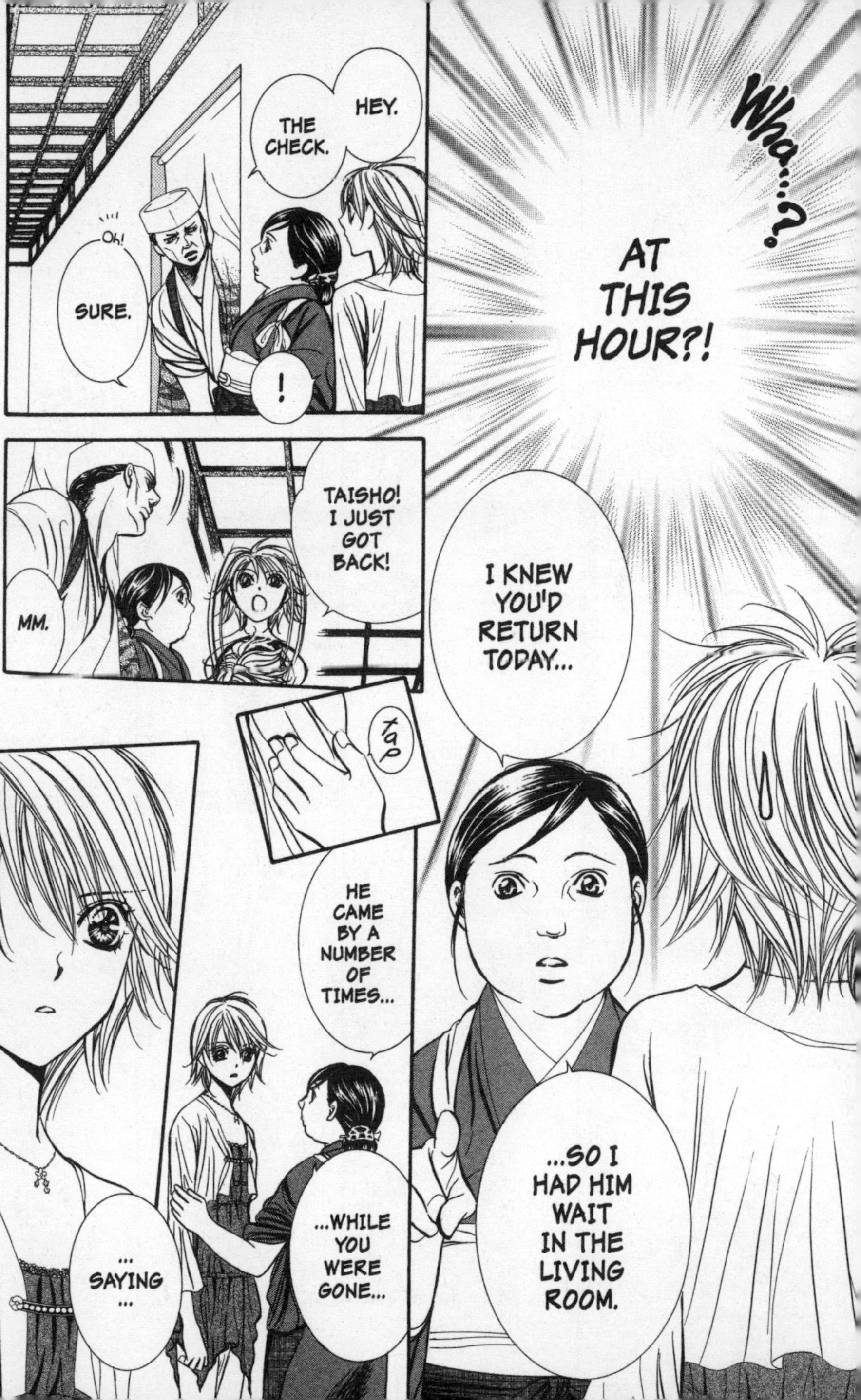
HEY.
THE CHECK.
Oh!
SURE.
!
TAISHO! I JUST GOT BACK!
MM.
tap
HE CAME BY A NUMBER OF TIMES...
...WHILE YOU WERE GONE...
...SAYING...
I KNEW YOU'D RETURN TODAY...
...SO I HAD HIM WAIT IN THE LIVING ROOM.
Wha...??
AT THIS HOUR?!

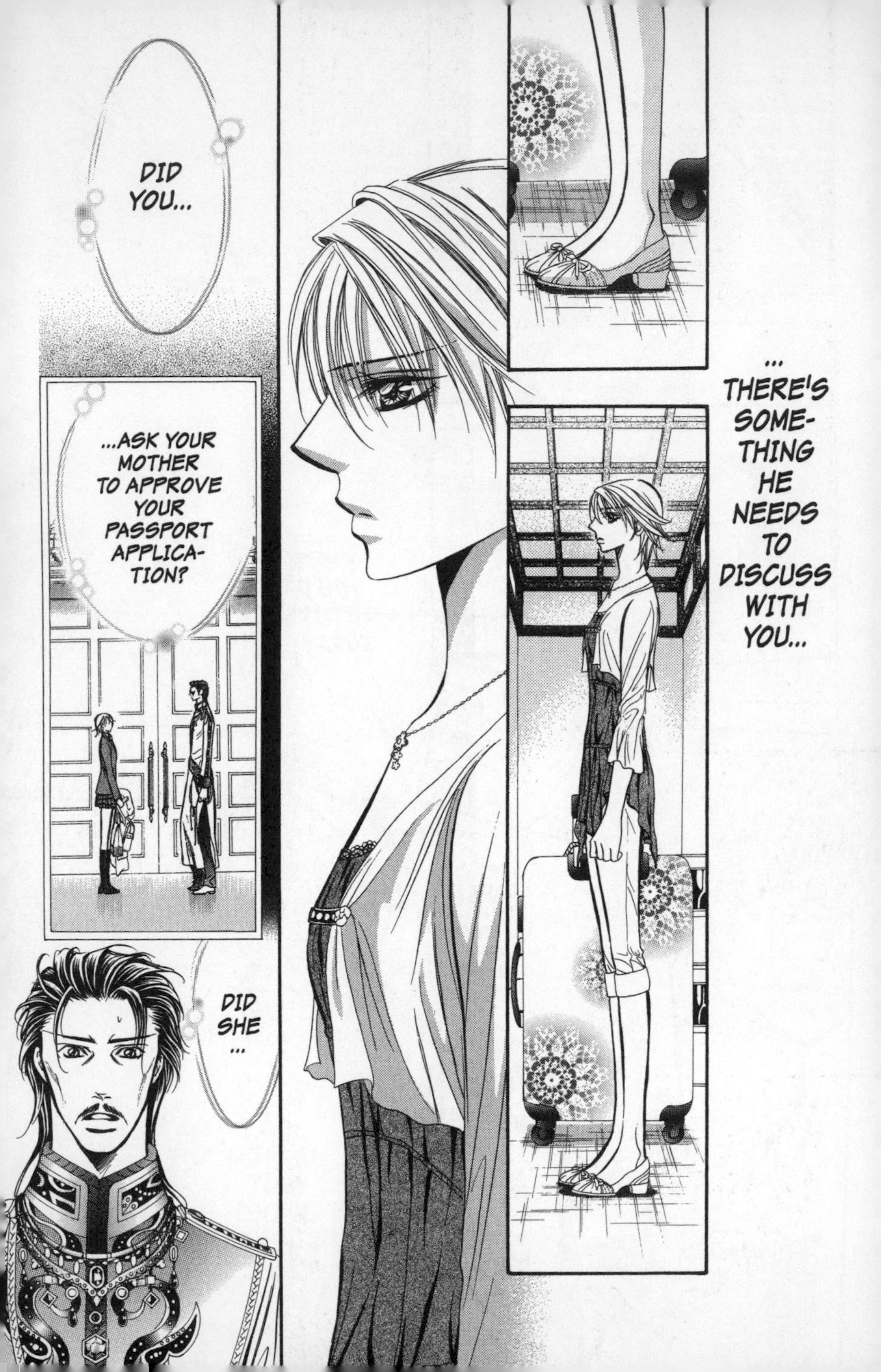
... THERE'S SOMETHING HE NEEDS TO DISCUSS WITH YOU...
DID YOU...
...ASK YOUR MOTHER TO APPROVE YOUR PASSPORT APPLICATION?
DID SHE ...

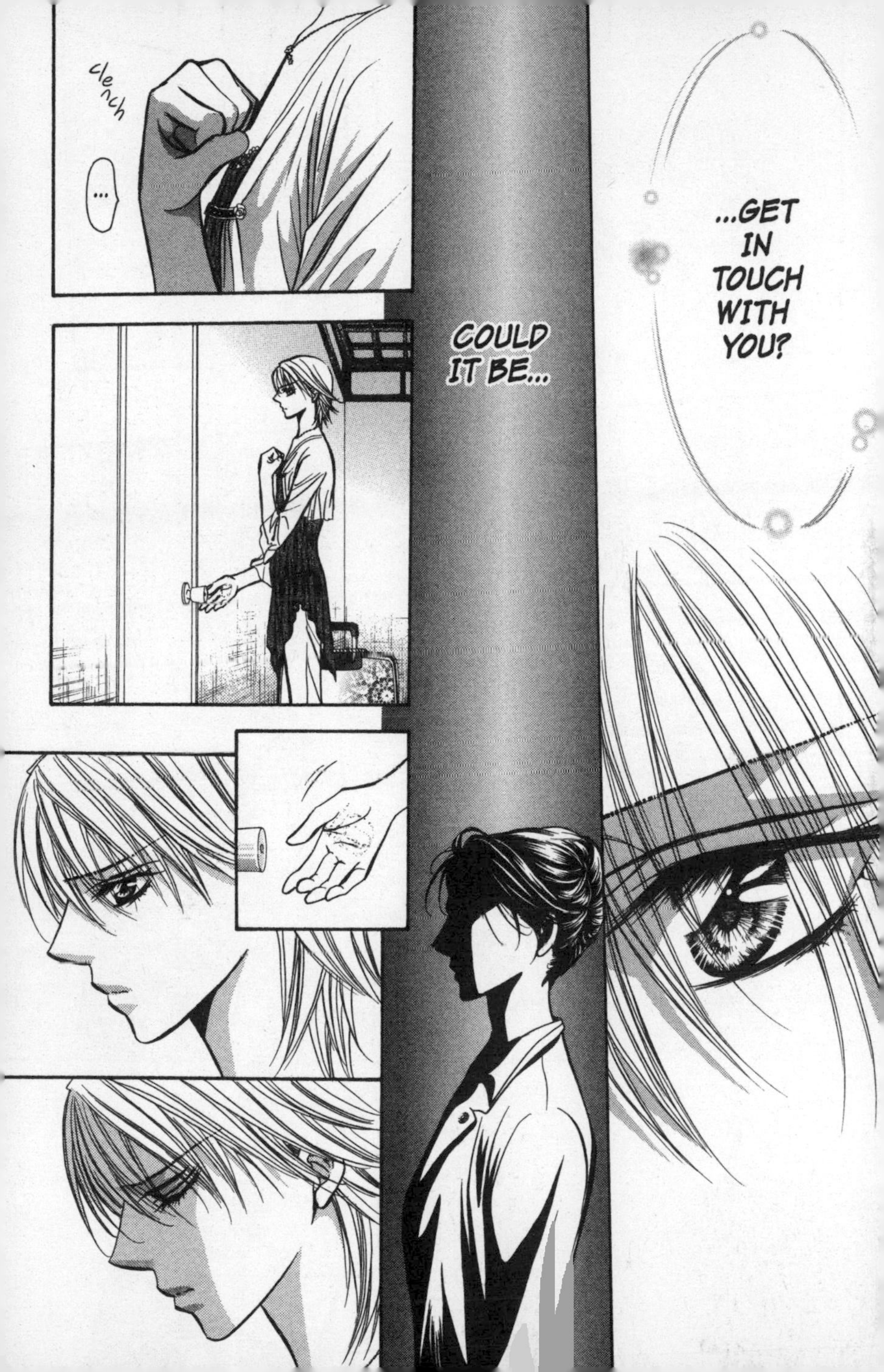

...GET IN TOUCH WITH YOU?
COULD IT BE...
clench
...

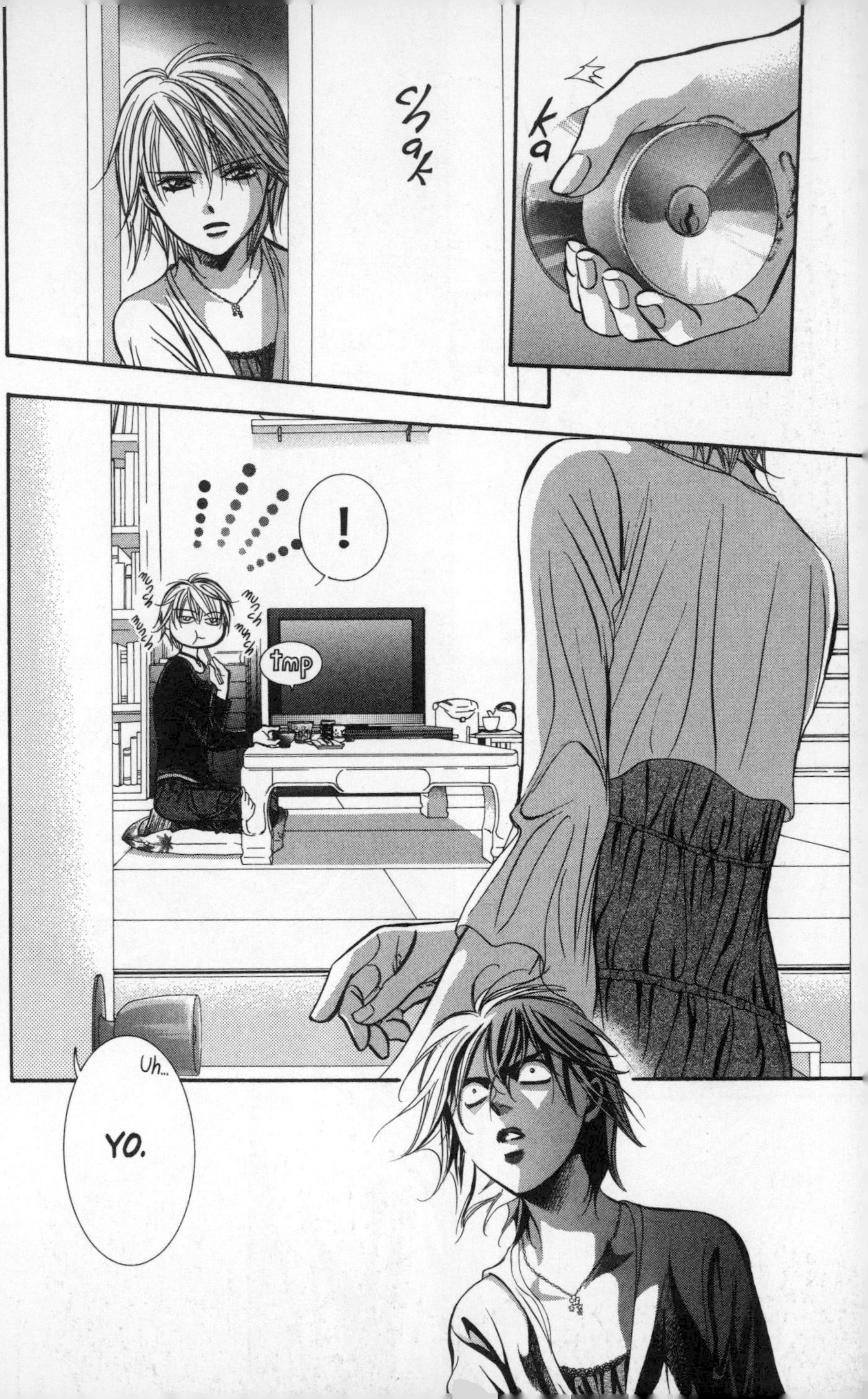
ka
chak
!
munch munch munch munch
tmp
Uh...
YO.

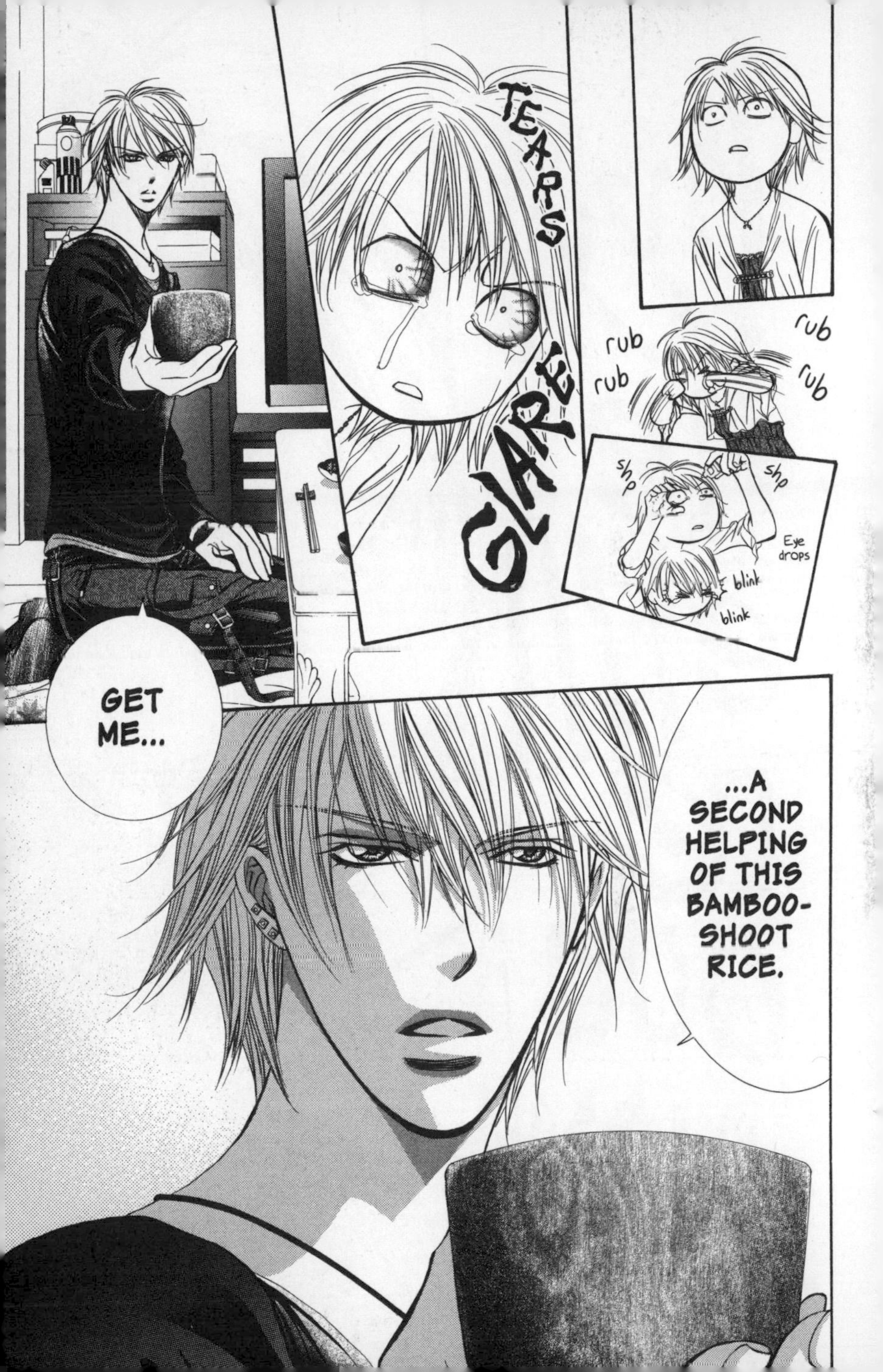

rub
rub
rub
rub
shp
shp
Eye drops
blink
blink
TEARS
GLARE
GET ME...
...A SECOND HELPING OF THIS BAMBOO-SHOOT RICE.

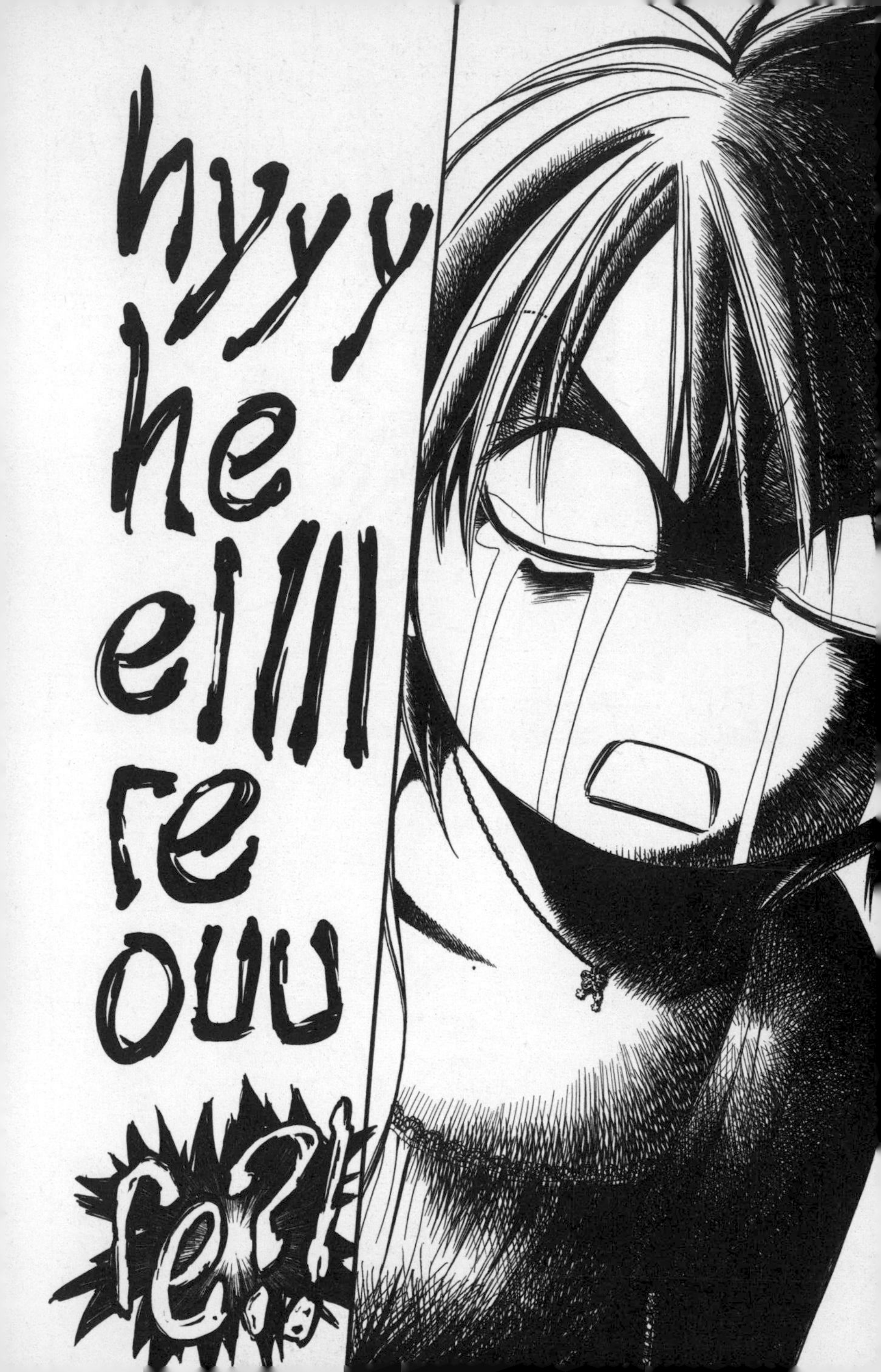
hyyy
he
elll
re
ouu
re?!

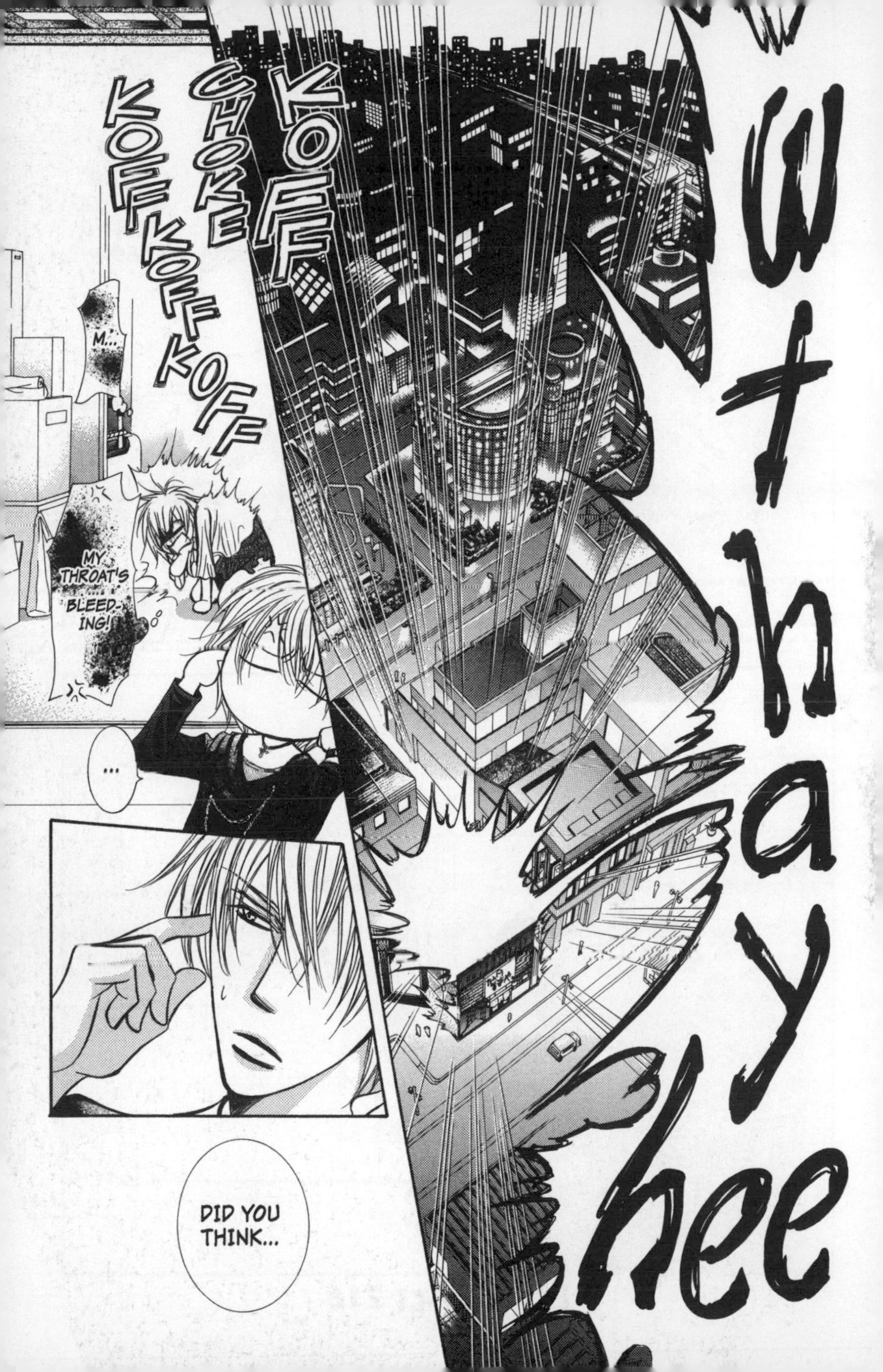

Wthay hee
KOFF
CHOKE
KOFF KOFF KOFF
M...
MY THROAT'S BLEEDING!
...
DID YOU THINK...

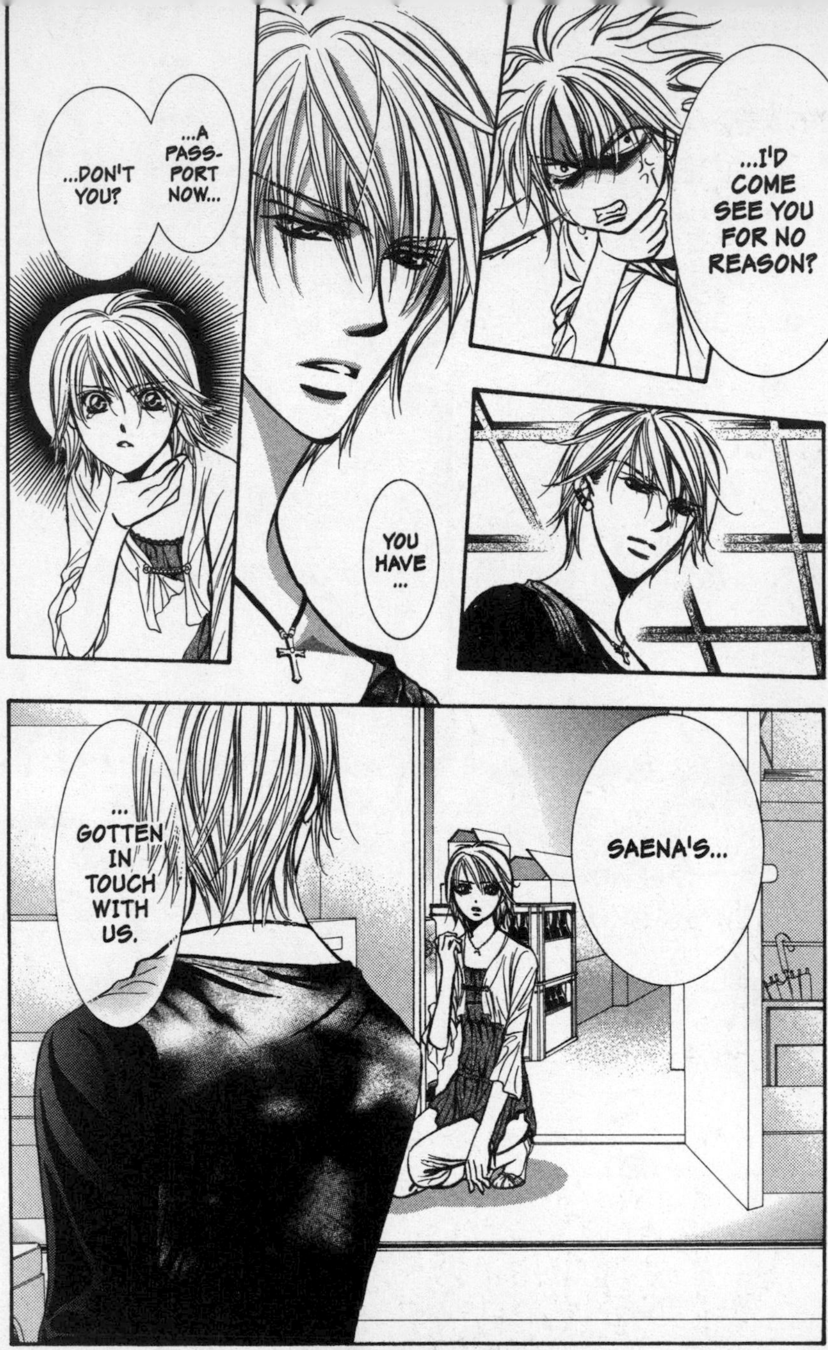
...I'D COME SEE YOU FOR NO REASON?
YOU HAVE ...
...A PASS-PORT NOW...
...DON'T YOU?
SAENA'S...
... GOTTEN IN TOUCH WITH US.

End of Act 216

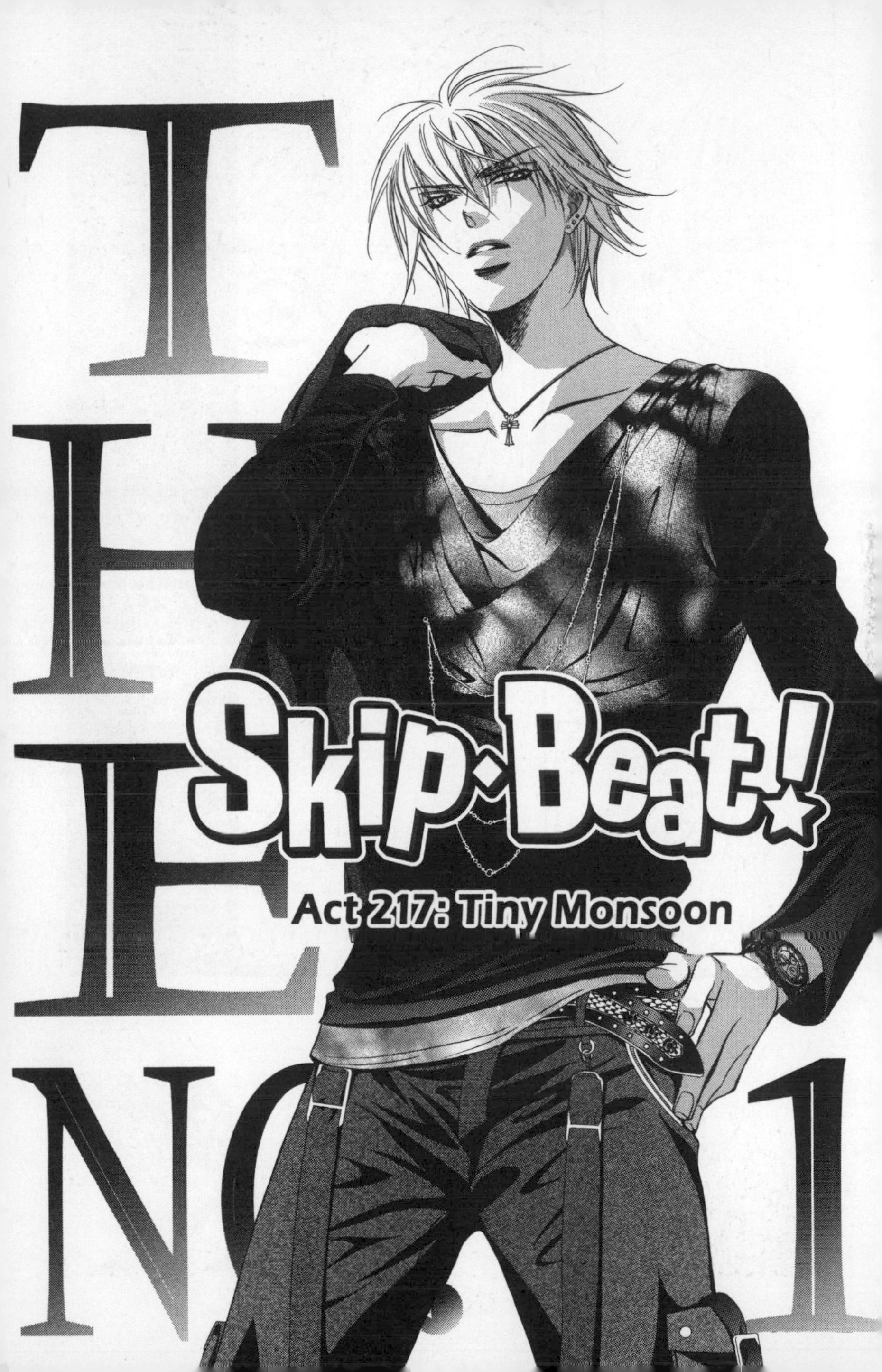
THE NO.1
Skip·Beat!
Act 217: Tiny Monsoon

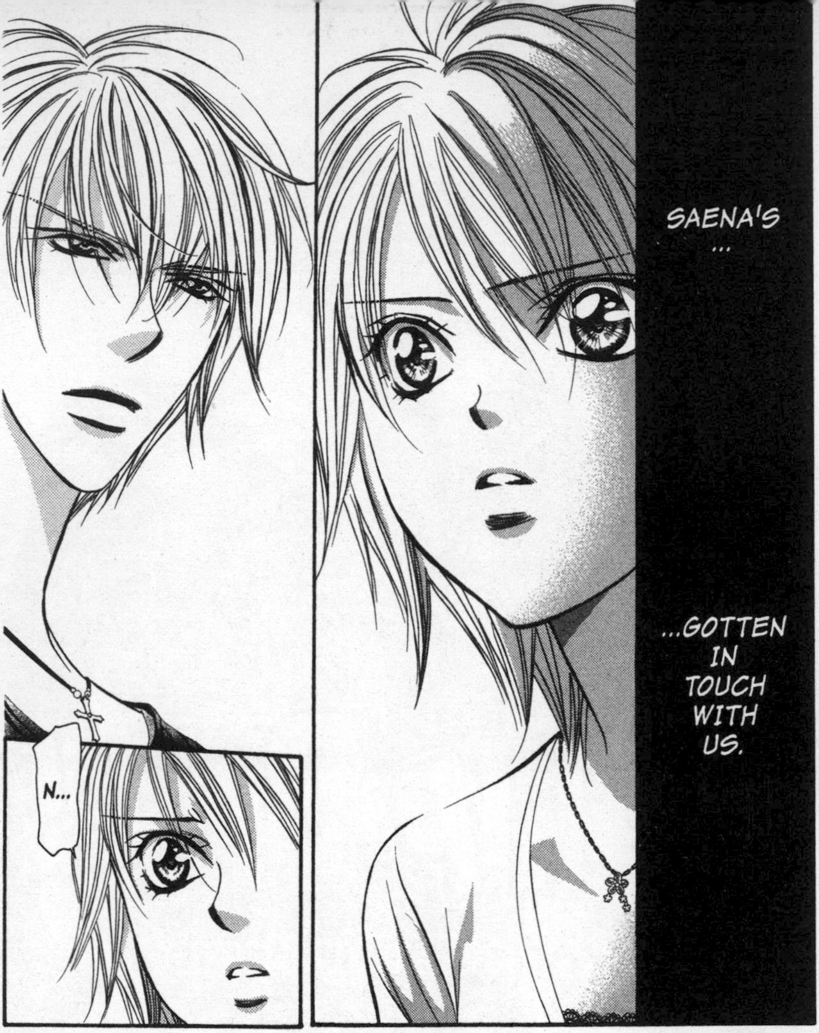
SAENA'S ...
...GOTTEN IN TOUCH WITH US.
N...

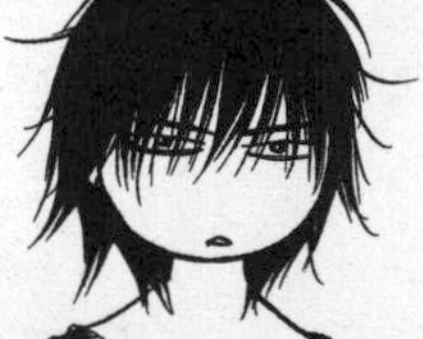

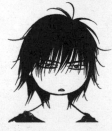

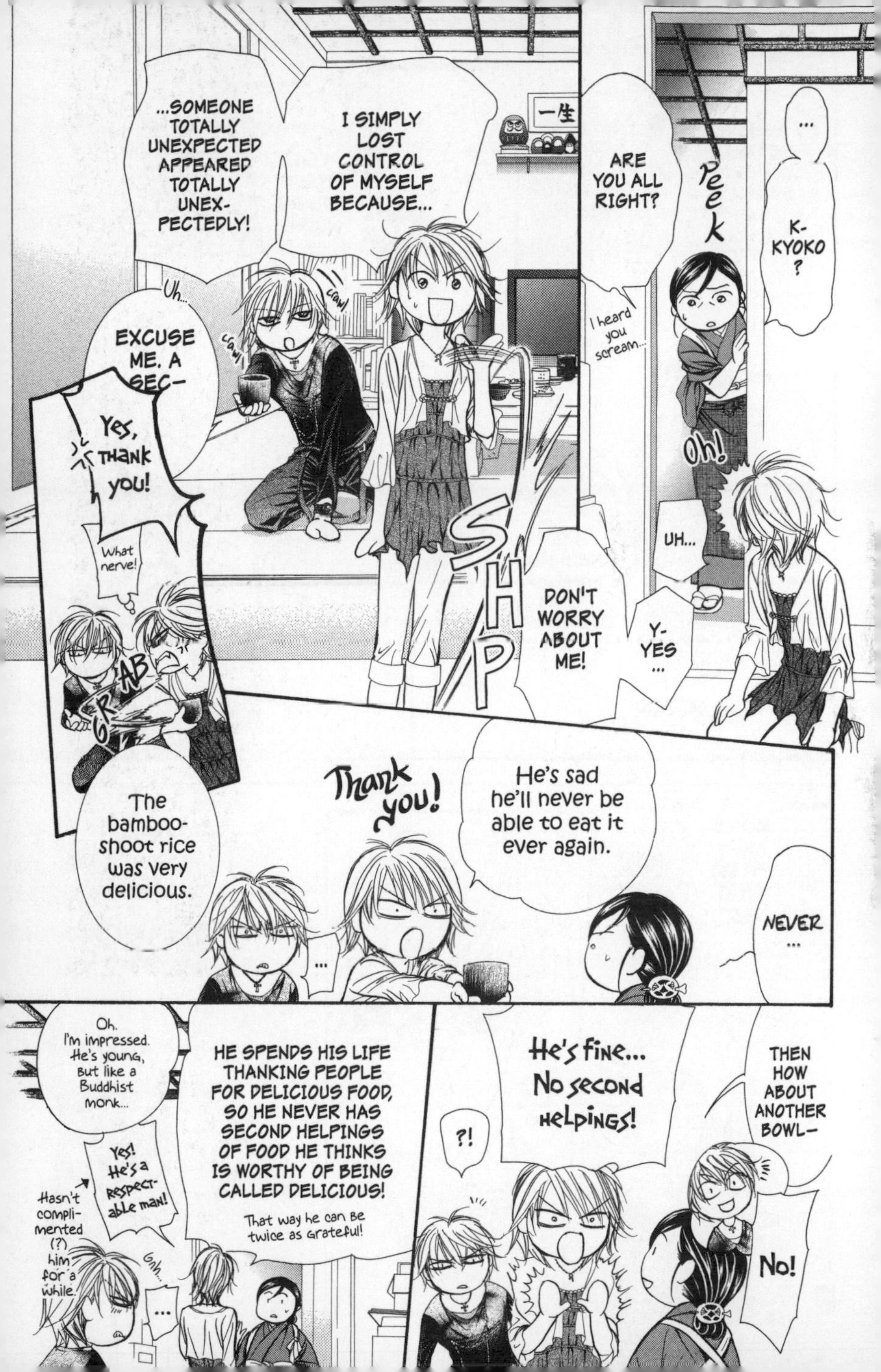
...
K-KYOKO?
ARE YOU ALL RIGHT?
Peek
I heard you scream...
Oh!
UH...
Y-YES...
DON'T WORRY ABOUT ME!
SHP
I SIMPLY LOST CONTROL OF MYSELF BECAUSE...
...SOMEONE TOTALLY UNEXPECTED APPEARED TOTALLY UNEX-PECTEDLY!
crawl
crawl
Uh...
EXCUSE ME. A SEC—
Yes, thank you!
What nerve!
GRAB
NEVER...
He's sad he'll never be able to eat it ever again.
Thank you!
...
The bamboo-shoot rice was very delicious.
THEN HOW ABOUT ANOTHER BOWL—
No!
He's fine... No second helpings!
?!
HE SPENDS HIS LIFE THANKING PEOPLE FOR DELICIOUS FOOD, SO HE NEVER HAS SECOND HELPINGS OF FOOD HE THINKS IS WORTHY OF BEING CALLED DELICIOUS!
That way he can be twice as grateful!
Oh. I'm impressed. He's young, but like a Buddhist monk...
Yes! He's a respect-able man!
Hasn't compli-mented (?) him for a while.
Gnh...
...

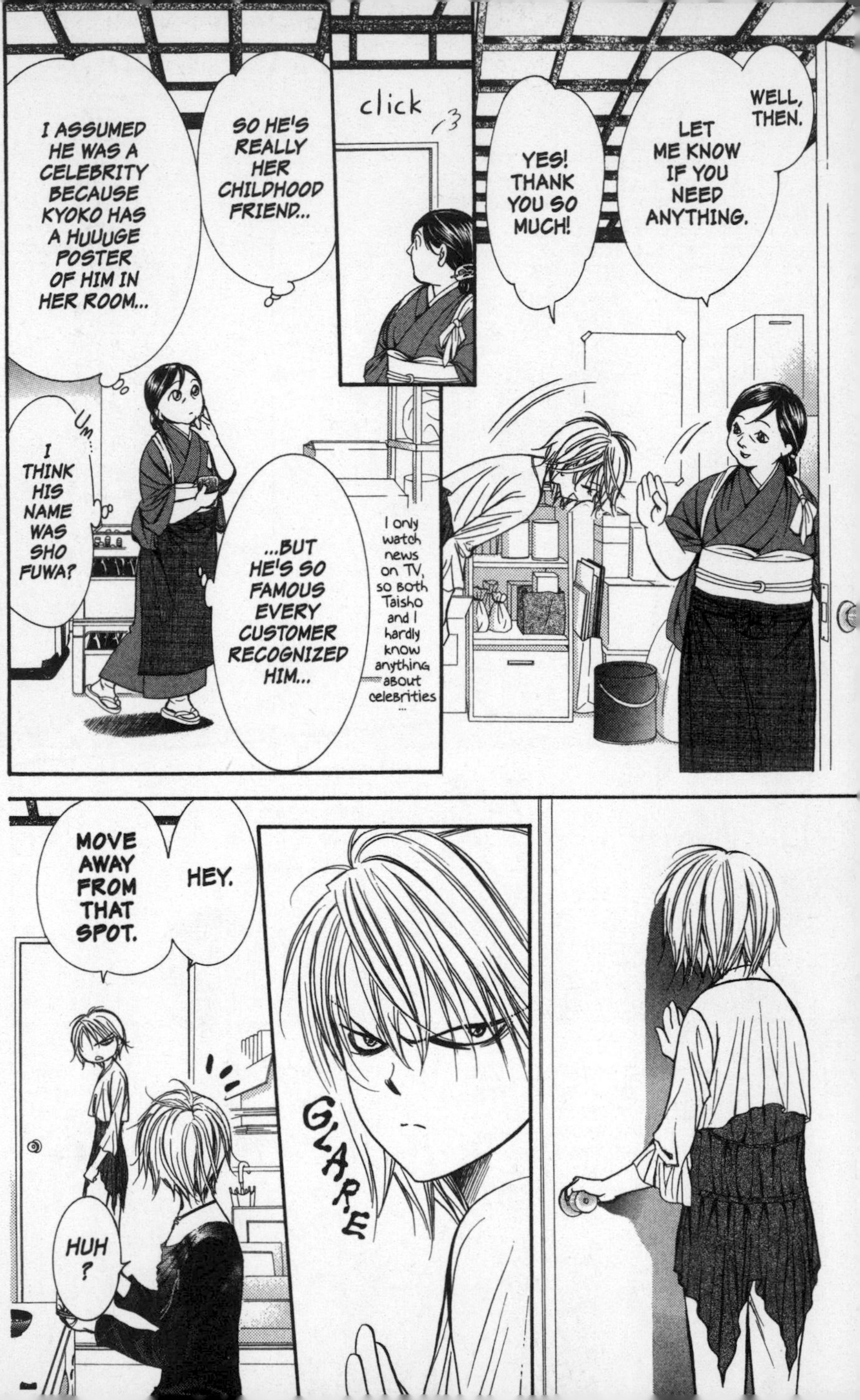
WELL, THEN.
LET ME KNOW IF YOU NEED ANYTHING.
YES! THANK YOU SO MUCH!
click
SO HE'S REALLY HER CHILDHOOD FRIEND...
I ASSUMED HE WAS A CELEBRITY BECAUSE KYOKO HAS A HUUUGE POSTER OF HIM IN HER ROOM...
Um...
I THINK HIS NAME WAS SHO FUWA?
...BUT HE'S SO FAMOUS EVERY CUSTOMER RECOGNIZED HIM...
I only watch news on TV, so both Taisho and I hardly know anything about celebrities...
GLARE
HEY.
MOVE AWAY FROM THAT SPOT.
HUH?

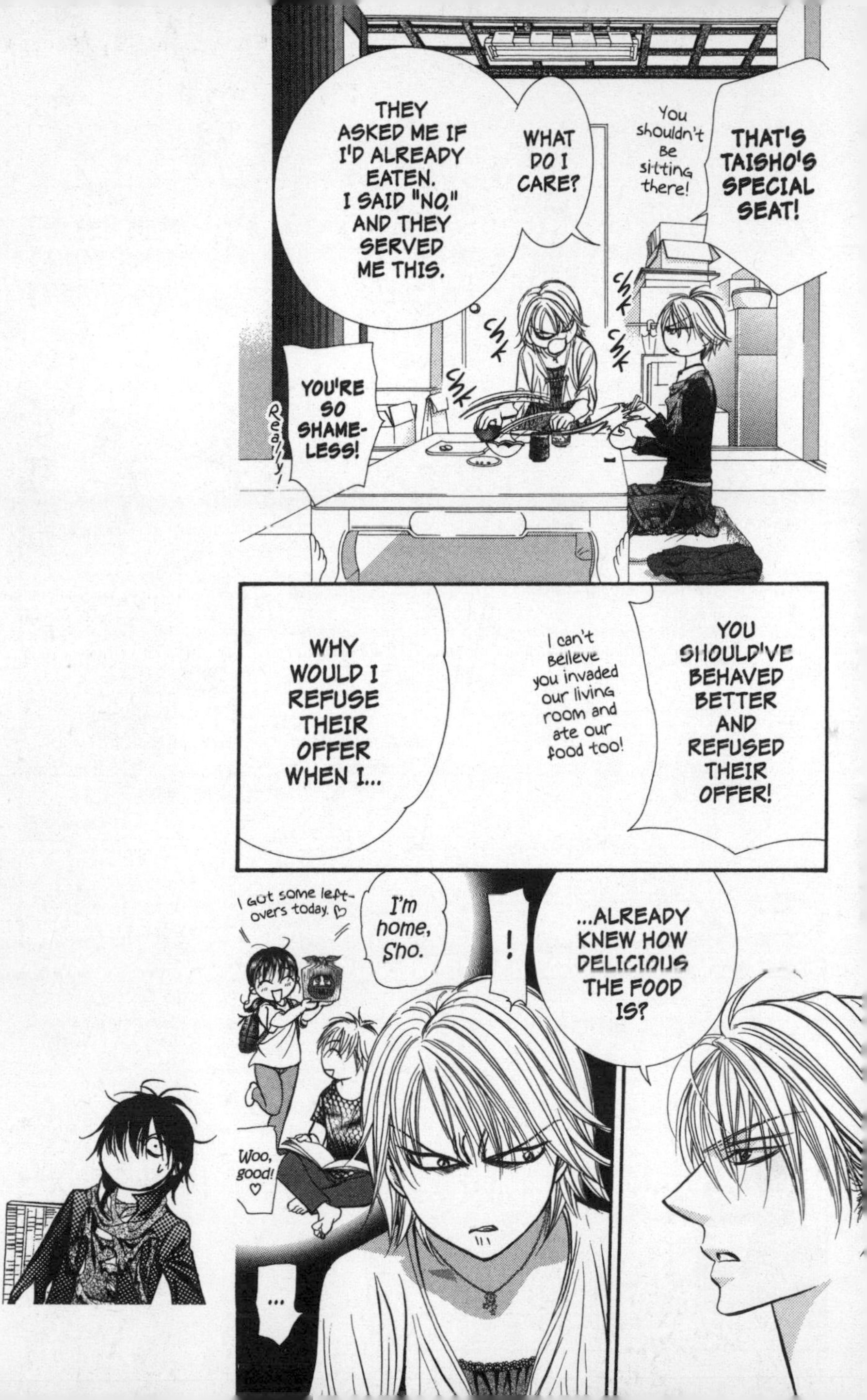
THAT'S TAISHO'S SPECIAL SEAT!
You shouldn't be sitting there!
WHAT DO I CARE?
THEY ASKED ME IF I'D ALREADY EATEN. I SAID "NO," AND THEY SERVED ME THIS.
CHK
CHK
CHK
CHK
YOU'RE SO SHAME-LESS!
Really!
YOU SHOULD'VE BEHAVED BETTER AND REFUSED THEIR OFFER!
I can't believe you invaded our living room and ate our food too!
WHY WOULD I REFUSE THEIR OFFER WHEN I...
...ALREADY KNEW HOW DELICIOUS THE FOOD IS?
!
I'm home, Sho.
I got some left-overs today.
Woo, good!
...

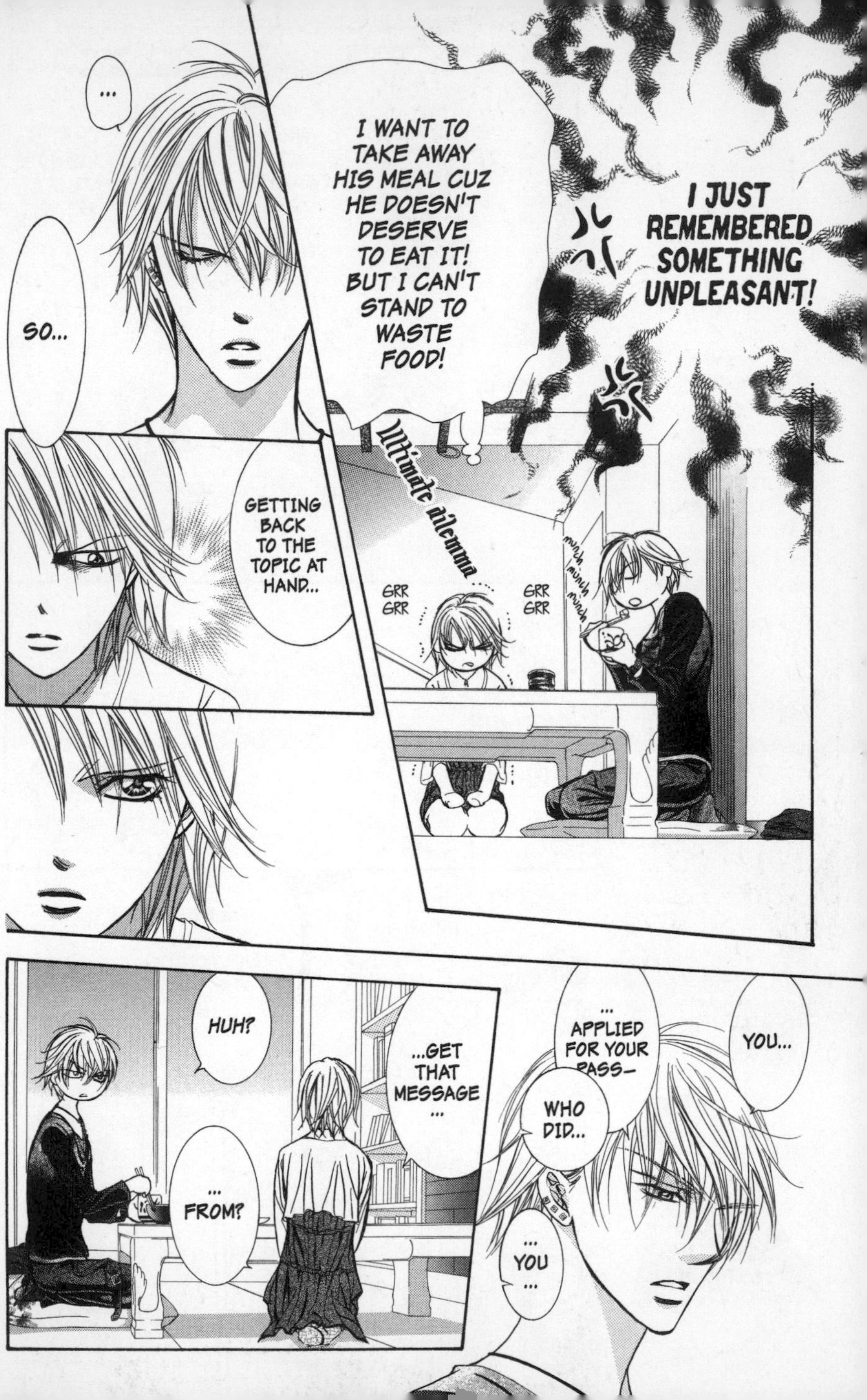
I JUST REMEMBERED SOMETHING UNPLEASANT!
I WANT TO TAKE AWAY HIS MEAL CUZ HE DOESN'T DESERVE TO EAT IT! BUT I CAN'T STAND TO WASTE FOOD!
Ultimate dilemma
GRR GRR
GRR GRR
munch munch munch
...
SO...
GETTING BACK TO THE TOPIC AT HAND...
YOU...
... APPLIED FOR YOUR PASS—
WHO DID...
... YOU ...
...GET THAT MESSAGE ...
HUH?
... FROM?

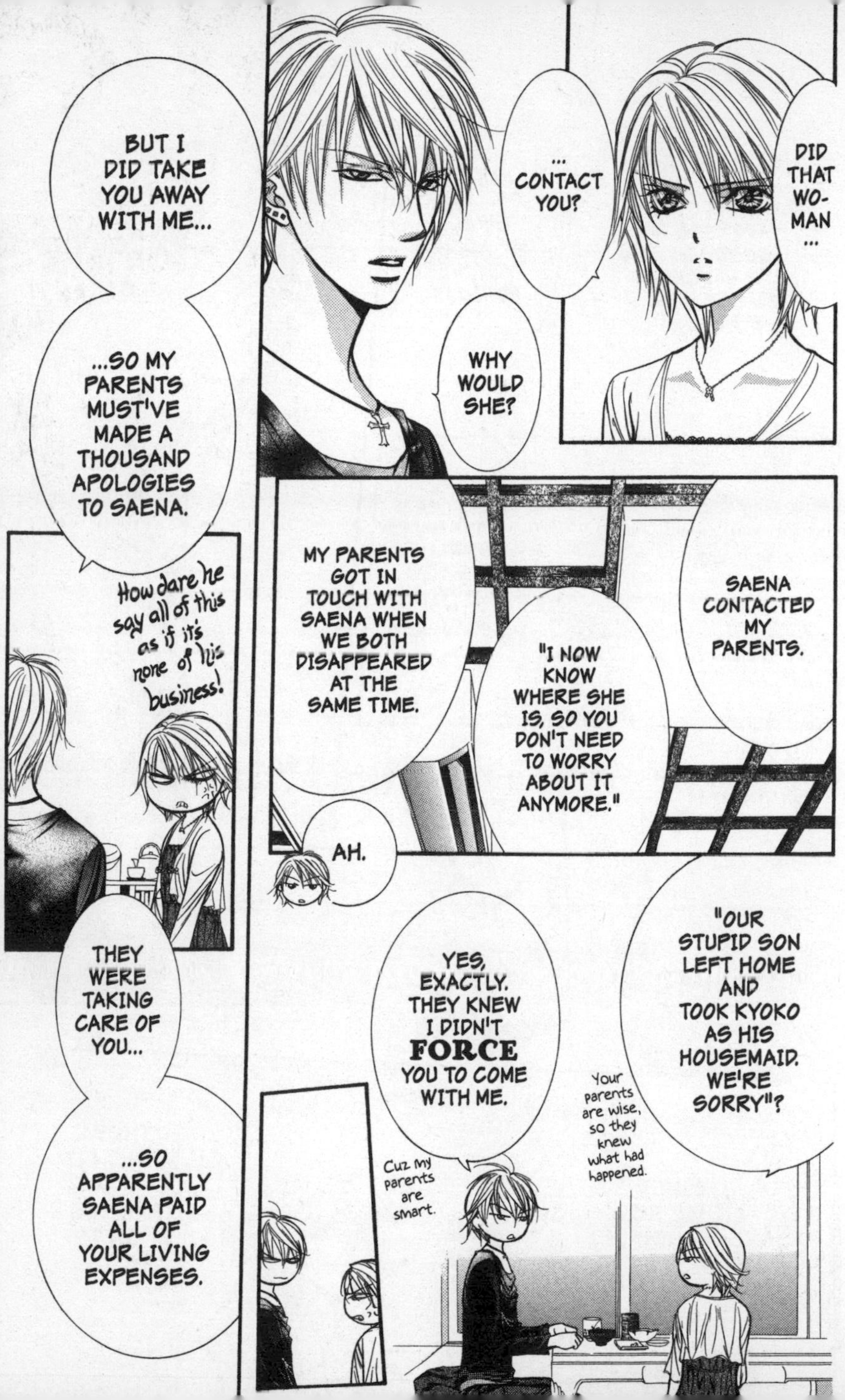

DID THAT WO-MAN ...
... CONTACT YOU?
WHY WOULD SHE?
SAENA CONTACTED MY PARENTS.
"I NOW KNOW WHERE SHE IS, SO YOU DON'T NEED TO WORRY ABOUT IT ANYMORE."
MY PARENTS GOT IN TOUCH WITH SAENA WHEN WE BOTH DISAPPEARED AT THE SAME TIME.
AH.
"OUR STUPID SON LEFT HOME AND TOOK KYOKO AS HIS HOUSEMAID. WE'RE SORRY"?
YES, EXACTLY. THEY KNEW I DIDN'T FORCE YOU TO COME WITH ME.
Your parents are wise, so they knew what had happened.
Cuz my parents are smart.
BUT I DID TAKE YOU AWAY WITH ME...
...SO MY PARENTS MUST'VE MADE A THOUSAND APOLOGIES TO SAENA.
How dare he say all of this as if it's none of his business!
THEY WERE TAKING CARE OF YOU...
...SO APPARENTLY SAENA PAID ALL OF YOUR LIVING EXPENSES.

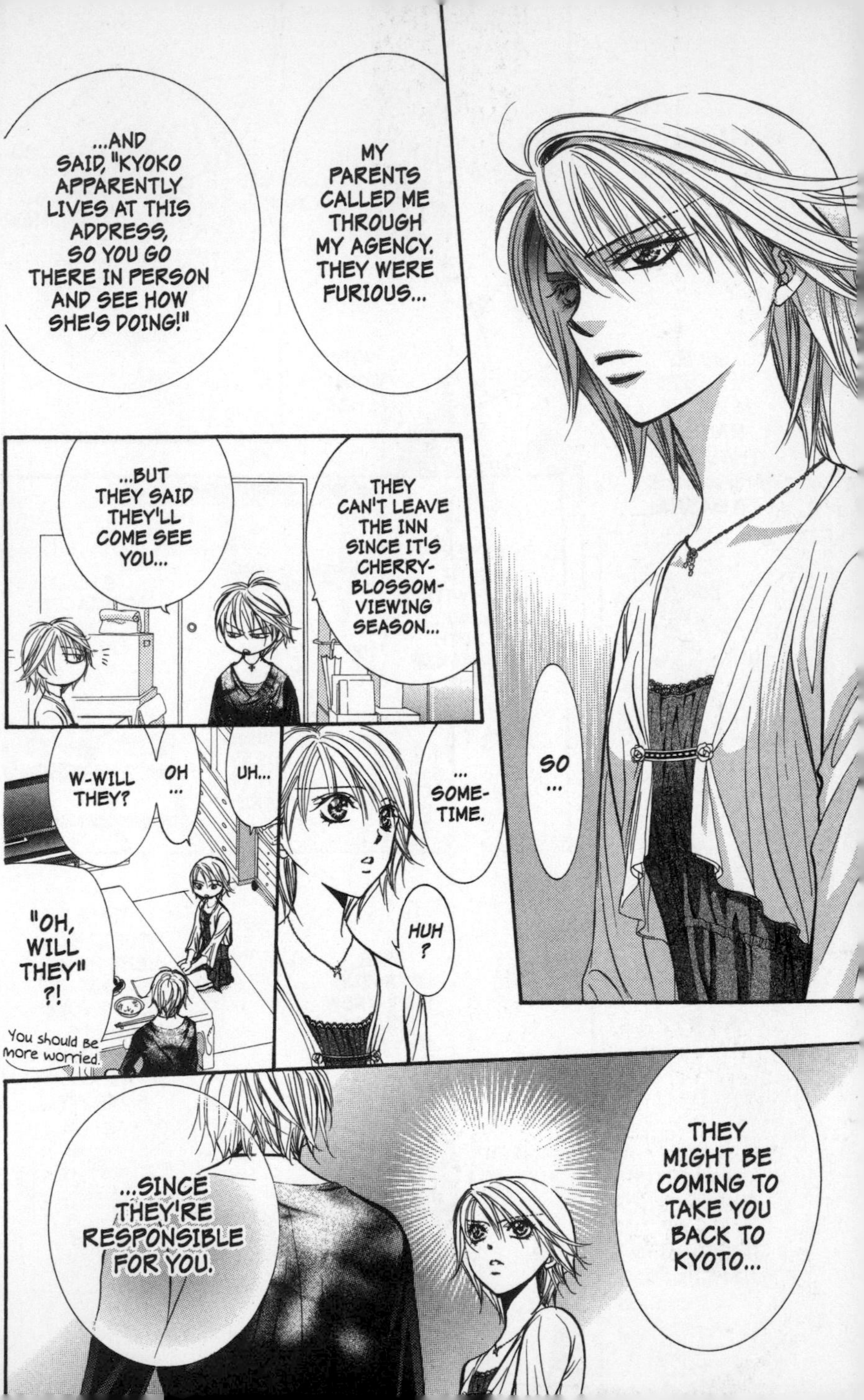
SO ...
MY PARENTS CALLED ME THROUGH MY AGENCY. THEY WERE FURIOUS...
...AND SAID, "KYOKO APPARENTLY LIVES AT THIS ADDRESS, SO YOU GO THERE IN PERSON AND SEE HOW SHE'S DOING!"
THEY CAN'T LEAVE THE INN SINCE IT'S CHERRY-BLOSSOM-VIEWING SEASON...
...BUT THEY SAID THEY'LL COME SEE YOU...
... SOME-TIME.
HUH ?
UH...
OH ...
W-WILL THEY?
"OH, WILL THEY" ?!
You should be more worried.
THEY MIGHT BE COMING TO TAKE YOU BACK TO KYOTO...
...SINCE THEY'RE RESPONSIBLE FOR YOU.

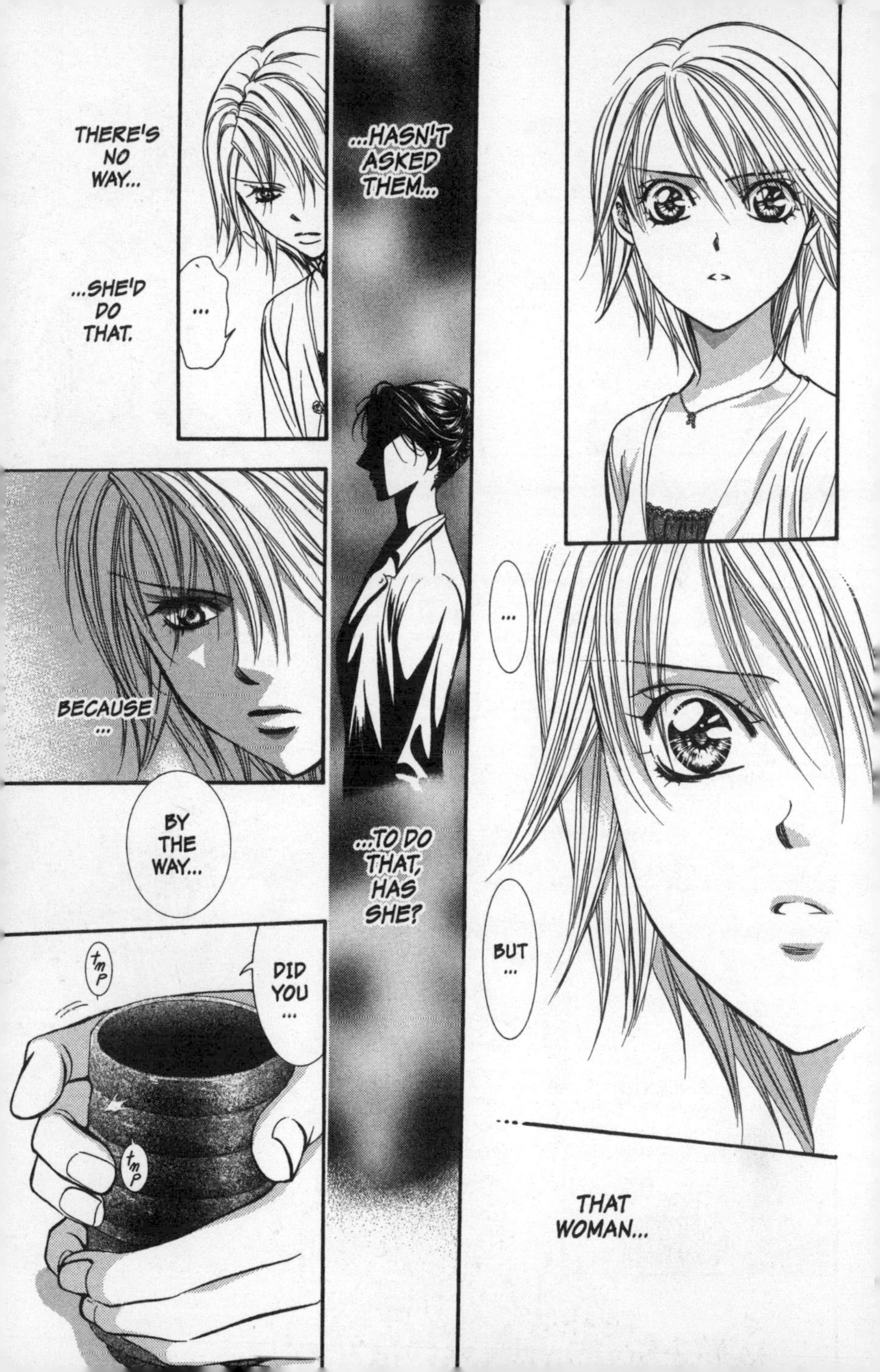
...
BUT...
...
THAT WOMAN...
...HASN'T ASKED THEM...
...TO DO THAT, HAS SHE?
THERE'S NO WAY...
...SHE'D DO THAT.
...
BECAUSE...
BY THE WAY...
DID YOU...
tmp
tmp

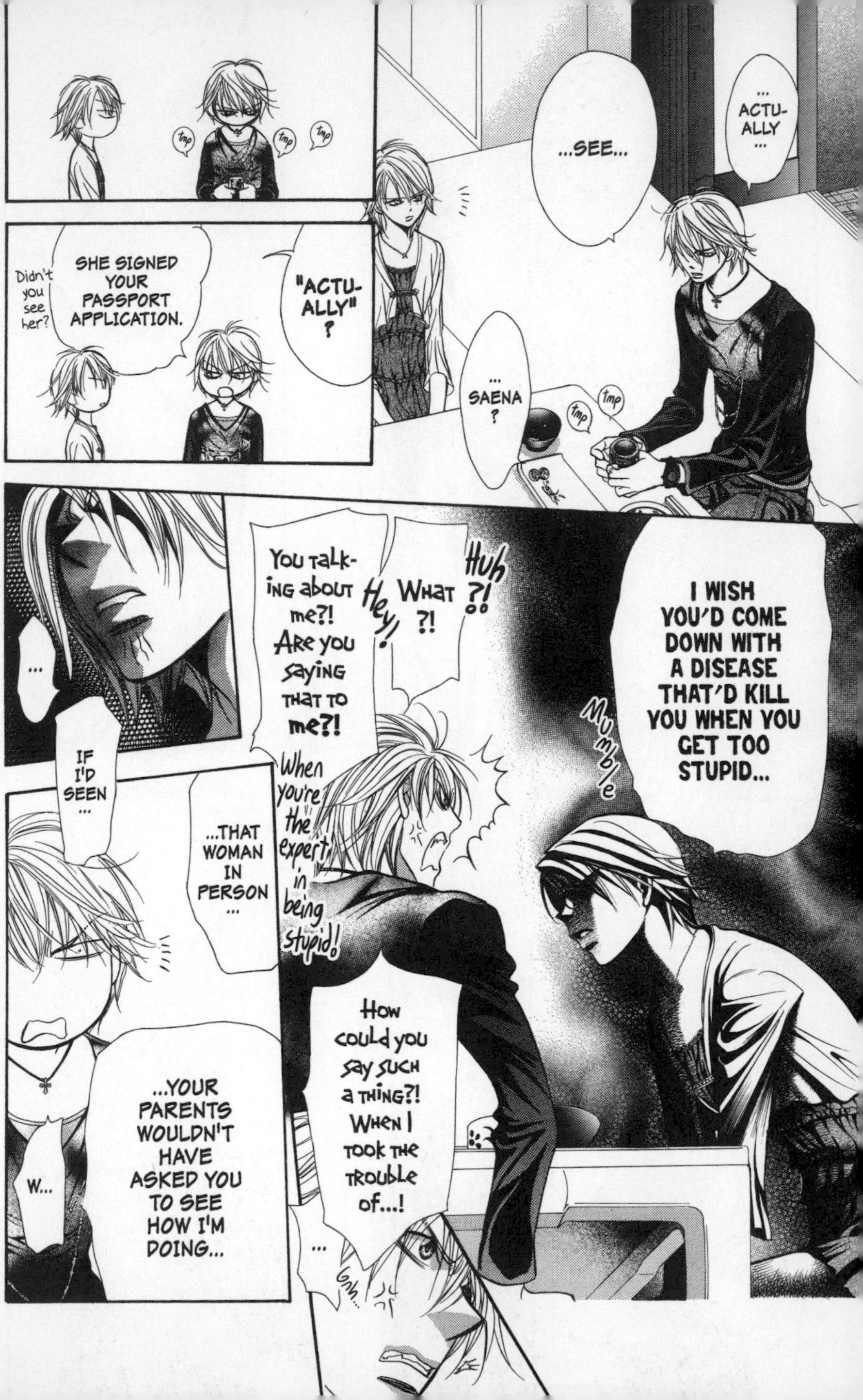
...ACTUALLY...
...SEE...
...SAENA?
tmp
tmp
tmp
tmp
tmp
"ACTUALLY"?
SHE SIGNED YOUR PASSPORT APPLICATION.
Didn't you see her?
I WISH YOU'D COME DOWN WITH A DISEASE THAT'D KILL YOU WHEN YOU GET TOO STUPID...
Mumble
Huh?!
WHAT?!
Hey!
You talking about me?! Are you saying that to me?!
When you're the expert in being stupid!
How could you say such a thing?! When I took the trouble of...!
...
Gnh...
...
IF I'D SEEN...
...THAT WOMAN IN PERSON...
...YOUR PARENTS WOULDN'T HAVE ASKED YOU TO SEE HOW I'M DOING...
W...

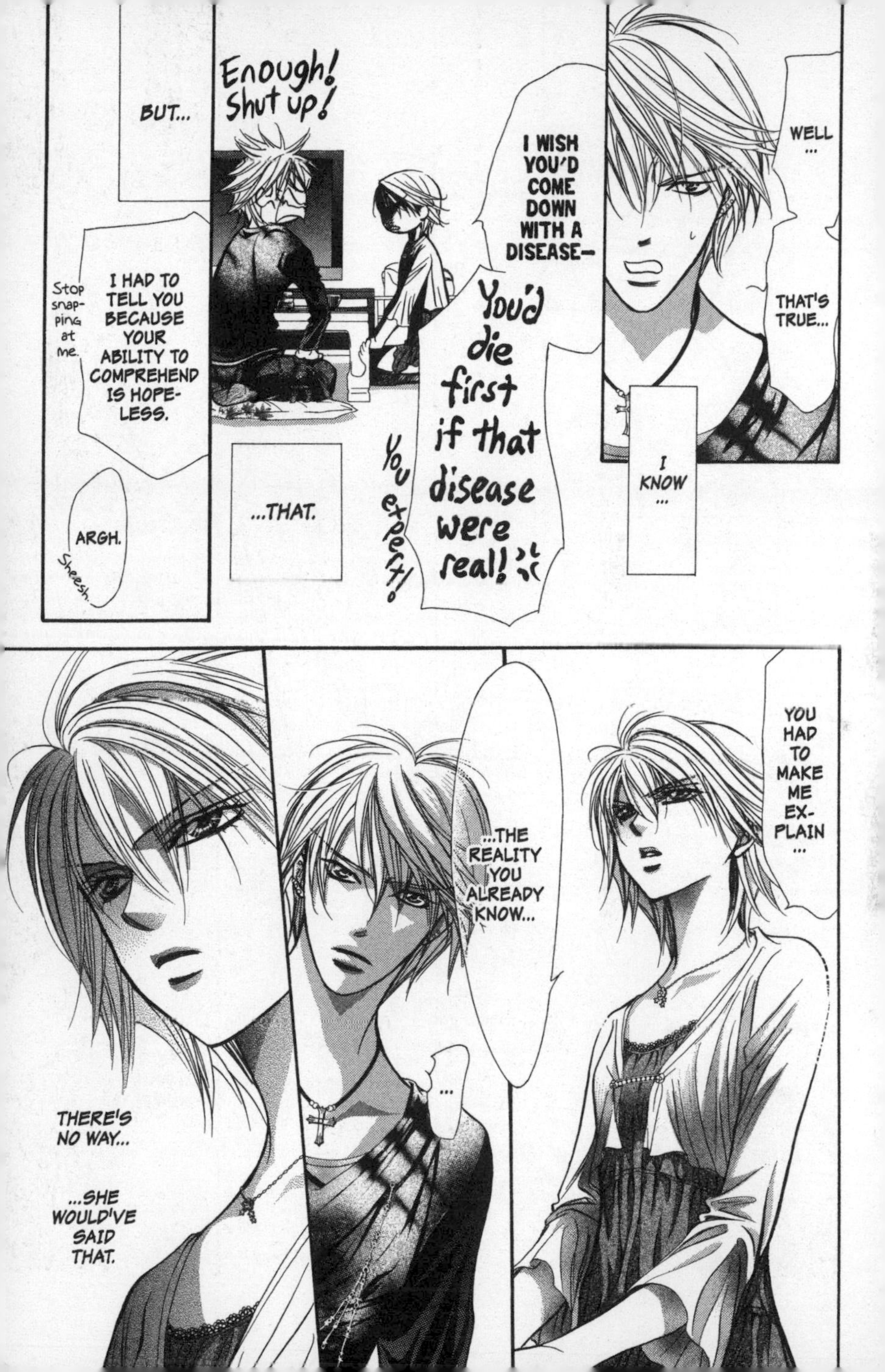
WELL ...
THAT'S TRUE...
I WISH YOU'D COME DOWN WITH A DISEASE—
I KNOW ...
You'd die first if that disease were real!
You expert!
Enough! Shut up!
...THAT.
BUT...
I HAD TO TELL YOU BECAUSE YOUR ABILITY TO COMPREHEND IS HOPELESS.
Stop snapping at me.
ARGH.
Sheesh.
YOU HAD TO MAKE ME EXPLAIN ...
...THE REALITY YOU ALREADY KNOW...
...
THERE'S NO WAY...
...SHE WOULD'VE SAID THAT.

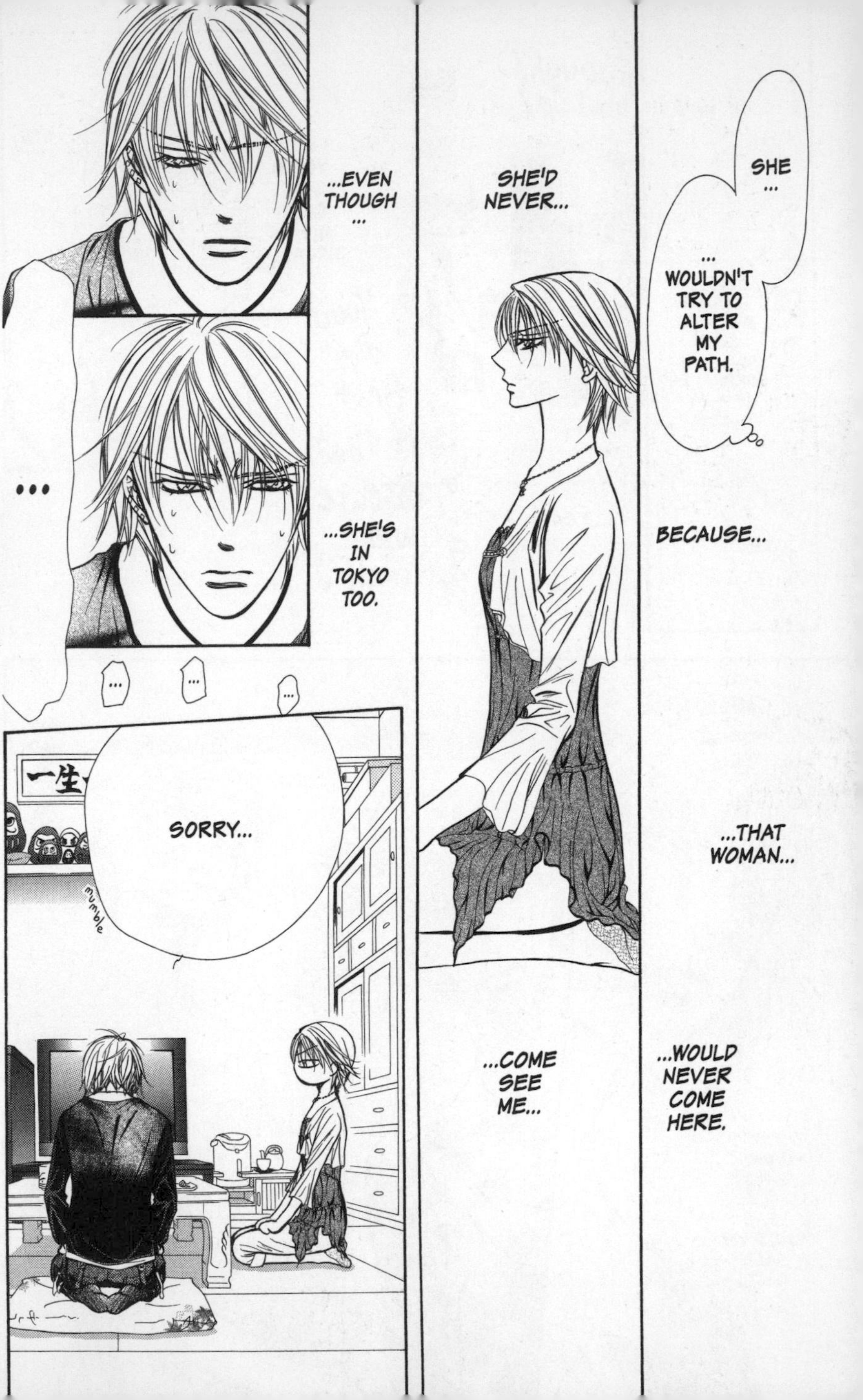
SHE ... ... WOULDN'T TRY TO ALTER MY PATH.
BECAUSE...
...THAT WOMAN...
...WOULD NEVER COME HERE.
SHE'D NEVER...
...COME SEE ME...
...EVEN THOUGH ...
...SHE'S IN TOKYO TOO.
...
...
...
...
SORRY...
mumble

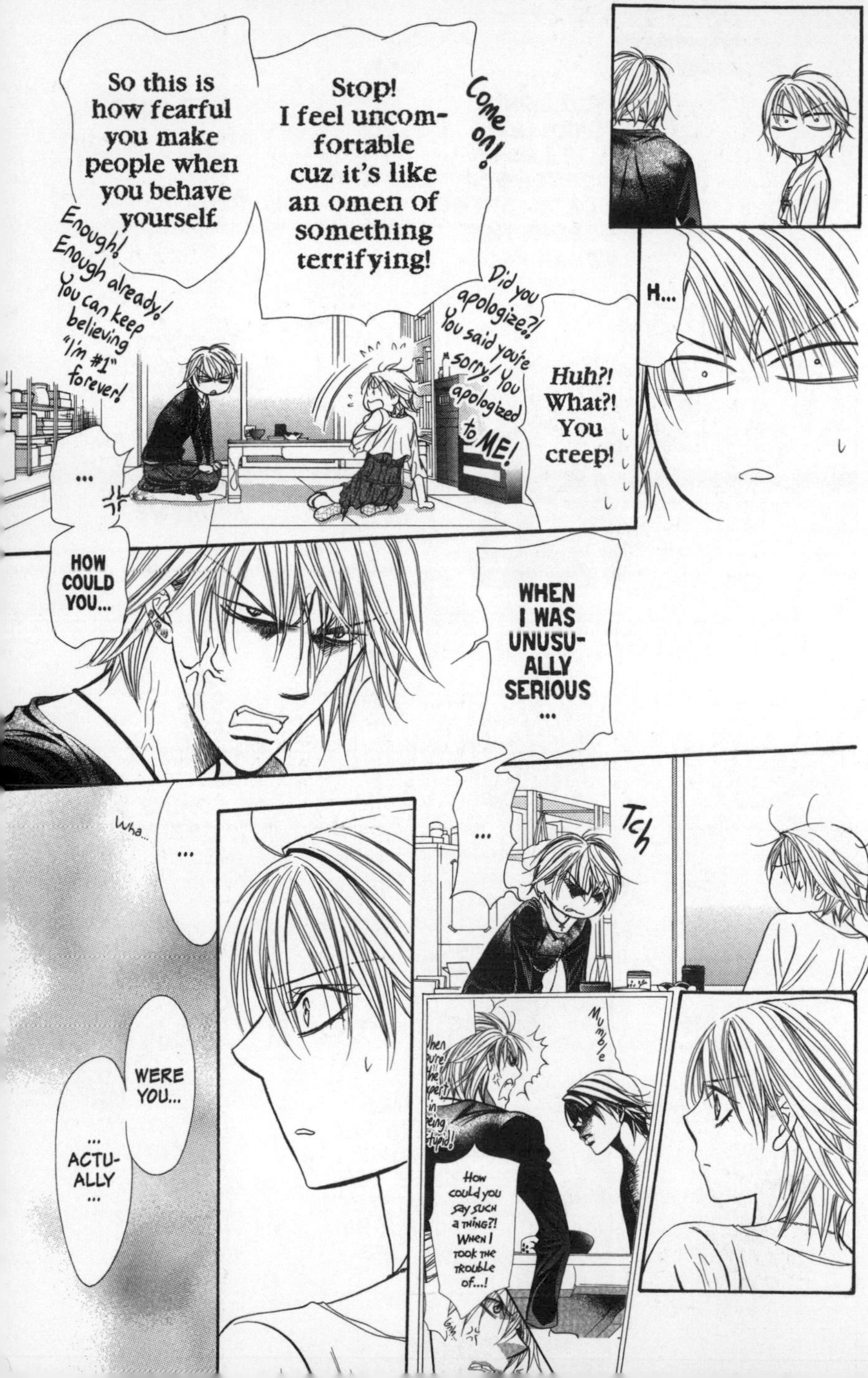
H...
Come on!
Stop! I feel uncomfortable cuz it's like an omen of something terrifying!
So this is how fearful you make people when you behave yourself.
Did you apologize?! You said you're sorry! You apologized to ME!
Huh?! What?! You creep!
Enough! Enough already! You can keep believing "I'm #1" forever!
...
WHEN I WAS UNUSUALLY SERIOUS...
HOW COULD YOU...
...
Tch
Mumble
When you're the expert in being stupid!
How could you say such a thing?! When I took the trouble of...!
Wha...
...
WERE YOU...
...ACTUALLY...

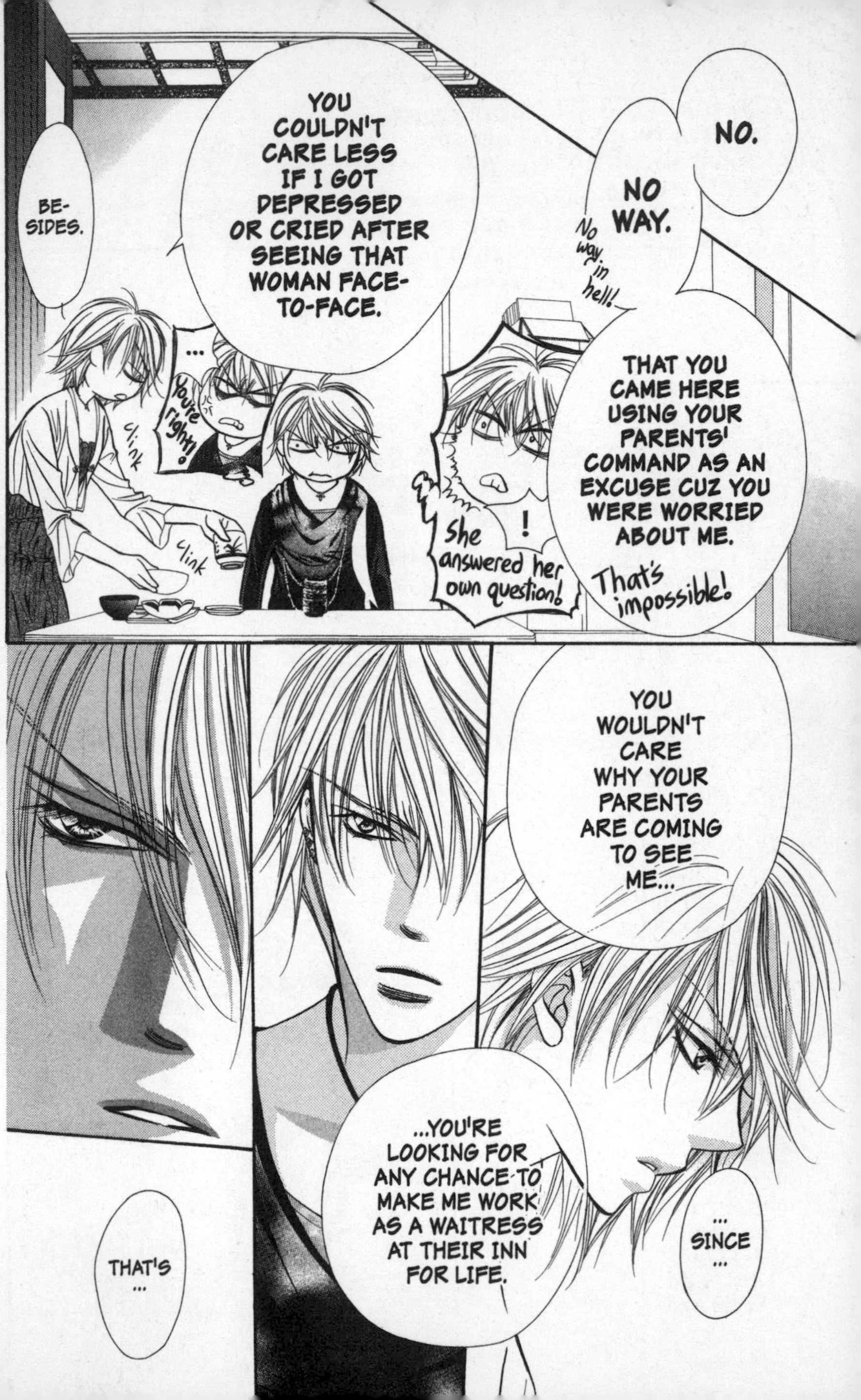

NO.
NO WAY.
No way in hell!
YOU COULDN'T CARE LESS IF I GOT DEPRESSED OR CRIED AFTER SEEING THAT WOMAN FACE-TO-FACE.
BE-SIDES.
THAT YOU CAME HERE USING YOUR PARENTS' COMMAND AS AN EXCUSE CUZ YOU WERE WORRIED ABOUT ME.
That's impossible!
!
She answered her own question!
...
You're right!!
clink
clink
YOU WOULDN'T CARE WHY YOUR PARENTS ARE COMING TO SEE ME...
...SINCE...
...YOU'RE LOOKING FOR ANY CHANCE TO MAKE ME WORK AS A WAITRESS AT THEIR INN FOR LIFE.
THAT'S...

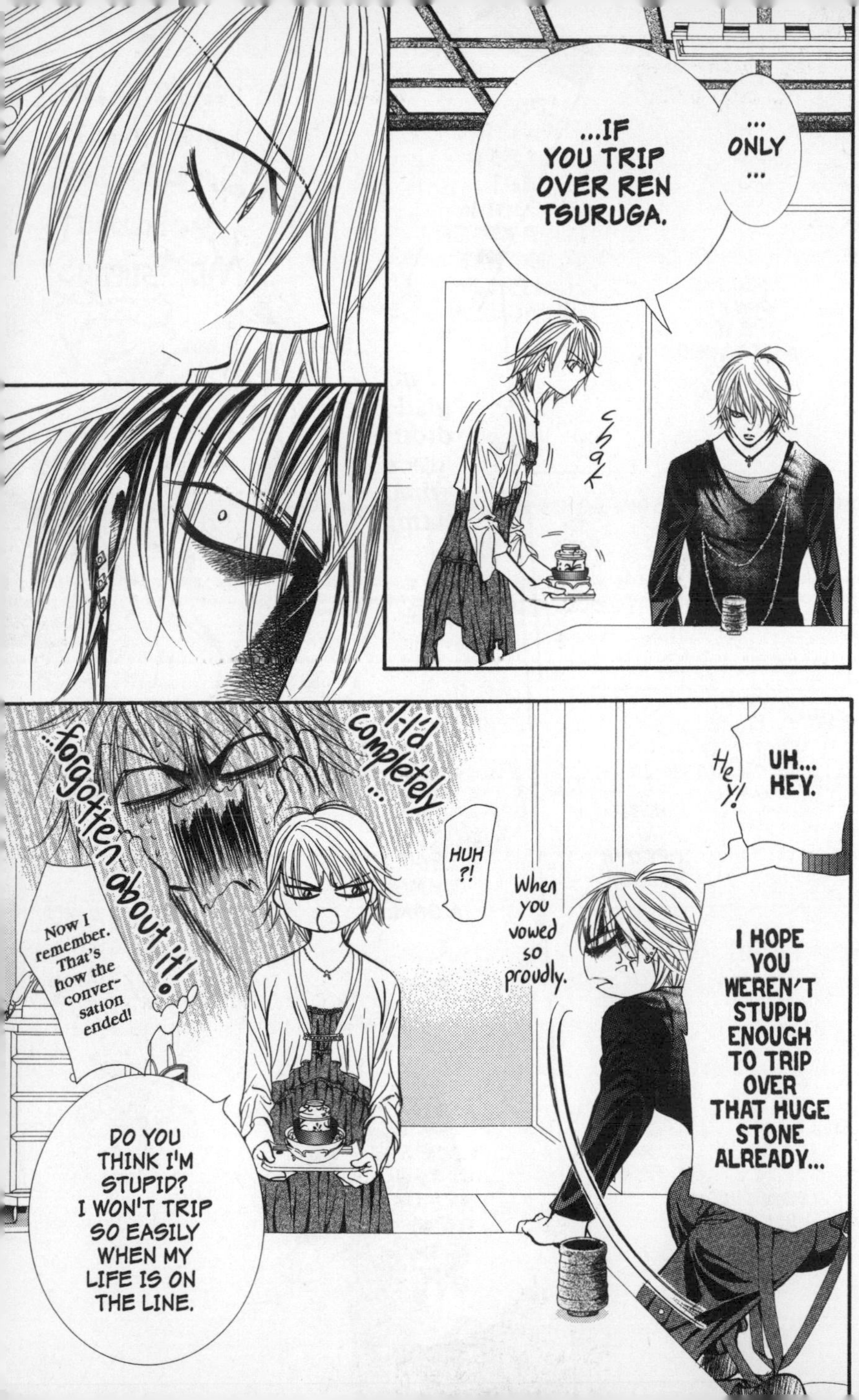

... ONLY ...
...IF YOU TRIP OVER REN TSURUGA.
chak
UH... HEY.
Hey!
I HOPE YOU WEREN'T STUPID ENOUGH TO TRIP OVER THAT HUGE STONE ALREADY...
When you vowed so proudly.
HUH ?!
I-I'd completely...
...forgotten about it!
Now I remember. That's how the conver-sation ended!
DO YOU THINK I'M STUPID? I WON'T TRIP SO EASILY WHEN MY LIFE IS ON THE LINE.

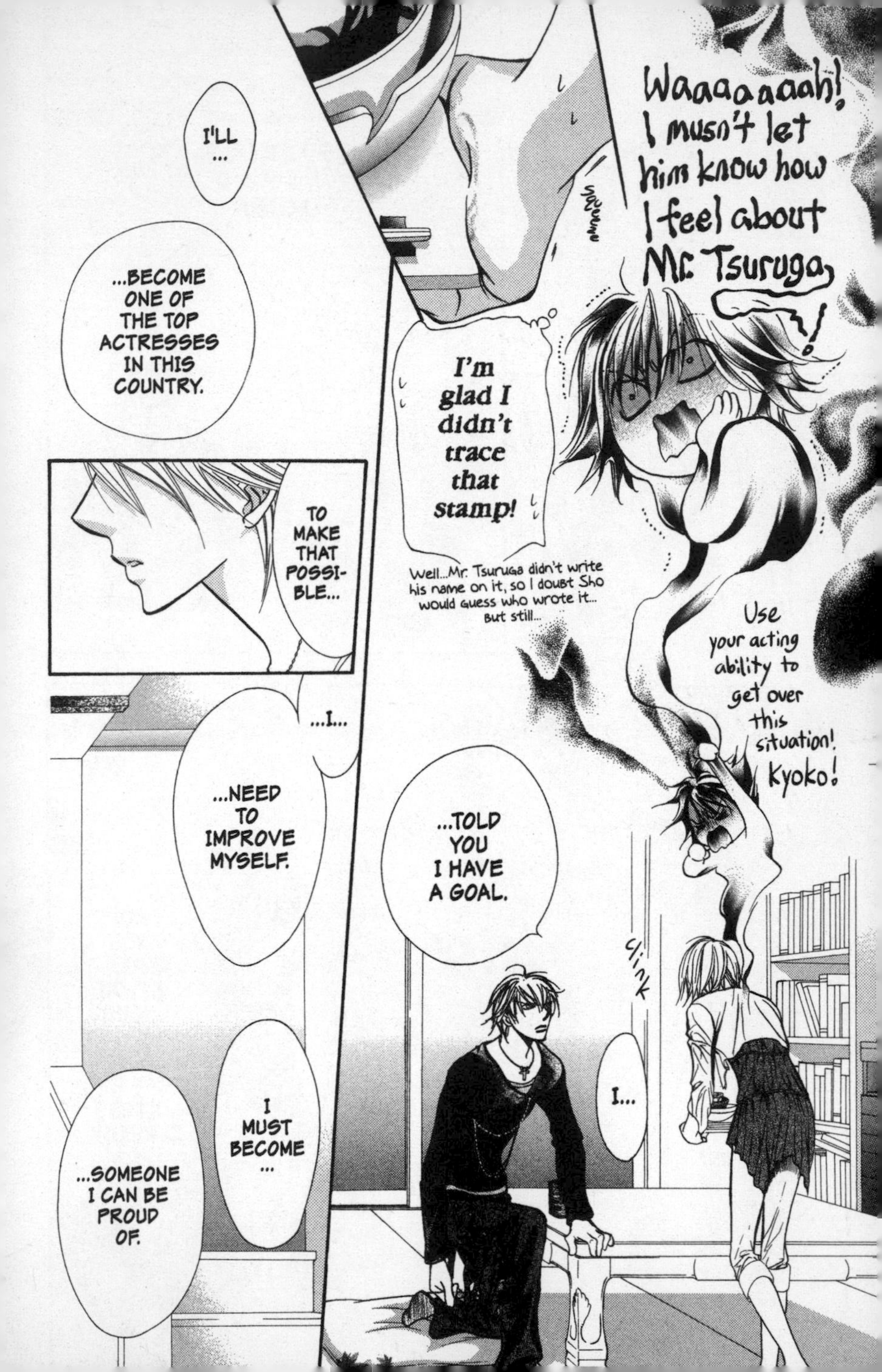
Waaaaaaah! I mustn't let him know how I feel about Mr. Tsuruga!
I'm glad I didn't trace that stamp!
Well...Mr. Tsuruga didn't write his name on it, so I doubt Sho would guess who wrote it... but still...
Use your acting ability to get over this situation! Kyoko!
clink
I...
...TOLD YOU I HAVE A GOAL.
I'LL ...
...BECOME ONE OF THE TOP ACTRESSES IN THIS COUNTRY.
TO MAKE THAT POSSIBLE...
...I...
...NEED TO IMPROVE MYSELF.
I MUST BECOME ...
...SOMEONE I CAN BE PROUD OF.

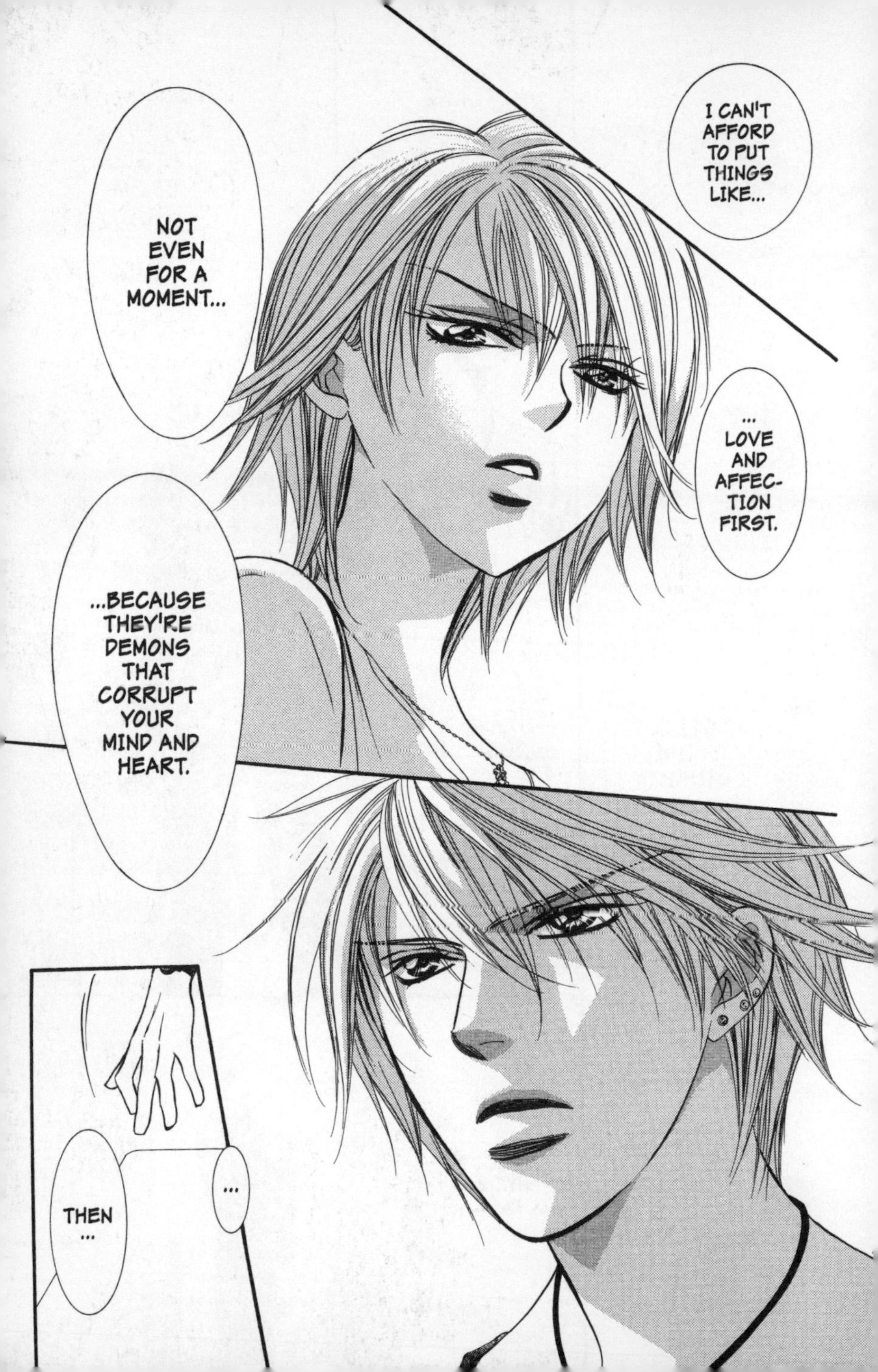
I CAN'T AFFORD TO PUT THINGS LIKE...
...LOVE AND AFFECTION FIRST.
NOT EVEN FOR A MOMENT...
...BECAUSE THEY'RE DEMONS THAT CORRUPT YOUR MIND AND HEART.
...
THEN...

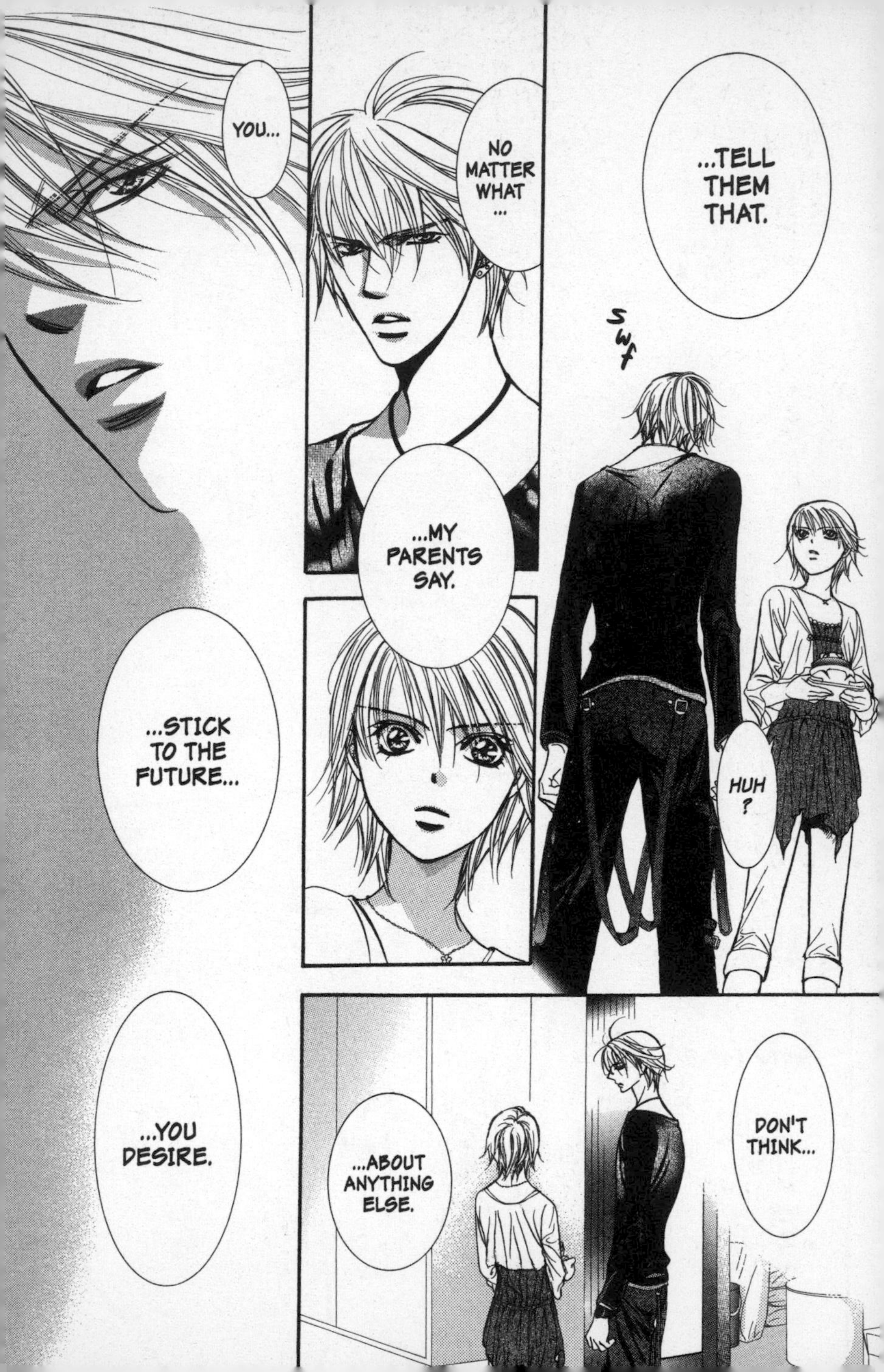
...TELL THEM THAT.
SWF
HUH?
NO MATTER WHAT...
...MY PARENTS SAY.
DON'T THINK...
...ABOUT ANYTHING ELSE.
YOU...
...STICK TO THE FUTURE...
...YOU DESIRE.

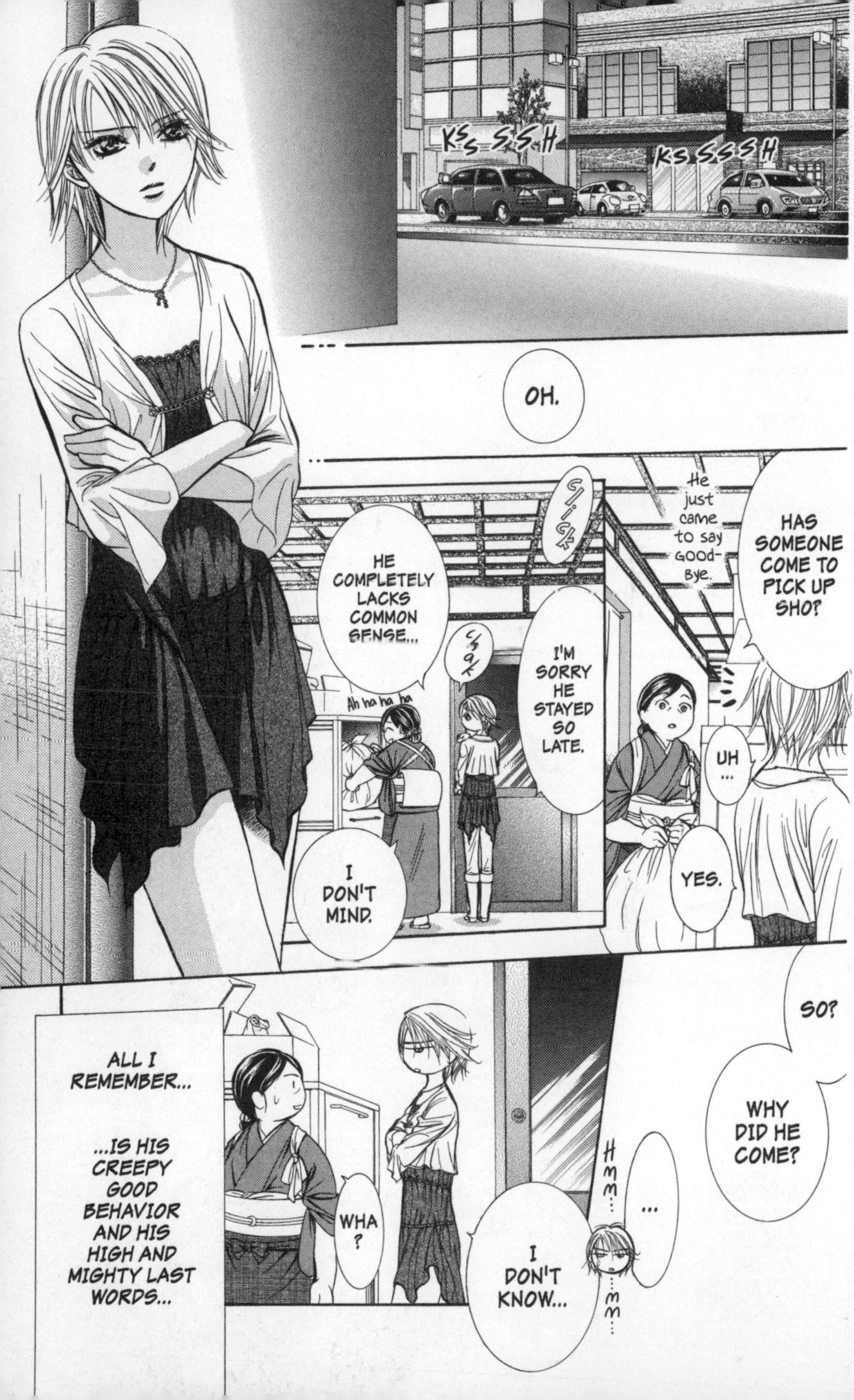
KSSSSH
KSSSSH
OH.
HAS SOMEONE COME TO PICK UP SHO?
He just came to say good-bye.
UH...
YES.
click
HE COMPLETELY LACKS COMMON SENSE...
I'M SORRY HE STAYED SO LATE.
creak
Ah ha ha ha
I DON'T MIND.
SO?
WHY DID HE COME?
...
Hmm... ...mm...
I DON'T KNOW...
WHA?
ALL I REMEMBER...
...IS HIS CREEPY GOOD BEHAVIOR AND HIS HIGH AND MIGHTY LAST WORDS...

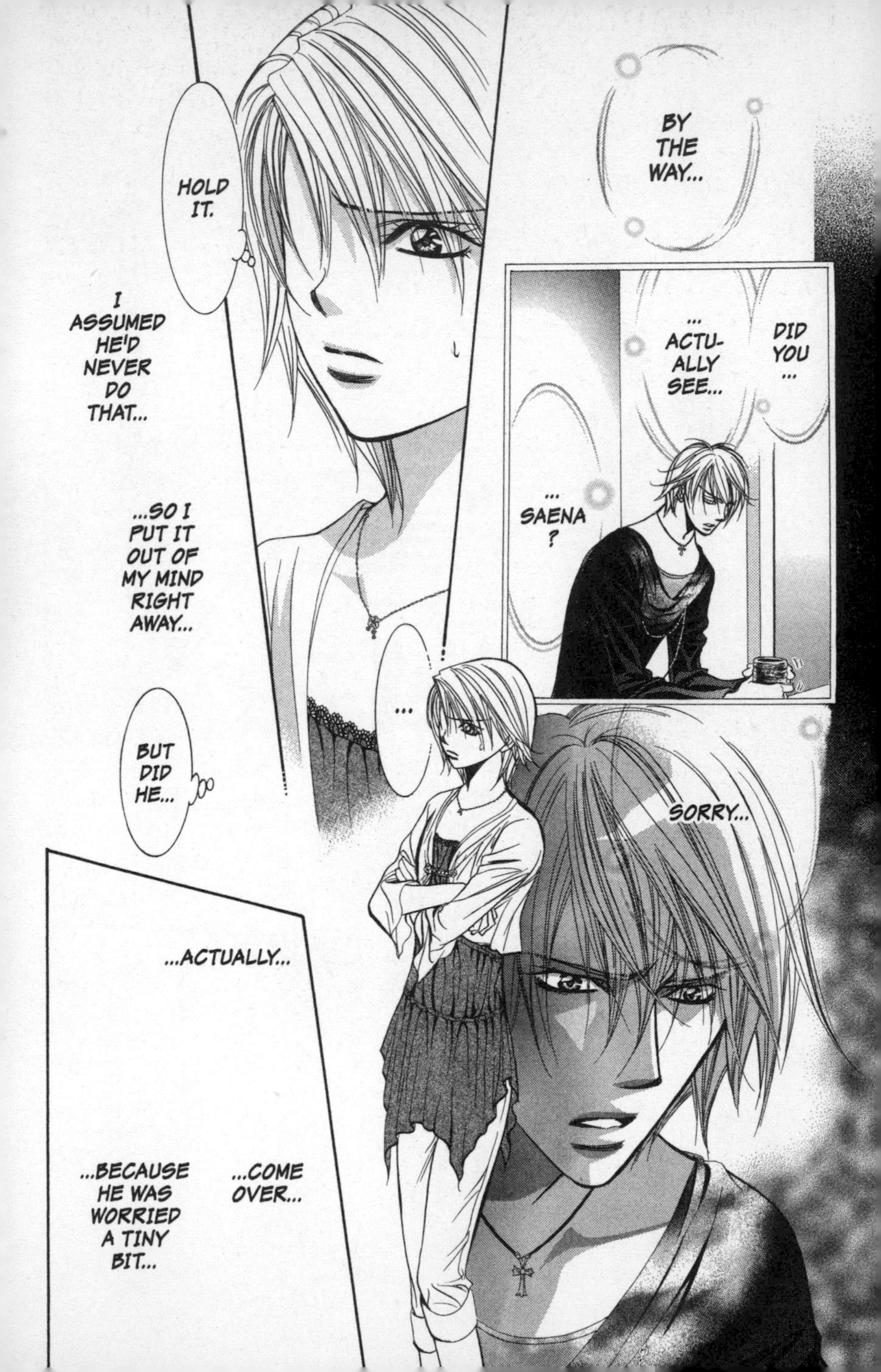

BY THE WAY...
DID YOU ...
... ACTU-ALLY SEE...
... SAENA ?
HOLD IT.
I ASSUMED HE'D NEVER DO THAT...
...SO I PUT IT OUT OF MY MIND RIGHT AWAY...
...
BUT DID HE...
SORRY...
...ACTUALLY...
...COME OVER...
...BECAUSE HE WAS WORRIED A TINY BIT...

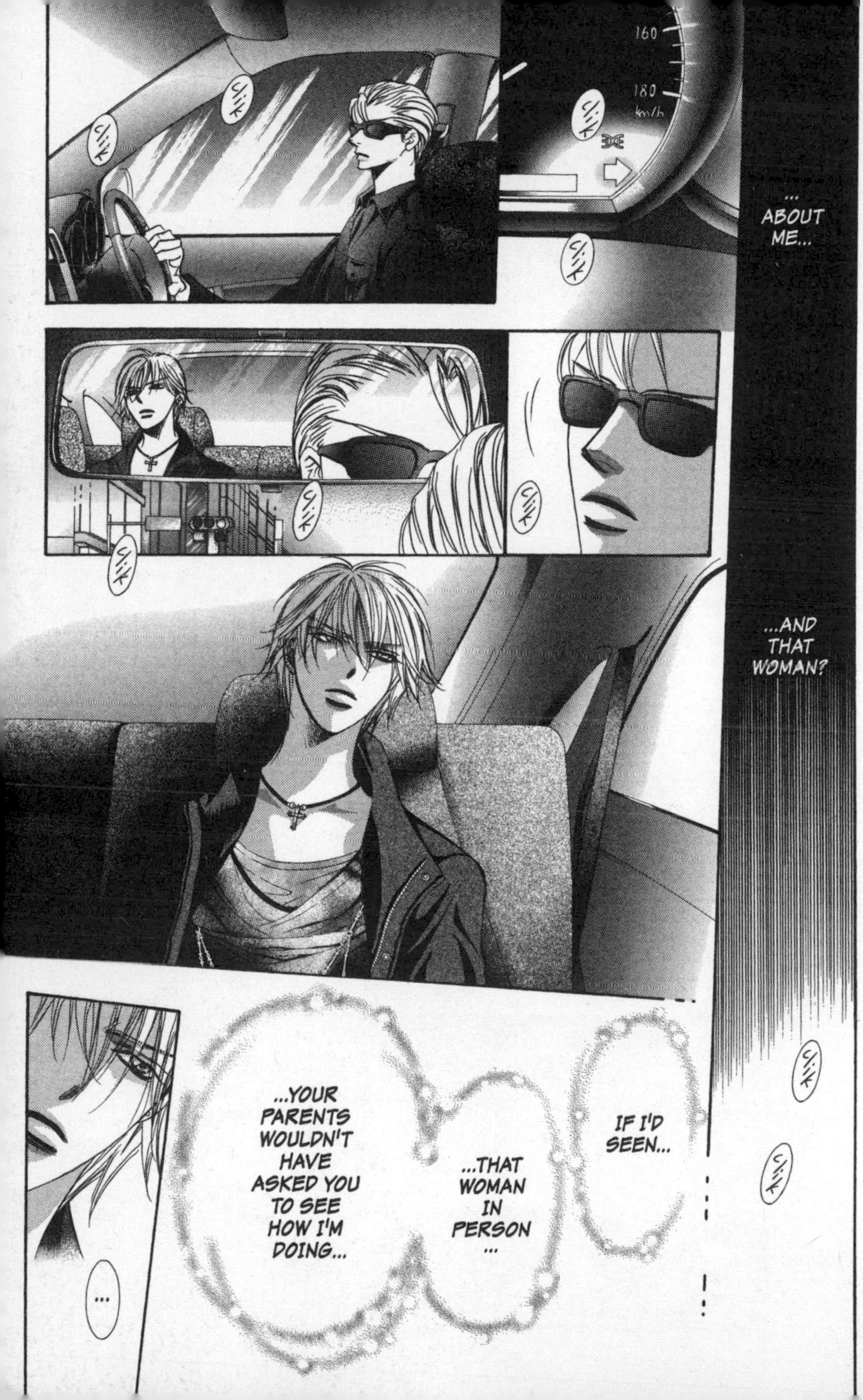

...ABOUT ME...
160
180
km/h
click
click
click
click
click
click
click
click
...AND THAT WOMAN?
click
click
IF I'D SEEN...
...THAT WOMAN IN PERSON...
...YOUR PARENTS WOULDN'T HAVE ASKED YOU TO SEE HOW I'M DOING...
...

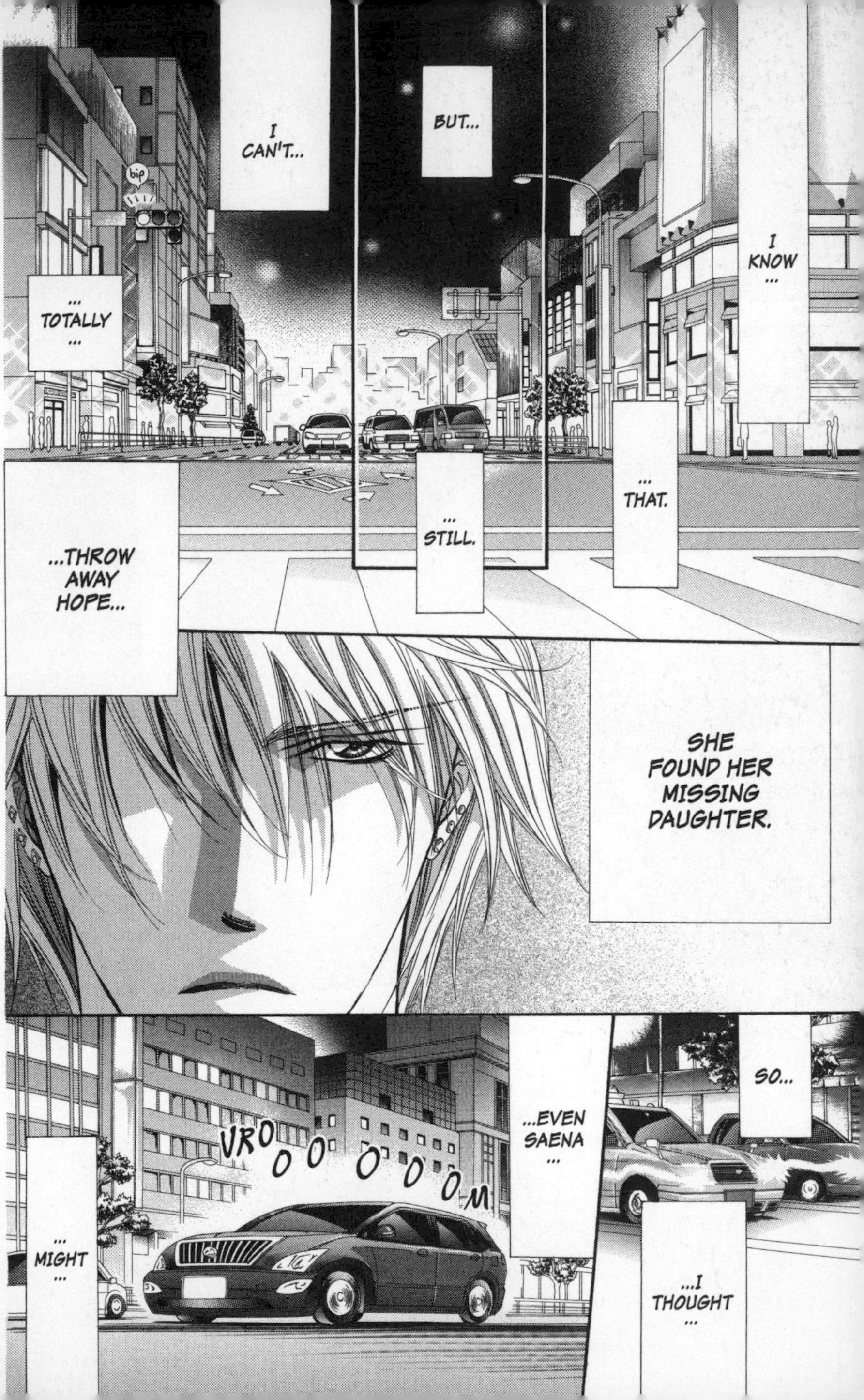

I KNOW...
...THAT.
BUT...
...STILL.
I CAN'T...
...TOTALLY...
...THROW AWAY HOPE...
bip
SHE FOUND HER MISSING DAUGHTER.
SO...
...I THOUGHT...
...EVEN SAENA...
VROOOOOOOM
...MIGHT...

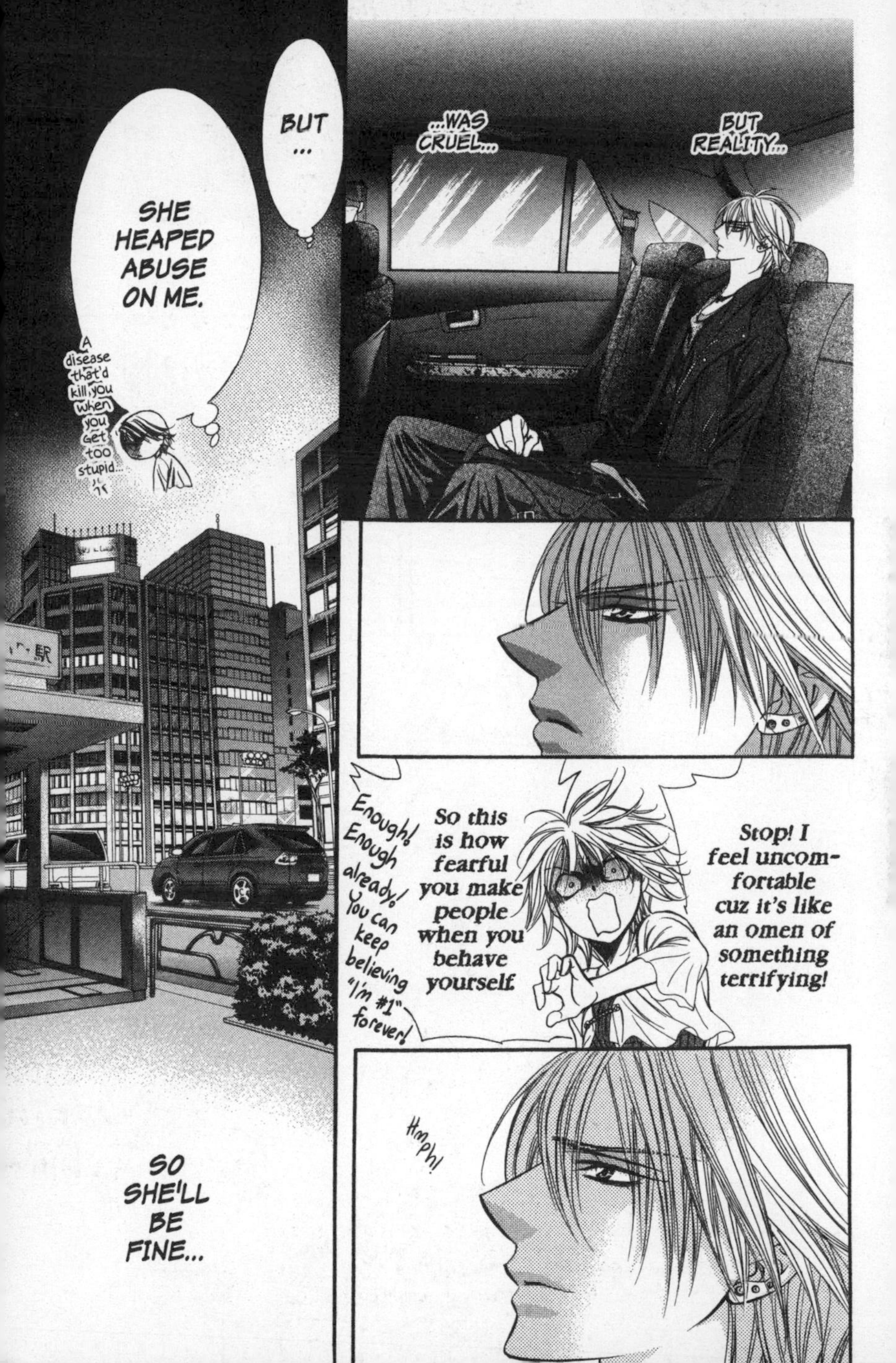
BUT REALITY...
...WAS CRUEL...
Stop! I feel uncom-fortable cuz it's like an omen of something terrifying!
So this is how fearful you make people when you behave yourself.
Enough! Enough already! You can keep believing "I'm #1" forever!
Hmph!
BUT ...
SHE HEAPED ABUSE ON ME.
A disease that'd kill you when you get too stupid...
SO SHE'LL BE FINE...

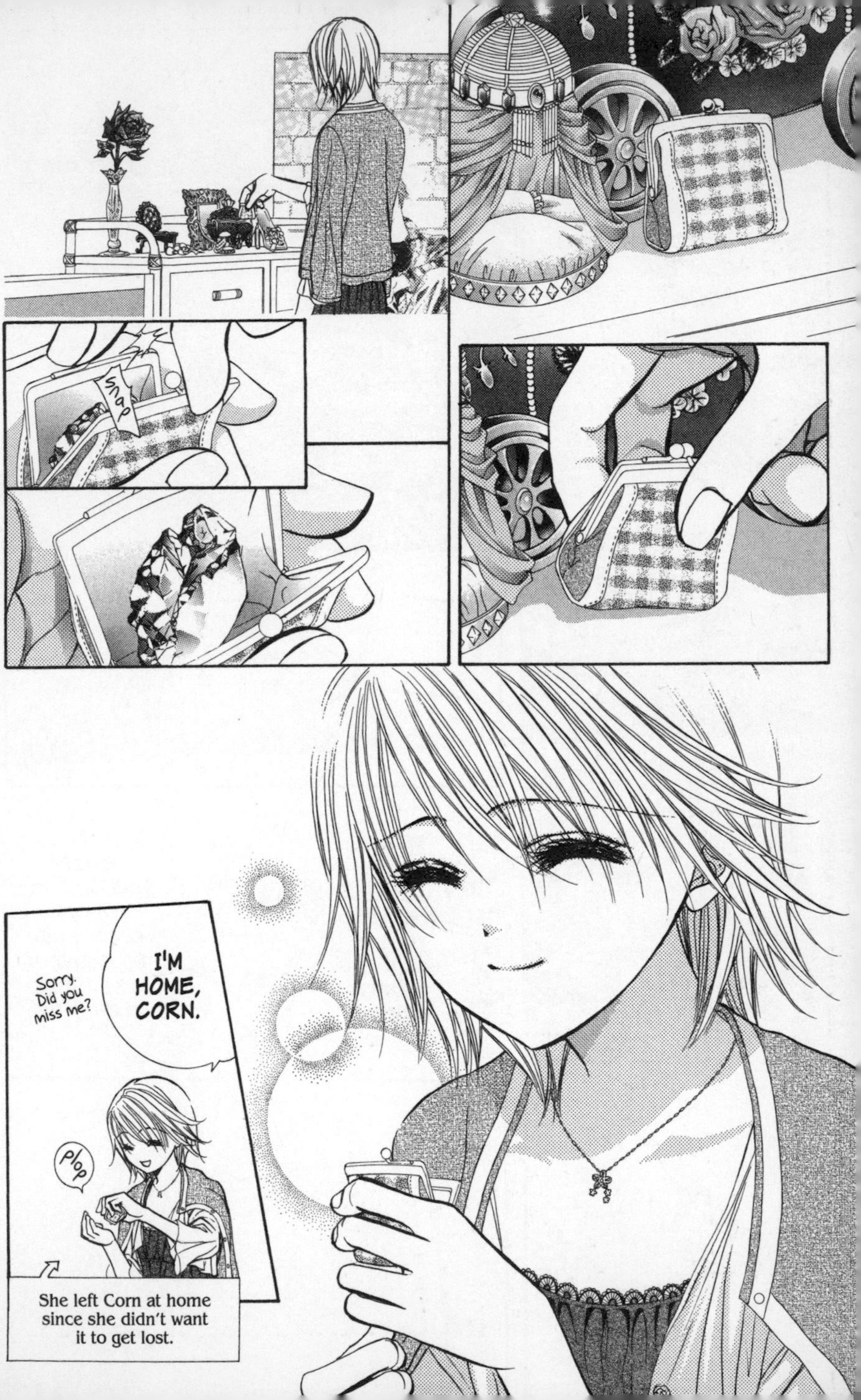
snap
I'M HOME, CORN.
Sorry. Did you miss me?
plop
She left Corn at home since she didn't want it to get lost.

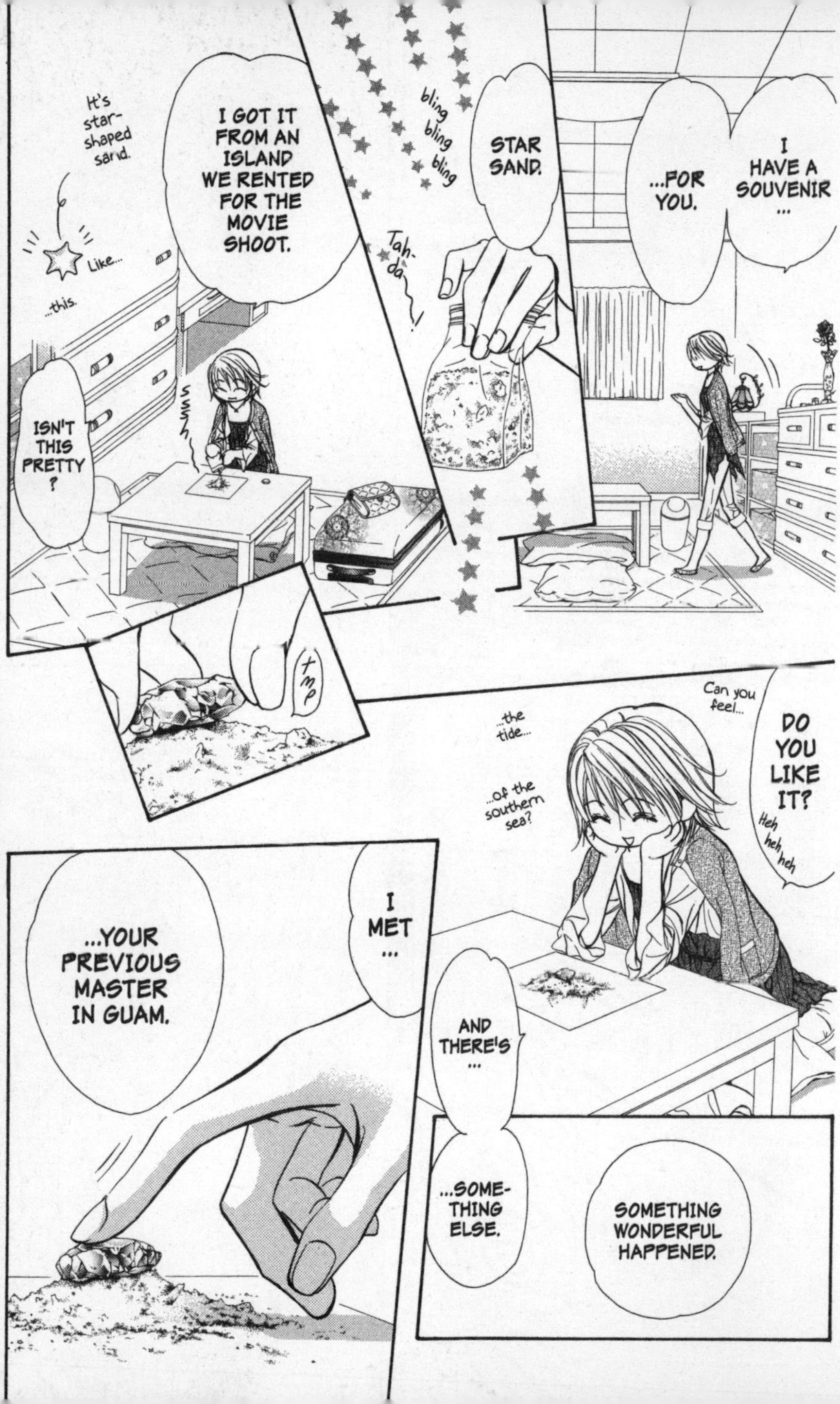
I HAVE A SOUVENIR...
...FOR YOU.
STAR SAND.
bling bling bling
Tah-da
I GOT IT FROM AN ISLAND WE RENTED FOR THE MOVIE SHOOT.
It's star-shaped sand.
Like...
...this.
ISN'T THIS PRETTY?
ssh
tmp
DO YOU LIKE IT?
Heh heh heh
Can you feel...
...the tide...
...of the southern sea?
AND THERE'S...
...SOME-THING ELSE.
SOMETHING WONDERFUL HAPPENED.
I MET...
...YOUR PREVIOUS MASTER IN GUAM.

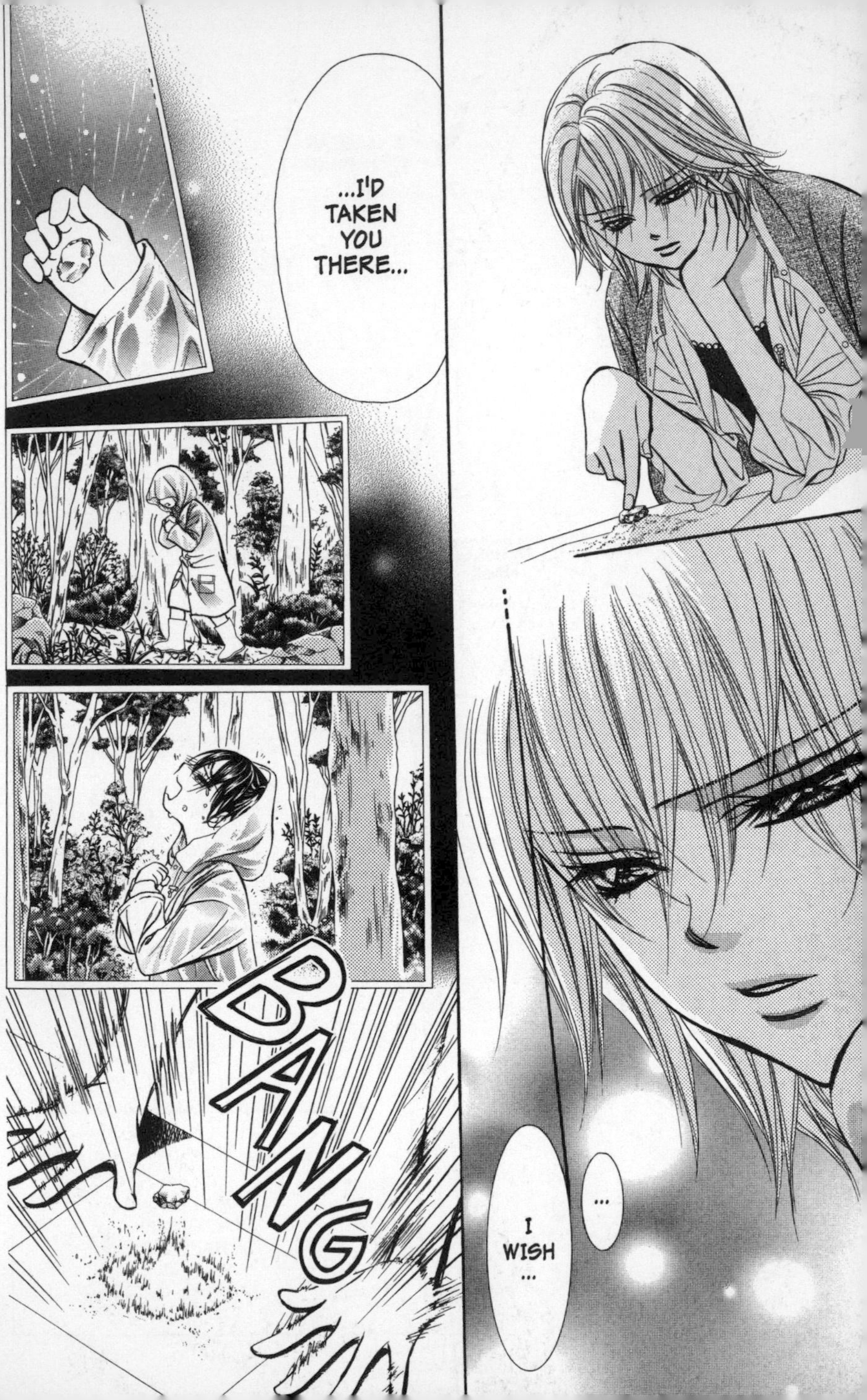
...
I WISH ...
...I'D TAKEN YOU THERE...
BANG

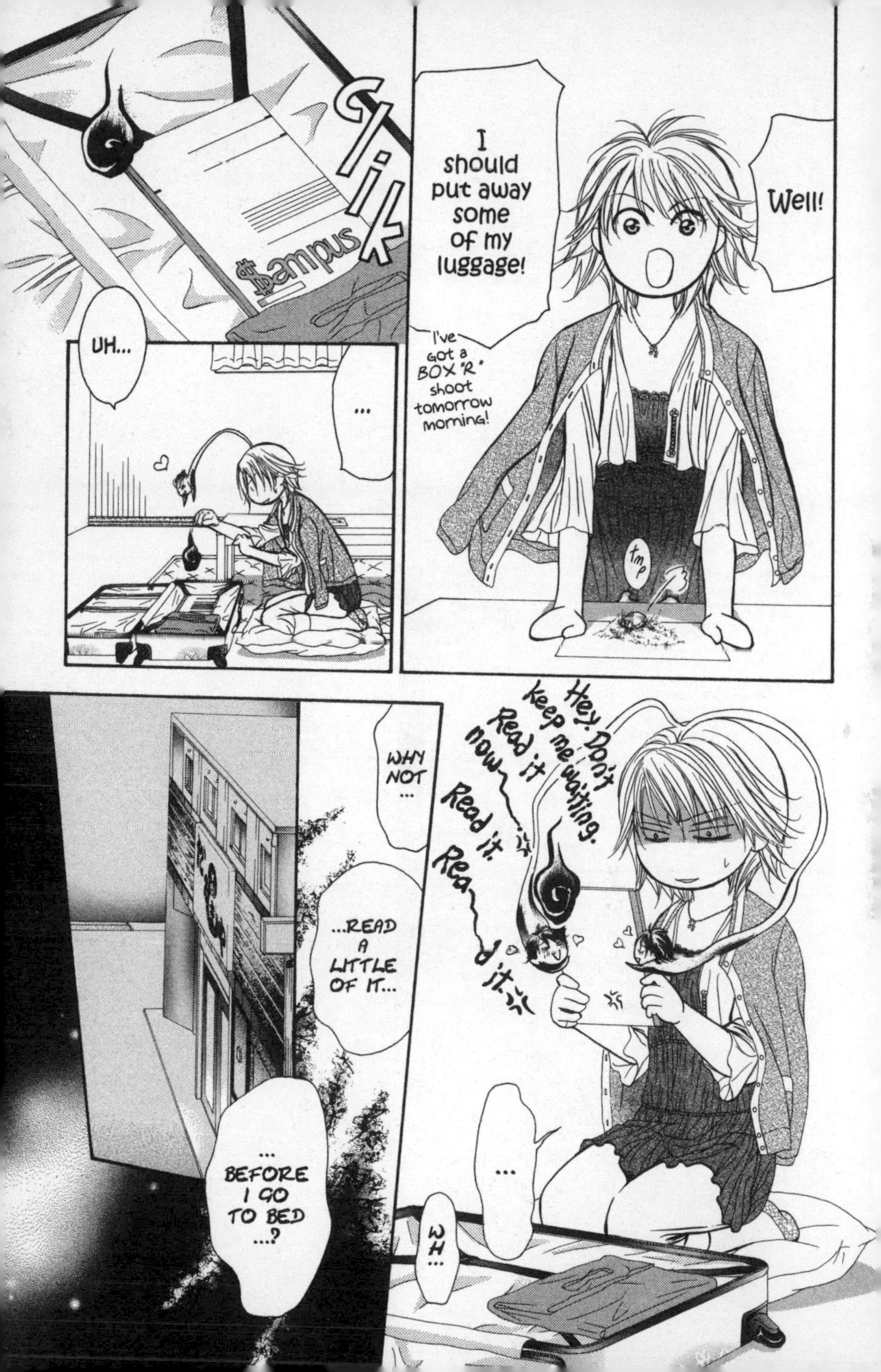
Well!
I should put away some of my luggage!
I've got a BOX "R" shoot tomorrow morning!
tmp
Clik
$ampus
UH...
...
Hey. Don't keep me waiting. Read it now~
Read it. Read it. Rea~d it.
...
WH...
WHY NOT ...
...READ A LITTLE OF IT...
... BEFORE I GO TO BED ...?

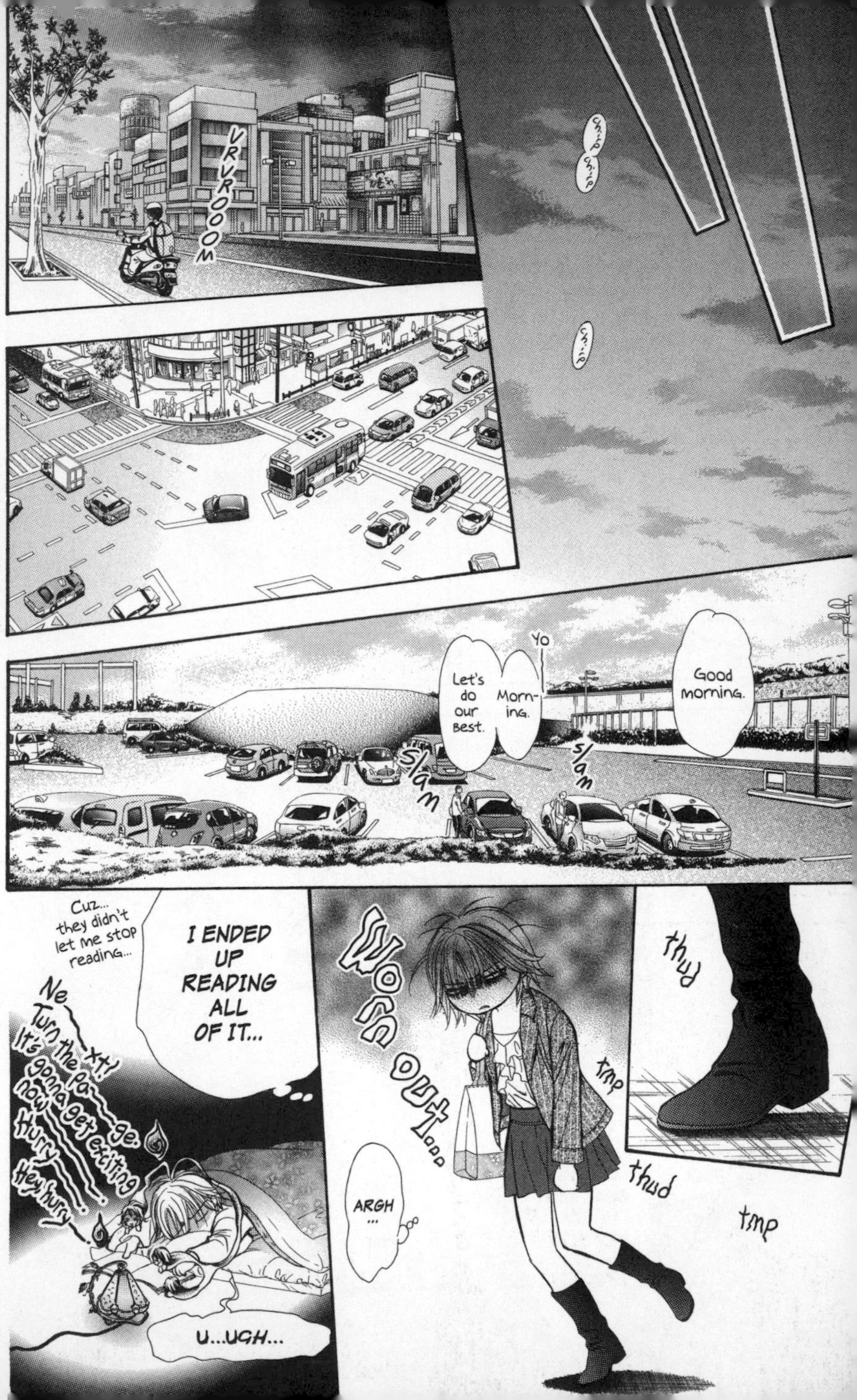
chirp chirp
chirp
VRVROOOOM
Good morning.
slam
Yo
Morning.
Let's do our best.
slam
thud
tmp
thud
tmp
Worn out...
ARGH...
I ENDED UP READING ALL OF IT...
Cuz... they didn't let me stop reading...
Ne~xt! Turn the pa~ge. It's gonna get exciting now. Hurry. Hey hurry.
U...UGH...

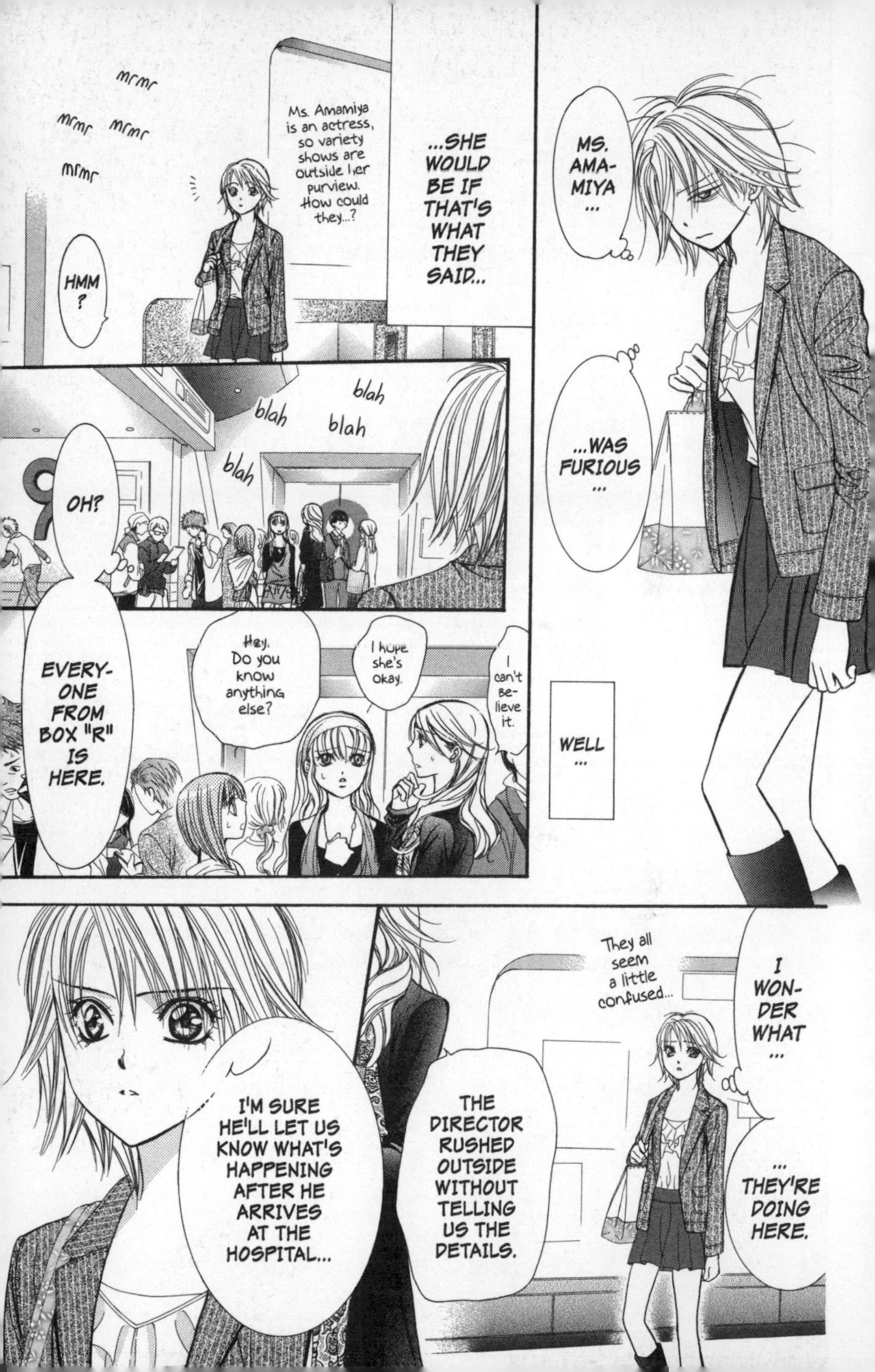
MS. AMAMIYA ...
...WAS FURIOUS ...
WELL ...
...SHE WOULD BE IF THAT'S WHAT THEY SAID...
Ms. Amamiya is an actress, so variety shows are outside her purview. How could they...?
mrmr
mrmr
mrmr
mrmr
HMM ?
blah
blah
blah
blah
OH?
I can't be-lieve it.
I hope she's okay.
Hey. Do you know anything else?
EVERY-ONE FROM BOX "R" IS HERE.
I WON-DER WHAT ...
... THEY'RE DOING HERE.
They all seem a little confused...
THE DIRECTOR RUSHED OUTSIDE WITHOUT TELLING US THE DETAILS.
I'M SURE HE'LL LET US KNOW WHAT'S HAPPENING AFTER HE ARRIVES AT THE HOSPITAL...

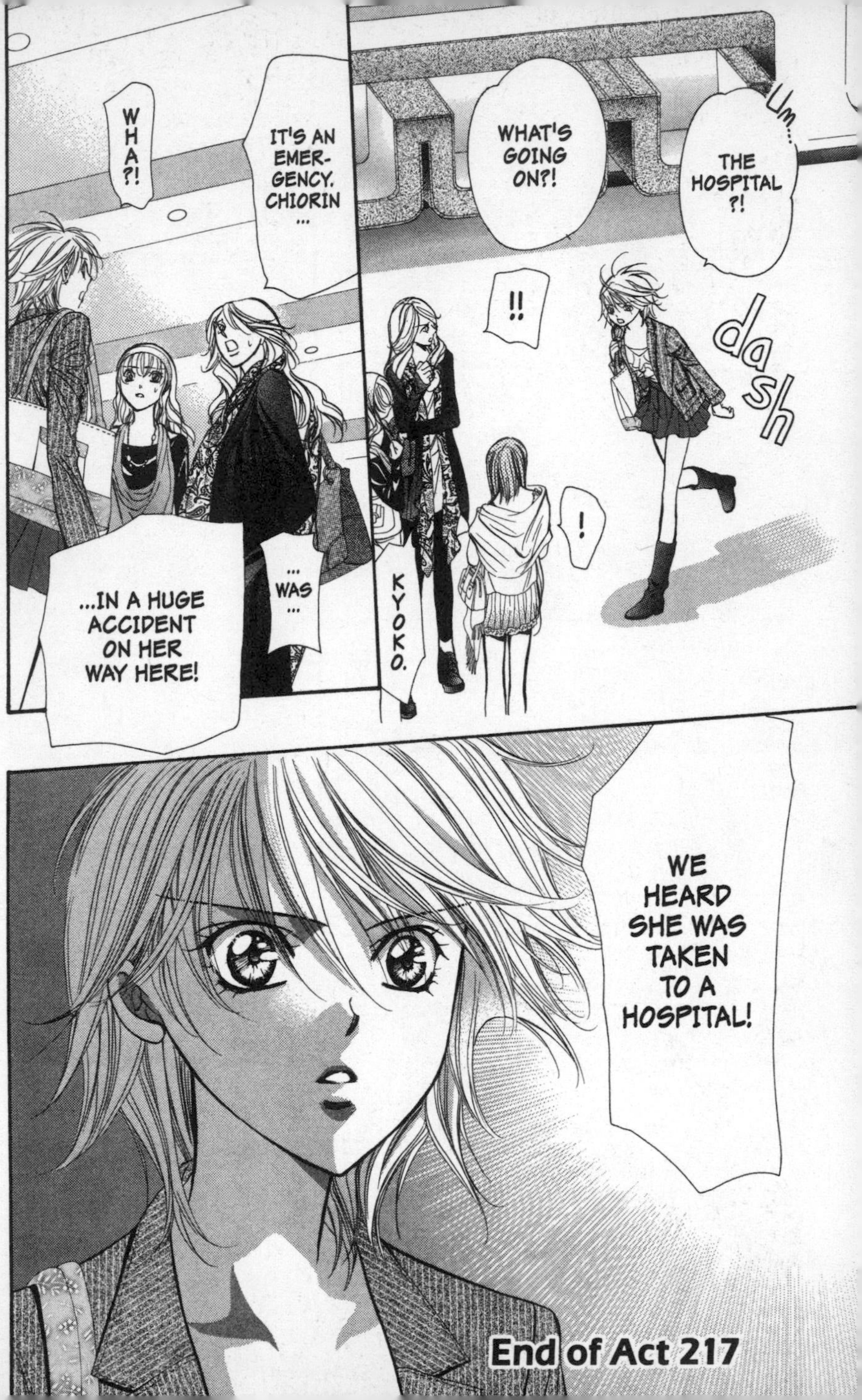
Um...
THE HOSPITAL ?!
WHAT'S GOING ON?!
!!
dash
!
KYOKO.
IT'S AN EMER-GENCY. CHIORIN ...
WHA ?!
... WAS ...
...IN A HUGE ACCIDENT ON HER WAY HERE!
WE HEARD SHE WAS TAKEN TO A HOSPITAL!

End of Act 217

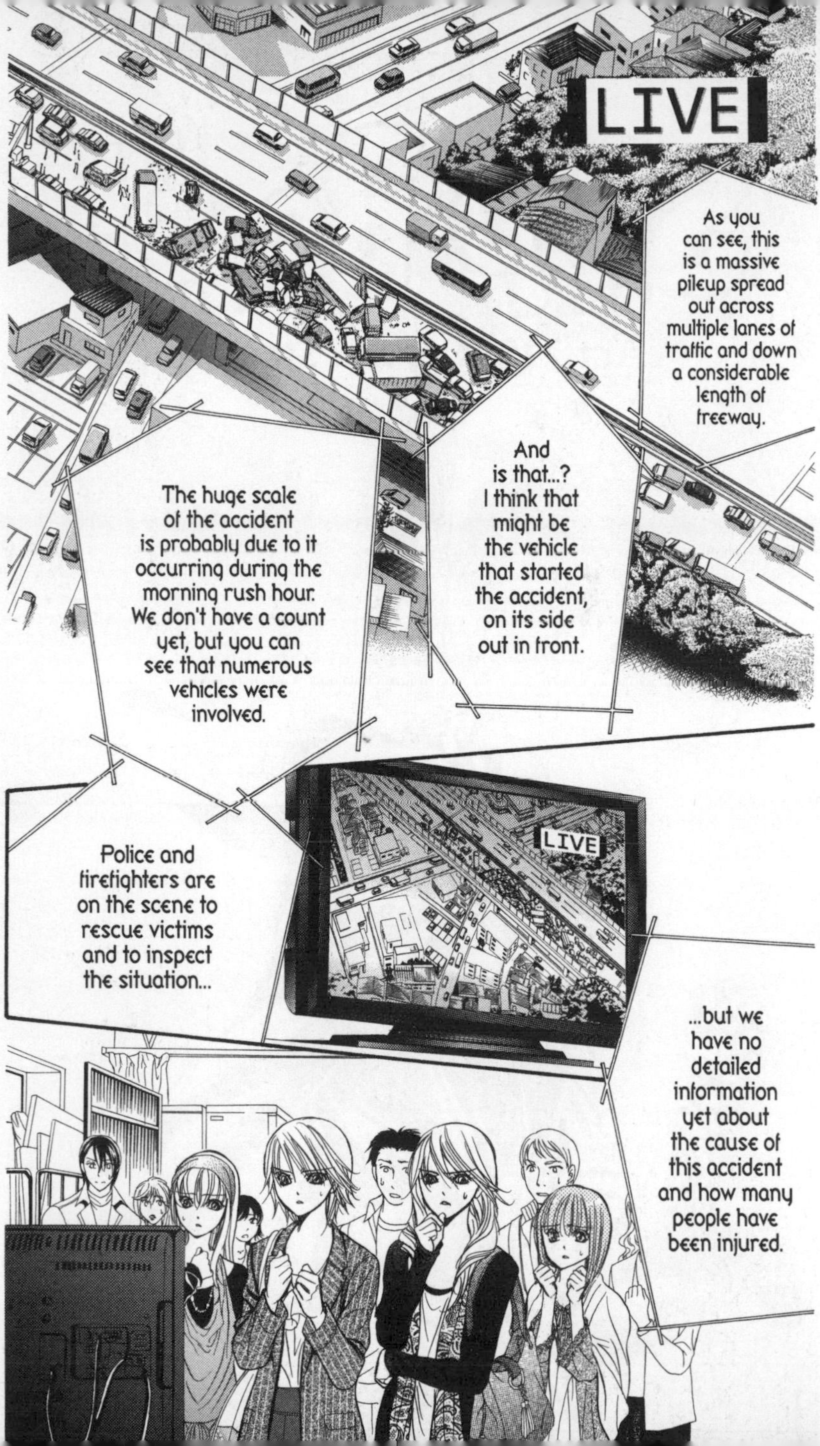
LIVE
As you can see, this is a massive pileup spread out across multiple lanes of traffic and down a considerable length of freeway.
And is that...? I think that might be the vehicle that started the accident, on its side out in front.
The huge scale of the accident is probably due to it occurring during the morning rush hour. We don't have a count yet, but you can see that numerous vehicles were involved.
LIVE
Police and firefighters are on the scene to rescue victims and to inspect the situation...
...but we have no detailed information yet about the cause of this accident and how many people have been injured.

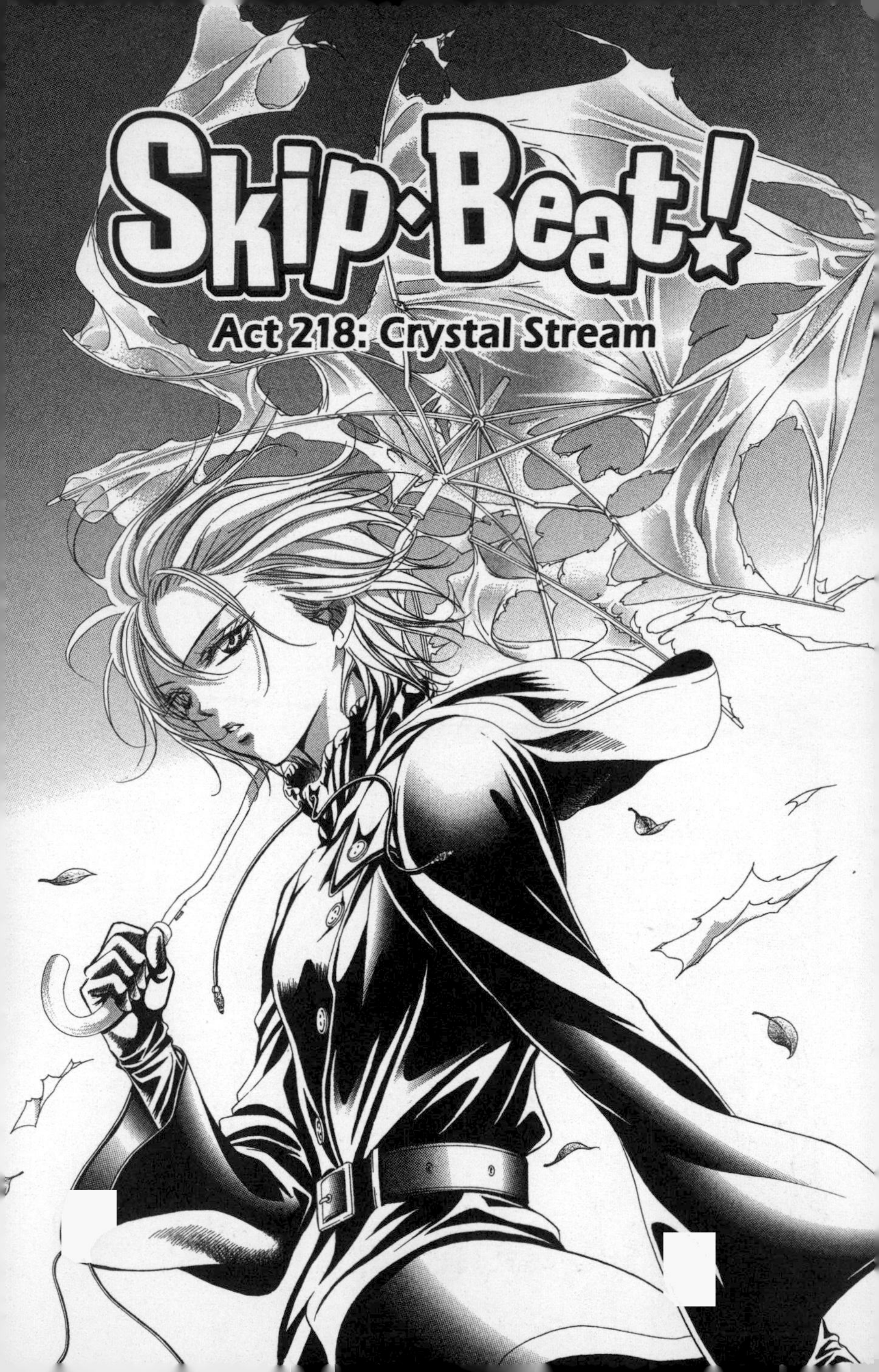
Skip·Beat!
Act 218: Crystal Stream

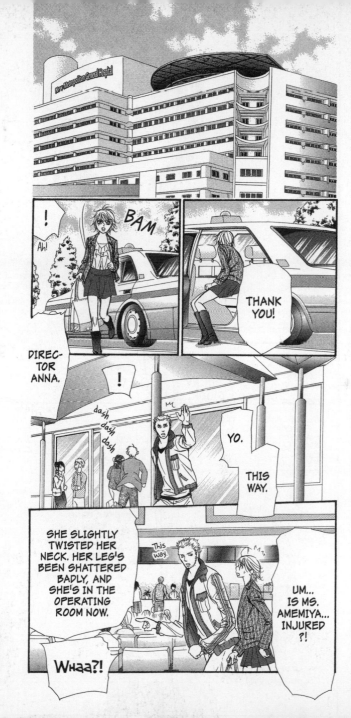

New Metropolitan General Hospital
THANK YOU!
!
Ah!
BAM
DIRECTOR ANNA.
!
YO.
THIS WAY.
dash dash dash
UM... IS MS. AMEMIYA... INJURED?!
This way.
SHE SLIGHTLY TWISTED HER NECK. HER LEG'S BEEN SHATTERED BADLY, AND SHE'S IN THE OPERATING ROOM NOW.
Whaa?!

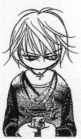

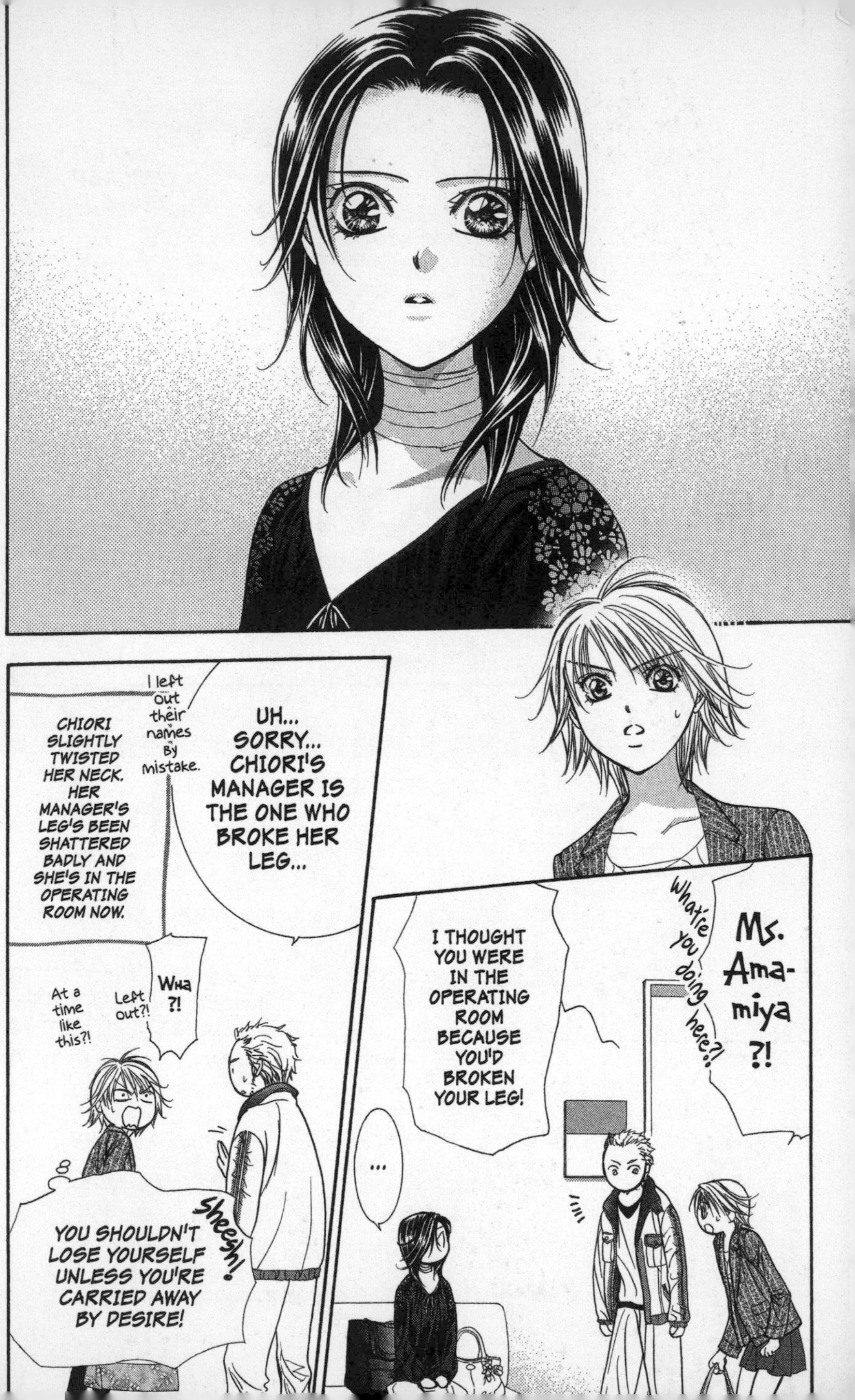
Ms. Amamiya ?!
What're you doing here?!
I THOUGHT YOU WERE IN THE OPERATING ROOM BECAUSE YOU'D BROKEN YOUR LEG!
...
UH... SORRY... CHIORI'S MANAGER IS THE ONE WHO BROKE HER LEG...
I left out their names By mistake.
CHIORI SLIGHTLY TWISTED HER NECK. HER MANAGER'S LEG'S BEEN SHATTERED BADLY AND SHE'S IN THE OPERATING ROOM NOW.
Wha ?!
Left out?!
At a time like this?!
Sheesh!
YOU SHOULDN'T LOSE YOURSELF UNLESS YOU'RE CARRIED AWAY BY DESIRE!

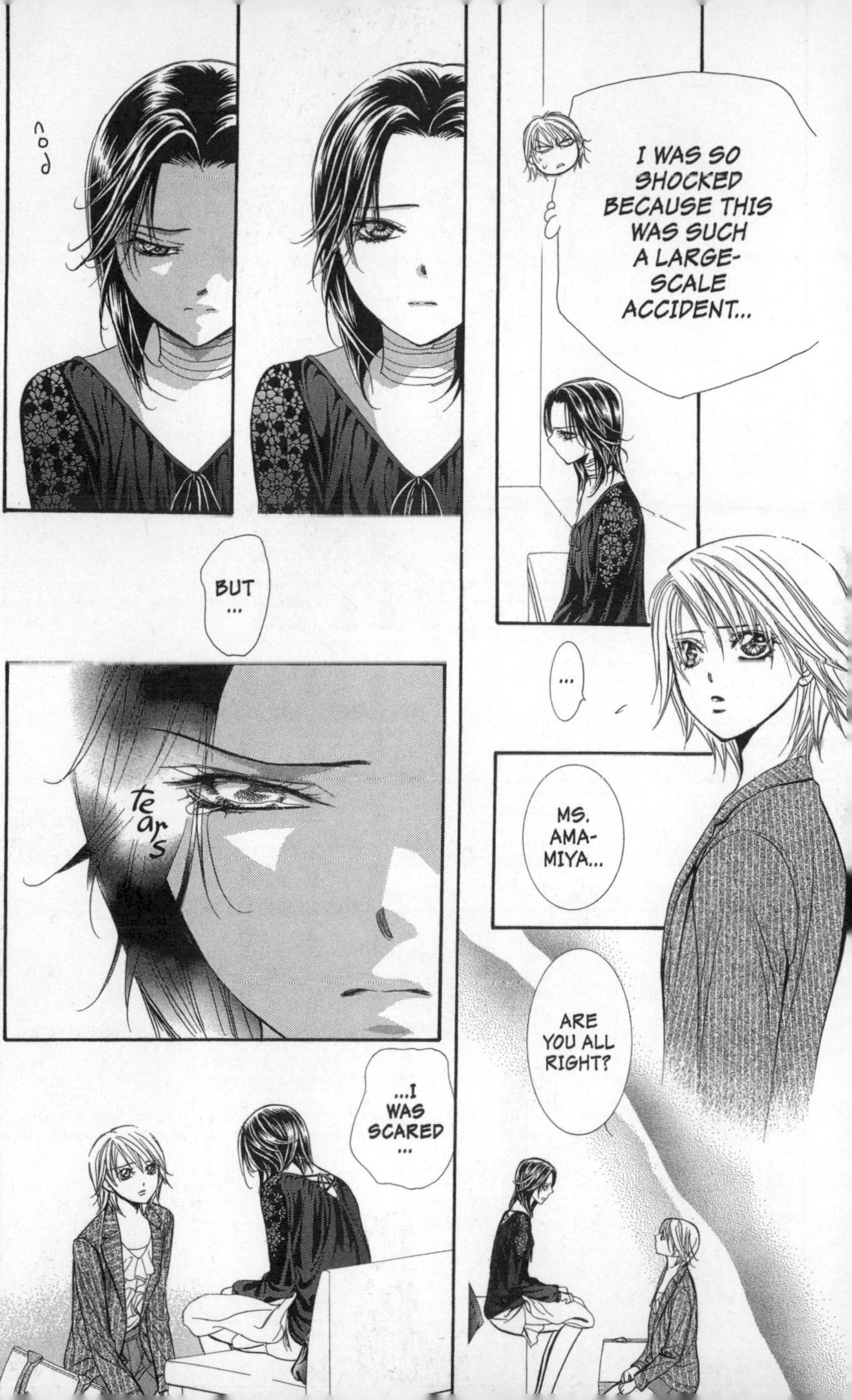
I WAS SO SHOCKED BECAUSE THIS WAS SUCH A LARGE-SCALE ACCIDENT...
...
MS. AMAMIYA...
ARE YOU ALL RIGHT?
nod
BUT ...
tears
...I WAS SCARED ...

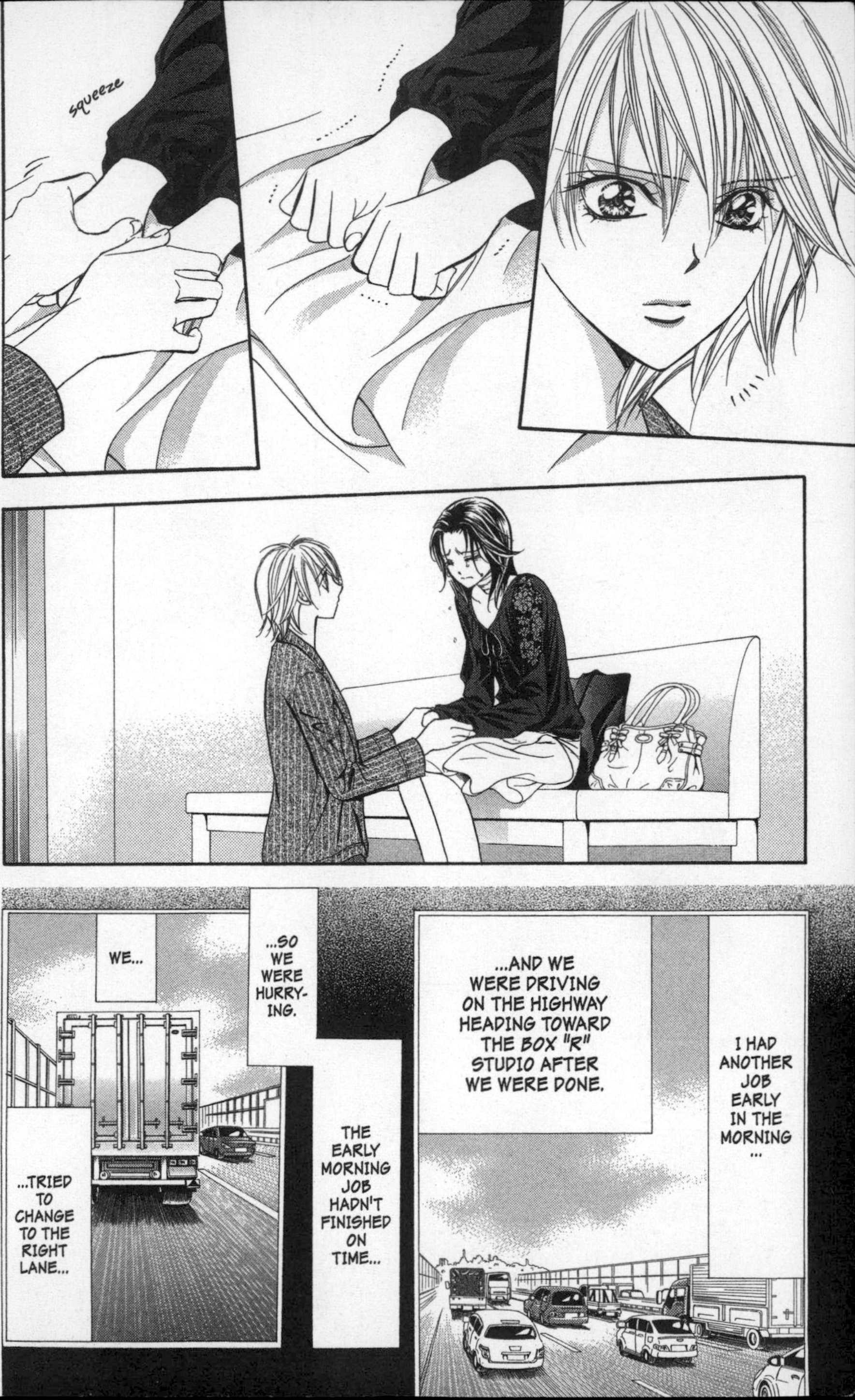
squeeze
I HAD ANOTHER JOB EARLY IN THE MORNING...
...AND WE WERE DRIVING ON THE HIGHWAY HEADING TOWARD THE BOX "R" STUDIO AFTER WE WERE DONE.
THE EARLY MORNING JOB HADN'T FINISHED ON TIME...
...SO WE WERE HURRYING.
WE...
...TRIED TO CHANGE TO THE RIGHT LANE...

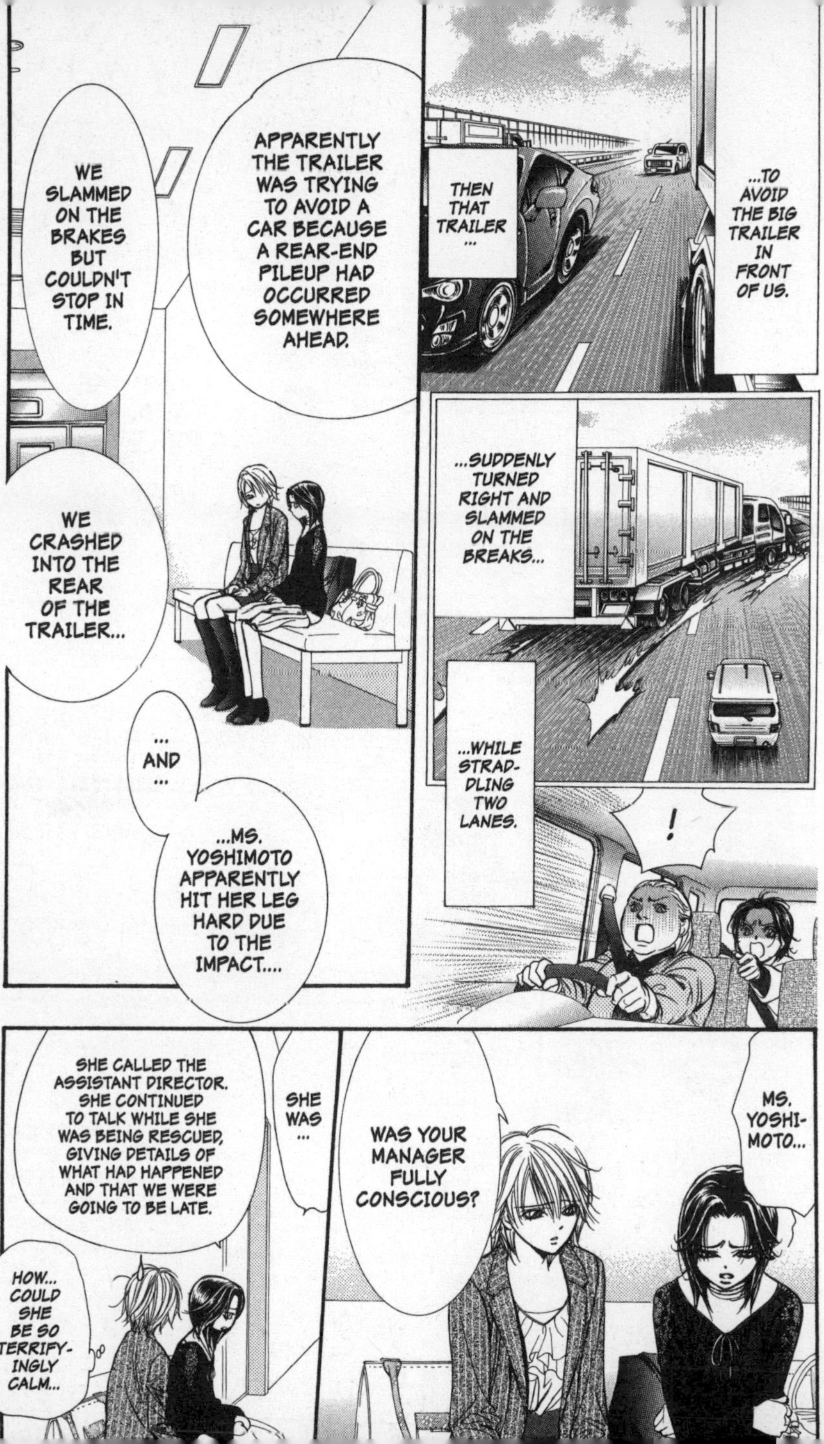
...TO AVOID THE BIG TRAILER IN FRONT OF US.
THEN THAT TRAILER ...
...SUDDENLY TURNED RIGHT AND SLAMMED ON THE BREAKS...
...WHILE STRAD-DLING TWO LANES.
!
APPARENTLY THE TRAILER WAS TRYING TO AVOID A CAR BECAUSE A REAR-END PILEUP HAD OCCURRED SOMEWHERE AHEAD.
WE SLAMMED ON THE BRAKES BUT COULDN'T STOP IN TIME.
WE CRASHED INTO THE REAR OF THE TRAILER...
... AND ...
...MS. YOSHIMOTO APPARENTLY HIT HER LEG HARD DUE TO THE IMPACT....
MS. YOSHI-MOTO...
WAS YOUR MANAGER FULLY CONSCIOUS?
SHE WAS ...
SHE CALLED THE ASSISTANT DIRECTOR. SHE CONTINUED TO TALK WHILE SHE WAS BEING RESCUED, GIVING DETAILS OF WHAT HAD HAPPENED AND THAT WE WERE GOING TO BE LATE.
HOW... COULD SHE BE SO TERRIFY-INGLY CALM...

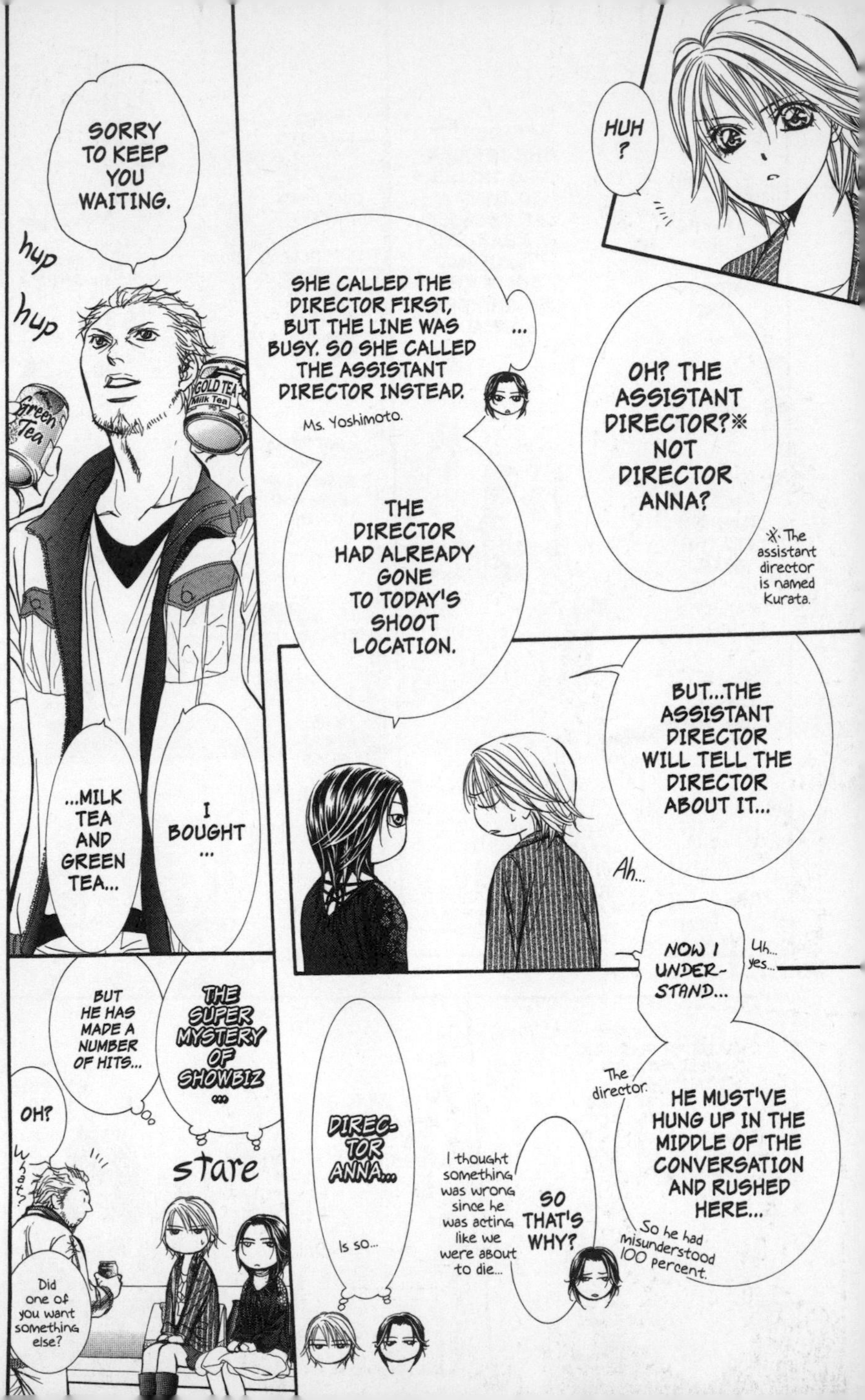
HUH?
OH? THE ASSISTANT DIRECTOR?※ NOT DIRECTOR ANNA?
※The assistant director is named Kurata.
...
SHE CALLED THE DIRECTOR FIRST, BUT THE LINE WAS BUSY. SO SHE CALLED THE ASSISTANT DIRECTOR INSTEAD.
Ms. Yoshimoto.
THE DIRECTOR HAD ALREADY GONE TO TODAY'S SHOOT LOCATION.
BUT...THE ASSISTANT DIRECTOR WILL TELL THE DIRECTOR ABOUT IT...
Ah...
NOW I UNDER-STAND...
Uh... yes...
The director.
HE MUST'VE HUNG UP IN THE MIDDLE OF THE CONVERSATION AND RUSHED HERE...
So he had misunderstood 100 percent.
SO THAT'S WHY?
I thought something was wrong since he was acting like we were about to die...
DIREC-TOR ANNA...
Is so...
SORRY TO KEEP YOU WAITING.
hup
hup
GOLD TEA Milk Tea
Green Tea
I BOUGHT...
...MILK TEA AND GREEN TEA...
THE SUPER MYSTERY OF SHOWBIZ...
BUT HE HAS MADE A NUMBER OF HITS...
stare
OH?
What?
Did one of you want something else?

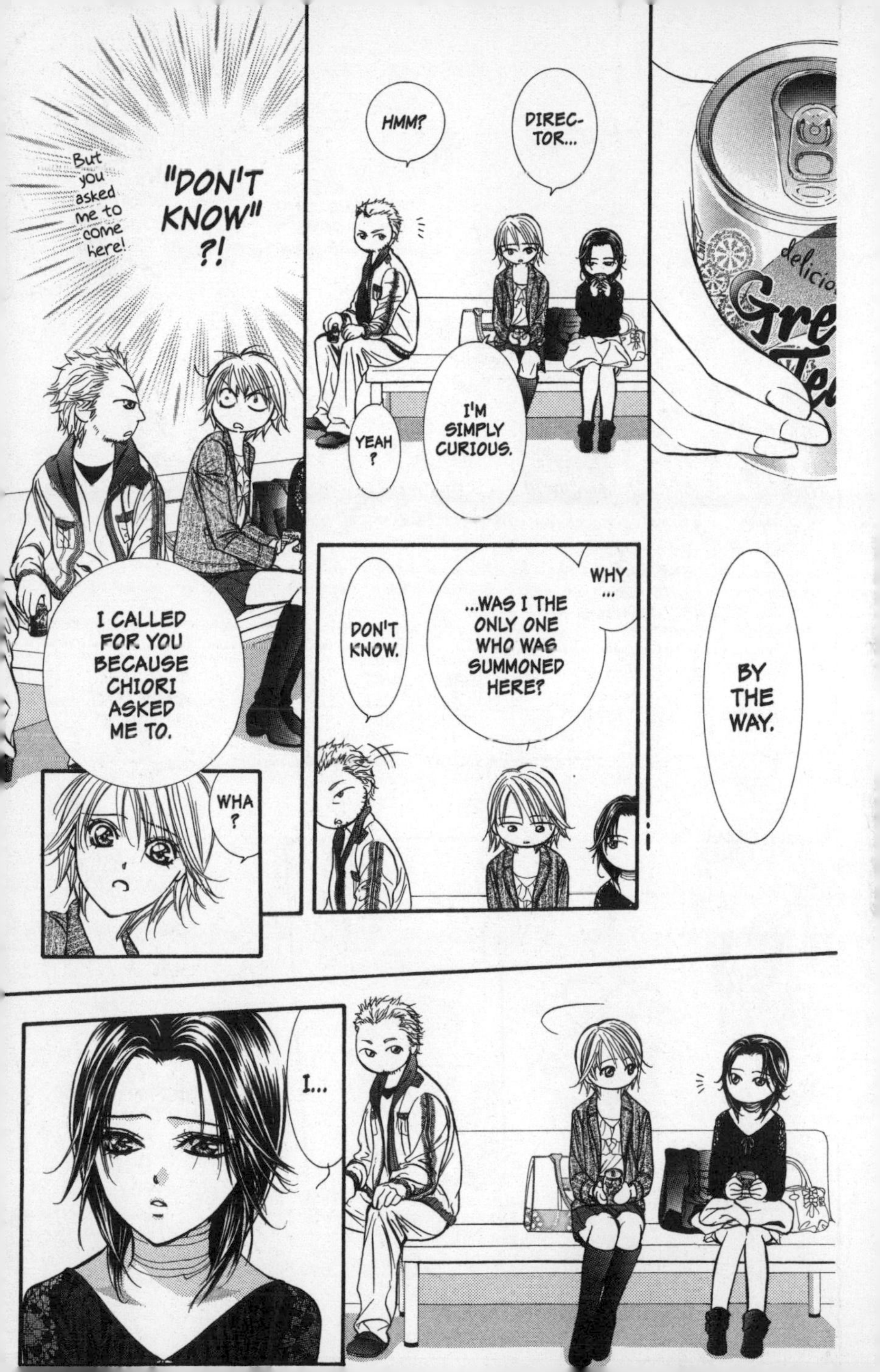
BY THE WAY.
DIREC-TOR...
HMM?
I'M SIMPLY CURIOUS.
YEAH?
WHY...
...WAS I THE ONLY ONE WHO WAS SUMMONED HERE?
DON'T KNOW.
"DON'T KNOW"?!
But you asked me to come here!
I CALLED FOR YOU BECAUSE CHIORI ASKED ME TO.
WHA?
I...

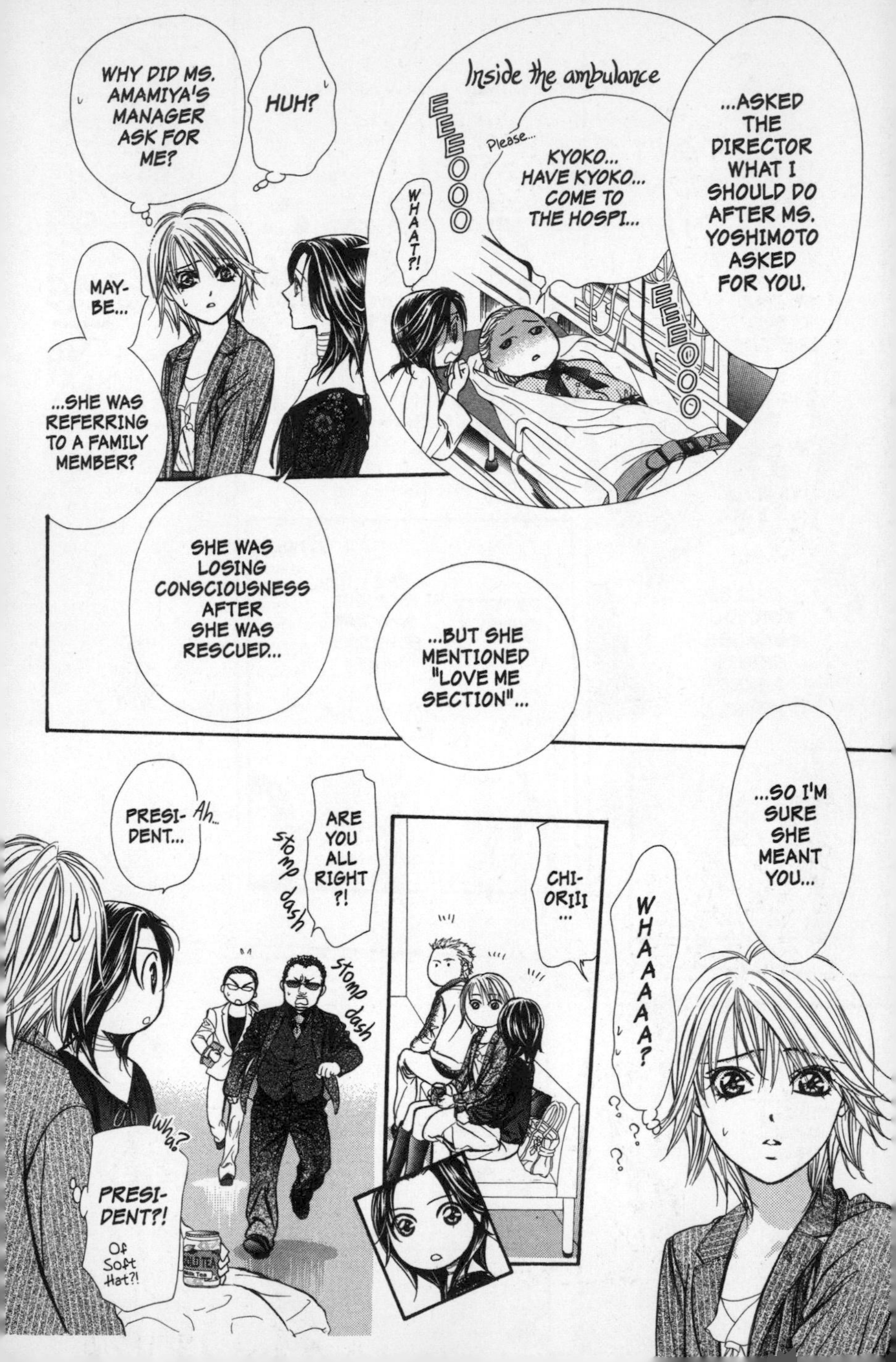
WHY DID MS. AMAMIYA'S MANAGER ASK FOR ME?
HUH?
MAY-BE...
...SHE WAS REFERRING TO A FAMILY MEMBER?
Inside the ambulance
EEEOOO
Please...
KYOKO... HAVE KYOKO... COME TO THE HOSPI...
WHAAT?!
EEEOOO
...ASKED THE DIRECTOR WHAT I SHOULD DO AFTER MS. YOSHIMOTO ASKED FOR YOU.
SHE WAS LOSING CONSCIOUSNESS AFTER SHE WAS RESCUED...
...BUT SHE MENTIONED "LOVE ME SECTION"...
...SO I'M SURE SHE MEANT YOU...
WHAAAAA?
CHI-ORIII...
PRESI-DENT...
Ah...
ARE YOU ALL RIGHT?!
stomp dash
stomp dash
Wha?
PRESI-DENT?!
Of Soft Hat?!

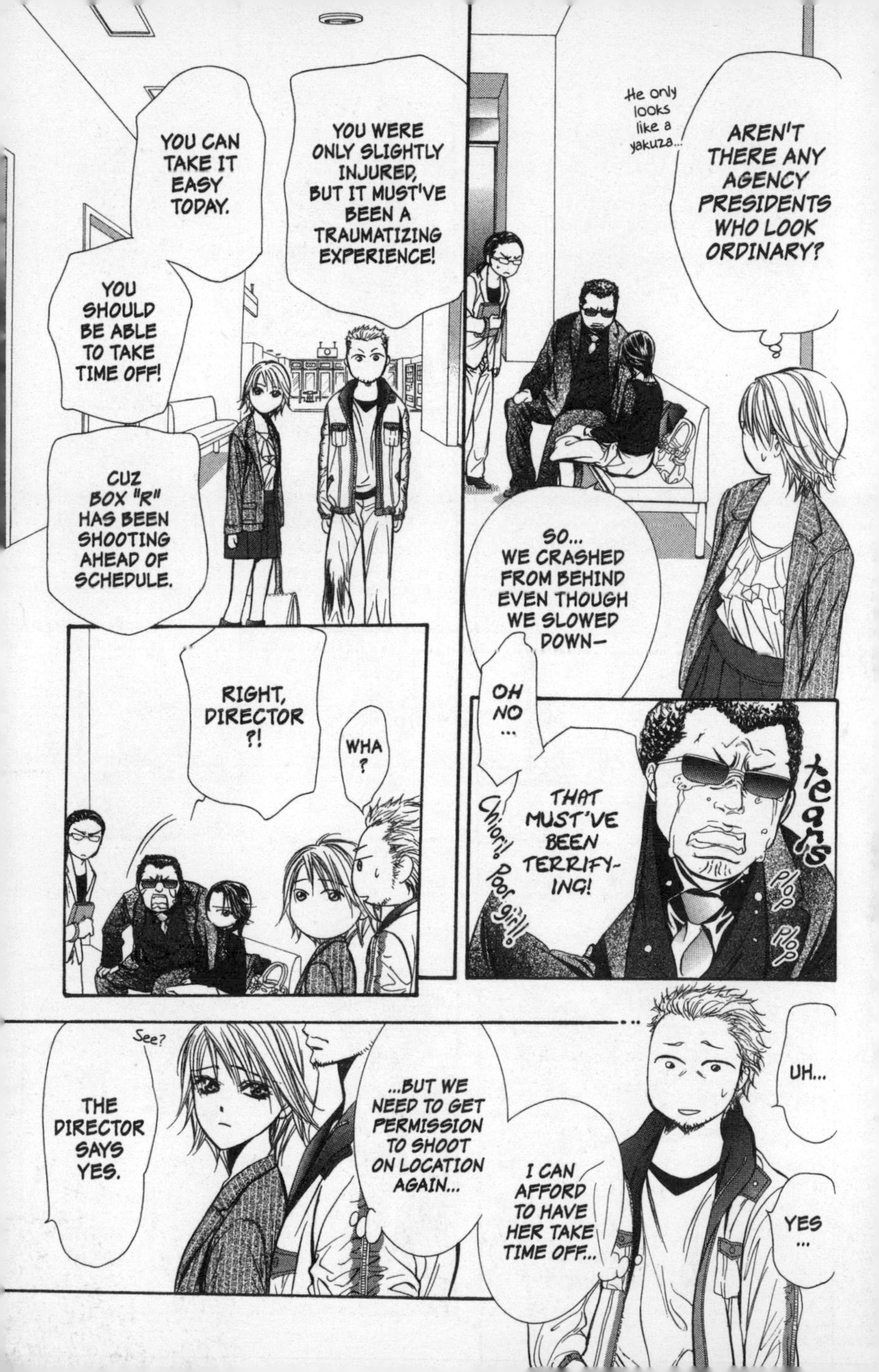
AREN'T THERE ANY AGENCY PRESIDENTS WHO LOOK ORDINARY?
He only looks like a yakuza...
SO... WE CRASHED FROM BEHIND EVEN THOUGH WE SLOWED DOWN—
YOU WERE ONLY SLIGHTLY INJURED, BUT IT MUST'VE BEEN A TRAUMATIZING EXPERIENCE!
YOU CAN TAKE IT EASY TODAY.
YOU SHOULD BE ABLE TO TAKE TIME OFF!
CUZ BOX "R" HAS BEEN SHOOTING AHEAD OF SCHEDULE.
tears
OH NO ...
THAT MUST'VE BEEN TERRIFY-ING!
Plop Plop
Chiori!! Poor girl!!
RIGHT, DIRECTOR ?!
WHA ?
UH...
...BUT WE NEED TO GET PERMISSION TO SHOOT ON LOCATION AGAIN...
I CAN AFFORD TO HAVE HER TAKE TIME OFF...
YES ...
See?
THE DIRECTOR SAYS YES.

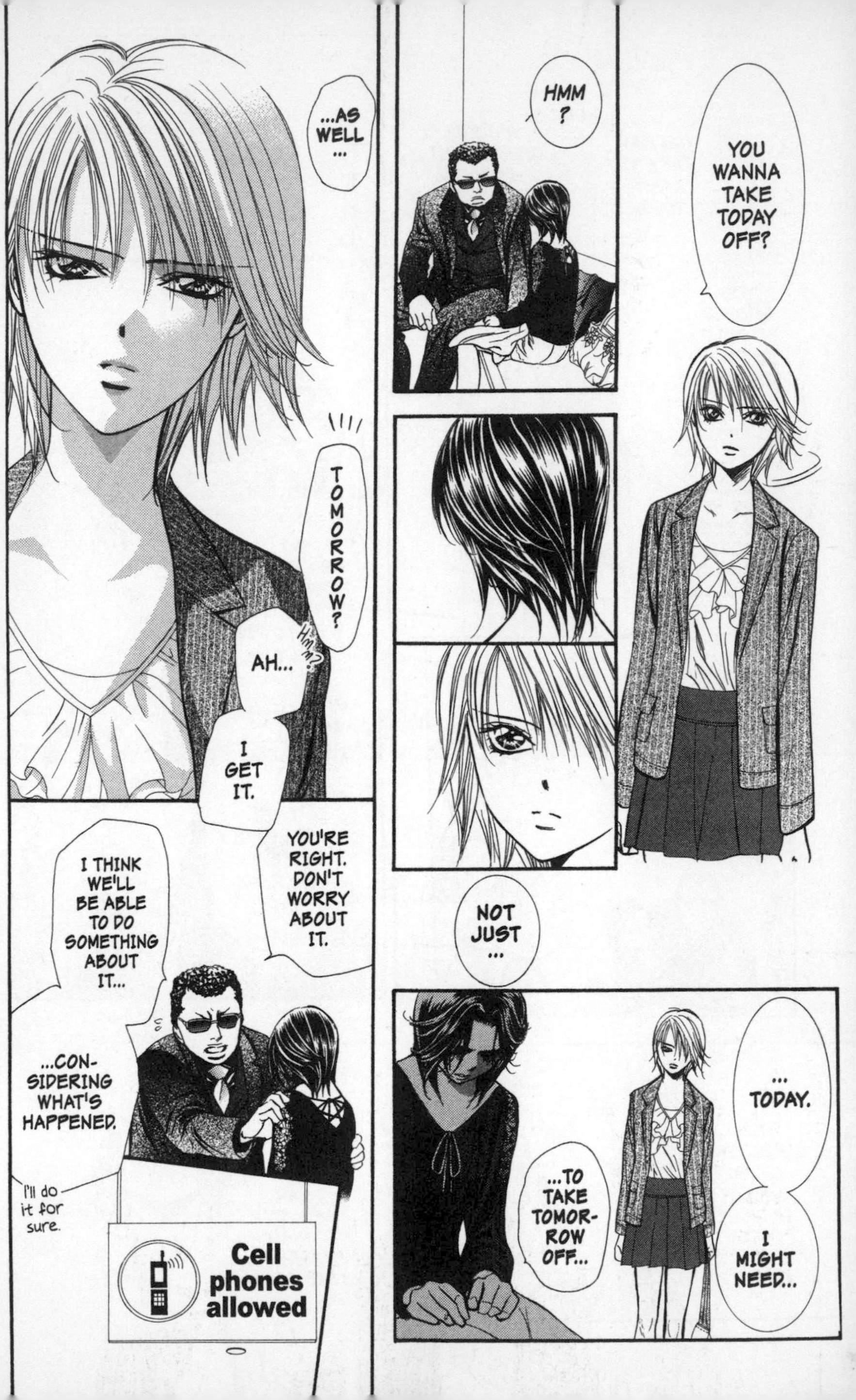
YOU WANNA TAKE TODAY OFF?
HMM?
NOT JUST...
...TODAY.
I MIGHT NEED...
...TO TAKE TOMOR-ROW OFF...
...AS WELL...
TOMORROW?
Hmm?
AH...
I GET IT.
YOU'RE RIGHT. DON'T WORRY ABOUT IT.
I THINK WE'LL BE ABLE TO DO SOMETHING ABOUT IT...
...CON-SIDERING WHAT'S HAPPENED.
I'll do it for sure.
Cell phones allowed

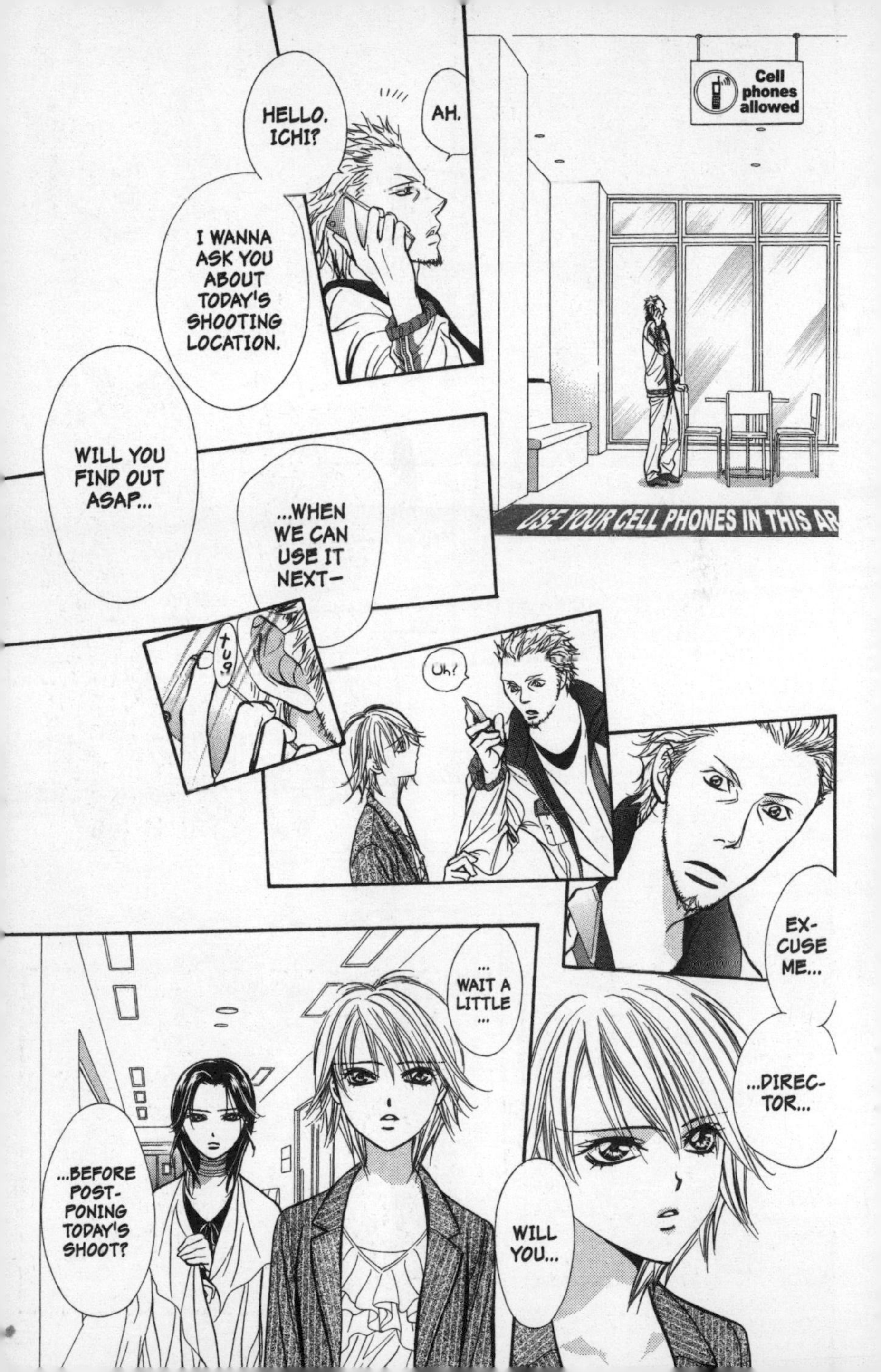
Cell phones allowed
USE YOUR CELL PHONES IN THIS AR
AH.
HELLO. ICHI?
I WANNA ASK YOU ABOUT TODAY'S SHOOTING LOCATION.
WILL YOU FIND OUT ASAP...
...WHEN WE CAN USE IT NEXT–
Uh?
tug
EX-CUSE ME...
...DIREC-TOR...
WILL YOU...
...WAIT A LITTLE...
...BEFORE POST-PONING TODAY'S SHOOT?

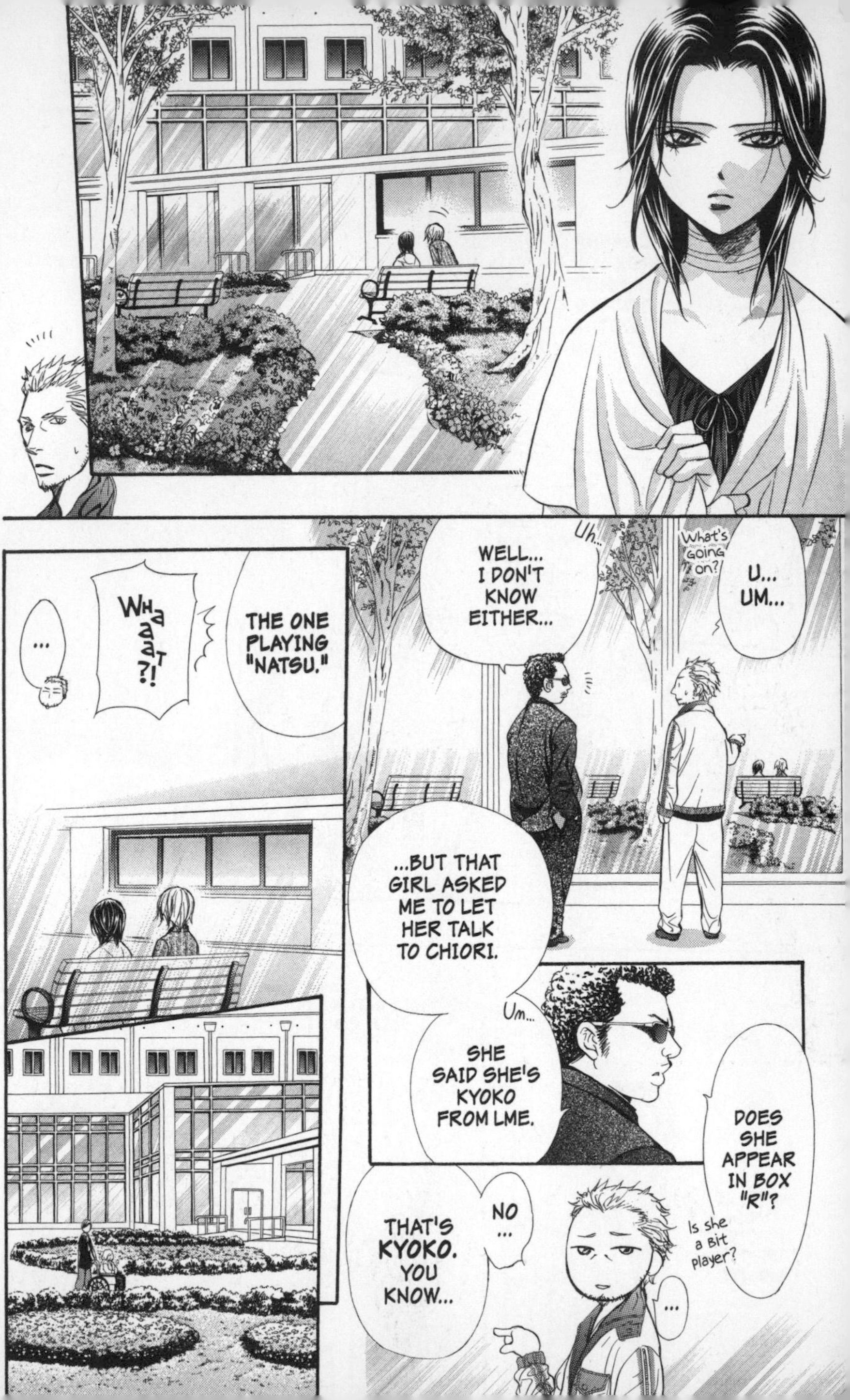

U... UM...
What's going on?
Uh...
WELL... I DON'T KNOW EITHER...
...BUT THAT GIRL ASKED ME TO LET HER TALK TO CHIORI.
Um...
SHE SAID SHE'S KYOKO FROM LME.
DOES SHE APPEAR IN BOX "R"?
Is she a bit player?
...
NO...
THAT'S KYOKO. YOU KNOW...
THE ONE PLAYING "NATSU."
Whaaat?!
...

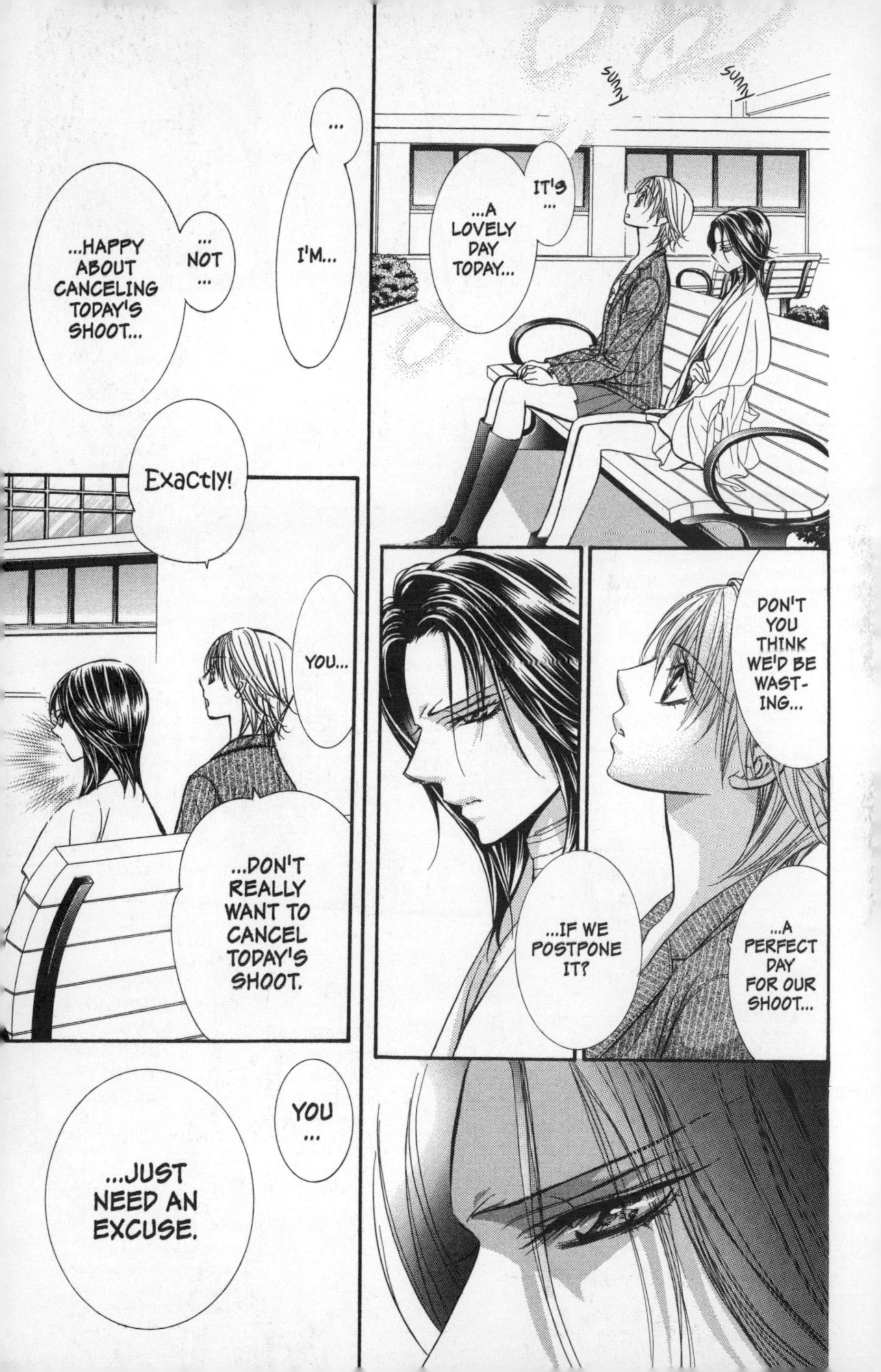
sunny
sunny
IT'S ...
...A LOVELY DAY TODAY...
DON'T YOU THINK WE'D BE WASTING...
...A PERFECT DAY FOR OUR SHOOT...
...IF WE POSTPONE IT?
...
I'M...
... NOT ...
...HAPPY ABOUT CANCELING TODAY'S SHOOT...
Exactly!
YOU...
...DON'T REALLY WANT TO CANCEL TODAY'S SHOOT.
YOU ...
...JUST NEED AN EXCUSE.

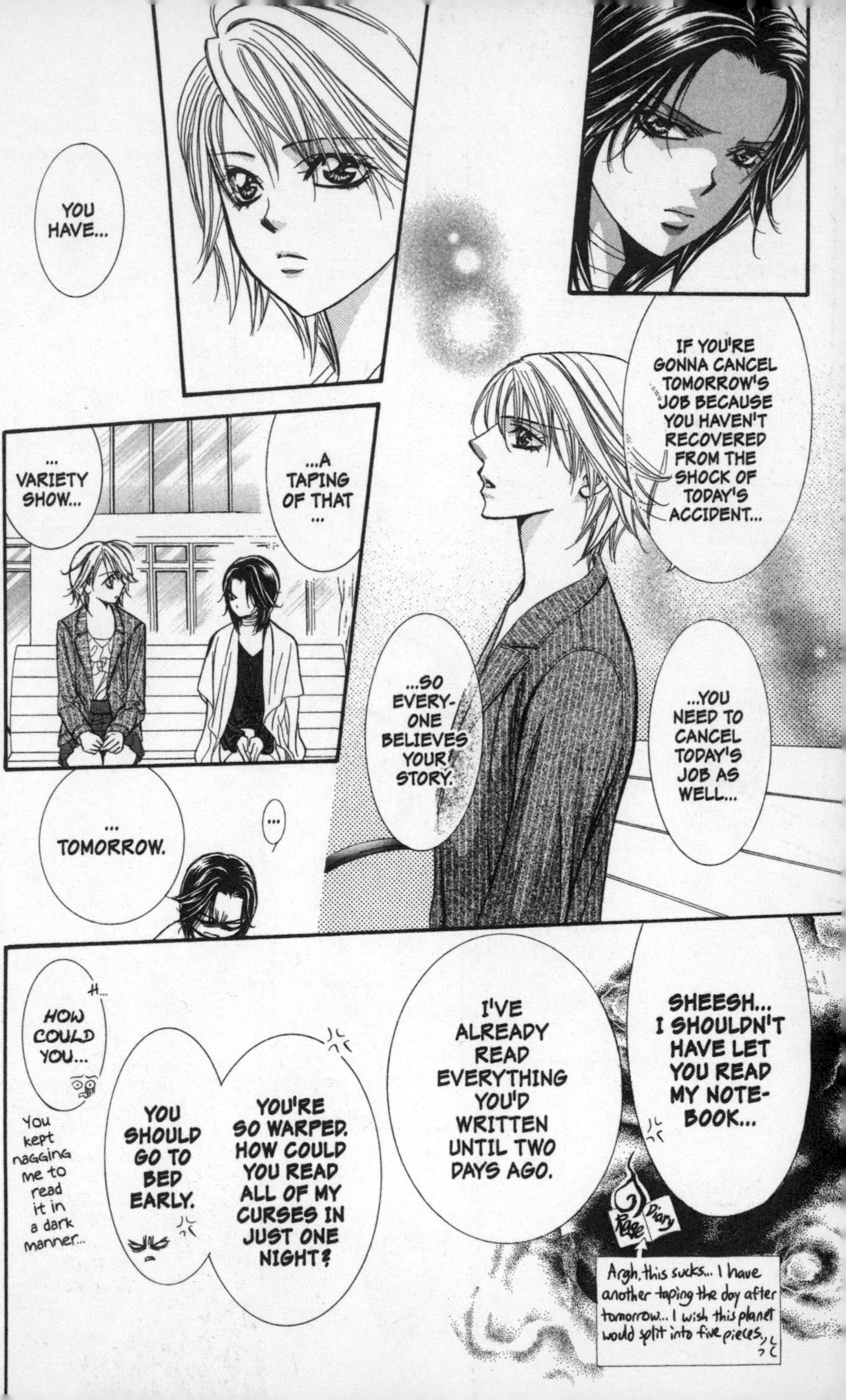
YOU HAVE...
IF YOU'RE GONNA CANCEL TOMORROW'S JOB BECAUSE YOU HAVEN'T RECOVERED FROM THE SHOCK OF TODAY'S ACCIDENT...
...YOU NEED TO CANCEL TODAY'S JOB AS WELL...
...SO EVERYONE BELIEVES YOUR STORY.
...A TAPING OF THAT ...
... VARIETY SHOW...
... TOMORROW.
...
SHEESH... I SHOULDN'T HAVE LET YOU READ MY NOTE-BOOK...
I'VE ALREADY READ EVERYTHING YOU'D WRITTEN UNTIL TWO DAYS AGO.
YOU'RE SO WARPED. HOW COULD YOU READ ALL OF MY CURSES IN JUST ONE NIGHT?
YOU SHOULD GO TO BED EARLY.
H... HOW COULD YOU...
You kept nagging me to read it in a dark manner...
Rage Diary
Argh, this sucks... I have another taping the day after tomorrow... I wish this planet would split into five pieces.

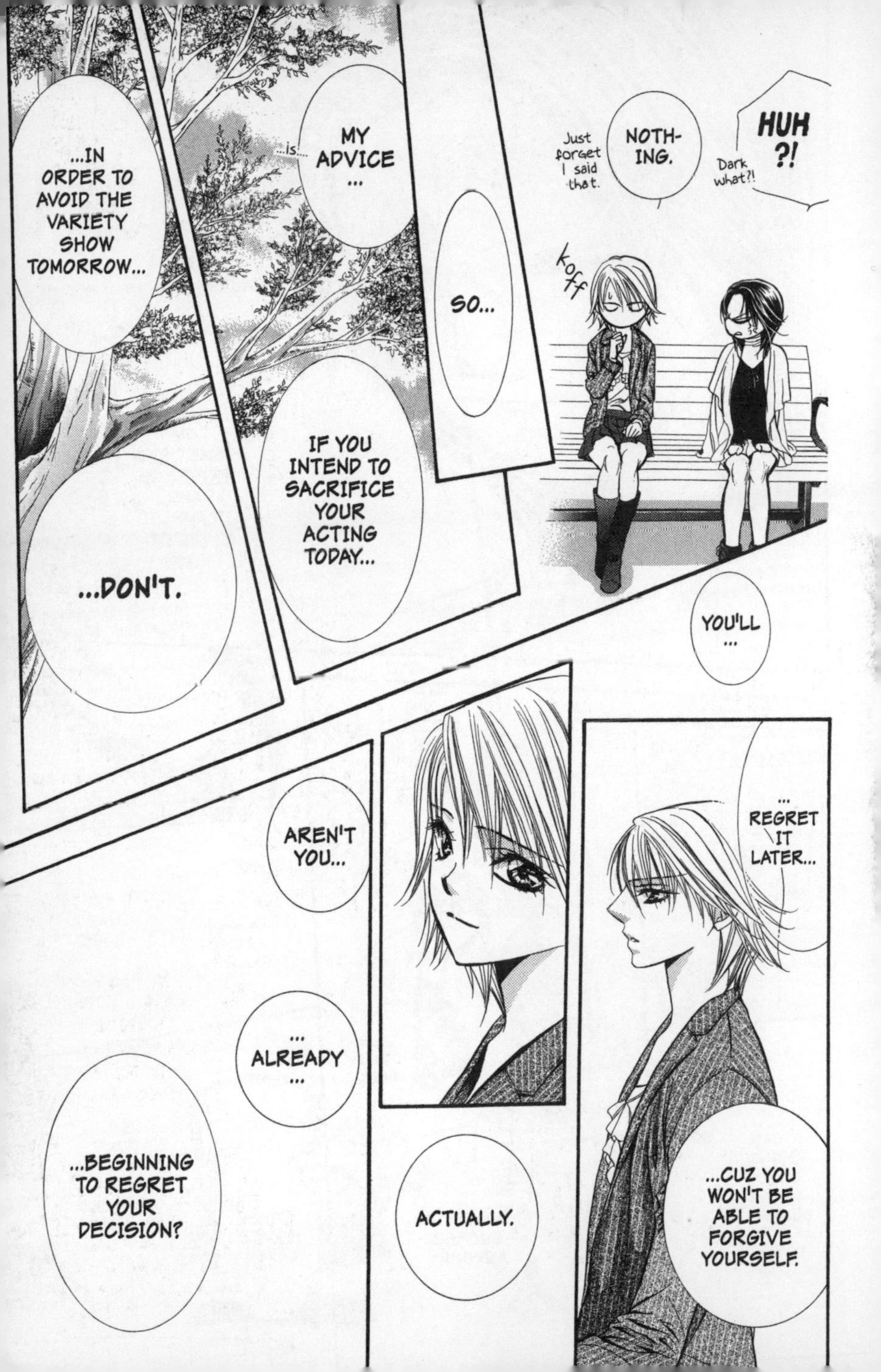
HUH?!
Dark what?!
NOTH-ING.
Just forget I said that.
koff
SO...
MY ADVICE...
...is...
IF YOU INTEND TO SACRIFICE YOUR ACTING TODAY...
...IN ORDER TO AVOID THE VARIETY SHOW TOMORROW...
...DON'T.
YOU'LL...
...REGRET IT LATER...
...CUZ YOU WON'T BE ABLE TO FORGIVE YOURSELF.
ACTUALLY.
AREN'T YOU...
...ALREADY...
...BEGINNING TO REGRET YOUR DECISION?

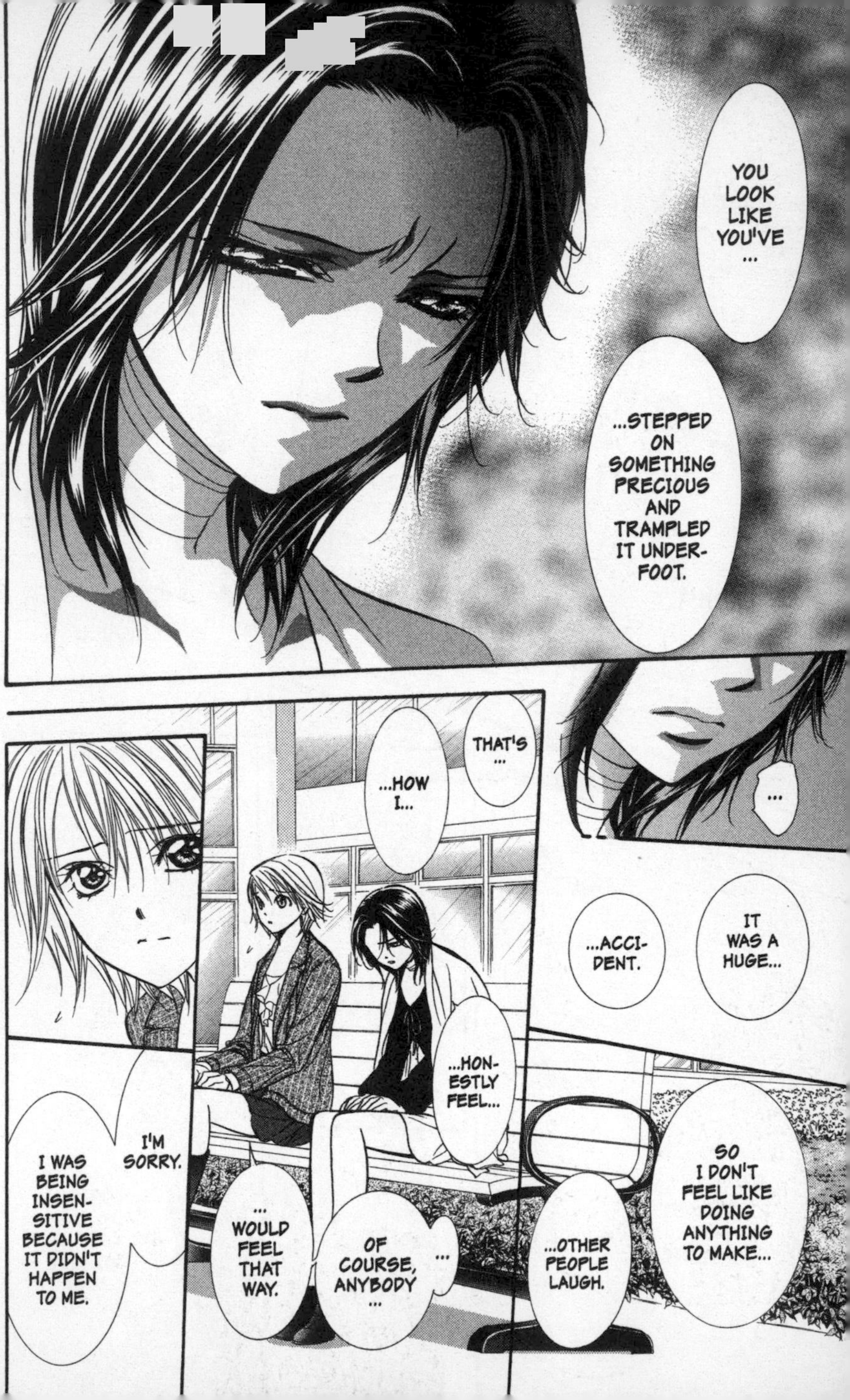
YOU LOOK LIKE YOU'VE ...
...STEPPED ON SOMETHING PRECIOUS AND TRAMPLED IT UNDER-FOOT.
...
IT WAS A HUGE...
...ACCI-DENT.
SO I DON'T FEEL LIKE DOING ANYTHING TO MAKE...
...OTHER PEOPLE LAUGH.
THAT'S ...
...HOW I...
...HON-ESTLY FEEL...
...
OF COURSE, ANYBODY ...
... WOULD FEEL THAT WAY.
I'M SORRY.
I WAS BEING INSEN-SITIVE BECAUSE IT DIDN'T HAPPEN TO ME.

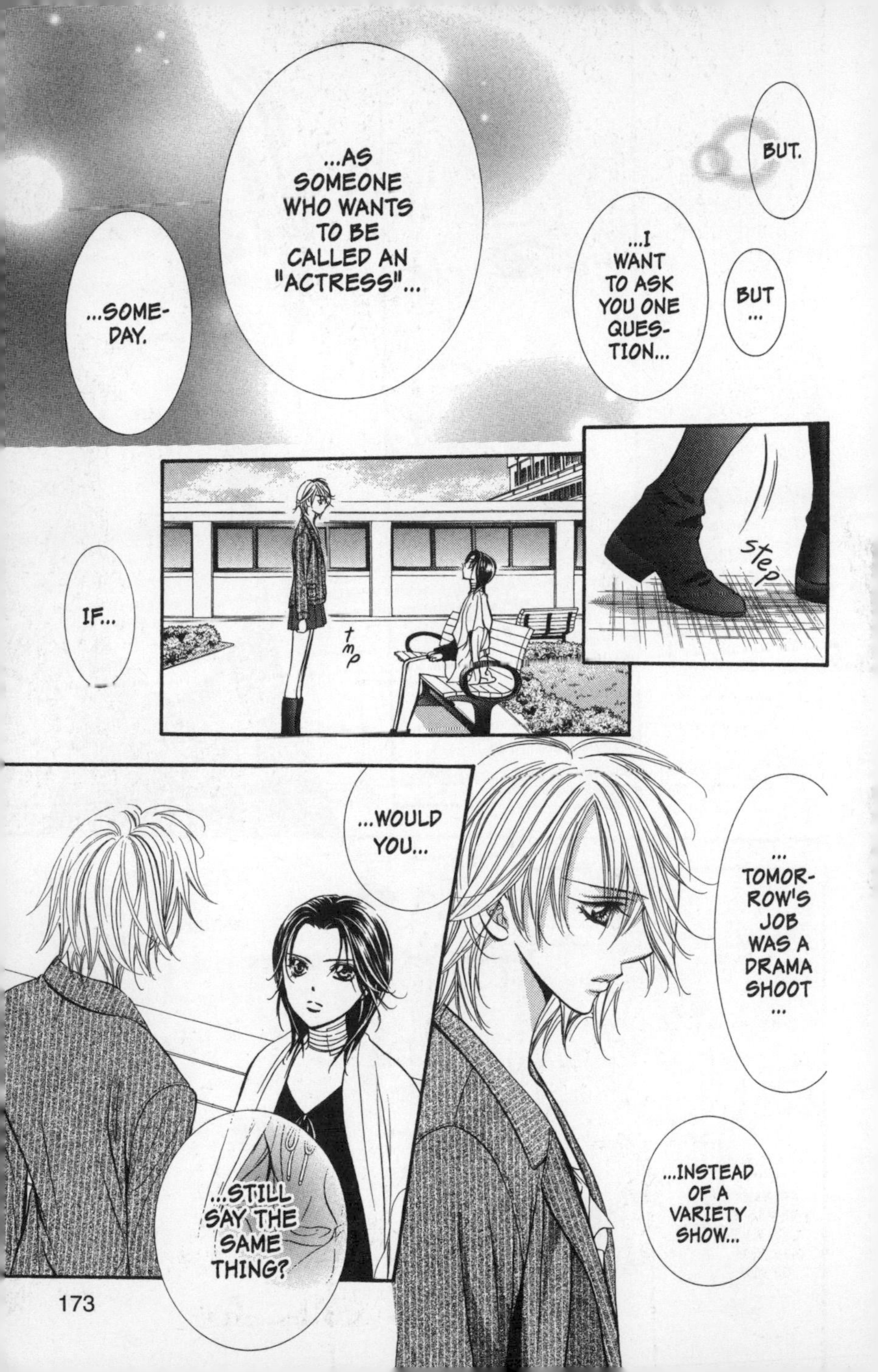
BUT.
BUT ...
...I WANT TO ASK YOU ONE QUES-TION...
...AS SOMEONE WHO WANTS TO BE CALLED AN "ACTRESS"...
...SOME-DAY.
step
tmp
IF...
... TOMOR-ROW'S JOB WAS A DRAMA SHOOT ...
...INSTEAD OF A VARIETY SHOW...
...WOULD YOU...
...STILL SAY THE SAME THING?

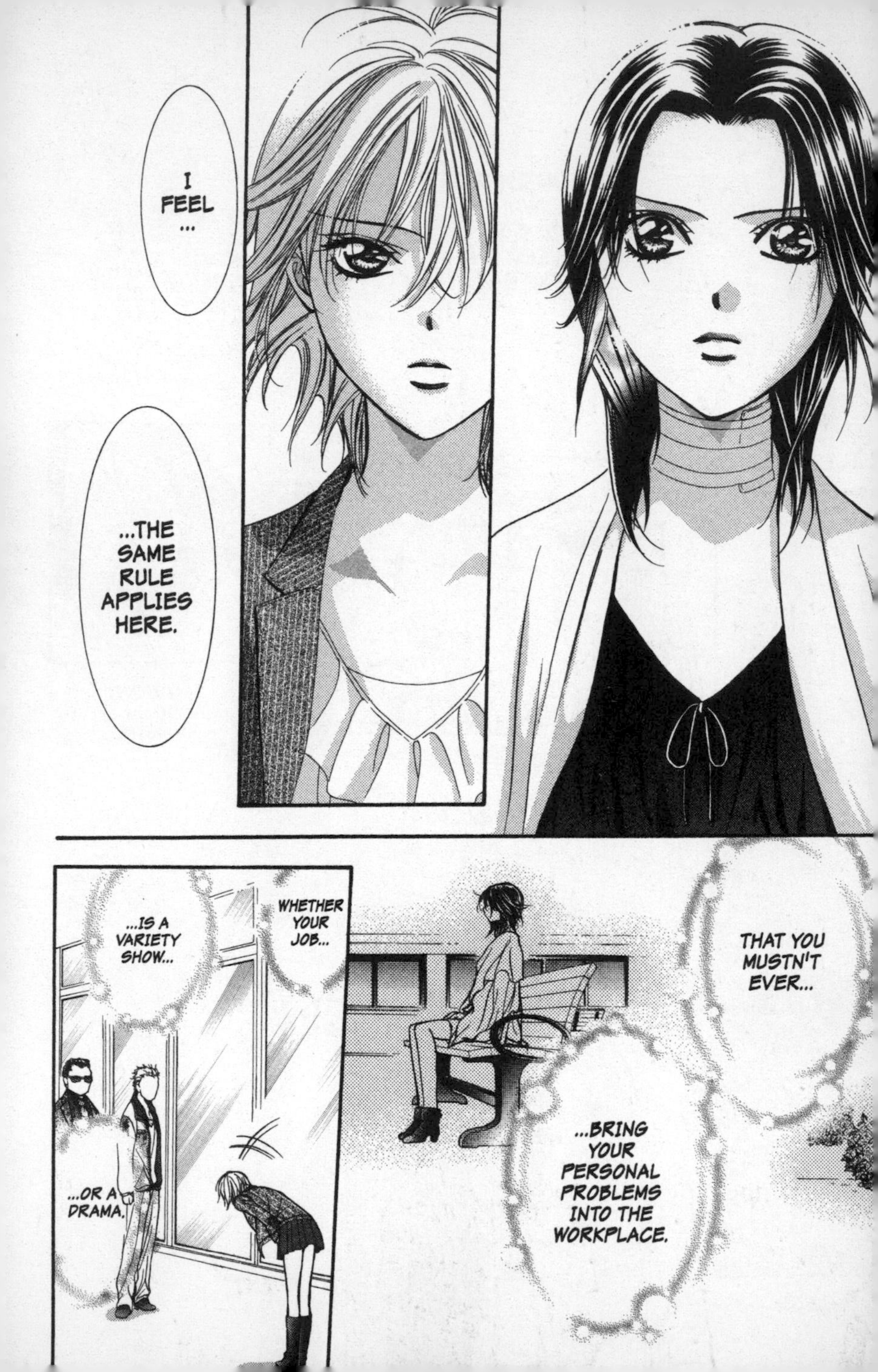
I FEEL ...
...THE SAME RULE APPLIES HERE.
THAT YOU MUSTN'T EVER...
...BRING YOUR PERSONAL PROBLEMS INTO THE WORKPLACE.
WHETHER YOUR JOB...
...IS A VARIETY SHOW...
...OR A DRAMA.

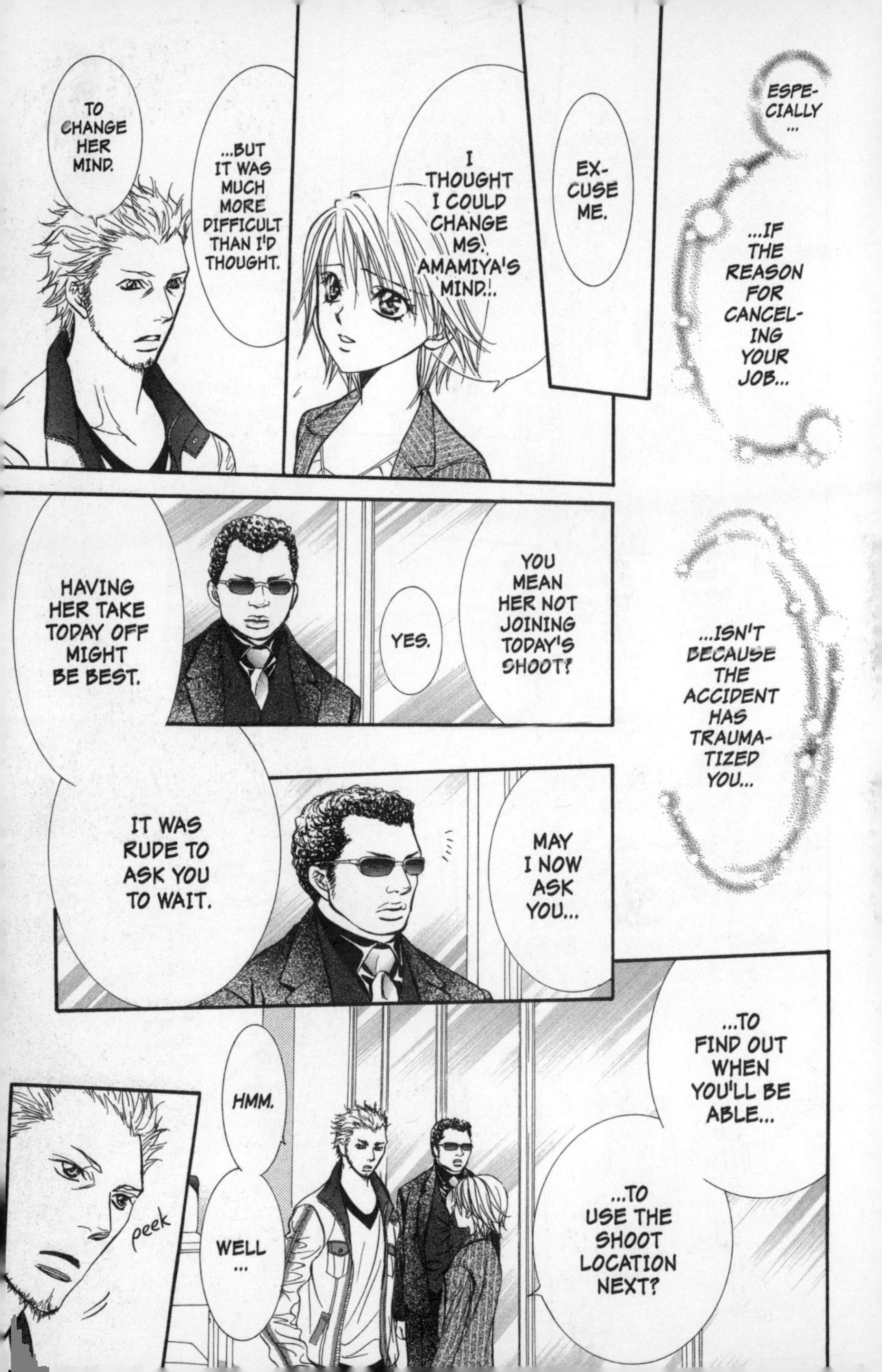
ESPE-CIALLY...
...IF THE REASON FOR CANCEL-ING YOUR JOB...
...ISN'T BECAUSE THE ACCIDENT HAS TRAUMA-TIZED YOU...
EX-CUSE ME.
I THOUGHT I COULD CHANGE MS. AMAMIYA'S MIND...
...BUT IT WAS MUCH MORE DIFFICULT THAN I'D THOUGHT.
TO CHANGE HER MIND.
YOU MEAN HER NOT JOINING TODAY'S SHOOT?
YES.
HAVING HER TAKE TODAY OFF MIGHT BE BEST.
MAY I NOW ASK YOU...
IT WAS RUDE TO ASK YOU TO WAIT.
...TO FIND OUT WHEN YOU'LL BE ABLE...
...TO USE THE SHOOT LOCATION NEXT?
HMM.
WELL...
peek

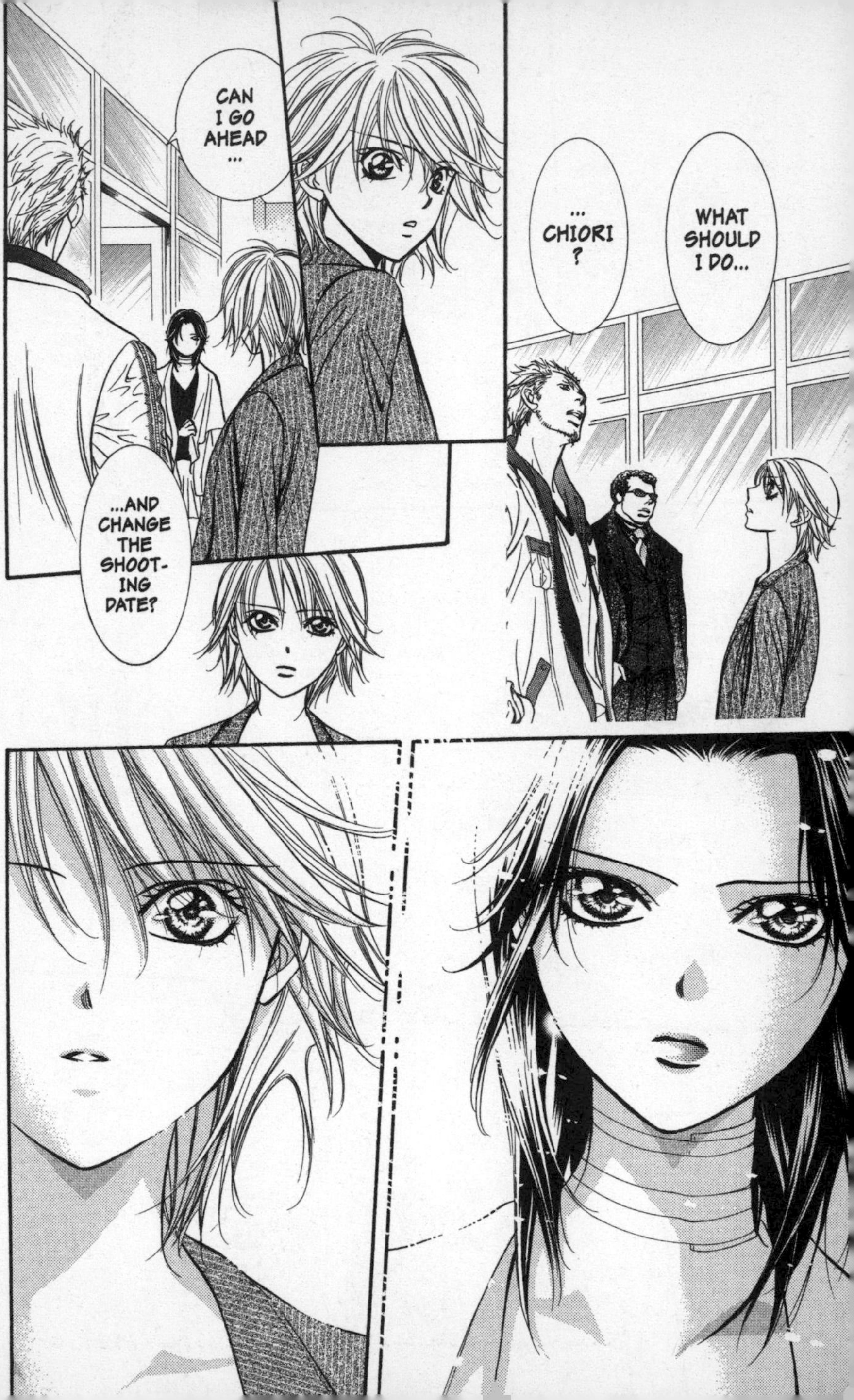
WHAT SHOULD I DO...
...CHIORI?
CAN I GO AHEAD...
...AND CHANGE THE SHOOTING DATE?

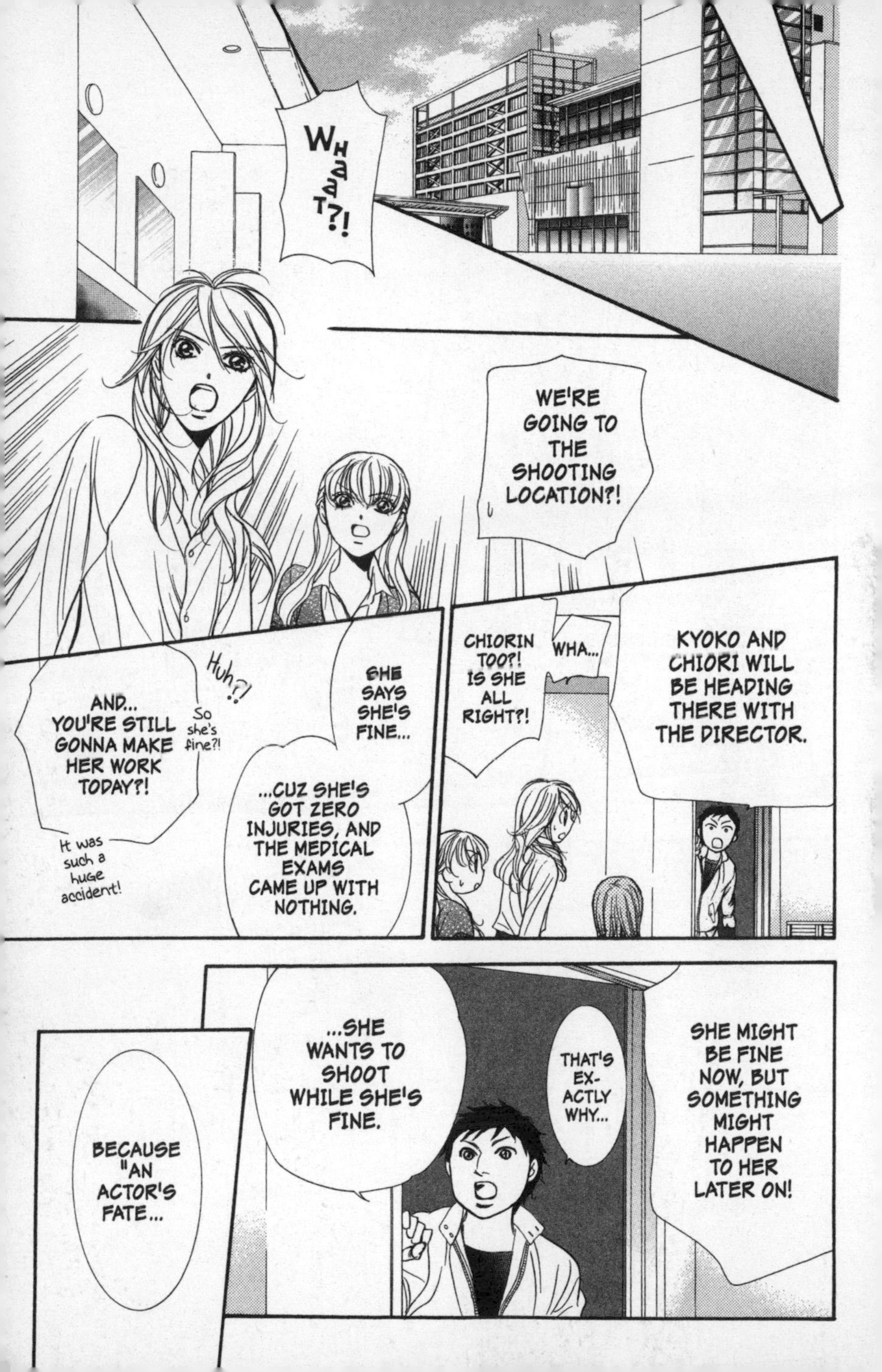
WHAAT?!
WE'RE GOING TO THE SHOOTING LOCATION?!
KYOKO AND CHIORI WILL BE HEADING THERE WITH THE DIRECTOR.
WHA...
CHIORIN TOO?! IS SHE ALL RIGHT?!
SHE SAYS SHE'S FINE...
...CUZ SHE'S GOT ZERO INJURIES, AND THE MEDICAL EXAMS CAME UP WITH NOTHING.
Huh?!
So she's fine?!
AND... YOU'RE STILL GONNA MAKE HER WORK TODAY?!
It was such a huge accident!
SHE MIGHT BE FINE NOW, BUT SOMETHING MIGHT HAPPEN TO HER LATER ON!
THAT'S EX-ACTLY WHY...
...SHE WANTS TO SHOOT WHILE SHE'S FINE.
BECAUSE "AN ACTOR'S FATE...

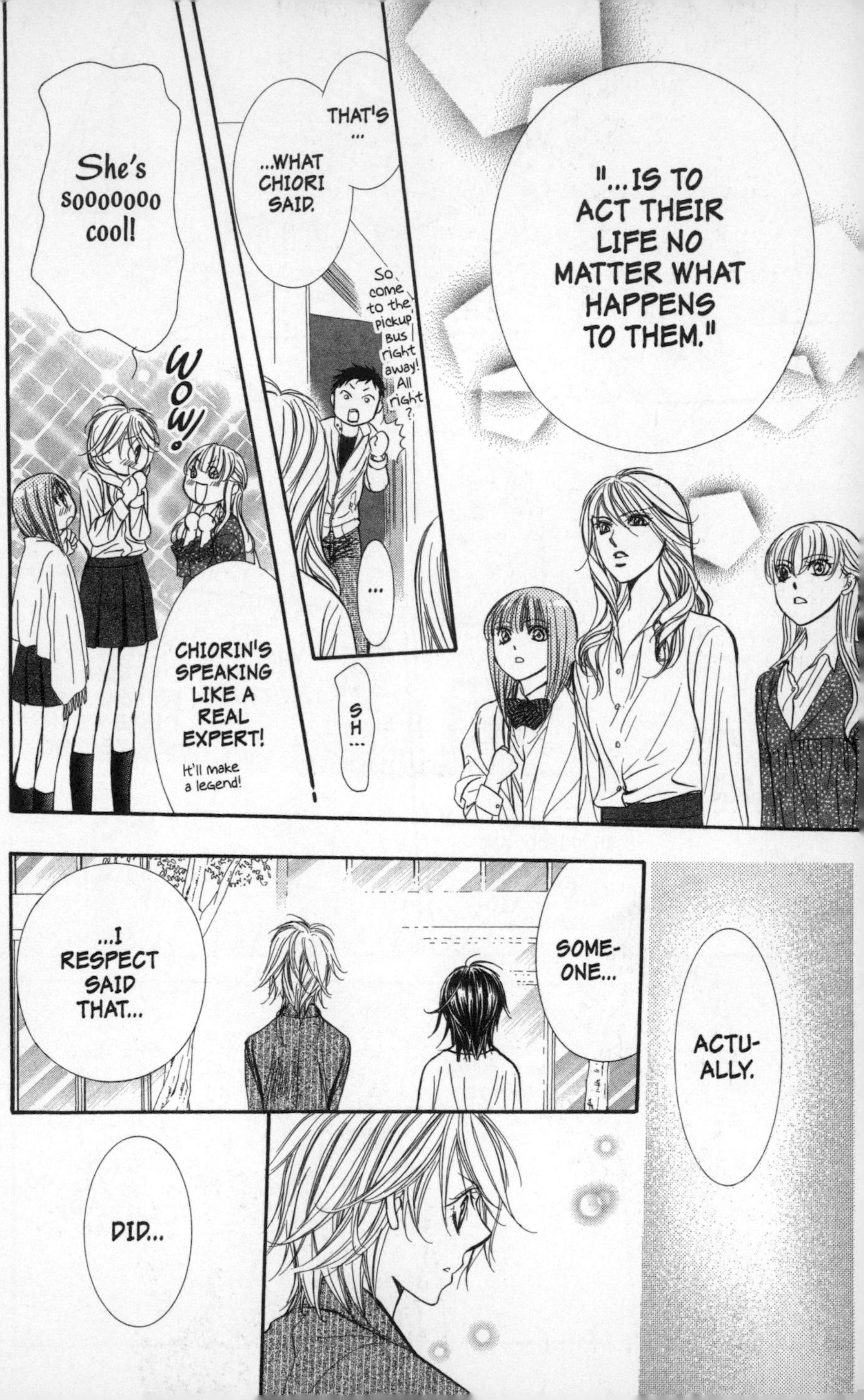
"...IS TO ACT THEIR LIFE NO MATTER WHAT HAPPENS TO THEM."
THAT'S ...
...WHAT CHIORI SAID.
So come to the pickup bus right away! All right?
...
SH...
She's soooooo cool!
WOW!
CHIORIN'S SPEAKING LIKE A REAL EXPERT!
It'll make a legend!
ACTU-ALLY.
SOME-ONE...
...I RESPECT SAID THAT...
DID...

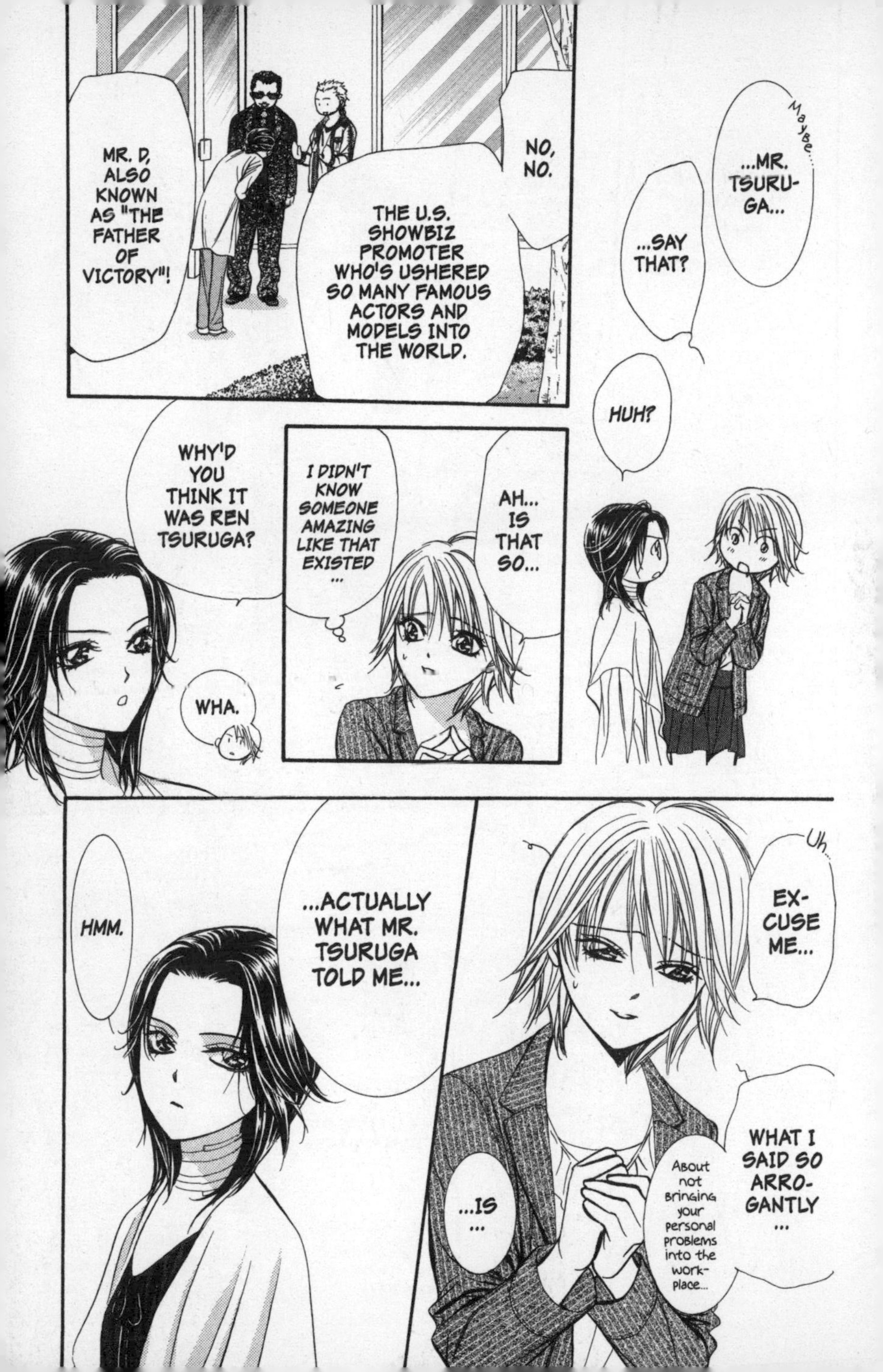
Maybe...
...MR. TSURUGA...
...SAY THAT?
NO, NO.
THE U.S. SHOWBIZ PROMOTER WHO'S USHERED SO MANY FAMOUS ACTORS AND MODELS INTO THE WORLD.
MR. D, ALSO KNOWN AS "THE FATHER OF VICTORY"!
HUH?
AH... IS THAT SO...
I DIDN'T KNOW SOMEONE AMAZING LIKE THAT EXISTED...
WHY'D YOU THINK IT WAS REN TSURUGA?
WHA.
Uh...
EX-CUSE ME...
WHAT I SAID SO ARRO-GANTLY...
About not bringing your personal problems into the work-place...
...IS...
...ACTUALLY WHAT MR. TSURUGA TOLD ME...
HMM.

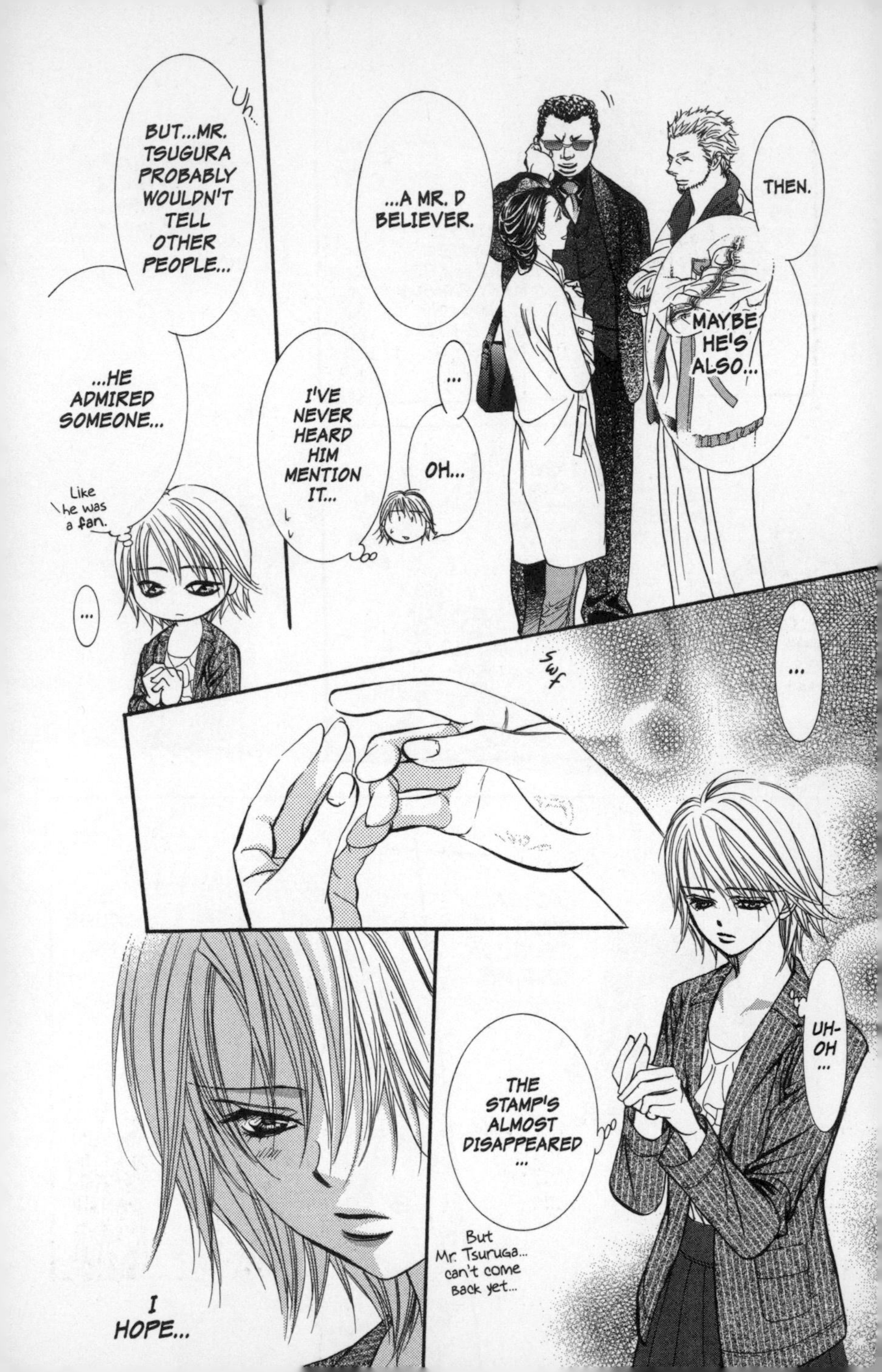
THEN.
MAYBE HE'S ALSO...
...A MR. D BELIEVER.
...
OH...
I'VE NEVER HEARD HIM MENTION IT...
Uh...
BUT...MR. TSUGURA PROBABLY WOULDN'T TELL OTHER PEOPLE...
...HE ADMIRED SOMEONE...
Like he was a fan.
...
...
swf
UH-OH...
THE STAMP'S ALMOST DISAPPEARED...
But Mr. Tsuruga... can't come back yet...
I HOPE...

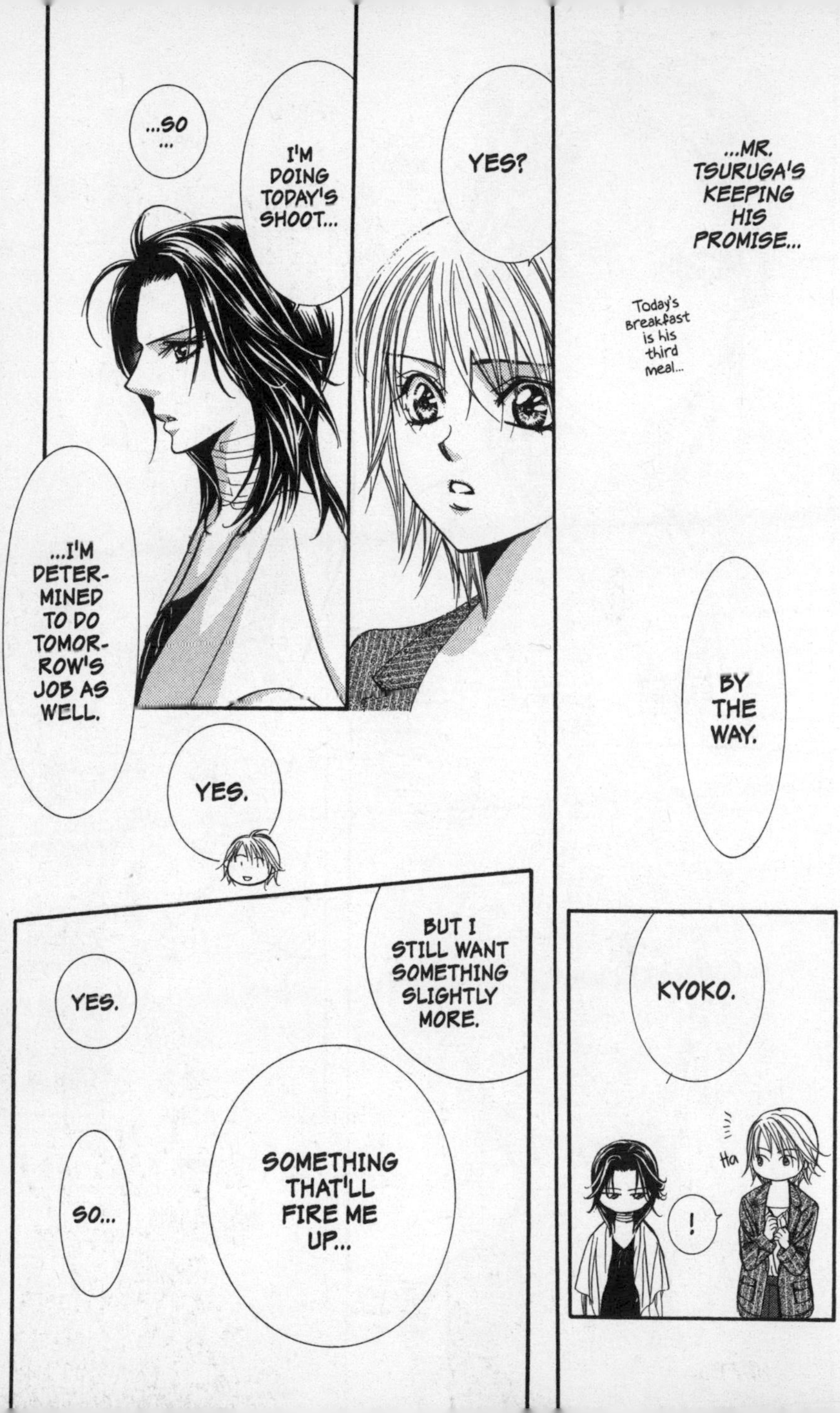
...MR. TSURUGA'S KEEPING HIS PROMISE...
Today's breakfast is his third meal...
BY THE WAY.
KYOKO.
Ha
!
YES?
...SO ...
I'M DOING TODAY'S SHOOT...
...I'M DETERMINED TO DO TOMORROW'S JOB AS WELL.
YES.
BUT I STILL WANT SOMETHING SLIGHTLY MORE.
YES.
SO...
SOMETHING THAT'LL FIRE ME UP...

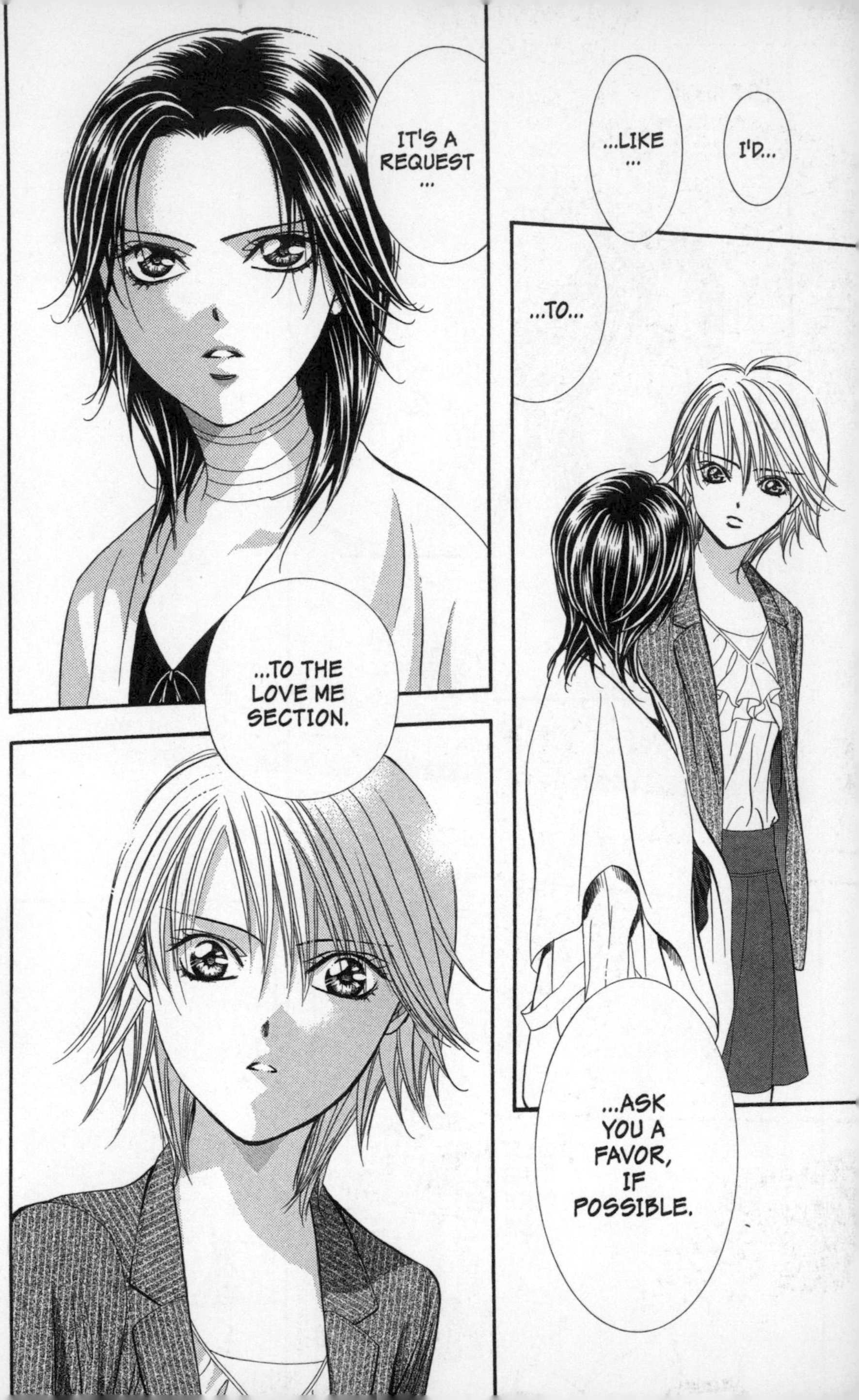
I'D...
...LIKE...
...TO...
...ASK YOU A FAVOR, IF POSSIBLE.
IT'S A REQUEST...
...TO THE LOVE ME SECTION.

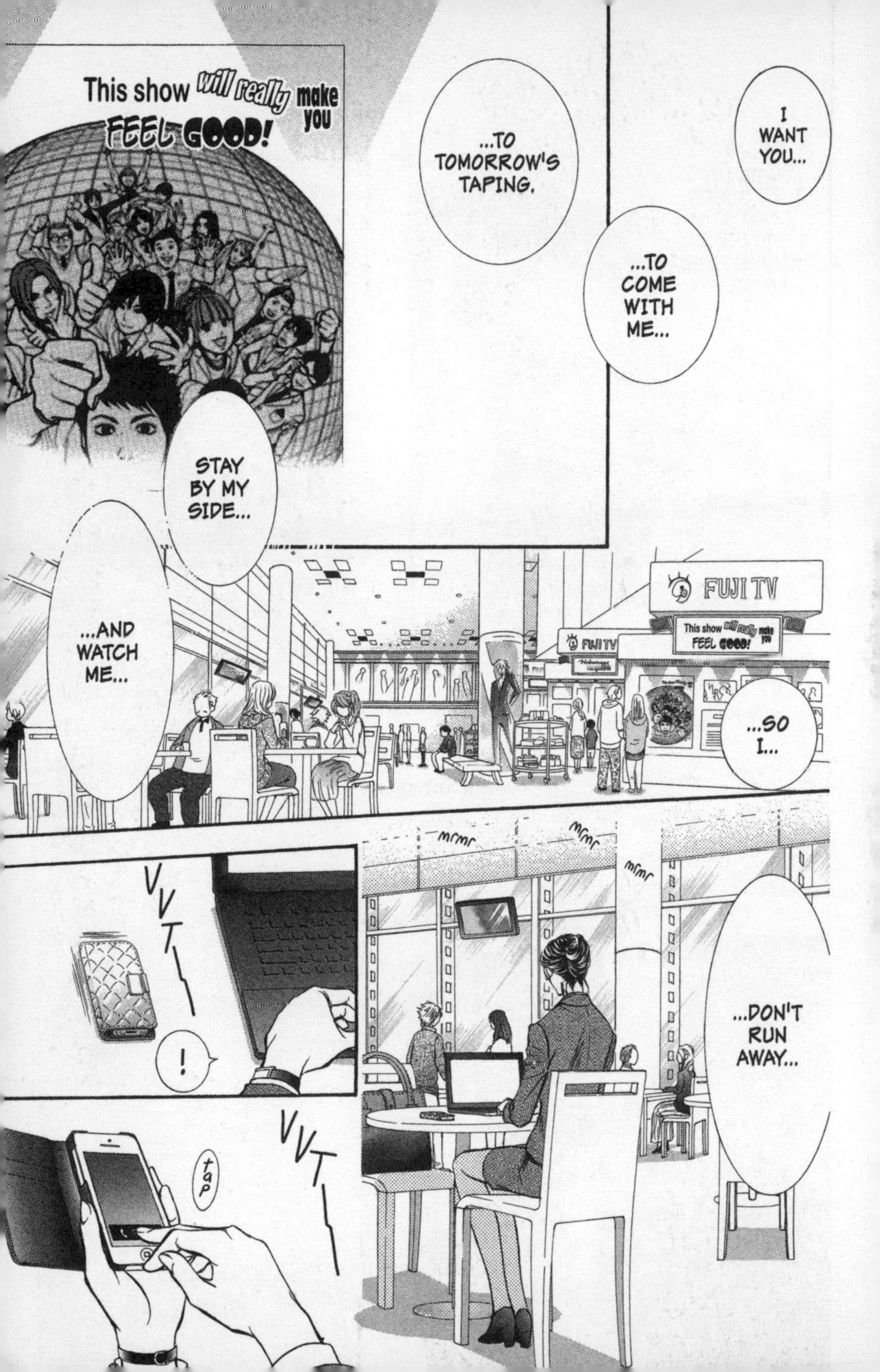
I WANT YOU...
...TO COME WITH ME...
...TO TOMORROW'S TAPING.
This show will really make you FEEL GOOD!
STAY BY MY SIDE...
FUJI TV
This show will really make you FEEL GOOD!
FUJI TV
...SO I...
...AND WATCH ME...
mrmr
mrmr
mrmr
...DON'T RUN AWAY...
VVT
!
VVT
tap

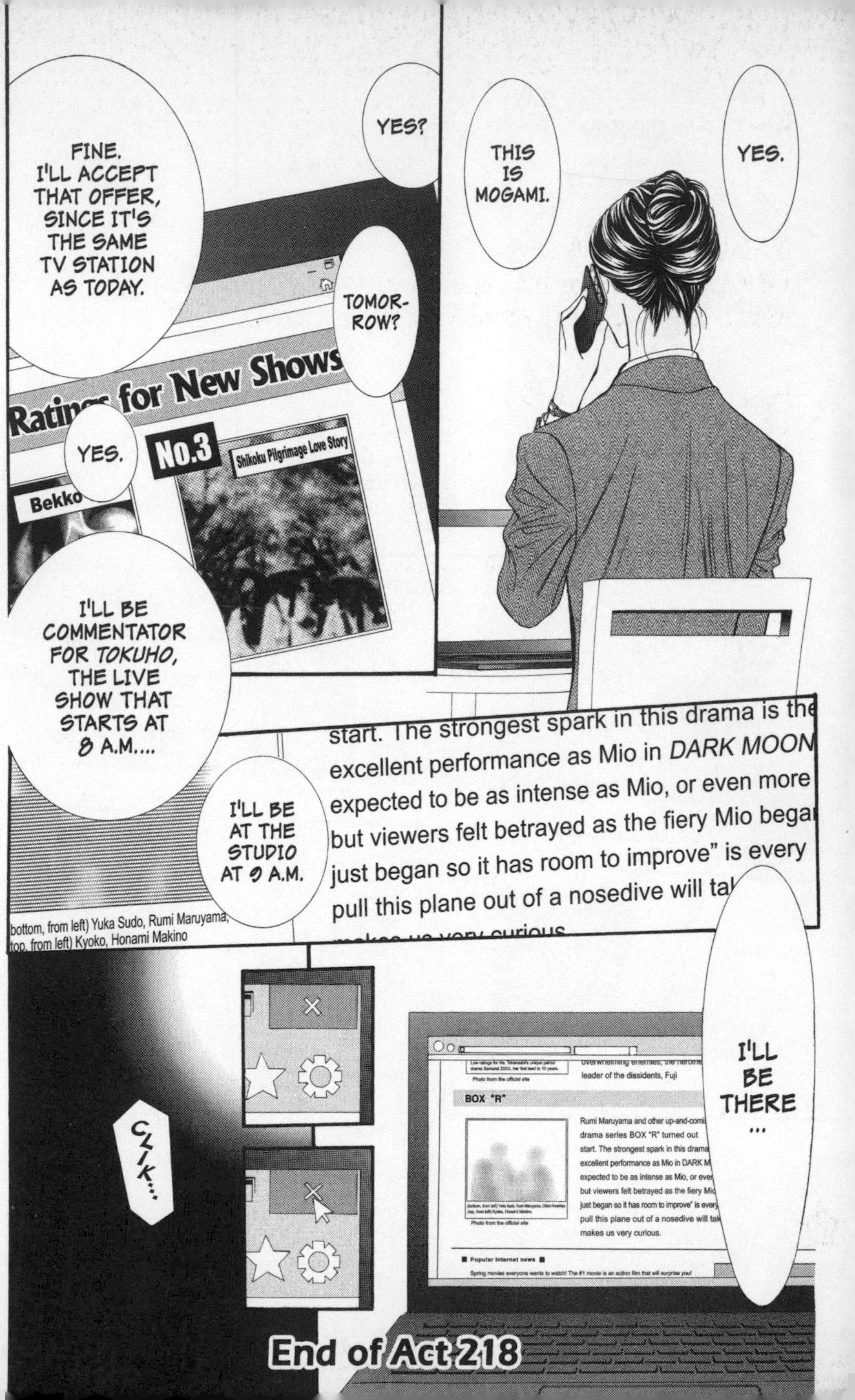
YES.
THIS IS MOGAMI.
YES?
TOMORROW?
YES.
FINE. I'LL ACCEPT THAT OFFER, SINCE IT'S THE SAME TV STATION AS TODAY.
Ratings for New Shows
No.3
Shikoku Pilgrimage Love Story
Bekko
I'LL BE COMMENTATOR FOR *TOKUHO*, THE LIVE SHOW THAT STARTS AT 8 A.M....
start. The strongest spark in this drama is the
excellent performance as Mio in *DARK MOON*
expected to be as intense as Mio, or even more
but viewers felt betrayed as the fiery Mio bega
just began so it has room to improve" is every
pull this plane out of a nosedive will ta
(bottom, from left) Yuka Sudo, Rumi Maruyama,
(top, from left) Kyoko, Honami Makino
I'LL BE AT THE STUDIO AT 9 A.M.
I'LL BE THERE...
CLIK...
BOX "R"
Rumi Maruyama and other up-and-comi
drama series BOX "R" turned out
start. The strongest spark in this drama
excellent performance as Mio in DARK M
expected to be as intense as Mio, or eve
but viewers felt betrayed as the fiery Mio
just began so it has room to improve" is every
pull this plane out of a nosedive will tak
makes us very curious.
Popular Internet news
Spring movies everyone wants to watch! The #1 movie is an action film that will surprise you!
End of Act 218

Skip-Beat! End Notes

Everyone knows how to be a fan, but sometimes cool things from other cultures need a little help crossing the language barrier.

Page 15, panel 1: Dondurma

Dondurma is a Turkish ice cream that includes salep (powdered orchid root) and mastic (a resin), which creates a thicker, chewier texture than plain ice cream.

Page 51, panel 4: Yanki

A *yanki* is a juvenile delinquent or young gangster.

Page 165, panel 1: Yakuza

A yakuza is a Japanese gangster.

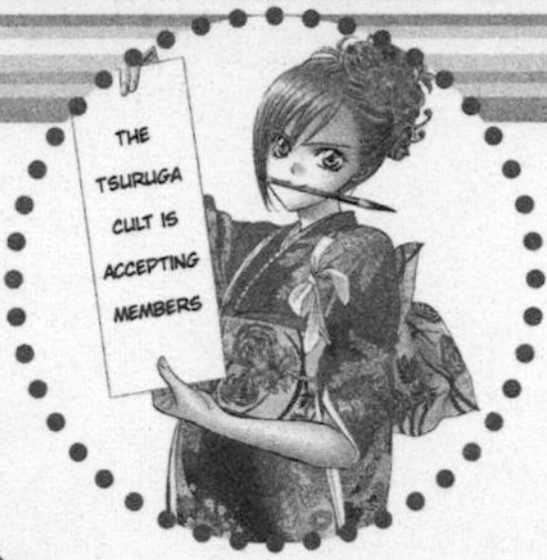
THE TSURUGA CULT IS ACCEPTING MEMBERS

Yoshiki Nakamura is originally from Tokushima Prefecture. She started drawing manga in elementary school, which eventually led to her 1993 debut of *Yume de Au yori Suteki* (Better than Seeing in a Dream) in *Hana to Yume* magazine. Her other works include the basketball series *Saint Love, MVP wa Yuzurenai* (Can't Give Up MVP), *Blue Wars* and *Tokyo Crazy Paradise*, a series about a female bodyguard in 2020 Tokyo.

SKIP·BEAT!

Vol. 36
Shojo Beat Edition

STORY AND ART BY YOSHIKI NAKAMURA

English Translation & Adaptation/Tomo Kimura
Touch-up Art & Lettering/Sabrina Heep
Design/Veronica Casson
Editor/Pancha Diaz

Skip-Beat! by Yoshiki Nakamura © Yoshiki Nakamura 2015
All rights reserved. First published in Japan in 2015 by HAKUSENSHA, Inc., Tokyo.
English language translation rights arranged with HAKUSENSHA, Inc., Tokyo.

The stories, characters and incidents mentioned in this publication are entirely fictional.

No portion of this book may be reproduced or transmitted in any form or by any means
without written permission from the copyright holders.

Printed in the U.S.A.

Published by VIZ Media, LLC
P.O. Box 77010
San Francisco, CA 94107

10 9 8 7 6 5 4 3 2 1
First printing, March 2016

www.viz.com

www.shojobeat.com

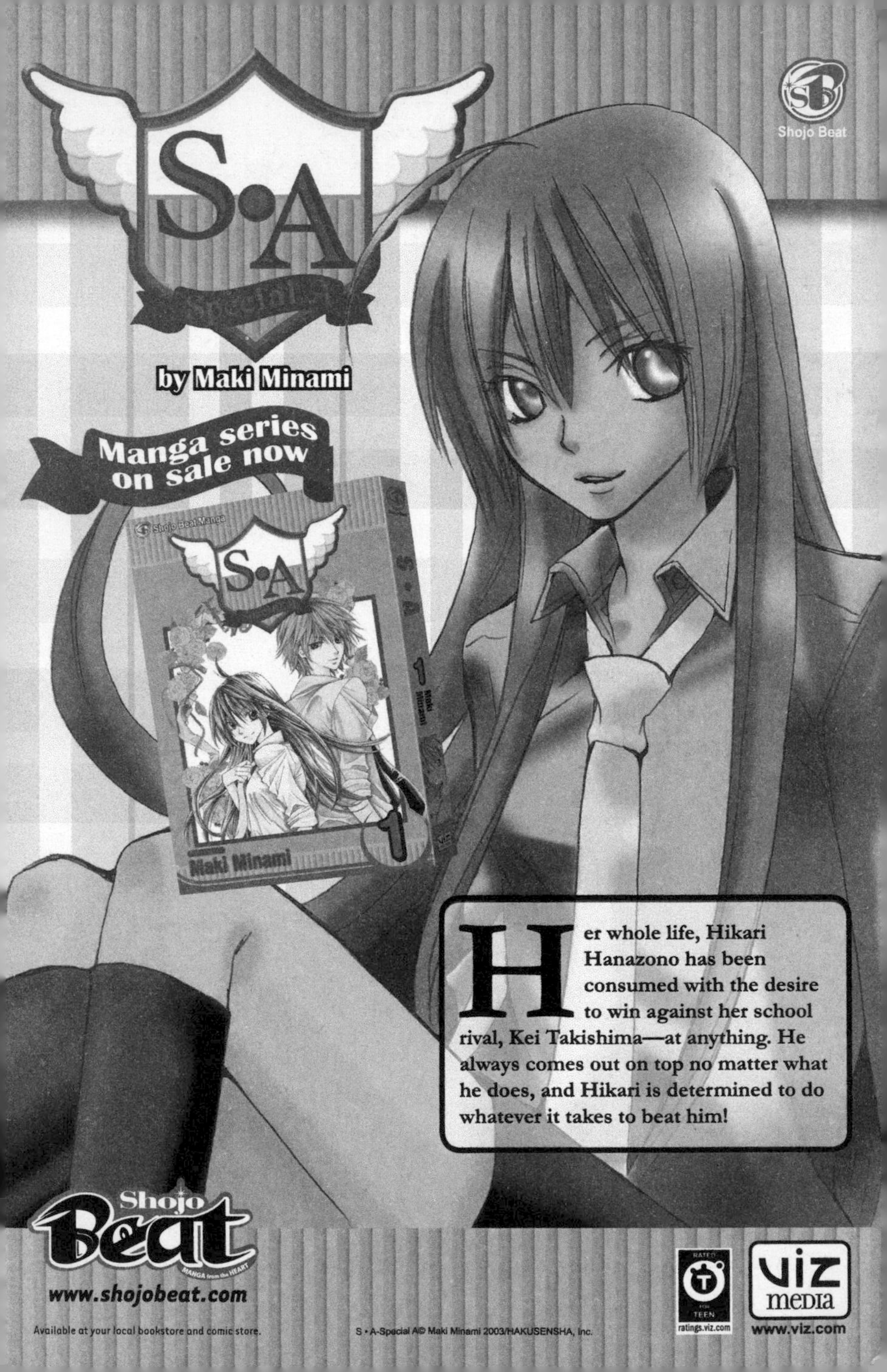

Shojo Beat
S•A
by Maki Minami
Manga series on sale now
Her whole life, Hikari Hanazono has been consumed with the desire to win against her school rival, Kei Takishima—at anything. He always comes out on top no matter what he does, and Hikari is determined to do whatever it takes to beat him!
Shojo Beat
MANGA from the HEART
www.shojobeat.com
Available at your local bookstore and comic store.
S • A-Special A© Maki Minami 2003/HAKUSENSHA, Inc.
RATED T FOR TEEN
ratings.viz.com
VIZ media
www.viz.com

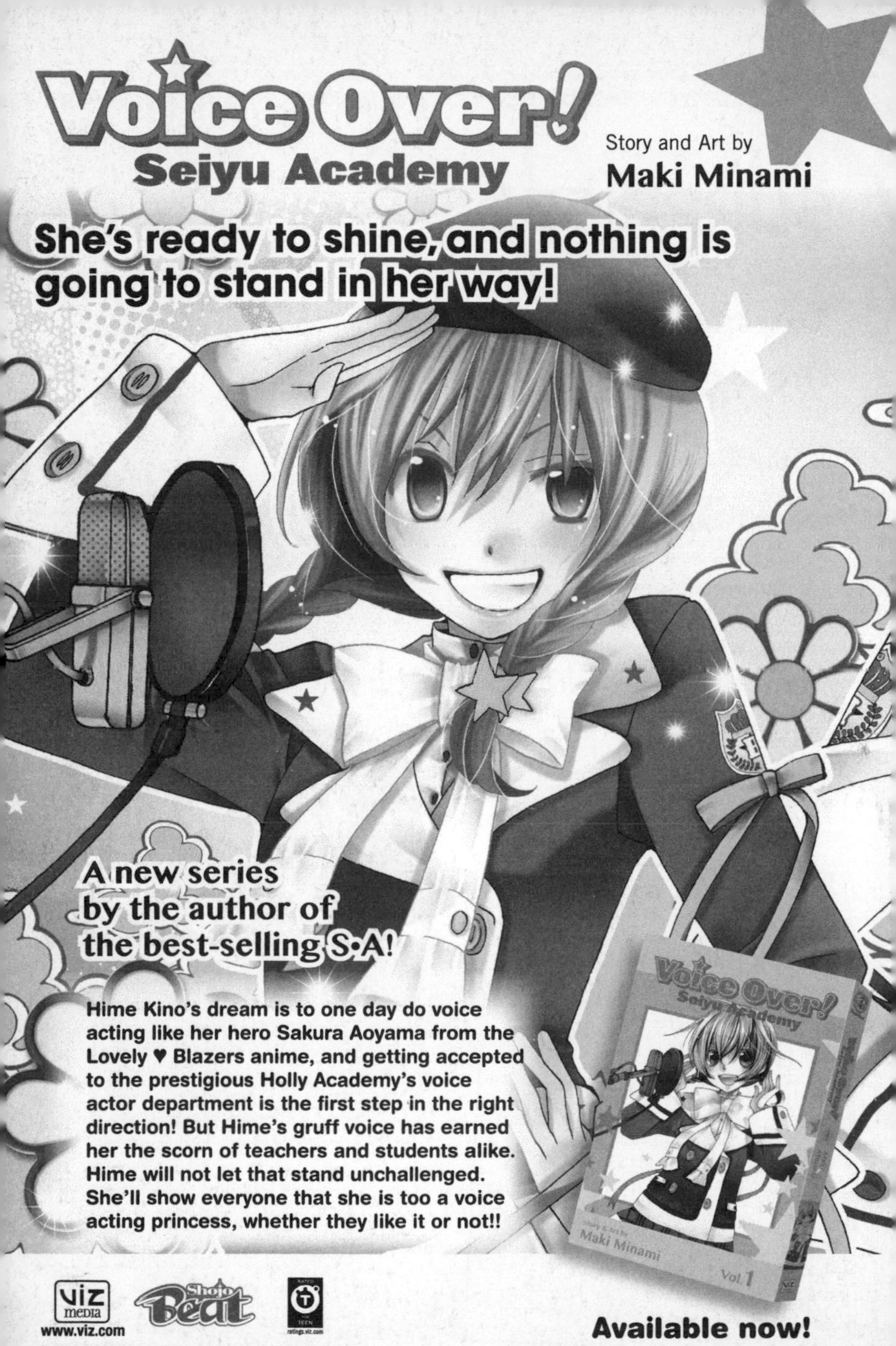
Voice Over!
Seiyu Academy
Story and Art by
Maki Minami
She's ready to shine, and nothing is going to stand in her way!
A new series by the author of the best-selling S•A!
Hime Kino's dream is to one day do voice acting like her hero Sakura Aoyama from the Lovely ♥ Blazers anime, and getting accepted to the prestigious Holly Academy's voice actor department is the first step in the right direction! But Hime's gruff voice has earned her the scorn of teachers and students alike. Hime will not let that stand unchallenged. She'll show everyone that she is too a voice acting princess, whether they like it or not!!
Voice Over! Seiyu Academy
Maki Minami
Vol. 1
viz media
Shojo Beat
www.viz.com
Available now!

SURPRISE!

You may be reading the wrong way!

It's true: In keeping with the original Japanese comic format, this book reads from right to left—so action, sound effects, and word balloons are completely reversed. This preserves the orientation of the original artwork—plus, it's fun! Check out the diagram shown here to get the hang of things, and then turn to the other side of the book to get started!

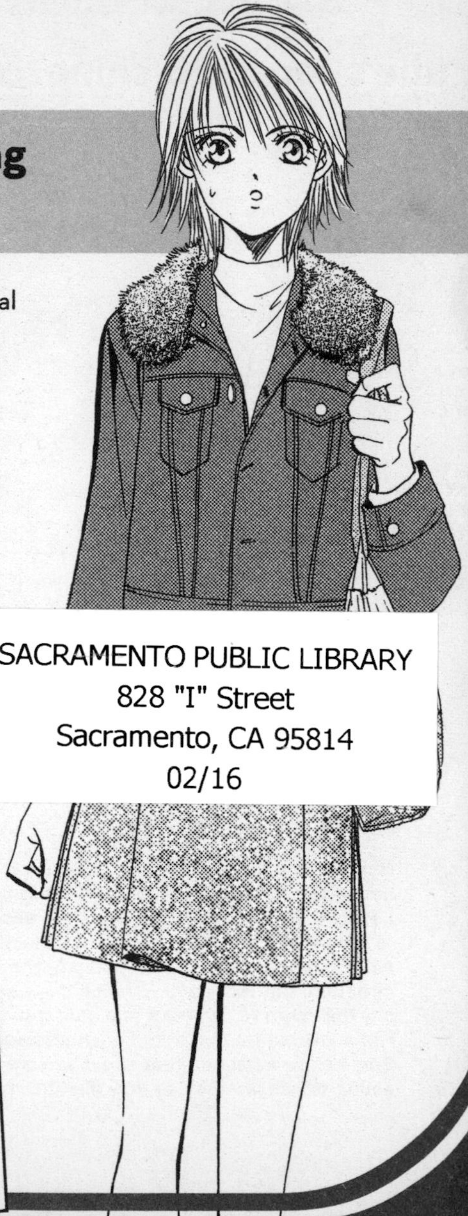

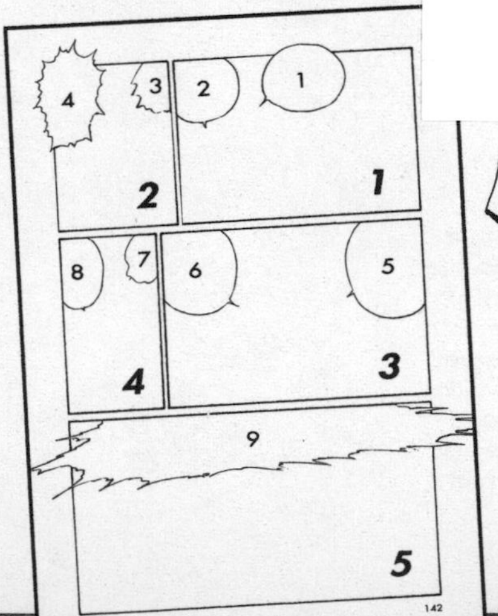
1
2
3
4
1
2
5
6
7
8
3
4
9
5
142